M000002444

Japanese
Pocket Dictionary

Japanese – English
English – Japanese

Berlitz Publishing
New York · Munich · Singapore

Original edition edited by the
Langenscheidt editorial staff

Compiled by LEXUS with:
Anthony P Newell
秋山真有子 (Mayuko Akiyama)
八幡尚子 (Takako Y Hyland)

Book in cover photo: © Punchstock/Medioimages

© 2011 Berlitz Publishing/APA Publications GmbH & Co.
Verlag KG, Singapore Branch, Singapore

Printed in Germany
ISBN 978-981-268-198-0

11010 (98333)

Preface

This Japanese Dictionary focuses on modern usage in English and Japanese.

The two sides of the book, the Japanese-English dictionary and the English-Japanese dictionary, are different in structure and purpose. The Japanese-English is a decoding dictionary, designed to enable the native speaker of English to understand Japanese. The English-Japanese is designed for productive usage, for self-expression in Japanese.

A system of signposting helps the user find the correct translation.

Grammar labels (*n, adj, v/t*) are given when it is necessary to identify *which* use or uses of an English word are being translated.

Indicators in *italics* (typical objects of verbs, synonyms of nouns etc) and subject area labels are given to clarify *which* sense or area of usage of a headword is being translated.

In the Japanese-English dictionary the Japanese headwords are alphabetically ordered according to their romanized pronunciation.

White lozenges (◊) are used in the Japanese-English dictionary to separate out different English grammatical categories, when all of these correspond to one single Japanese word.

The pronunciation of Japanese

All Japanese characters in this dictionary are accompanied by a romanized script known as romaji. Not all romaji letters are pronounced as you would normally expect on the basis of English. The following is a guide to the pronunciation of romaji.

Vowels

There are only five vowel sounds in Japanese:

a	as in f*a*ther	o	as in p*o*rt (but shorter)
e	as in g*e*t or b*e*d	u	as in p*u*t
i	as in h*ea*t (but shorter)		

Remember that there are no silent letters. So when 'e', for example, comes at the end of a word it must be pronounced: 'are' is ah-reh' (not as in 'are' in English).

A bar, or macron, over a vowel means that it has twice the length of a vowel without a bar. Distinguish carefully between obasan (aunt) and obāsan (grandmother) or koji (orphan) and kōji (construction).

When two vowels are adjacent they should not be made into a single sound (as in English), but each should be pronounced separately:

ai	like Thai	ie	pronounced ee-eh
ae	pronounced ah-eh	oh	pronounced o-oo
ei	like the ay of pay	ue	pronounced oo-eh

Consonants

g	as in *g*o or *g*irl	s	always as in ma*ss* (never z)
j	as in *j*ar	y	as in *y*et

Note that 'y' is never a long 'i' sound. For example, the Kyū of Kyūshū is like the 'cu' of cute and never like the 'ki' of kite.

The letter 'r' sounds more like an 'l'.

Double consonants are an important feature of Japanese. Each part of a double consonant should be pronounced separately: anna is pronounced an-na; kippu is kip-pu; gakkō is gak-kō.

An apostrophe is used to indicate a slight pause when speaking.

Stress

To all intents and purposes there is no stress in Japanese. So give the same value to all syllables: say Yo-ko-ha-ma not Yo-ko-HA-ma.

Notes

1. **Object particles**

   Object particles such as 'no' and 'ni' are included with translations of transitive verbs in the English-Japanese half of the dictionary. If an object particle is not given, then you can assume that the correct particle to use is 'o'.

   > **win 2** *v/t* ... ni katsu ...に勝つ; *lottery, money, prize* ateru 当てる

2. **(no) and (na)**

   Where the Japanese translation of an adjective is given with (no) or (na) the general rule is that the 'no' or 'na' is only used if the adjective is placed before its noun:

   > **quiet** shizuka (na) 静か(な)

   > *a quiet room* shizuka na heya 静かな部屋

   > *the room was quiet* heya wa shizuka deshita 部屋は静かでした

   Verbs of activity and verbs of being

   translation of some basic prepositions (or postpositions anese) depends on the type of verb used with the ion. Verbs of activity are verbs like: work, run, eat. being are verbs like: live, be.

   > *to work in Tokyo* watashi wa Tōkyō de imashita 私は東京で働いていました

   > *till live in Tokyo?* kare wa mada Tōkyō ni ka 彼はまだ東京に住んでいますか

Abbreviations

adj	adjective	MIL	military
adv	adverb	MUS	music
ANAT	anatomy	*n*	noun
AUTO	motoring	NAUT	nautical
BIOL	biology	*pej*	pejorative
BOT	botany	PHOT	photography
Br	British English	POL	politics
COMM	commerce, business	*prep*	preposition
COMPUT	computers, IT term	*pron*	pronoun
conj	conjunction	®	registered trademark
ELEC	electricity,	RADIO	radio
	electronics	RAIL	railroad
fig	figurative	REL	religion
FIN	financial	sb	somebody
form	formal usage	SCHOOL	education
GRAM	grammar	SPORTS	sports
H	humble, showing	sth	something
	humility to the	TEL	telecommunications
	listener	THEAT	theater
infml	familiar, colloquial	TV	television
JUR	law	*v/i*	intransitive verb
MATH	mathematics	*v/t*	transitive verb
MED	medicine	→	see

Japanese – English

A

ああ **ā** ah!
暴く **abaku** expose
暴れる **abareru** become violent
浴びる **abiru** take *shower*
危ない **abunai** dangerous
脂 **abura** fat
油 **abura** oil
脂っこい **aburakkoi** fatty
あちこち **achikochi** here
and there
あちら **achira** over there
アダプター **adaputā** adapter
アドバイス **adobaisu** advice
あえぐ **aegu** pant
あふれる **afureru** overflow
アフリカ **Afurika** Africa
アフターサービス **afutā
sābisu** after sales service
あがる **agaru** get nervous
上がる **agaru** rise
あげる **ageru** give; let out
groan
上げる **ageru** raise
揚げる **ageru** deep-fry; hoist
あご **ago** chin; jaw
あぐらをかく **agura o kaku**
sit cross-legged

阿呆 **ahō** fool
愛 **ai** love
間 **aida** between; during
◊ interval
アイディア **aidia** idea
愛人 **aijin** lover
愛情 **aijō** affection
合い鍵 **aikagi** duplicate key
相変わらず **aikawarazu** the
same as ever
愛国 **aikoku** patriotism
あいまい（な）**aimai (na)**
ambiguous
あいにく **ainiku** unfortunately
アイロン **airon** iron
アイロン台 **airondai** ironing
board
アイルランド **Airurando**
Ireland
あいさつ **aisatsu** greeting
アイシャドウ **aishadō** eye
shadow
愛想のいい **aisō no ī** amiable
愛想の悪い **aisō no warui**
unfriendly
アイスホッケー **aisuhokkē**
(ice) hockey

アイスコーヒー **aisukōhī**
iced coffee

アイスクリーム **aisukurīmu**
ice cream

愛する **ai suru** love

アイスティー **aisutī** iced tea

相手 **aite** companion; opponent

あいつ **aitsu** that guy

合図 **aizu** signal

味 **aji** taste

アジア **Ajia** Asia

アジア人 **Ajiajin** Asian

味をする **ajimi suru** taste

あじさい **ajisai** hydrangea

味わう **ajiwau** taste

あか **aka** grime

赤ちゃん **akachan** baby

赤い **akai** red

赤字 **akaji** deficit

あからさま（な）**akarasama
(na)** frank

明り **akari** light

明るい **akarui** bright

赤信号 **akashingō** red light

明けましておめでとう
　ございます **akemashite
omedetō gozaimasu** Happy
New Year!

明ける **akeru** open

空ける **akeru** vacate

明ける **akeru**: 夜が明ける
yo ga akeru dawn is breaking

秋 **aki** fall

空き部屋 **akibeya** unoccupied

room

明らか（な）**akiraka (na)**
obvious

あきらめる **akirameru**
give up

あきれる **akireru** be shocked

飽きる **akiru** be tired of

悪化 **akka** deterioration

あこがれ **akogare** yearning

あこがれる **akogareru**
yearn for

空く **aku** be empty

開く **aku** open

悪 **aku** evil

あくび **akubi** yawn

悪意 **akui** malice

悪魔 **akuma** devil

あくまでも **akumade mo** to
the (bitter) end

悪夢 **akumu** nightmare

悪性（の）**akusei (no)**
malignant

アクセル **akuseru** gas pedal

アクセサリー **akusesarī**
accessory

握手 **akushu** handshake

悪態 **akutai** verbal abuse

悪用 **akuyō** misuse

尼 **ama** nun

アマチュア **amachua**
amateur

甘える **amaeru** act like a
spoilt child

甘い **amai** sweet; indulgent

甘口 (の) **amakuchi (no)**
mild

あまり **amari** (not) so much

余る **amaru** be left over

甘やかす **amayakasu** pamper

甘酒 **amazake** sweet sake

甘酸っぱい **amazuppai**
sweet and sour

あめ **ame** candy

雨 **ame** rain

アメリカ **Amerika** America

アメリカ人 **Amerikajin**
American

網 **ami** net

編み物 **amimono** knitting

編む **amu** knit

案 **an** plan

穴 **ana** hole

あなご **anago** eel

あなた **anata** you

あなたの **anata no** your

あなたたち **anatatachi** you
(plural)

あなたたちの **anatatachi no**
your *(plural)*

姉 **ane** big sister

案外 **angai** unexpectedly

暗号 **angō** code

兄 **ani** big brother

アニメ **anime** cartoon

暗示 **anji** hint

アンケート **ankēto**
questionnaire

暗記 **anki** memorizing

あんこ **anko** sweet bean paste

アンコール **ankōru** encore

あんな **anna** that sort of

案内 **annai** information

案内係 **annaigakari** guide

案内人 **annainin** guide

あの **ano** that; those

あのね **anone** well...

アノラック **anorakku** parka

アンプ **anpu** amplifier

暗殺 **ansatsu** assassination

安静 **ansei** rest cure

安心 **anshin** peace of mind

暗証番号 **anshō-bangō** PIN

安定 **antei** stability

アンテナ **antena** antenna

暗算 **anzan** mental arithmetic

安全 (な) **anzen (na)** safe

安全ピン **anzenpin** safety pin

あんず **anzu** apricot

青い **aoi** blue

青白い **aojiroi** pale

青信号 **aoshingō** green light

アパート **apāto** apartment

圧迫 **appaku** oppression

アラブ (の) **Arabu (no)** Arab

荒い **arai** rough

粗い **arai** coarse

あらかじめ **arakajime** in
advance

あらまし **aramashi** outline

アラーム **arāmu** alarm

あられ **arare** hail

あらし **arashi** storm

争い **arasoi** conflict

争う **arasou** fight

荒す **arasu** ruin

改める **aratameru** renew

改めて **aratamete** anew

洗う **arau** wash

現れる **arawareru** appear

表す **arawasu** show *emotion*

あらゆる **arayuru** all kinds of

あれ **are** that (one)

荒れる **areru** get rough

アレルギー **arerugī** allergy

あり **ari** ant

ありがたい **arigatai** grateful

ありがとう **arigatō** thanks

ある **aru** be; be located ◊ certain; …がある *... ga aru* have...; there is / are

アルバイト **arubaito** part-time work

アルバム **arubamu** album

アルファベット **arufabetto** letter; alphabet

歩いて **aruite** on foot

あるいは **arui wa** or

アルコール **arukōru** alcohol

アルコール中毒 **arukōru chūdoku** alcoholism

歩く **aruku** walk

麻 **asa** hemp

朝 **asa** morning

朝ごはん **asagohan** breakfast

浅薄 (な) **asahaka (na)** shallow *person*

朝日 **asahi** rising sun

浅い **asai** shallow

朝飯 **asameshi** breakfast *(colloquial)*

朝寝坊 **asanebō** late riser

あさって **asatte** the day after tomorrow

汗 **ase** sweat

あせる **aseru** get impatient; fade

足 **ashi** foot; leg

脚 **ashi** leg *(of table etc)*

足跡 **ashiato** footprint

足首 **ashikubi** ankle

足元に気をつけて **ashimoto ni ki o tsukete** mind the step!

明日 **ashita** tomorrow

遊び **asobi** fun

遊ぶ **asobu** have fun

あそこ **asoko** over there

あっさり (と) **assari (to)** plainly

明日 **asu** tomorrow

アスピリン **asupirin** aspirin

与える **ataeru** give

値 **atai** price

頭 **atama** head

頭金 **atamakin** down payment

新しい **atarashī** new

辺り **atari** vicinity

当たり **atari** success

あたり前 **atarimae** natural

当たる **ataru** strike; be right

温かい、暖かい **atatakai** warm

温まる、暖まる **atatamaru** warm up

温める、暖める **atatameru** warm up

あっち **atchi** over there

…宛て **-ate** addressed to

当てはまる **atehamaru** applicable to

宛て名 **atena** address

当てる **ateru** win

跡 **ato** trace

後で **ato de** afterward

厚い **atsui** heavy; thick

暑い **atsui** hot *weather*

熱い **atsui** hot *object*

厚かましい **atsukamashī** impudent

扱う **atsukau** handle

集まり **atsumari** gathering

集まる **atsumaru** gather

集める **atsumeru** collect

圧力 **atsuryoku** pressure

厚さ **atsusa** thickness

暑さ **atsusa** heat *(weather)*

あっという間に **atto iu ma ni** in a flash

圧倒的(な) **attōteki (na)** overpowering

あう **au** meet with *sth unfavorable*

合う **au** fit

会う **au** meet

泡 **awa** bubble

あわび **awabi** abalone

淡い **awai** faint

哀れ(な) **aware (na)** pitiful

合わせる **awaseru** join; tune in

合わせて **awasete** all together

あわただしい **awatadashī** hurried

あわてる **awateru** be flustered

過ち **ayamachi** error

誤り **ayamari** mistake

謝る **ayamaru** apologize

誤る **ayamaru** make a mistake

誤った **ayamatta** mistaken

怪しい **ayashī** fishy

あやす **ayasu** dandle

操る **ayatsuru** manipulate

危うく **ayauku** narrowly escape

あざ **aza** bruise; birthmark

あざける **azakeru** ridicule

欺く **azamuku** deceive

鮮やか(な) **azayaka (na)** vivid

預ける **azukeru** deposit *luggage*

B

場 **ba** place

バーベキュー **bābekyū**
barbecue

バッジ **badji** badge

バーゲン（セール）**bāgen
(sēru)** sale

倍 **bai** double

場合 **bāi** circumstance

バイバイ **baibai** bye-bye

売買 **baibai** buying and selling

ばい菌 **baikin** germ

バイク **baiku** motorbike

バインダー **baindā** binder

バイオリン **baiorin** violin

陪審 **baishin** jury

賠償 **baishō** recompense

売春 **baishun** prostitution

売春婦 **baishunfu** prostitute

売店 **baiten** booth

バイト **baito** byte; part-time
job

梅雨 **baiu** rainy season

ばか **baka** fool

ばかばかしい **bakabakashī**
ridiculous

ばか（な）**baka (na)** idiotic

ばかり **bakari** just;
approximately

化け物 **bakemono** monster

バケツ **baketsu** bucket

罰金 **bakkin** fine *(money)*

バック **bakku** background;
reverse AUTO

バックミラー **bakkumirā**
rear-view mirror

バックル **bakkuru** buckle

ばく大（な）**bakudai (na)**
vast

爆弾 **bakudan** bomb

爆撃 **bakugeki** bomb attack

爆発 **bakuhatsu** explosion

漠然とした **bakuzen to
shita** vague

バン **ban** van

晩 **ban** evening

番 **ban** number; turn

バナナ **banana** banana

バンド **bando** strap; band
(music)

ばね **bane** spring

番号 **bangō** number

晩ごはん **bangohan** evening
meal

番組 **bangumi** program

バニラ **banira** vanilla

バンパー **banpā** bumper

伴奏 **bansō** accompaniment

ばんそうこう **bansōkō**
adhesive plaster

万歳 **banzai** hurray!

ばら **bara** rose

ばらばら(の) **barabara (no)** in pieces

バランス **baransu** balance

バレエ **barē** ballet

バレーボール **barēbōru** volleyball

ばれる **bareru** be found out

馬力 **bariki** horsepower

バルコニー **barukonī** balcony

場所 **basho** place

罰する **bassuru** punish

バス **basu** bus ; bass

バスケットボール **basukettobōru** basketball

バスローブ **basurōbu** bathrobe

バス停 **basutei** bus stop

バター **batā** butter

罰 **batsu** penalty

抜群 **batsugun** outstanding

ばつ(印) **batsu(jirushi)** cross

バッテリー **batterī** battery

バット **batto** bat

ベッド **beddo** bed

ベッドカバー **beddokabā** bedspread

米国 **beikoku** America

…べき **-beki** should

別館 **bekkan** annex

別居 **bekkyo** separation

ベーコン **bēkon** bacon

弁 **ben** dialect ◀

ベンチ **benchi** bench

弁護 **bengo** defense JUR

弁護士 **bengoshi** lawyer

紅 **beni** rouge

便所 **benjo** toilet

弁解 **benkai** excuse

勉強 **benkyō** study

便秘 **benpi** constipation

便利(な) **benri (na)** convenient

弁償 **benshō** recompense

弁当 **bentō** lunch box

ベランダ **beranda** veranda

ベル **beru** bell

ベール **bēru** veil

ベルギー **Berugī** Belgium

ベルト **beruto** belt

別荘 **bessō** villa

ベテラン(の) **beteran (no)** expert

べとべとした **betobeto shita** sticky

別々に **betsubetsu ni** separately

別(の) **betsu (no)** separate

ビデオ **bideo** video

ビデオカメラ **bideo-kamera** video camera

ビデオテープ **bideo-tēpu** videotape

美人 **bijin** beautiful woman

ビジネスクラス **bijinesu-kurasu** business class

美術 **bijutsu** art

美術館 **bijutsukan** art gallery

ビキニ **bikini** bikini

びっくりする **bikkuri suru** be shocked

微妙(な) **bimyō (na)** subtle

びん **bin** bottle

便 **bin** flight

貧乏 **binbō** poverty

ビニール袋 **binīru-bukuro** plastic bag

敏感(な) **binkan (na)** sensitive

便せん **binsen** writing paper

ビラ **bira** handout

ビル **biru** building

ビール **bīru** beer

微笑 **bishō** smile

ビスケット **bisuketto** biscuit

ビタミン **bitamin** vitamin

美徳 **bitoku** virtue

美容院 **biyōin** beauty parlor

美容師 **biyōshi** beautician

ビザ **biza** visa

棒 **bō** rod

墓地 **bochi** cemetery

膨張 **bōchō** expansion

膨大(な) **bōdai (na)** vast

暴動 **bōdō** riot

防衛 **bōei** defense

貿易 **bōeki** trade

望遠鏡 **bōenkyō** telescope

暴風雨 **bōfū-u** hurricane

妨害 **bōgai** interference

ボーイ **bōi** bellhop

ボーイフレンド **bōifurendo** boyfriend

ボイコット **boikotto** boycott

ボイラー **boirā** boiler

ボーイスカウト **bōi-sukauto** scout

ぼかす **bokasu** blur

冒険 **bōken** adventure

簿記 **boki** bookkeeping

簿記係 **bokigakari** bookkeeper

募金 **bokin** fundraising

暴行 **bōkō** assault

膀胱 **bōkō** bladder

母国 **bokoku** native country

ぼく **boku** I

牧場 **bokujō** ranch

ボクサー **bokusā** boxer

牧師 **bokushi** clergyman

ボクシング **bokushingu** boxing

亡命 **bōmei** exile

盆 **bon** tray

ボーナス **bōnasu** bonus

忘年会 **bōnen-kai** year-end party

ボンネット **bonnetto** hood

盆踊り **bon'odori** festival dance

盆栽 **bonsai** bonsai

ぼんやりした **bon'yari shita** absent-minded

防音(の) **bō-on (no)** soundproof

ぼっ発 **boppatsu** outbreak

ボランティア **borantia** volunteer

ぼろ **boro** rag

ぼろぼろ（の）**boroboro (no)** ragged

ボール **bōru** ball; bowl

ボールペン **bōrupen** ballpoint pen

ボルト **boruto** bolt; volt

暴力 **bōryoku** violence

暴力的（な）**bōryokuteki (na)** violent

ボリューム **boryūmu** volume

帽子 **bōshi** cap; hat

防止 **bōshi** prevention

募集 **boshū** recruitment

没収する **bosshū suru** confiscate

防水（の）**bōsui (no)** waterproof

ボタン **botan** button

ボート **bōto** boat

没落 **botsuraku** downfall

ぼやけた **boyaketa** hazy

ぼう然として **bōzen to shite** in a daze

坊主 **bōzu** Buddhist monk

部 **bu** section

無愛想（な）**buaisō (na)** surly

部分 **bubun** part

部分的（な）**bubunteki (na)** partial

部長 **buchō** chief

ぶどう **budō** grape

部品 **buhin** part

無事に **buji ni** safely

侮辱 **bujoku** insult

部下 **buka** subordinate

武器 **buki** weapon

無気味（な），不気味（な）**bukimi (na)** weird

不器用（な）**bukiyō (na)** clumsy

物価 **bukka** commodity prices

ぶっきらぼう（な）**bukkirabō (na)** blunt

仏教 **Bukkyō** Buddhism

部門 **bumon** sector

ブーム **būmu** boom

文 **bun** sentence

分 **bun** portion

文房具 **bunbōgu** stationery

文房具屋 **bunbōguya** stationery store

文学 **bungaku** literature

分譲マンション **bunjō-manshon** condo

文化 **bunka** culture

分解する **bunkai suru** dismantle

分割 **bunkatsu** division

分割払い **bunkatsu-barai** paying by installments

文庫本 **bunkobon** pocket-sized book

文明 **bunmei** civilization

文脈 **bunmyaku** context

分配 **bunpai** distribution

文法 **bunpō** grammar

文楽 **bunraku** *traditional Japanese puppet play*

分裂 **bunretsu** split

分離 **bunri** separation

分類 **bunrui** classification

分量 **bunryō** amount

分析 **bunseki** analysis

文書 **bunsho** document

文章 **bunshō** writing

分数 **bunsū** fraction

文体 **buntai** style of writing

分担する **buntan suru** share

文通 **buntsū** correspondence

分野 **bun'ya** field *(academic)*

ぶらぶらする **burabura suru** lounge around

ブラインド **buraindo** shades

ブラジャー **burajā** brassiere

ブランデー **burandē** brandy

ブランド **burando** brand

ブランコ **buranko** swing

ぶら下がる **burasagaru** dangle

ブラシ **burashi** brush

ぶらつく **buratsuku** wander

ブラウス **burausu** blouse

無礼 **burei** rudeness

ブレーキ **burēki** brake

ブレスレット **buresuretto** bracelet

ブリーフケース **burīfukēsu** briefcase

ブローチ **burōchi** brooch

ブロッコリ **burokkori** broccoli

部類 **burui** category, class

不作法(な) **busahō (na)** ill-mannered

武士 **bushi** samurai

部署 **busho** place of duty

部首 **bushu** radical *(in Chinese character)*

…不足 **-busoku** shortage

物質 **busshitsu** substance

物質的(な) **busshitsuteki (na)** material

ぶす **busu** ugly

豚 **buta** pig

舞台 **butai** stage THEAT

部隊 **butai** corps

豚肉 **butaniku** pork

ぶつ **butsu** smack

ブーツ **būtsu** boot

仏壇 **butsudan** Buddhist altar

ぶつかる **butsukaru** bump into

ぶつける **butsukeru** bump

物理学 **butsurigaku** physics

仏像 **butsuzō** statue of Buddha

ブザー **buzā** buzzer

びょう **byō** tack

秒 **byō** second *(of time)*

屏風 **byōbu** folding screen

平等 **byōdō** equality
病院 **byōin** hospital
病気 **byōki** illness

病人 **byōnin** invalid
描写 **byōsha** description
病棟 **byōtō** hospital ward

C

茶 **cha** tea
チャイム **chaimu** chime
茶色(の) **chairo (no)** brown
…着 **-chaku** arrival;
◊ *countword for clothes*
着実(な) **chakujitsu (na)**
reliable
着陸 **chakuriku** landing
着色剤 **chakushokuzai**
coloring agent
…ちゃん **-chan** *affectionate
suffix added to names*
チャンネル **channeru** TV
channel
茶の湯 **chanoyu** tea
ceremony
チャンピオン **chanpion**
champion
チャンス **chansu** chance
ちゃんと **chanto** properly
チャレンジ **charenji**
challenge
チャーター便 **chātā-bin**
charter flight
茶わん **chawan** bowl
チェック **chekku** check
チェックアウトする

チェックアウトする **chekku-auto suru** check out
チェックイン(カウンター)
chekku-in (kauntā) check-in
(counter)
チェックインする **chekku-
in suru** check in
チェーン **chēn** chain
チェーンストア **chēn-sutoa**
chain store
チェロ **chero** cello
血 **chi** blood
治安 **chian** law and order
乳房 **chibusa** breast
父 **chichi** father
乳 **chichi** milk; breast
父親 **chichioya** father
知恵 **chie** wisdom
違い **chigai** difference
…違いない **-chigai nai**
surely
違う **chigau** be different
ちぎる **chigiru** tear into small
pieces
地平線 **chiheisen** horizon
地方 **chihō** region
地位 **chi-i** rank
地域 **chi-iki** area

知事 **chiji** governor

縮まる **chijimaru** shrink

縮める **chijimeru** shrink

縮む **chijimu** shrink

知人 **chijin** acquaintance

地下道 **chikadō** underpass

地階 **chikai** basement

近い **chikai** near

誓い **chikai** vow

知覚 **chikaku** perception

近くに **chikaku ni** nearby

近道 **chikamichi** short cut

ちかん **chikan** groper

地下(の) **chika (no)** underground

力 **chikara** strength

力強い **chikarazuyoi** strong

地下鉄 **chikatetsu** subway

誓う **chikau** vow

近寄る **chikayoru** approach

近づける **chikazukeru** have access to

近づく **chikazuku** approach

チキン **chikin** chicken

遅刻する **chikoku suru** arrive late

地区 **chiku** district

乳首 **chikubi** nipple

チクチクする **chikuchiku suru** prickle

畜生 **chikushō** damn it!

地球 **chikyū** the earth

地球儀 **chikyūgi** globe *(model)*

地名 **chimei** place name

チーム **chīmu** team

チームワーク **chīmuwāku** teamwork

沈没 **chinbotsu** sinking

賃金 **chingin** wages

陳述 **chinjutsu** statement *(to police)*

珍味 **chinmi** delicacy

沈黙 **chinmoku** silence

知能 **chinō** intelligence

陳列する **chinretsu suru** display

鎮静剤 **chinseizai** sedative

賃借 **chinshaku** lease

賃貸 **chintai** lease

賃貸料 **chintai-ryō** rent

チップ **chippu** chip *(in gambling)*; tip *(money)*

ちらちらする **chirachira suru** flicker

散らかす **chirakasu** scatter

ちらし **chirashi** leaflet

散らす **chirasu** scatter

ちらっと見る **chiratto miru** glance at

ちり **chiri** litter; dust

地理学 **chirigaku** geography *(subject)*

ちり紙 **chirigami** tissue paper

ちりとり **chiritori** dustpan

散る **chiru** be scattered

治療 **chiryō** treatment

治療法 **chiryōhō** cure

小さい **chīsai** small

小さ(な) **chīsa (na)** small

知性 **chisei** intellect

知識 **chishiki** knowledge

致死(の) **chishi (no)** lethal

地質学 **chishitsugaku**
  geology *(subject)*

窒息 **chissoku** suffocation

地帯 **chitai** zone

知的(な) **chiteki (na)**
  intellectual

秩序 **chitsujo** order

ちっとも…ない **chittomo
  … nai** not at all

地図 **chizu** map

チーズ **chīzu** cheese

地図帳 **chizuchō** atlas

チーズケーキ **chīzukēki**
  cheesecake

腸 **chō** intestines

長 **chō** chief

兆 **chō** trillion

町 **chō** city area

庁 **chō** government agency

超… **chō-** ultra-

貯蓄 **chochiku** saving

提灯 **chōchin** paper lantern

ちょうだい **chōdai** please

ちょうど **chōdo** exactly

重複 **chōfuku** repetition

徴兵 **chōhei** conscription

長方形 **chōhōkei** rectangle

諜報機関 **chōhō kikan** secret
  service

長女 **chōjo** eldest daughter

頂上 **chōjō** summit

超過 **chōka** excess

朝刊 **chōkan** morning paper

超過料金 **chōka-ryōkin**
  excess fare

帳消しにする **chōkeshi ni
  suru** write off

貯金 **chokin** savings

貯金箱 **chokinbako** piggy
  bank

長期(の) **chōki (no)** long-term

直角 **chokkaku** right angle

直感 **chokkan** intuition

直径 **chokkei** diameter

直行便 **chokkō-bin** nonstop
  flight

徴候, 兆候 **chōkō** indication

彫刻 **chōkoku** sculpture

彫刻家 **chōkokuka** sculptor

チョコレート **chokorēto**
  chocolate

超高層ビル **chōkōsō-biru**
  skyscraper

チョーク **chōku** chalk

直立した **chokuritsu shita**
  upright

直線 **chokusen** straight line

直接(の) **chokusetsu (no)**
  direct

直通(の) **chokutsū (no)**
  direct

長距離電話 **chōkyori denwa**
  long-distance call

長距離(の) **chōkyori (no)**
long-distance

丁目 **chōme** district subsection
(in addresses)

調味料 **chōmiryō** seasoning

弔問 **chōmon** condolence
visit

蝶結び **chōmusubi** bow *(in
hair etc)*

長男 **chōnan** eldest son

ちょんまげ **chonmage**
topknot

調律する **chōritsu suru**
tune

調査 **chōsa** investigation

調整 **chōsei** adjustment

挑戦 **chōsen** challenge

調節 **chōsetsu** regulation

著者 **chosha** author

調子 **chōshi** condition; tone
MUS

長所 **chōsho** strong point

調書 **chōsho** record

朝食 **chōshoku** breakfast

聴衆 **chōshū** audience

徴収する **chōshū suru** levy

貯水池 **chosuichi** reservoir

調停 **chōtei** mediation

頂点 **chōten** peak

ちょっと **chotto** a little
◊ excuse me!

調和 **chōwa** harmony

貯蔵品 **chozōhin** supplies
(food)

貯蔵室 **chozōshitsu**
stockroom

注 **chū** annotation

…中 **-chū** during

チューブ **chūbu** tube

中断 **chūdan** interruption

中毒 **chūdoku** poisoning

中学校 **chūgakkō** junior high
school

中元 **chūgen** midsummer gift

中国 **Chūgoku** China; western
region of Honshu

中国人 **Chūgokujin** Chinese

注意 **chūi** attention

注意深い **chūi-bukai** careful

チューインガム **chūin-
gamu** (chewing) gum

忠実(な) **chūjitsu (na)** loyal

中旬 **chūjun** middle 10 days
of a month

仲介者 **chūkaisha**
go-between

中間(の) **chūkan (no)**
halfway; neutral *(color)*

中華料理 **Chūka-ryōri**
Chinese cuisine

中継放送 **chūkei-hōsō**
outside broadcast

中近東 **Chūkintō** Middle East

忠告 **chūkoku** advice

中古(の) **chūko (no)**
secondhand

中級(の) **chūkyū (no)**
intermediate

注目 **chūmoku** attention

注文 **chūmon** order

中年(の) **chūnen (no)**
middle-aged

注入 **chūnyū** infusion

中央 **chūō** center

中立 **chūritsu** neutrality

仲裁 **chūsai** arbitration

忠誠 **chūsei** allegiance

中世 **Chūsei** the Middle Ages

注射 **chūsha** injection

駐車 **chūsha** parking

駐車場 **chūshajō** parking lot

駐車禁止 **chūsha-kinshi** no
parking

中止 **chūshi** stoppage

中心 **chūshin** center

中傷 **chūshō** slander

昼食 **chūshoku** lunch

抽象的(な) **chūshōteki (na)**
abstract

中東 **Chūtō** the Middle East

中絶 **chūzetsu** interruption;
abortion

D

だ **da** be

打撲症 **dabokushō** bruise

だぶだぶ(の) **dabudabu
(no)** baggy

ダブルベッド **daburu-
beddo** double bed

ダブル(の) **daburu (no)**
double

だ液 **daeki** saliva

打楽器 **dagakki** percussion
instrument

駄菓子屋 **dagashiya**
confectionery

打撃 **dageki** hit

台 **dai** pedestal

題 **dai** title

…代 **-dai** generation

大 **dai** large

第… **dai-** (ordinal prefix): 第
一 **dai-ichi** first

ダイバー **daibā** diver

大便 **daiben** feces

ダイビング **daibingu** dive
(underwater)

大分 **daibu** very

大部分 **daibubun** bulk

大仏 **daibutsu** great statue of
Buddha

台地 **daichi** plateau

台所 **daidokoro** kitchen

ダイエット **daietto** diet

大学 **daigaku** university

大学院 **daigakuin** graduate
school

大学生 **daigakusei** college
student

代表 **daihyō** representative

大臣 **daijin** minister POL

大事(な) **daiji (na)** important

大丈夫 **daijōbu** OK

代金 **daikin** price

大根 **daikon** white radish

大人気 **daininki** phenomenon

代理 **dairi** representative

代理人 **dairinin** agent

大理石 **dairiseki** marble

代理店 **dairiten** agency

大聖堂 **daiseidō** cathedral

大好き(な) **daisuki (na)** favorite

だいたい **daitai** approximately

大胆(な) **daitan (na)** bold

大統領 **daitōryō** president

大都市 **daitoshi** metropolis

ダイヤモンド **daiyamondo** diamond

代用品 **daiyōhin** substitute

大豆 **daizu** soy bean

だから **dakara** therefore; because

…だけ ... **dake** only

だけど **dakedo** but

抱き合う **dakiau** embrace

抱き締める **dakishimeru** hug

抱く **daku** embrace

妥協 **dakyō** compromise

黙る **damaru** shut up

だます **damasu** deceive

駄目(な) **dame (na)** no good

ダム **damu** dam

段 **dan** step

暖房 **danbō** heating

段ボール **danbōru** cardboard

団地 **danchi** public apartment complex

だんだん **dandan** gradually

断言 **dangen** declaration

だんご **dango** dumpling

断食 **danjiki** fast *(not eating)*

男女 **danjo** men and women

段階 **dankai** stage

団結 **danketsu** solidarity

断固とした **danko to shita** determined

旦那 **danna** master; husband

段落 **danraku** paragraph

暖炉 **danro** fireplace

弾力性 **danryokusei** elasticity

男性 **dansei** male

男性的(な) **danseiteki (na)** masculine

男子 **danshi** boy

男尊女卑 **danson-johi** male domination

ダンス **dansu** dance

団体 **dantai** group

断定 **dantei** conclusion

だらしない **darashinai** untidy; loose *morals*

誰 **dare** who

誰でも **dare demo** whoever

誰か **dareka** somebody

誰も **dare mo** anybody; nobody

誰(の) **dare (no)** whose

だろう **darō** will probably (be) ◊ suppose

だるい **darui** listless

だるま **daruma** Dharma figurine

ダサい **dasai** provincial

打算的(な) **dasanteki (na)** crafty

脱線 **dassen** digression

脱走 **dassō** escape

脱水する **dassui suru** spin dry

出す **dasu** put out; issue *warning etc*

妥当(な) **datō (na)** appropriate

打倒する **datō suru** overturn

だった **datta** was, were

脱退 **dattai** withdraw

…で … **de** ◊ in; at; on ◊ by; with

出会い **deai** encounter

…である … **de aru** be

出会う **deau** happen to meet

でぶ **debu** fatso

出口 **deguchi** exit

出入口 **deiriguchi** doorway

出かける **dekakeru** go out

出来上がる **dekiagaru** be finished

出来事 **dekigoto** event

できれば **dekireba** if possible

できる **dekiru** be able to

できるだけ **dekiru dake** as … as possible

でこぼこ(な) **dekoboko (na)** uneven

出前 **demae** home delivery

デモ **demo** demonstration

でも **demo** ◊ but; though ◊: 誰でも **dare demo** anyone; どこでも **doko demo** anywhere

出迎える **demukaeru** go and meet

電圧 **den'atsu** voltage

電池 **denchi** battery

電源 **dengen** power supply

伝言 **dengon** message

電化製品 **denka-seihin** appliance

伝記 **denki** biography

電気 **denki** electricity

電気屋 **denkiya** appliance store

電球 **denkyū** (light) bulb

電熱器 **dennetsuki** hotplate

電報 **denpō** telegram, wire

伝票 **denpyō** slip *(paper)*

電力 **denryoku** power

電流 **denryū** current

電線 **densen** power line

伝染 **densen** infection

伝染性(の) **densensei (no)** contagious

伝説 **densetsu** legend

電車 **densha** train

電子工学 **denshi-kōgaku** electronics

電子レンジ **denshi-renji** microwave (oven)

電卓 **dentaku** pocket calculator

伝統 **dentō** tradition

伝統(な) **dentōteki (na)** traditional

電話 **denwa** phone; phone call

電話番号 **denwa-bangō** phone number

電話帳 **denwachō** phone directory

電話機 **denwaki** phone

デオドラント **deodoranto** deodorant

デパート **depāto** department store

デリケート(な) **derikēto (na)** delicate

出る **deru** come out

弟子 **deshi** disciple

でした **deshita** polite form of datta

でしょう **deshō** polite form of darō will probably (be)

です **desu** polite form of da be

データ **dēta** data

データベース **dēta-bēsu** database

データ保護 **dēta-hogo** data

protection

データ処理 **dēta-shori** data processing

デート **dēto** date (romantic)

では **dewa** well then

デザイン **dezain** design

デザート **dezāto** dessert

ディスコ **disuko** disco

ディスク **disuku** disk

ディスクドライブ **disuku-doraibu** disk drive

ディーゼル **dīzeru** diesel

度 **do** degree

どう **dō** how; what; どうでもいい **dō demo ī** it doesn't make any difference; どうしたの **dō shita no** what's the matter?

銅 **dō** copper

胴 **dō** trunk (of body)

同… **dō-** same

ドア **doa** door

動物 **dōbutsu** animal

動物園 **dōbutsuen** zoo

どちら **dochira** which

どちらでも **dochira demo** whichever

どちらも **dochira mo** both

どちら(の) **dochira (no)** which

同封する **dōfū suru** enclose (in letter)

道具 **dōgu** tool

土俵 **dohyō** sumo ring

同意 **dōi** agreement

どういたしまして **dō itashimashite** you're welcome

ドイツ **Doitsu** Germany

ドイツ語 **Doitsugo** German (language)

ドイツ人 **Doitsujin** German

同時に **dōji ni** at the same time

同情 **dōjō** sympathy

どうか **dō ka** ◊ please; どうか手伝ってください **dō ka tetsudatte kudasai** please help ◊ whether (or not);買うかどうか **kau ka dō ka** whether to buy or not

動機 **dōki** motivation

動悸 **dōki** palpitations

どきどきする **dokidoki suru** pound (of heart)

ドック **dokku** dock

どこ **doko** where

瞳孔 **dōkō** pupil (eye)

同行 **dōkō** accompany

どこでも **doko demo** wherever

どこか **dokoka** somewhere

どこも **doko mo** anywhere; nowhere

どこに **doko ni** where

どこにも **doko nimo** anywhere; nowhere

毒 **doku** poison

独自 (の) **dokuji (no)** original

独立 **dokuritsu** independence

独立記念日 **Dokuritsu-kinenbi** Independence Day

独立 (の) **dokuritsu (no)** independent

独裁者 **dokusaisha** dictator

独裁的 (な) **dokusaiteki (na)** dictatorial

独占 **dokusen** monopoly

読者 **dokusha** reader

独身 (の) **dokushin (no)** unmarried

読書 **dokusho** reading

独奏 **dokusō** solo

独創性 **dokusōsei** originality

独特 (な) **dokutoku (na)** distinctive

同級生 **dōkyūsei** classmate

同盟 **dōmei** alliance

どうも **dōmo** ◊ thank you ◊ very much; どうもありがとう **dōmo arigatō** thanks very much

どう猛 (な) **dōmō (na)** ferocious

どもる **domoru** stammer

ドーム **dōmu** dome

動脈 **dōmyaku** artery

どなる **donaru** shout

どなた **donata** polite form of **dare** who

ドーナツ **dōnatsu** doughnut

丼 **donburi** bowl of rice

どうにか **dōnika** somehow

鈍感(な) **donkan (na)**
insensitive

どんな **donna** what kind of?

どの **dono** which どのくら
い **dono kurai** how much?;
how long?

…殿 **-dono** polite title suffix
used in formal letters after
addressee's name

どんよりした **don'yori shita**
lackluster

導入 **dōnyū** introduction

ドライバー **doraibā** driver;
screwdriver

ドライブ **doraibu** drive (also
COMPUT)

ドライクリーニング **dorai-
kurīningu** dry cleaning

ドラマ **dorama** drama

ドラム **doramu** drum

どれ **dore** which

どれでも **dore demo**
whichever

どれくらい **dore kurai** how
much?; how long?

ドレッシング **doresshingu**
(salad) dressing

ドレス **doresu** dress

泥 **doro** mud

道路 **dōro** road

泥棒 **dorobō** thief

ドル **doru** dollar

同僚 **dōryō** colleague

努力 **doryoku** effort

動作 **dōsa** movement

どうせ **dōse** anyhow; at best

同棲 **dōsei** cohabitation

同性愛(の) **dōseiai (no)**
homosexual

同性愛者 **dōseiaisha**
homosexual

同志 **dōshi** comrade

動詞 **dōshi** verb

どうして **dōshite** why?

どうしても **dōshite mo** by
any means

同窓会 **dōsōkai** reunion

どっしりした **dosshiri shita**
massive

どっち **dotchi** which?

同点 **dōten** tie (in sports)

道徳 **dōtoku** ethics

道徳的(な) **dōtokuteki (na)**
ethical

同等(の) **dōtō (no)**
equivalent

ドット **dotto** dot

童話 **dōwa** fairy tale

どうやって **dō yatte** how?

童謡 **dōyō** nursery rhyme

同様(の) **dōyō** same

土曜日 **doyōbi** Saturday

どうぞ **dōzo** please; come in!;
go ahead!

E

絵 **e** painting

へ **e** to

ええ **ē** yes

エーッ **ē'** *(expression of surprise, doubt or hesitation)* eh?

エアコン **eakon** air conditioning

えび **ebi** shrimp; prawn

枝 **eda** branch

江戸時代 **Edo-jidai** Edo period (1603-1867)

絵筆 **efude** paintbrush

描く **egaku** depict

笑顔 **egao** smiling face

絵はがき **ehagaki** (picture) postcard

絵本 **ehon** picture book

永遠 **eien** eternity

映画 **eiga** movie

映画館 **eigakan** movie theater

英語 **Eigo** English *(language)*

営業 **eigyō** business

営業中(の) **eigyōchū (no)** open for business

営業時間 **eigyō-jikan** business hours

英国 **Eikoku** Britain

英国人 **Eikokujin** British person

英国(の) **Eikoku (no)** British

影響 **eikyō** influence

永久に **eikyū ni** permanently

衛生 **eisei** hygiene

衛星 **eisei** satellite

衛星テレビ **eisei-terebi** satellite TV

英和辞典 **Eiwa jiten** English-Japanese dictionary

栄養 **eiyō** nourishment

英雄 **eiyū** hero

エイズ **eizu** Aids

絵かき **ekaki** painter

駅 **eki** (railroad) station

駅弁 **ekiben** (railroad) lunch box

疫病 **ekibyō** plague

エキスパート **ekisupāto** expert

液体 **ekitai** liquid

エキゾチック(な) **ekizochikku (na)** exotic

エコノミークラス **ekonomī-kurasu** economy class

エメラルド **emerarudo** emerald

エムサイズ **em-saizu** medium

円 **en** circle; yen

縁 **en** fate

延長 **enchō** extension

延長コード **enchō-kōdo** extension cable

円高 **endaka** appreciation of the yen

演壇 **endan** platform

えんどう豆 **endōmame** pea

えんえんと **en'en to** endlessly

エネルギー **enerugī** energy

沿岸(の) **engan (no)** coastal

縁側 **engawa** veranda

演劇 **engeki** drama

演技 **engi** performance

縁起 **engi** omen

エンジン **enjin** engine

エンジニア **enjinia** engineer

演じる **enjiru** play *role*

援助 **enjo** aid

宴会 **enkai** banquet

円形(の) **enkei (no)** circular

延期 **enki** postponement

円満(な) **enman (na)** peaceful

絵の具 **enogu** paint

鉛筆 **enpitsu** pencil

鉛筆削り **enpitsu-kezuri** pencil sharpener

遠慮 **enryo** personal restraint;

ご遠慮なく **go-enryo naku** go ahead; help yourself

遠視(の) **enshi (no)** far-sighted

炎症 **enshō** inflammation

円周 **enshū** circumference

演出 **enshutsu** direction *(movies)*

塩素 **enso** chlorine

演奏 **ensō** performance

遠足 **ensoku** excursion

煙突 **entotsu** chimney

円安 **en'yasu** depreciation of the yen

演説 **enzetsu** public speech

選ぶ **erabu** choose

偉い **erai** eminent

エラーメッセージ **erā-messēji** error message

エレベーター **erebētā** elevator

エレガント(な) **ereganto (na)** elegant

襟 **eri** collar

エリート **erīto** elite

得る **eru** obtain

えさ **esa** bait

エッセイ **essei** essay

エース **ēsu** ace

エスカレーター **esukarētā** escalator

エッチ(な) **etchi (na)** dirty-minded

えーっと **ētto** well ...

F

ファインダー **faindā**
viewfinder

ファイル **fairu** file

ファックス **fakkusu** fax

ファン **fan** fan *(sports etc)*

ファッション **fasshon**
fashion

ファスナー **fasunā** fastener

ファーストフード **fāsuto
fūdo** fast food

ファーストクラス **fāsuto
kurasu** first class

ファウル **fauru** foul

フェリー **ferī** ferry

フィリピン(の) **Firipin (no)**
Philippine

フィルム **firumu** film

フィルター **firutā** filter

フォーク **fōku** fork

不… **fu-** non-; un-

風(な) **fū** style

不安 **fuan** insecurity

不安(な) **fuan (na)** uneasy

不安定 **fuantei** instability

不安定(な) **fuantei (na)**
unstable

不便(な) **fuben (na)**
inconvenient

不備(な) **fubi (na)** defective

吹雪 **fubuki** blizzard

不平等(な) **fubyōdō (na)**
unequal

縁 **fuchi** frame; edge

不注意(な) **fuchūi (na)**
careless

札 **fuda** tag

普段着 **fudangi** casual wear

不断(の) **fudan (no)** perpetual

筆 **fude** writing brush

フード **fūdo** hood *(on head)*

不動産 **fudōsan** real estate

不動産屋 **fudōsan'ya** real
estate agent

笛 **fue** whistle

増える **fueru** increase

夫婦 **fūfu** married couple

風変わり(な) **fūgawari (na)**
eccentric

不合理(な) **fugōri (na)**
illogical

ふぐ **fugu** blowfish

不平 **fuhei** complaint

普遍的(な) **fuhenteki (na)**
universal

不法(な) **fuhō (na)** illicit

不評(な) **fuhyō (na)** unpopular

不意に **fui ni** unexpectedly

藤 **fuji** wisteria

不時着 **fujichaku** crash
landing

夫人 **fujin** wife

婦人 **fujin** lady

婦人科 **fujinka** gynecologist

富士山 **Fuji-san** Mt. Fuji

不自由 (な) **fujiyū (na)** physically handicapped

不十分 (な) **fujūbun (na)** inadequate

負荷 **fuka** load ELEC

深い **fukai** deep

不快 (な) **fukai (na)** unpleasant

不可解 (な) **fukakai (na)** baffling

深まる **fukamaru** deepen

不可能 (な) **fukanō (na)** impossible

深さ **fukasa** depth

ふけ **fuke** dandruff

風景 **fūkei** scenery

不景気 **fukeiki** slump

ふける **fukeru** indulge in; grow old

不潔 (な) **fuketsu (na)** filthy

不機嫌である **fukigen de aru** be in a temper

吹替えする **fukikae suru** dub

ふきん **fukin** cloth

付近 **fukin** neighborhood

不謹慎 (な) **fukinshin (na)** indiscreet

吹き飛ばす **fukitobasu** blow away

不吉 (な) **fukitsu (na)** ominous

復活 **fukkatsu** revival

復活祭 **Fukkatsusai** Easter

フック **fukku** hook

ふっくらする **fukkura suru** plump up

不公平 (な) **fukōhei (na)** unfair

不幸 (な) **fukō (na)** unfortunate

不公正 **fukōsei** injustice

ふく **fuku** mop up; wipe

吹く **fuku** blow

服 **fuku** clothes

福 **fuku** good fortune

副… **fuku-** vice-; deputy

副業 **fukugyō** sideline

服従 **fukujū** obedience

含める **fukumeru** include

含めて **fukumete** including

含む **fukumu** include

ふくらはぎ **fukurahagi** calf (of leg)

膨らみ **fukurami** bulge

膨れる **fukureru** bulge

袋 **fukuro** bag

ふくろう **fukurō** owl

副作用 **fukusayō** side effect

複製 **fukusei** copy

副詞 **fukushi** adverb

福祉 **fukushi** welfare

復習 **fukushū** review (of lessons)

復しゅう **fukushū** revenge

服装 **fukusō** clothing

服用法 **fukuyōhō** directions
MED

複雑（な）**fukuzatsu (na)**
complicated

不況 **fukyō** depression
(economic)

普及 **fukyū** spread

不満（な）**fuman (na)**
dissatisfied

不満足（な）**fumanzoku (na)**
unsatisfactory

不明（の）**fumei (no)**
unclear

不名誉（な）**fumeiyo (na)**
dishonorable

踏み入れる **fumi-ireru**
step into

踏切 **fumikiri** grade crossing

不眠 **fumin** insomnia

不毛（の）**fumō (no)** barren

ふもと **fumoto** bottom

踏む **fumu** tread on

ふん **fun** dung

分 **fun** minute

船便 **funabin** shipping

船旅 **funatabi** cruise

分別のある **funbetsu no aru**
sensible

船 **fune** ship

憤慨 **fungai** indignation

雰囲気 **fun'iki** atmosphere

噴火 **funka** eruption

噴火口 **funkakō** crater

紛失 **funshitsu** loss

噴出 **funshutsu** eruption

紛争 **funsō** dispute

噴水 **funsui** fountain

ふらふら（の）**furafura (no)**
unsteady

フライドポテト **furaido-
poteto** French fries

フライパン **furaipan** frying
pan

フランス **Furansu** France

フランス語 **Furansugo**
French *(language)*

フランス人 **Furansujin**
French person

フランス（の）**Furansu (no)**
French

フラッシュ **furasshu**
flash(light)

フレーム **furēmu** frame

触れる **fureru** touch

不利 **furi** disadvantage

ふりがな **furigana** *small
kana written beside kanji as a
pronunciation aid*

振り返る **furikaeru** turn
around

ふりかける **furikakeru**
sprinkle

風呂 **furo** bath

風呂場 **furoba** bathroom

フロント **furonto** reception
desk

フロント係 **furonto-gakari** receptionist

フロントガラス **furonto-garasu** windshield

浮浪者 **furōsha** tramp

風呂敷 **furoshiki** wrapping cloth

降る **furu** fall *(of rain, snow)*

振る **furu** shake; swing

震える **furueru** shake *(of voice, hand)*; shiver

古本屋 **furuhon'ya** secondhand bookstore

古い **furui** old

古くさい **furukusai** old-fashioned

ふるまい **furumai** behavior

ふるまう **furumau** behave; treat *(to food and drink)*

古里 **furusato** hometown

フルート **furūto** flute

フルーツ **furūtsu** fruit

不良 **furyō** juvenile delinquent

房 **fusa** lock *(of hair)*; tassel

封鎖 **fūsa** blockade

ふさぐ **fusagu** obstruct

夫妻 **fusai** husband and wife

不採用 **fusaiyō** rejection

ふさわしい **fusawashī** suitable

防ぐ **fusegu** prevent

不正 **fusei** injustice

不正(な) **fusei (na)** unjust

風船 **fūsen** balloon

風車 **fūsha** windmill

不思議(な) **fushigi (na)** mysterious

不審(な) **fushin (na)** questionable

不親切(な) **fushinsetsu (na)** unkind

不自然(な) **fushizen (na)** unnatural

負傷 **fushō** injury

不正直(な) **fushōjiki (na)** dishonest

腐食 **fushoku** corrosion

負傷者 **fushōsha** the injured

不足 **fusoku** shortage

ふすま **fusuma** sliding screen

ふた **futa** lid

双子 **futago** twin

二けた(の) **futaketa no** double-digit

負担 **futan** burden

負担する **futan suru** bear *(costs)*

二人 **futari** two people

再び **futatabi** again

二つ **futatsu** two

不定期(の) **futeiki (no)** irregular

不定(の) **futei (no)** indefinite

ふと **futo** suddenly

封筒 **fūtō** envelope

不凍液 **futōeki** antifreeze

太い **futoi** thick *rope*; deep *voice*

不透明 (な) **futōmei (na)**
opaque

ふとん **futon** futon

不当 (な) **futō (na)** unfair

太る **futoru** put on weight

太った **futotta** fat

二日 **futsuka** two days;
the 2nd

二日酔い **futsukayoi**
hangover

普通 (の) **futsū (no)** usual

普通は **futsū wa** usually

普通預金口座 **futsū-yokin-kōza** savings account

不運 **fu-un** bad luck

ふわふわした **fuwafuwa
shita** fluffy

増やす **fuyasu** increase

扶養 **fuyō** support

不用 (の) **fuyō (no)** waste

冬 **fuyu** winter

不愉快 (な) **fuyukai (na)**
unpleasant

冬休み **fuyuyasumi** winter
vacation

不在 (の) **fuzai (no)** absent

ふざける **fuzakeru** fool
around

ふざけて **fuzakete** jokingly

風俗 **fūzoku** manners

付属 (の) **fuzoku (no)**
affiliated

ふぞろい (の) **fuzoroi (no)**
uneven

G

が **ga** but ◊ *(subject particle)*:
私がやった *watashi ga
yatta* I did it

蛾 **ga** moth

画びょう **gabyō** thumbtack

がちょう **gachō** goose

ガードマン **gādoman**
guard

害 **gai** harm

外部 **gaibu** exterior

害虫 **gaichū** pest

ガイド **gaido** guide

ガイドブック **gaidobukku**

guidebook

外人 **gaijin** foreigner *pej*

外貨 **gaika** foreign currency

外観 **gaikan** façade

外見 **gaiken** appearance

外交 **gaikō** diplomacy

外交官 **gaikōkan** diplomat

外国 **gaikoku** foreign
country

外国語 **gaikokugo** foreign
language

外国人 **gaikokujin**
foreigner

外国人登録証明書 **gaikokujin tōroku shōmeisho** alien registration card

外国為替 **gaiku-kawase** foreign exchange

がい骨 **gaikotsu** skeleton

外務省 **Gaimushō** (Japanese) State Department

概念 **gainen** concept

外来語 **gairaigo** loanword

概算で **gaisan de** approximately

概して **gaishite** as a rule

外食する **gaishoku suru** eat out

外出する **gaishutsu suru** go out

街灯 **gaitō** streetlight

概要 **gaiyō** outline

画家 **gaka** artist

がけ **gake** cliff

学科 **gakka** academic department

学会 **gakkai** academic association

がっかりした **gakkari shita** disappointed

楽器 **gakki** musical instrument

学期 **gakki** semester

学校 **gakkō** school

額 **gaku** sum; frame

学 **gaku** learning

学部 **gakubu** department (in college)

学長 **gakuchō** college president

楽団 **gakudan** orchestra

楽譜 **gakufu** score MUS

学費 **gakuhi** tuition fees

学位 **gakui** degree

学問 **gakumon** scholarship

学年 **gakunen** academic year

学歴 **gakureki** educational background

学生 **gakusei** student

学生寮 **gakuseiryō** college dorm

学者 **gakusha** scholar

学習 **gakushū** learning

我慢 **gaman** patience

我慢強い **gamanzuyoi** patient

画面 **gamen** screen

ガム **gamu** gum

がん **gan** cancer

がんばる **ganbaru** persevere

がんばって **ganbatte** good luck!

願望 **ganbō** longing

元日 **Ganjitsu** New Year's Day

頑丈（な）**ganjō (na)** robust

眼科医 **gankai** ophthalmologist

頑固（な）**ganko (na)** stubborn

願書 **gansho** application form

元旦 **Gantan** New Year's Day

合併 **gappei** merger

合併症 **gappeishō**

complications MED

柄 **gara** character; pattern

がらくた **garakuta** junk

ガラス **garasu** glass

ガレージ **garēji** garage

画廊 **garō** art gallery

ガールフレンド
 gārufurendo girlfriend

ガソリン **gasorin** gasoline

ガソリンスタンド **gasorin-
 sutando** gas station

がっしりした **gasshiri shita**
 sturdy

合唱団 **gasshōdan** chorus

合宿 **gasshuku** lodging
 together

ガス **gasu** gas

がたがた(の) **gatagata (no)**
 ramshackle

側 **gawa** side

ガーゼ **gāze** gauze

下品(な) **gehin (na)** vulgar

芸術 **geijutsu** art

芸術家 **geijutsuka** artist

芸術作品 **geijutsu-sakuhin**
 work of art

芸術的(な) **geijutsuteki
 (na)** artistic

芸者 **geisha** geisha

下旬 **gejun** last 10 days of
 a month

外科 **geka** surgery

外科医 **gekai** surgeon

劇 **geki** play

激怒 **gekido** fury

劇場 **gekijō** theater

撃退する **gekitai suru** repel

劇的(な) **gekiteki (na)**
 dramatic

月刊(の) **gekkan (no)**
 monthly

月刊誌 **gekkanshi** monthly
 (magazine)

月給 **gekkyū** monthly salary

ゲーム **gēmu** game

ゲームセンター **gēmu-
 sentā** arcade

現場 **genba** scene

原爆 **genbaku** atom bomb

現地時間 **genchi-jikan**
 local time

現代(の) **gendai (no)**
 contemporary

現代的(な) **gendaiteki (na)**
 modern *way of thinking*

限度 **gendo** limit

弦楽器 **gengakki** stringed
 instrument

言語 **gengo** language

原因 **gen'in** cause

現実 **genjitsu** reality

原住民 **genjūmin** native

厳重に **genjū ni** strictly

限界 **genkai** limitation

厳格(な) **genkaku (na)**
 austere

玄関 **genkan** entrance hall

元気 **genki** vigor

現金 **genkin** cash

元気(な) **genki (na)** vigorous

現金自動支払機 **genkin-jidō-shiharaiki** ATM

原稿 **genkō** manuscript

原告 **genkoku** plaintiff

言及する **genkyū suru** refer to

玄米 **genmai** unpolished rice

幻滅 **genmetsu** disillusionment

厳密(な) **genmitsu (na)** strict

原理 **genri** principle

原料 **genryō** raw materials

原子 **genshi** atom

原子力 **genshiryoku** atomic energy

原子力爆弾 **genshiryoku-bakudan** atom bomb

原子力発電所 **genshiryoku-hatsudensho** nuclear power station

減少 **genshō** decrease

現象 **genshō** phenomenon

厳粛(な) **genshuku (na)** solemn

幻想 **gensō** fantasy

原則 **gensoku** general principle

原則的には **gensokuteki ni wa** in principle

限定 **gentei** limitation

原油 **gen'yu** crude (oil)

現在 **genzai** right now ◊ the present

現在(の) **genzai (no)** current

現像 **genzō** development (photo)

げっぷ **geppu** belch

下落 **geraku** decline

ゲレンデ **gerende** ski run

下痢 **geri** diarrhea

下宿 **geshuku** lodgings

下水 **gesui** sewage

下水道 **gesuidō** sewer

下駄 **geta** thonged clogs

ゲート **gēto** gate

月末 **getsumatsu** end of the month

月曜日 **getsuyōbi** Monday

下剤 **gezai** laxative

ギア **gia** gear

議案 **gian** bill POL

議長 **gichō** chairperson

議題 **gidai** agenda

ギフト **gifuto** gift

議員 **gi-in** member of the Diet

議事録 **gijiroku** minutes (of meeting)

技術 **gijutsu** technique

議会 **gikai** national assembly

疑問 **gimon** doubt

疑問符 **gimonfu** question mark

義務 **gimu** duty

義務教育 **gimu-kyōiku** compulsory education

銀 **gin** silver

銀行 **ginkō** bank FIN

銀行口座 **ginkō-kōza** bank

account

銀めっき（の）**gin-mekki (no)** silver-plated

ギプス **gipusu** plaster cast

義理 **giri** obligation

ギリシア **Girishia** Greece

義理と人情 **giri to ninjō** duty and emotion

議論 **giron** argument

犠牲 **gisei** sacrifice

犠牲者 **giseisha** victim

技師 **gishi** engineer

儀式 **gishiki** ceremony

ぎっしり詰まって **gisshiri tsumatte** chock-full

ギター **gitā** guitar

ぎざぎざ（の）**gizagiza (no)** jagged

偽善 **gizen** hypocrisy

偽善者 **gizensha** hypocrite

偽造（の）**gizō (no)** counterfeit

五 **go** five

語 **go** word

碁 **go** game of Go

…go **-go** after

御…；ご…**go-** (honorific prefix): ご家族 **gokazoku** your family

ごちゃごちゃ **gochagocha** muddle

ごちそうさまでした **gochisōsama deshita** thank you, that was delicious

語学 **gogaku** language study

五月 **gogatsu** May

午後 **gogo** afternoon

ゴーグル **gōguru** goggles

ご飯 **gohan** rice (cooked)

合法的（な）**gōhōteki (na)** legal

語い **goi** vocabulary

合意 **gōi** consensus

強情（な）**gōjō (na)** pigheaded

五十 **gojū** fifty

五重の塔 **gojūnotō** five-story pagoda

誤解 **gokai** misunderstanding

合格 **gōkaku** pass (an exam)

強かん **gōkan** rape

豪華（な）**gōka (na)** luxurious

互換性 **gokansei** compatibility

合計 **gōkei** total

ごきぶり **gokiburi** cockroach

ごく **goku** extremely

ご苦労さま **gokurōsama** thanks for your help

胡麻 **goma** sesame

ごまかし **gomakashi** deception

ごまかす **gomakasu** deceive

ごう慢（な）**gōman (na)** arrogant

ごめんなさい **gomen nasai** I'm sorry

ごみ **gomi** garbage

塵箱 **gomibako** trash can

拷問 **gōmon** torture

ゴム **gomu** rubber

ゴムひも **gomuhimo** piece
of elastic

娯楽 **goraku** recreation

御覧 **goran** look! *(polite form)*

合理化 **gōrika** rationalization

合理的（な）**gōriteki (na)** rational

…頃 **...goro** around

ゴール **gōru** goal

ゴールデンウィーク
gōruden-wīku Golden Week
(string of national holidays between April 29 and May 5)

ゴルフ **gorufu** golf

ゴルフクラブ **gorufu-kurabu** golf club

ゴールキーパー **gōru-kīpā** goalkeeper

合成（の）**gōsei (no)** synthetic

誤植 **goshoku** misprint

強盗 **gōtō** robber; holdup

…ごとに **-goto ni** each

御用 **goyō** order; business

ございます **gozaimasu** polite form of **aru**

午前 **gozen** a.m.

具合 **guai** condition

ぐち **guchi** complaint

郡 **gun** county

軍 **gun** army

軍人 **gunjin** soldier

軍事（の）**gunji (no)** military

軍艦 **gunkan** warship

群衆 **gunshū** crowd

軍隊 **guntai** armed forces

グラフ **gurafu** graph

ぐらい **gurai** around

グラム **guramu** gram

グラス **gurasu** tumbler

グレープフルーツ
gurēpufurūtsu grapefruit

グリーン車 **gurīnsha** first
class car *(on bullet train)*

グリル **guriru** grill

ぐるぐる巻く **guruguru maku** coil (up)

グルメ **gurume** gourmet

グループ **gurūpu** group

ぐっすり **gussuri** soundly

偶数（の）**gūsū (no)** even

具体的（な）**gutaiteki (na)** concrete

偶然 **gūzen** coincidence

ぐずぐずする **guzuguzu suru** dawdle

逆 **gyaku** opposite

逆風 **gyakufū** headwind

虐殺 **gyakusatsu** massacre

逆説 **gyakusetsu** paradox

逆説的（な）**gyakusetsuteki (na)** paradoxical

虐待 **gyakutai** abuse

行 **gyō** line *(of text)*

行儀 **gyōgi** manners

行事 **gyōji** event; festivities

魚介類 **gyokairui** seafood

凝固する **gyōko suru**

coagulate
行列 **gyōretsu** procession
行政 **gyōsei** administration
業績 **gyōseki** achievement
凝視する **gyōshi suru** stare ·

ギョウザ **gyōza** Chinese dumpling
牛肉 **gyūniku** beef
牛乳 **gyūnyū** milk
ぎゅっと **gyutto** firmly

H

刃 **ha** blade
歯 **ha** tooth; cog
葉 **ha** leaf
把握する **ha-aku suru** comprehend
幅 **haba** breadth; range ·
幅跳び **habatobi** long jump
派閥 **habatsu** in-group
ハーブ **hābu** herb
省く **habuku** leave out
歯ブラシ **haburashi** toothbrush
はち **hachi** wasp
鉢 **hachi** bowl
八 **hachi** eight
八月 **hachigatsu** August
はちまき **hachimaki** headband
はちみつ **hachimitsu** honey
肌 **hada** skin
裸(の) **hadaka (no)** naked
裸足(の) **hadashi (no)** barefoot
肌寒い **hadazamui** chilly
派手(な) **hade (na)** showy

ハードディスク **hādo disuku** hard disk
ハエ **hae** fly
生える **haeru** grow
葉書 **hagaki** postcard
はがれる **hagareru** come off
はがす **hagasu** peel off
励ます **hagemasu** encourage
励む **hagemu** make a big effort
激しい **hageshī** violent *emotion, storm*; acute *pain*; heavy *rain*
はげた **hageta** bald
歯ぐき **haguki** gum *(in mouth)*
母 **haha** mother
母親 **hahaoya** mother
破片 **hahen** fragment
はい **hai** yes; no *(to negative question)*; uh-huh *(I'm listening)*
灰 **hai** ash
肺 **hai** lung
杯 **hai** cup
敗北 **haiboku** defeat

配置 **haichi** arrangement
肺炎 **haien** pneumonia
配布 **haifu** distribution
肺がん **haigan** lung cancer
灰色(の) **hai-iro (no)** gray
ハイジャック **haijakku** hijack
配管 **haikan** plumbing
配管工 **haikankō** plumber
背景 **haikei** background .
拝啓 **haikei** Dear Sir
拝見する **haiken suru** H see
廃棄 **haiki** disposal
廃棄物 **haikibutsu** waste product
排気ガス **haikigasu** exhaust fumes
排気管 **haikikan** exhaust (pipe)
ハイキング **haikingu** hiking
俳句 **haiku** haiku
入る **hairu** enter
歯医者 **haisha** dentist
敗者 **haisha** loser
廃止 **haishi** abolition
排水 **haisui** drainage
排水管 **haisuikan** drainpipe
敗退 **haitai** defeat
配達 **haitatsu** delivery
俳優 **haiyū** actor
灰皿 **haizara** ashtray
恥 **haji** shame
はじく **hajiku** flip
初まり **hajimari** beginning

始まる **hajimaru** begin
初め **hajime** beginning
はじめまして **hajimemashite** how do you do?
始める **hajimeru** begin
初めて **hajimete** for the first time
初めは **hajime wa** at first
墓 **haka** grave
破壊 **hakai** destruction
破壊的(な) **hakaiteki (na)** destructive
はかま **hakama** *traditional pants, like culottes*
はかり **hakari** scales
測る **hakaru** measure
量る **hakaru** weigh
図る **hakaru** plan
博士号 **hakasegō** doctorate
はけ **hake** paintbrush
派遣 **haken** temp
吐き出す **hakidasu** spew out
吐き気 **hakike** vomiting
はきもの **hakimono** footwear
発覚 **hakkaku** disclosure
発見 **hakken** discovery
はっきり **hakkiri** clearly
発酵 **hakkō** fermentation
発行 **hakkō** issue
発行者 **hakkōsha** publisher
発掘 **hakkutsu** excavation
箱 **hako** box
運ぶ **hakobu** carry

はく **haku** wear; put on *footwear, pants*

吐く **haku** vomit

掃く **haku** sweep

…泊 **-haku** overnight stay

博物館 **hakubutsukan** museum

白鳥 **hakuchō** swan

迫害 **hakugai** persecution

白人 **hakujin** Caucasian

白状 **hakujō** confession

拍手 **hakushu** applause

浜辺 **hamabe** beach

はめる **hameru** wear *gloves, rings*

破滅 **hametsu** ruin

歯みがき粉 **hamigakiko** toothpaste

ハム **hamu** ham

班 **han** squad

版 **han** edition

判 **han** stamp; seal

半 **han** half

反… **han-** anti-

花 **hana** flower

鼻 **hana** nose

花火 **hanabi** fireworks

花びら **hanabira** petal

鼻血 **hanaji** nosebleed

花見 **hanami** blossom viewing

鼻水 **hanamizu** mucus

花婿 **hanamuko** bridegroom

離れる **hanareru** break away

離れた **hanareta** remote

話 **hanashi** talk

話し合い **hanashiai** discussion

話し合う **hanashiau** discuss

話中(の) **hanashi-chū (no)** busy *(phone line)*

話しかける **hanashikakeru** speak to

話し言葉 **hanashi-kotoba** vernacular

離す **hanasu** disengage

放す **hanasu** release

話す **hanasu** speak

花束 **hanataba** bunch of flowers

花屋 **hanaya** florist

華やか(な) **hanayaka (na)** gorgeous

花嫁 **hanayome** bride

花盛り(の) **hanazakari (no)** in full bloom

鼻詰まり **hanazumari** nasal congestion

ハンバーガー **hanbāgā** hamburger

販売 **hanbai** selling

販売店 **hanbaiten** outlet

半分 **hanbun** half

判断 **handan** judgment

反動 **handō** backlash

ハンドバッグ **handobaggu** handbag

ハンドル **handoru** (steering) wheel; handlebars

羽 **hane** wing; feather

羽根 **hane** shuttlecock

繁栄 **han'ei** prosperity

はね返る **hanekaeru** rebound

ハネムーン **hanemūn** honeymoon

半円 **han'en** semicircle

はねる **haneru** leap

版画 **hanga** woodblock print

ハンガー **hangā** clothes hanger

半額(の) **hangaku (no)** half-price

反撃 **hangeki** counter-attack

反逆 **hangyaku** revolt

反逆者 **hangyakusha** rebel

範囲 **han'i** scope

判事 **hanji** judge

繁盛している **hanjō shite iru** prospering

ハンカチ **hankachi** handkerchief

繁華街 **hankagai** busy shopping district

反感 **hankan** antipathy

判決 **hanketsu** judgment

はんこ **hanko** signature seal

反抗 **hankō** defiance

犯人 **hannin** culprit

反応 **hannō** reaction

反乱 **hanran** rebellion

反論する **hanron suru** refute

ハンサム(な) **hansamu (na)** handsome

反省 **hansei** self-reflection

帆船 **hansen** sailing ship

反射 **hansha** reflection

繁殖 **hanshoku** breeding

半そで(の) **hansode (no)** short-sleeved

反則 **hansoku** infringement

反則する **hansoku suru** foul SPORTS

半数(の) **hansū (no)** half

反対 **hantai** opposition

半島 **hantō** peninsula

犯罪 **hanzai** crime

半ズボン **hanzubon** shorts

はおり **haori** half-length Japanese coat

葉っぱ **happa** leaf

発砲される **happō sareru** go off *(of gun)*

発表 **happyō** announcement

腹 **hara** abdomen

払い込む **haraikomu** pay in

払い戻す **haraimodosu** repay

払う **harau** pay

腫れ **hare** swelling

晴れ(の) **hare (no)** fine *day*

晴れる **hareru** brighten up

腫れる **hareru** swell

破裂 **haretsu** rupture

針 **hari** needle; hand *(of clock)*

張り **hari** tension

はり治療 **harichiryō** acupuncture

はり紙 **harigami** notice

針金 **harigane** wire
張り付く **haritsuku** stick to
張り詰めた **haritsumeta** tense
はる **haru** stick onto
張る **haru** stretch; pitch *tent*
春 **haru** spring
春一番 **haruichiban** first south wind of spring
はるかに **haruka ni** far; by far
はさみ **hasami** scissors
挟む **hasamu** put between
破産 **hasan** bankruptcy
はし **hashi** chopsticks
橋 **hashi** bridge
端 **hashi** edge; end
はしご **hashigo** ladder
はしか **hashika** measles
はし置き **hashioki** chopstick rest
柱 **hashira** pillar
走り書き **hashirigaki** scribble
走る **hashiru** run
破損 **hason** damage
発生 **hassei** outbreak
発車 **hassha** departure
発射 **hassha** launch
発しん **hasshin** rash
発送 **hassō** dispatch
発する **hassuru** emit; issue
はす **hasu** lotus
旗 **hata** flag
はたち、二十歳 **hatachi** twenty (years old)

畑 **hatake** field
はためく **hatameku** flutter
働く **hataraku** work
果たす **hatasu** fulfill
はと **hato** dove; pigeon
波止場 **hatoba** wharf
発売 **hatsubai** launch *(of product)*
発電機 **hatsudenki** generator
発電所 **hatsudensho** power station
発言 **hatsugen** public statement
二十日 **hatsuka** 20th *(of month)*
発明 **hatsumei** invention
発明者 **hatsumeisha** inventor
初耳 **hatsumimi** first time to hear something
初詣 **hatsumōde** first shrine visit at New Year
発音 **hatsuon** pronunciation
発達 **hattatsu** growth
発展 **hatten** development
発展途上国 **hatten-tojōkoku** developing country
はう **hau** crawl
早い **hayai** early
速い **hayai** fast
早く **hayaku** early
速く **hayaku** fast
早目に **hayame ni** ahead of time
早める **hayameru** hasten

早起き **hayaoki** getting up
early

はやり(の) **hayari (no)**
trendy

はやる **hayaru** become
popular

速さ **hayasa** speed

林 **hayashi** woods

…はず **-hazu** should

恥ずかしがり(の)
hazukashigari (no) shy

恥ずかしい **hazukashī**
ashamed

弾み **hazumi** bounce;
momentum

弾む **hazumu** bounce

はずれ **hazure** miss; outskirts

はずす **hazusu** undo

屁 **he** fart

ヘアブラシ **heaburashi**
hairbrush

ヘアピンカーブ **heapin-
kābu** hairpin curve

ヘアスタイル **heasutairu**
hairstyle

へび **hebi** snake

ヘッドホン **heddohon**
headphones

ヘッドライト **heddoraito**
headlamp

平凡(な) **heibon (na)**
mediocre

平地 **heichi** plain

兵役 **heieki** military service

平服 **heifuku** clothes for
everyday wear

平日 **heijitsu** weekday

陛下 **Heika** Your Majesty

兵器 **heiki** armaments

平均 **heikin** average

平気(な) **heiki (na)** OK

平行(の) **heikō (no)** parallel

平面図 **heimenzu** ground plan

平穏(な) **heion (na)** tranquil

閉鎖 **heisa** closure

平静 **heisei** calm

平成時代 **Heisei-jidai** Heisei
era *(1989-)*

兵士 **heishi** soldier

閉店 **heiten** closure

閉店時間 **heiten-jikan**
closing time

平和 **heiwa** peace

平然と **heizen to** calmly

へこみ **hekomi** dent

へま **hema** blunder

偏 **hen** radical of a Chinese
character

変圧器 **hen'atsuki** transformer

変動 **hendō** fluctuation

返事 **henji** reply

変化 **henka** change

変換 **henkan** conversion

偏見 **henken** prejudice

変更 **henkō** change

返却 **henkyaku** return

変(な) **hen (na)** weird

返済 **hensai** repayment

変色する **henshoku suru** change color

編集 **henshū** editing

編集者 **henshūsha** editor *(of book)*

変装 **hensō** disguise

変態 **hentai** pervert

扁桃腺 **hentōsen** tonsils

扁桃腺炎 **hentōsen'en** tonsillitis

偏頭痛 **henzutsū** migraine

減らす **herasu** reduce

ヘリコプター **herikoputā** helicopter

ヘロイン **heroin** heroin

減る **heru** decline

ヘルメット **herumetto** helmet

へそ **heso** navel

下手(な) **heta (na)** incompetent

へとへと(の) **hetoheto (no)** exhausted

へつらう **hetsurau** flatter

部屋 **heya** room

部屋代 **heyadai** rent

日 **hi** day

火 **hi** fire

…費 **-hi** expenses

非… **hi-** non-; un-

火花 **hibana** spark

ひび **hibi** crack

響き **hibiki** ring *(of voice)*

響く **hibiku** reverberate

非暴力(の) **hibōryoku (no)** nonviolent

左 **hidari** left

左側 **hidarigawa** left

左利き(の) **hidarikiki (no)** left-handed

左手 **hidarite** left hand

ひどい **hidoi** terrible

冷え **hie** chill

非衛生的(な) **hieiseiteki (na)** unhygienic

冷える **hieru** freeze

皮膚 **hifu** skin

日帰り旅行 **higaeri-ryokō** day-trip

被害 **higai** damage

被害者 **higaisha** victim

彼岸 **higan** the equinoctial week

日傘 **higasa** sunshade

東 **higashi** east

ひげ **hige** beard; whiskers

悲劇 **higeki** tragedy

ひげそり **higesori** shaver; razor

日ごとに **higoto ni** by day

批判 **hihan** criticism

批判的(な) **hihanteki (na)** critical

批評 **hihyō** review

ひじ **hiji** elbow

非常口 **hijōguchi** emergency exit

非常階段 **hijō-kaidan** fire escape

非常勤(の) **hijōkin (no)** part-time

非情(な) **hijō (na)** heartless

非常に **hijō ni** very

控え目(な) **hikaeme (no)** moderate; modest

日陰 **hikage** shade

比較 **hikaku** comparison

比較的(に) **hikakuteki (ni)** comparatively

悲観的(な) **hikanteki (na)** pessimistic

光 **hikari** light

光る **hikaru** shine

…ひき **-hiki** countword for animals, fish etc

引き上げる **hikiageru** raise wages; withdraw army

引き出し **hikidashi** drawer; withdrawal

引き出す **hikidasu** withdraw

引き戸 **hikido** sliding door

引き離す **hikihanasu** pull apart

引き返す **hikikaesu** turn back

ひき肉 **hikiniku** ground meat

引き伸ばし **hikinobashi** enlargement (of photo)

引き伸ばす **hikinobasu** enlarge; prolong

引き抜く **hikinuku** extract

引き落し **hikiotoshi** debit

率いる **hikīru** lead

引き裂く **hikisaku** tear paper, cloth

引き潮 **hikishio** ebb tide

引き継ぐ **hikitsugu** take over

引き付ける **hikitsukeru** attract

引き受ける **hikiukeru** undertake

引き分け **hikiwake** draw SPORTS

引きずる **hikizuru** drag

引っかく **hikkaku** scratch

ひっきりなしに **hikkirinashi ni** incessantly

引っ込める **hikkomeru** retract

引っ越す **hikkosu** move house

ひっくり返る **hikkurikaeru** overturn

ひっくり返す **hikkurikaesu** overturn

飛行 **hikō** flight

飛行場 **hikōjō** airfield

飛行機 **hikōki** airplane

被告 **hikoku** defendant

被告弁護人 **hikoku-bengonin** defense lawyer

引く **hiku** knock down; grind coffee, meat; saw wood

引く **hiku** subtract; go down (of swelling); pull

弾く **hiku** play MUS

低い **hikui** low

卑き**きょう**（な）**hikyō (na)** cowardly

暇 **hima** leisure

ひ孫 **himago** great-grandchild

肥満 **himan** obesity

悲鳴 **himei** scream

秘密 **himitsu** secret

ひも **himo** string; cord

ひな祭り **Hina-matsuri** Girls' Festival

非難 **hinan** blame

避難 **hinan** shelter

ひな人形 **hinaningyō** set of ornamental dolls

頻度 **hindo** frequency

皮肉 **hiniku** irony

避妊 **hinin** birth control

避妊薬 **hinin'yaku** contraceptive

貧弱（な）**hinjaku (na)** lamentable

貧血 **hinketsu** anemia

貧困 **hinkon** poverty

品目 **hinmoku** item

日の出 **hinode** sunrise

日の丸 **hinomaru** Japanese national flag

頻繁（な）**hinpan (na)** frequent

品質 **hinshitsu** quality

品種 **hinshu** breed

ヒント **hinto** hint

引っ張る **hipparu** pull

ひらがな **hiragana** the rounded Japanese syllabary

避雷針 **hiraishin** lightning conductor

開く **hiraku** open; throw party

ひらめ **hirame** plaice

ひらめき **hirameki** flash; brainstorm

ひらめく **hirameku** have a flash of inspiration

平泳ぎ **hiraoyogi** breaststroke

ひれ **hire** fin

ヒレ肉 **hireniku** fillet

卑劣（な）**hiretsu (na)** contemptible

疲労 **hirō** fatigue

ヒーロー **hīrō** hero

広場 **hiroba** square

披露宴 **hirōen** wedding reception

広がる **hirogaru** extend

広げる **hirogeru** broaden

広い **hiroi** wide

広まる **hiromaru** become widespread

広める **hiromeru** spread

広さ **hirosa** width

拾う **hirou** pick up

昼 **hiru** midday; daytime

ヒール **hīru** heel

昼ごはん **hirugohan** lunch

昼間 **hiruma** daytime

昼寝 **hirune** siesta

昼休み **hiruyasumi** lunch break

肥料 **hiryō** manure

悲惨(な) **hisan (na)** disastrous

ひさしぶり **hisashiburi** a long time; ひさしぶりです **hisashiburi desu** long time no see

秘書 **hisho** secretary

ひそか(な) **hisoka (na)** stealthy

筆跡 **hisseki** handwriting

必死に **hisshi ni** madly

必修(の) **hisshū (no)** compulsory

ひすい **hisui** jade

ヒーター **hītā** heater

額 **hitai** forehead

浸す **hitasu** dip; soak

ヒッチハイクする **hitchihaiku suru** hitchhike

否定 **hitei** denial

人 **hito** person

一… **hito-** *(prefix)* one; a; 一きれ **hitokire** a slice

人々 **hitobito** people

人柄 **hitogara** character

人込み **hitogomi** crowd

人質 **hitojichi** hostage

一言 **hitokoto** a (brief) word

一口 **hitokuchi** mouthful

ひとり **hitori** one person

ひとりで **hitori de** by oneself

ひとりっこ **hitorikko** only child

等しい **hitoshī** equal

一つ **hitotsu** one

ひつぎ **hitsugi** coffin

羊 **hitsuji** sheep

必要 **hitsuyō** need

必然的に **hitsuzenteki ni** inevitably

ヒット **hitto** hit

引っつく **hittsuku** stick to

冷やかす **hiyakasu** make fun of

日焼け **hiyake** sunburn; suntan

日焼け止め **hiyakedome** sunblock

飛躍的発展 **hiyakuteki-hatten** breakthrough

冷やす **hiyasu** chill *wine*

費用 **hiyō** expense

肥沃(な) **hiyoku (na)** fertile

比喩的(な) **hiyuteki (na)** figurative

膝 **hiza** knee

ひざまずく **hizamazuku** kneel down

日差し **hizashi** sunlight

日付 **hizuke** date

帆 **ho** sail

法 **hō** law

方 **hō** direction

法案 **hōan** bill POL

ほうび **hōbi** reward

保母 **hobo** kindergarten teacher

ほぼ **hobo** about

放置 **hōchi** neglect

ホチキス **hochikisu** stapler

包丁 **hōchō** kitchen knife

補聴器 **hochōki** hearing aid

程 **hodo** around; 早ければ早い程いい **hayakereba hayai hodo ī** the sooner the better

歩道 **hodō** sidewalk

報道 **hōdō** journalism

報道陣 **hōdōjin** the press

ほどく **hodoku** disentangle

歩道橋 **hodōkyō** footbridge

放映する **hōei suru** televise

ほえる **hoeru** bark

報復 **hōfuku** retaliation

豊富 (な) **hōfu (na)** abundant

捕鯨 **hogei** whaling

砲撃 **hōgeki** shellfire

方言 **hōgen** dialect

保護 **hogo** conservation

方法 **hōhō** way; method

ほほ笑み **hohoemi** smile

ほほ笑む **hohoemu** smile

保育園 **hoikuen** nursery (school)

ホイル **hoiru** tinfoil

補助(の) **hojo (no)** auxiliary

他、 **hoka** etc

放火 **hōka** arson

放課後 **hōkago** after school

崩壊 **hōkai** collapse *(of government)*

保管 **hokan** storage

他に **hoka ni** in addition

他(の) **hoka (no)** other

保険 **hoken** insurance

保険会社 **hoken-gaisha** insurance company

保険料 **hokenryō** insurance premium

ほうき **hōki** broom

放棄する **hōki suru** renounce

北海道 **Hokkaidō** Hokkaido

北極 **Hokkyoku** North Pole

方向 **hōkō** direction

報告 **hōkoku** report

報告書 **hōkoku-sho** written report

ほこり **hokori** dust

誇り **hokori** pride

歩行者 **hokōsha** pedestrian

ほくろ **hokuro** mole *(on skin)*

北西 **hokusei** northwest

北東 **hokutō** northeast

方面 **hōmen** direction; district; line *(of business)*

ほめる **homeru** praise

ホモ **homo** homosexual

訪問 **hōmon** visit

訪問者 **hōmonsha** caller

ホーム **hōmu** home; (railroad) platform

法務省 **Hōmushō** Justice Department

本 **hon** book

…本 **-hon** countword for long thin things

本… **hon-** genuine

本部 **honbu** headquarters

本棚 **hondana** bookcase

骨 **hone** bone

本日 **honjitsu** today

本気 **honki** earnest

本物 **honmono** the real thing

本音 **honne** what you really think

本人 **honnin** the person in question

ほんの **hon no** mere

本能 **honnō** instinct

ほのお **honō** flame

ほのか(な) **honoka (na)** faint

ほのめかす **honomekasu** imply

本社 **honsha** head office

本質 **honshitsu** essence

本州 **Honshū** Honshu

本店 **honten** main store

本当 **hontō** truth

本屋 **hon'ya** bookstore

翻訳 **hon'yaku** translation

翻訳者 **hon'yakusha** translator

ほら **hora** hey

洞穴 **hora-ana** cave

ほうれん草 **hōrensō** spinach

掘り出し物 **horidashimono** lucky find

法律 **hōritsu** law

ほうろう **hōrō** enamel

滅びる **horobiru** be ruined

放浪する **hōrō suru** wander around

掘る **horu** dig

彫る **horu** engrave

ホール **hōru** hall

ホルモン **horumon** hormone

捕虜 **horyo** prisoner of war

保留する **horyū suru** reserve

補佐官 **hosakan** aide

宝石 **hōseki** jewel

宝石商 **hōsekishō** jeweler

保釈 **hoshaku** bail

放射能 **hōshanō** radiation

放射性(の) **hōshasei (no)** radioactive

星 **hoshi** star

欲しい **hoshī** want

干しぶどう **hoshibudō** raisin

星印 **hoshijirushi** asterisk

方針 **hōshin** policy

星占い **hoshiuranai** astrology

保証 **hoshō** guarantee

補償金 **hoshōkin** compensation

保証人 **hoshōnin** guarantor

報酬 **hōshū** remuneration

保守的(な) **hoshuteki (na)** conservative

放送 **hōsō** broadcast

包装 **hōsō** packaging

細い **hosoi** fine; thin

包装紙 **hōsōshi** wrapping paper

発作 **hossa** seizure MED

ほっそりした **hossori shita** slim

干す **hosu** dry

ホース **hōsu** hose

ホステス **hosutesu** hostess

包帯 **hōtai** bandage

ほたる **hotaru** firefly

ホッチキス **hotchikisu®** stapler

法廷 **hōtei** court

ほてる **hoteru** feel warm

ホテル **hoteru** hotel

仏 **hotoke** Buddha; departed soul

ほとんど **hotondo** nearly

ホットケーキ **hotto-kēki** pancake

ほっとした **hotto shita** that's a relief

ホワイトカラー **howaito-karā** white-collar worker

保存 **hozon** preservation

百科辞典 **hyakka-jiten** encyclopedia

百貨店 **hyakkaten** department store

百 **hyaku** hundred

百万 **hyakuman** million

百万長者 **hyakuman-chōja** millionaire

百周年 **hyakushūnen** centenary

ひょう **hyō** hail; leopard

表 **hyō** table *(of figures)*

票 **hyō** vote

評判 **hyōban** reputation

氷河 **hyōga** glacier

表現 **hyōgen** expression

標本 **hyōhon** specimen MED

表示 **hyōji** sign

表情 **hyōjō** facial expression

標準 **hyōjun** standard

標準語 **hyōjungo** standard language

評価 **hyōka** valuation

標高 **hyōkō** altitude

表面 **hyōmen** surface

表面的(な) **hyōmenteki (na)** superficial

評論 **hyōron** criticism

評論家 **hyōronka** critic

漂流する **hyōryū suru** drift

表紙 **hyōshi** (front) cover

標識 **hyōshiki** sign

氷点 **hyōten** freezing point

氷山 **hyōzan** iceberg

ヒューズ **hyūzu** fuse

I

胃 **i** stomach

いい **ī** good

…位 **-i** rank

…医 **-i** doctor

言い表す **īarawasu** describe

いばる **ibaru** brag

いびき **ibiki** snoring

いぼ **ibo** wart

いぶす **ibusu** smoke *bacon*

一 **ichi** one

位置 **ichi** position

市場 **ichiba** market

一番 **ichiban** the best

一部 **ichibu** part

一度 **ichido** once

一月 **ichigatsu** January

いちご **ichigo** strawberry

一時 **ichiji** one o'clock; for now

いちじく **ichijiku** fig

著しい **ichijirushī** remarkable

一時的(な) **ichijiteki (na)** momentary

一枚 **ichimai** one sheet; a copy *(of record, CD)*

一万 **ichiman** ten thousand

一年 **ichinen** one year

一日 **ichinichi** one day

一応 **ichiō** for the time being; roughly

一億 **ichioku** one hundred million

一流(の) **ichiryū (no)** first-rate

いちょう **ichō** gingko tree

偉大(な) **idai (na)** great

遺伝 **iden** inheritance

遺伝性(の) **idensei (no)** hereditary

遺伝子 **idenshi** gene

遺伝子工学 **idenshi-kōgaku** genetic engineering

イデオロギー **ideorogī** ideology

緯度 **ido** latitude

井戸 **ido** well

移動 **idō** migration; transfer

家 **ie** house

いいえ **īe** no; yes *(to negative question)*

家元 **iemoto** *principal of a school of one of the Japanese arts*

イエスキリスト **Iesu Kirisuto** Jesus Christ

衣服 **ifuku** garment

以外 **igai** except

意外(な) **igai (na)** unexpected

医学 **igaku** medicine

異議 **igi** objection

意義 **igi** significance

イギリス **Igirisu** Britain

イギリス人 **Igirisujin** British person

囲碁 **igo** the game of Go

居心地 **igokochi** comfort

違反 **ihan** violation

言い張る **īharu** insist

違法(の) **ihō (no)** illegal

委員 **i-in** committee member

委員長 **i-inchō** chairperson

委員会 **i-inkai** committee

維持 **iji** maintenance

意地 **iji** will-power; nature

いじめ **ijime** bullying

いじめる **ijimeru** bully

意地悪(な) **ijiwaru (na)** spiteful

以上 **ijō** above; not less than; that's all

異常(な) **ijō (na)** abnormal

異常に **ijō ni** extraordinarily

移住 **ijū** emigration; immigration

移住者 **ijūsha** emigrant; immigrant

いか **ika** squid

以下 **ika** below; not more than

言いかえる **īkaeru** paraphrase

言い返す **īkaesu** retort

いかが **ikaga** how?; how about?

いかがわしい **ikagawashī** disreputable

いい加減(な) **īkagen (na)** proper; irresponsible; いいか げんにしなさい **ikagen ni shinasai** that's enough, calm down!; いいかげんにして よ **ikagen ni shite yo** do me a favor!

いかに **ika ni** how

いかにも **ika ni mo** indeed

怒り **ikari** anger

いかさま **ikasama** deception

言い方 **īkata** phrase

池 **ike** pond

生け花 **ikebana** flower arranging

生け垣 **ikegaki** hedge

意見 **iken** opinion

息 **iki** breath

…行き **…iki** be bound for

行き止まり **ikidomari** dead end

息苦しい **ikigurushī** suffocating

生き生きした **iki-iki shita** lively

生き返る **ikikaeru** be resurrected

生き物 **ikimono** being; creature

いきなり **ikinari** suddenly

生き残る **ikinokoru** survive

勢い **ikioi** energy

生きる **ikiru** live

行き先 **ikisaki** destination

一ヵ月 **ikkagetsu** one month

一回 **ikkai** once; one episode

一階 **ikkai** first floor

一気に **ikki ni** in one go

遺骨 **ikotsu** ashes

行く **iku** go; cover *distance*

意気地のない **ikuji no nai** cowardly

いくら **ikura** how much?

いくらか（の）**ikuraka (no)** a number of

いくつ **ikutsu** how many; how old

いくつか（の）**ikutsuka (no)** several

今 **ima** now

居間 **ima** living room

いまいましい **imaimashī** vexing

います **imasu** *polite form of iru* be

今すぐ **ima sugu** straight away

イメージ **imēji** image

Eメール **īmēru** email

意味 **imi** meaning

移民 **imin** emigrant; immigrant

芋 **imo** sweet potato

妹 **imōto** (younger) sister

印 **in** seal; stamp

…以内で …**inai de** within

田舎 **inaka** countryside

稲荷神社 **inari-jinja** *shrine for the celebration of the harvest*

陰謀 **inbō** plot

いんちき（の）**inchiki (no)** bogus

稲 **ine** rice plant

居眠り **inemuri** snooze

インフレ **infure** inflation

インフルエンザ **infuruenza** influenza

イングランド **Ingurando** England

印鑑 **inkan** signature seal

陰険（な）**inken (na)** sneaky

陰気（な）**inki (na)** dismal

インク **inku** ink

命 **inochi** life

命取り **inochitori** killer

祈り **inori** prayer

祈る **inoru** pray

飲料水 **inryōsui** drinking water

印刷 **insatsu** printing

印刷物 **insatsubutsu** printed matter

印象 **inshō** impression

印象的（な）**inshōteki (na)** impressive

飲酒運転 **inshu-unten** drunk driving

インスタント食品 **insutanto-shokuhin** convenience food

インタビュー **intabyū** interview

インターチェンジ

intāchenji interchange

インターネット **intānetto** Internet

インテリア **interia** décor

犬 **inu** dog

引用 **in'yō** quotation

引用符 **in'yōfu** quotation marks

…一杯 … **ippai** a cup / glass of

いっぱい(の) **ippai (no)** full

一泊 **ippaku** one night

一般(の) **ippan (no)** general; usual

一般的(な) **ippanteki (na)** usual

一片 **ippen** one piece

一品 **ippin** one dish

一歩 **ippo** one step

一本 **ippon** one piece, length *(of cloth etc)*

一方的(な) **ippōteki (na)** unilateral

一方通行 **ippō-tsūkō** one-way street

いらだたせる **iradataseru** vex

依頼 **irai** request

以来 **irai** since

いらいらする **iraira suru** frustrating ◊ get worked up

いらっしゃいませ **irasshaimase** welcome!

いらっしゃる **irassharu** *(polite)* be; come; go

入れ歯 **ireba** dentures

入れ物 **iremono** container

入れる **ireru** put into; admit; brew; turn on *faucet, heater*

いれずみ **irezumi** tattoo

入り江 **irie** inlet

入り口 **iriguchi** entrance

色 **iro** color

色々(な) **iroiro (na)** various

いる **iru** be; be present; live; have; …がいる *… ga iru* there is / are

要る **iru** need

衣類 **irui** clothing

いるか **iruka** dolphin

医療 **iryō** medical treatment

遺産 **isan** inheritance

遺跡 **iseki** ruins

医者 **isha** doctor

石 **ishi** stone

意志 **ishi** will; willpower

医師 **ishi** doctor

意識 **ishiki** consciousness

意識不明(の) **ishiki-fumei (no)** unconscious

遺失物取扱所 **ishitsubutsu-toriatsukaijo** lost-and-found (office)

衣装 **ishō** costume; clothes

移植 **ishoku** transplant

急がせる **isogaseru** rush *person*

忙しい **isogashī** busy

急ぐ **isogu** hurry

一冊 **issatsu** one volume;
one copy
一斉に **issei ni** in unison
一生 **isshō** life; lifetime
一生懸命 **isshōkenmei** with
great determination
一緒に **issho ni** together
一週間 **isshūkan** one week
いす **isu** chair
イスラム教 **Isuramukyō**
Islam
イースト **īsuto** yeast
板 **ita** plank
いただきます **itadakimasu**
words spoken before eating
痛い **itai** painful
遺体 **itai** remains
痛ましい **itamashī** pitiful
傷める **itameru** hurt
炒める **itameru** (stir-)fry
痛み **itami** pain
痛み止め **itamidome**
painkiller
痛む, 傷む **itamu** hurt
イタリア **Itaria** Italy
いたします **itashimasu** H do
いたずら **itazura** prank
一致 **itchi** agreement
意図 **ito** intention
糸 **ito** thread
いとこ **itoko** cousin
糸巻き **itomaki** spool
意図的な **itoteki (na)**
intentional

いつ **itsu** when
いつか **itsuka** sometime
いつも **itsumo** always
五つ **itsutsu** five
一体 **ittai** in general; ... on
earth; 一体誰が **ittai dare
ga...** who on earth...?
一定(の) **ittei (no)** fixed;
definite
いってきます **itte kimasu**
see you; I'm off now
いってらっしゃい
itterasshai have a nice day
一等 **ittō** first class
言う **iu** say
岩 **iwa** rock
祝い **iwai** celebration
言い訳 **īwake** excuse
いわし **iwashi** sardine
祝う **iwau** celebrate
いわゆる **iwayuru** so-called
いやがらせ **iyagarase**
harassment
イヤホン **iyahon** earphones
嫌み **iyami** unpleasantness;
sarcasm
嫌み(な) **iyami (na)** sarcastic
嫌(な) **iya (na)** nasty
いやらしい **iyarashī** indecent
イヤリング **iyaringu** earring
卑しい **iyashī** humble; vulgar
卑しめる **iyashimeru**
degrade
いよいよ **iyoiyo** at last

意欲 **iyoku** will; desire

居酒屋 **izakaya** bar

以前 **izen** before

遺族 **izoku** the bereaved

依存 **izon** dependence

泉 **izumi** spring *(of water)*

いずれ **izure** some day; いず
れも *izure mo* any

J

じゃあ **jā** well; in that case;
じゃあ、また *jā, mata* see
you later!

じゃがいも **jagaimo** potato

蛇口 **jaguchi** faucet

ジャケット **jaketto** jacket

弱点 **jakuten** weakness

邪魔 **jama** intrusion

ジャム **jamu** jam

じゃんけん **janken** *game of
stone, paper, scissors*

ジャンプ **janpu** jump

砂利 **jari** gravel

ジェットコースター **jetto-
kōsutā** roller coaster

字 **ji** written character

…時 **-ji** o'clock

痔 **ji** piles MED

耳鼻科 **jibika** ear and nose
department

自分 **jibun** oneself

自治権 **jichiken** autonomy

時代 **jidai** era

時代劇 **jidaigeki** historical
drama

時代後れ(の) **jidaiokure
(no)** outdated

自動販売機 **jidōhanbaiki**
vending machine

自動(の) **jidō (no)**
automatic

自動車 **jidōsha** automobile

自動車教習所 **jidōsha-
kyōshūjo** driving school

自動的(な) **jidōteki (na)**
automatic

自営業(の) **jieigyō (no)** self-
employed

自衛隊 **jieitai** Japan Self-
Defense Forces

地獄 **jigoku** hell

事業 **jigyō** business enterprise

自白 **jihaku** confession

自発的(な) **jihatsuteki (na)**
voluntary; spontaneous

慈悲 **jihi** mercy

事実 **jijitsu** reality; fact

事情 **jijō** circumstances

自覚 **jikaku** self-awareness

時間 **jikan** time; hour

時間割 **jikanwari** schedule

自家製(の) **jikasei (no)** homemade

自活する **jikatsu suru** support oneself

事件 **jiken** case *(for police)*

時期 **jiki** season; time

磁器 **jiki** porcelain

実感 **jikkan** realization

実験 **jikken** experiment

実行 **jikkō** execution

実況放送 **jikkyō-hōsō** live broadcast

事故 **jiko** accident

自己 **jiko** self

自己中心的(な) **jiko-chūshinteki (na)** egocentric

時刻 **jikoku** time

時刻表 **jikokuhyō** schedule

軸 **jiku** axle

字幕 **jimaku** subtitles

自慢 **jiman** pride

自明(の) **jimei (no)** self-evident

じめじめした **jimejime shita** swampy

地面 **jimen** ground

地味(な) **jimi (na)** modest; plain

地元(の) **jimoto (no)** local

ジム **jimu** gym

事務 **jimu** office work

事務員 **jimuin** clerk

事務所 **jimusho** office

事務的(な) **jimuteki (na)** businesslike; mechanical

…人 **-jin** person

人文科学 **jinbun-kagaku** the arts

人道的(な) **jindōteki (na)** humanitarian

人員 **jin'in** personnel

辞任 **jinin** resignation

人為的(な) **jin'iteki (na)** man-made

神社 **jinja** shrine

人格 **jinkaku** personality

人権 **jinken** human rights

人口 **jinkō** population

人工衛星 **jinkō-eisei** satellite

人工(の) **jinkō (no)** artificial

尋問 **jinmon** interrogation

人類 **jinrui** mankind

人生 **jinsei** life

人種 **jinshu** race

迅速(な) **jinsoku (na)** rapid

腎臓 **jinzō** kidney

ジーンズ **jīnzu** jeans

地雷 **jirai** landmine

じらした **jirashita** tantalizing

自立した **jiritsu shita** emancipated

時差ぼけ **jisaboke** jetlag

自殺 **jisatsu** suicide

自制 **jisei** self-control

磁石 **jishaku** magnet

自信 **jishin** confidence

地震 **jishin** earthquake

辞書 **jisho** dictionary

自主的(な) jishuteki (na) independent

実際は jissai wa in fact

実践 jissen practice

実施する jisshi suru put into effect

実質的(な) jisshitsuteki (na) substantive

地滑り jisuberi landslide

自炊 jisui self-catering

辞退する jitai suru refuse

自宅 jitaku home

時点 jiten point in time

辞典 jiten dictionary

自転車 jitensha bicycle

実物 jitsubutsu the real thing

実現 jitsugen realization

実業家 jitsugyōka businessman

実力 jitsuryoku capability

じっと jitto quietly

自由 jiyū freedom

自由経済 jiyūkeizai free market economy

自由民主党 Jiyūminshutō LDP, Liberal Democratic Party

自由(な) jiyū (na) free

自由主義(の) jiyū-shugi (no) liberalism

慈善 jizen charity

地蔵 jizō guardian deity of children and travelers

持続 jizoku persistence

上 jō best; top

情 jō emotion

…状 -jō letter; card

丈夫 jōbu robust

助長する jochō suru encourage

冗談 jōdan joke

上映する jōei suru show movie

上演する jōen suru put on play

除外 jogai exclusion

助言 jogen advice

ジョギング jogingu jogging

蒸発 jōhatsu evaporation

上品(な) jōhin (na) dignified

譲歩 jōho concession

情報 jōhō information

情報工学 jōhō-kōgaku information technology, IT

女医 joi woman doctor

上位(の) jōi (no) senior

徐々(の) jojo (no) gradual

上旬 jōjun first ten days of a month

ジョーカー jōkā joker

条件 jōken condition

蒸気 jōki steam

上機嫌(の) jōkigen (no) good-humored

上記(の) jōki (no) above-mentioned

常勤(の) jōkin (no) full-time

ジョッキ jokki jockey; beer mug

条項 **jōkō** article *(section)*; clause *(in agreement)*

乗客 **jōkyaku** passenger

除去 **jokyo** removal

状況 **jōkyō** circumstances

助教授 **jokyōju** associate professor

上級(の) **jōkyū (no)** advanced

乗務員 **jōmuin** crew; crew member

静脈 **jōmyaku** vein

情熱 **jōnetsu** passion

女王 **joō** queen

常連 **jōren** regular (customer)

上陸する **jōriku suru** go ashore

上流(の) **jōryū (no)** upper-class

助産婦 **josanpu** midwife

女性 **josei** woman; female

情勢 **jōsei** state of affairs

助成金 **joseikin** subsidy

女性(の) **josei (no)** female

女性らしい **joseirashī** feminine

乗車 **jōsha** aboard a train

乗車券 **jōshaken** train [bus] ticket

女子 **joshi** girl; woman

上司 **jōshi** boss

常識 **jōshiki** (common) sense

上昇 **jōshō** rise

助手 **joshu** assistant

助手席 **joshuseki** passenger seat

状態 **jōtai** circumstances

上達 **jōtatsu** improvement

条約 **jōyaku** treaty

常用漢字 **Jōyō kanji** *Chinese characters in common use*

女優 **joyū** actress

錠剤 **jōzai** tablet

醸造所 **jōzōjo** brewery

上手(な) **jōzu (na)** skillful

銃 **jū** gun

十 **jū** ten

…中 **-jū** throughout

十分(な) **jūbun (na)** adequate

十代 **jūdai** teenage years

重大(な) **jūdai (na)** important

充電する **jūden suru** recharge

柔道 **jūdō** judo

十月 **jūgatsu** October

授業 **jugyō** lesson

従業員 **jūgyōin** employee

獣医 **jūi** veterinary surgeon

十一月 **jūichigatsu** November

十字架 **jūjika** cross REL

従順(な) **jūjun (na)** submissive

受験 **juken** taking an exam

受験者 **jukensha** exam candidate

塾 **juku** crammer

熟練 **jukuren** proficiency

熟練した **jukuren shita** accomplished

儒教 **Jukyō** Confucianism

住民 **jūmin** inhabitants

寿命 **jumyō** life; lifespan

順 **jun** sequence

柔軟(な) **jūnan (na)** flexible

順番に **junban ni** in sequence

準備 **junbi** preparation(s)

準備中 **junbichū** in
preparation

順調(な) **junchō (na)**
trouble-free

順位 **jun'i** position *(in race etc)*

十二月 **jūnigatsu** December

十二支 **jūnishi** *the twelve
Chinese year signs*

順序 **junjo** sequence

準々決勝 **junjunkesshō**
quarterfinals

巡回 **junkai** rounds *(of
mailman, doctor)*

循環 **junkan** circulation

準決勝 **junkesshō** semifinals

純潔(な) **junketsu (na)** pure

順応する **junnō suru** adapt

巡礼 **junrei** pilgrimage

純粋(な) **junsui (na)** pure

十億 **jūoku** one billion

重力 **jūryoku** gravity

受領書 **juryōsho** receipt

受信 **jushin** receiving TV, RADIO

受信機 **jushinki** receiver
TV, RADIO

住所 **jūsho** address

重傷 **jūshō** serious injury

受賞者 **jushōsha** prizewinner

渋滞 **jūtai** traffic congestion

住宅 **jūtaku** housing

住宅地 **jūtakuchi** residential
district

じゅうたん **jūtan** carpet

重点 **jūten** emphasis

受話器 **juwaki** receiver TEL

重役 **jūyaku** executive

需要 **juyō** demand COMM

重要(な) **jūyō (na)** important

じゅず **juzu** prayer beads

K

か **ka** ◊ *(question particle)*: い
いですか **ī desu ka** is it
OK? ◊: …か…か… **... ka ...
ka** either … or …

…日 **-ka** *(countword for days)*;
二日 **futsuka** two days; the
second *(of the month)*

…下 **-ka** below

…化 **-ka** transform into

…科 **-ka** department

…家 **-ka** person

課 **ka** section; lesson

蚊 **ka** mosquito

かば **kaba** hippopotamus

カバー **kabā** cover; jacket *(of book)*

かばん **kaban** bag

かばう **kabau** protect

かばやき **kabayaki** broiled eel

壁 **kabe** wall

壁紙 **kabegami** wallpaper

かび **kabi** mold

花瓶 **kabin** vase

かぼちゃ **kabocha** pumpkin

かぶ **kabu** turnip

株 **kabu** share FIN

カーブ **kābu** curve

歌舞伎 **Kabuki** Kabuki

株主 **kabunushi** stockholder

かぶる **kaburu** wear *hat*

株式会社 **kabushiki-gaisha** incorporated ◊ limited company

株式市場 **kabushiki-shijō** stock market

かぶと **kabuto** helmet

かぶと虫 **kabutomushi** beetle

価値 **kachi** value

勝ち **kachi** win

家畜 **kachiku** domestic animal

かちんと鳴る **kachin to naru** clink; click

課長 **kachō** section chief

課題 **kadai** assignment

過大評価された **kadai-hyōka sareta** overrated

花壇 **kadan** (flower)bed

角 **kado** corner

カード **kādo** card

…かどうか **…ka dō ka** whether

門松 **kadomatsu** New Year's pine decoration

帰り **kaeri** return journey

かえる **kaeru** frog ◊ hatch out *(of eggs)*

変える **kaeru** change

代える，替える **kaeru** replace; convert

帰る **kaeru** return

返す **kaesu** give back

花粉 **kafun** pollen

花粉症 **kafunshō** hay fever

化学 **kagaku** chemistry

科学 **kagaku** science

科学技術 **kagaku-gijutsu** technology

化学者 **kagakusha** chemist

科学者 **kagakusha** scientist

科学的（な）**kagakuteki (na)** scientific

鏡 **kagami** mirror

輝く **kagayaku** sparkle

陰 **kage** shade

影 **kage** shadow

過激派 **kagekiha** extremist

過激（な）**kageki (na)** extreme

加減 **kagen** adjustment; physical condition

鍵 **kagi** key; lock

鍵穴 **kagiana** keyhole

限られた **kagirareta** restricted

限り **kagiri** limit

限る **kagiru** set a limit

かご **kago** basket; cage

かぐ **kagu** sniff

家具 **kagu** furniture

下半身麻痺の人 **kahanshin-mahi no hito** paraplegic

会 **kai** association

階 **kai** story

回 **kai** round *(of drinks)*; occasion

貝 **kai** shellfish

怪物 **kaibutsu** monster

会長 **kaichō** chairman

懐中電灯 **kaichū-dentō** flashlight

階段 **kaidan** stairs

解読する **kaidoku suru** decipher

回復 **kaifuku** recovery

絵画 **kaiga** painting

海外(の) **kaigai (no)** overseas

海岸 **kaigan** coast

貝殻 **kaigara** shell

会議 **kaigi** meeting

会議室 **kaigishitsu** conference room

介護 **kaigo** nursing *(of the elderly)*

海軍 **kaigun** navy

開発 **kaihatsu** development

回避 **kaihi** evasion

会費 **kaihi** membership fee

解放 **kaihō** emancipation

会員 **kai-in** member

会員証 **kai-inshō** pass

会場 **kaijō** venue

改革 **kaikaku** reform

快感 **kaikan** pleasant feeling

快活(な) **kaikatsu (na)** cheerful

会計 **kaikei** accounts

会計係 **kaikeigakari** cashier

会計士 **kaikeishi** accountant

会見 **kaiken** interview

解決 **kaiketsu** resolution

解雇 **kaiko** dismissal

海峡 **kaikyō** strait

階級 **kaikyū** social class

解明する **kaimei suru** unravel

買い物 **kaimono** shopping

下位(の) **kai (no)** inferior

飼い主 **kainushi** owner

介入 **kainyū** intervention

改良 **kairyō** improvement

海流 **kairyū** current *(in sea)*

開催地 **kaisaichi** venue

開催する **kaisai suru** hold *(meeting etc)*

解散する **kaisan suru** dismiss

改札係 **kaisatsugakari** ticket collector

改札口 **kaisatsuguchi** ticket barrier

改正 **kaisei** reform

懐石料理 **kaiseki-ryōri** Japanese-style haute cuisine

回戦 **kaisen** round *(in tournament)*

回線 **kaisen** telephone line

解説 **kaisetsu** commentary

会社 **kaisha** business company

会社員 **kaishain** employee

解釈 **kaishaku** interpretation

開始 **kaishi** start

回収 **kaishū** recovery; recall

階層 **kaisō** layer

海草 **kaisō** seaweed

快速 **kaisoku** fast train

回数 **kaisū** frequency

回数券 **kaisūken** multi-journey ticket

開拓する **kaitaku suru** open up *(land)*

買い手 **kaite** buyer

快適(な) **kaiteki (na)** pleasant

回転 **kaiten** rotation

解答 **kaitō** answer

解凍する **kaitō suru** defrost; unzip *(file)*

会話 **kaiwa** conversation

かいよう **kaiyō** ulcer

改善 **kaizen** improvement

火事 **kaji** blaze

家事 **kaji** housekeeping; housework

かじき **kajiki** swordfish

かじる **kajiru** gnaw; nibble

過剰(の) **kajō (no)** excess; excessive

価格 **kakaku** value

係り **kakari** person in charge

かかる **kakaru** cost; take *time*

掛かる **kakaru** hang

かかと **kakato** heel

かかわる **kakawaru** get involved with

駆け足 **kakeashi** running

掛け布団 **kakebuton** duvet

賭け事 **kakegoto** gambling

家計 **kakei** household budget

家系 **kakei** lineage

掛け軸 **kakejiku** hanging scroll

かけら **kakera** fragment

かける **kakeru** put on *glasses, necklace*; build; cover; sprinkle; impose *tax*; switch on

賭ける **kakeru** bet

掛ける **kakeru** hang; multiply; sit down

欠ける **kakeru** lack; wane

掛け算 **kakezan** multiplication

かき **kaki** oyster

柿 **kaki** persimmon

夏期 **kaki** summer semester

かき氷 **kakigōri** *crushed ice with syrup*

かき混ぜる **kakimazeru** stir; toss

書き直す **kakinaosu** rewrite

書留めで送る **kakitome de okuru** send a letter registered

書き留める **kakitomeru** write down

書き初め **kakizome** New Year calligraphy

かっこ **kakko** bracket

格好 **kakkō** appearance

格好いい **kakkō ī** stylish

過去 **kako** past

下降 **kakō** downturn

囲む **kakomu** surround

かく **kaku** scratch

欠く **kaku** be lacking; neglect

描く **kaku** paint; draw

書く **kaku** write

核 **kaku** nucleus

各 **kaku** each

拡張 **kakuchō** expansion

拡大 **kakudai** enlargement

拡大鏡 **kakudaikyō** magnifying glass

角度 **kakudo** angle

覚悟 **kakugo** readiness

核兵器 **kakuheiki** nuclear weapon

確保する **kakuho suru** ensure

確実（な）**kakujitsu (na)** definite

革命 **kakumei** revolution

確認 **kakunin** confirmation

核（の）**kaku (no)** nuclear

隠れる **kakureru** hide

隔離 **kakuri** seclusion; quarantine

確率 **kakuritsu** probability

確信 **kakushin** assurance

革新 **kakushin** innovation

隠す **kakusu** hide

確定する **kakutei suru** determine

カクテル **kakuteru** cocktail

獲得する **kakutoku suru** acquire

窯 **kama** kiln

かまう **kamau** mind

かめ **kame** tortoise; turtle

カメラ **kamera** camera

神 **kami** god

紙 **kami** paper

髪 **kami** hair

紙袋 **kamibukuro** paper bag

髪型 **kamigata** hairdo

神風 **kamikaze** kamikaze

雷 **kaminari** bolt *(of lightning)*; thunder

神様 **kamisama** God; god; champion

かみそり **kamisori** razor

かも **kamo** duck; sucker *(person)*

科目 **kamoku** subject

かもめ **kamome** (sea)gull

…かもしれない **… kamo shirenai** may, might

貨物 **kamotsu** freight

かむ **kamu** bite
缶 **kan** can
勘 **kan** intuition
…間 **-kan** for; during; between
かな **ka na** *(question particle)*
仮名 **kana** Japanese syllabary
かなえる **kanaeru** grant
家内 **kanai** wife
必ず **kanarazu** without fail
かなり **kanari** considerably
悲しい **kanashī** sad
悲しみ **kanashimi** sadness
悲しむ **kanashimu** feel sad
かなづち **kanazuchi** hammer; nonswimmer
看板 **kanban** signboard
勘弁 **kanben** forgiveness
干潮 **kanchō** low tide
館長 **kanchō** director; curator
寛大(な) **kandai (na)** generous
感動的(な) **kandōteki (na)** moving
金 **kane** money
鐘 **kane** bell
金持ち **kanemochi** the rich
兼ねる **kaneru** serve several functions
考え **kangae** idea
考え方 **kangaekata** way of thinking
考え込む **kangaekomu** brood
考え直す **kangaenaosu** reconsider

考えられない **kangaerarenai** unthinkable
考える **kangaeru** think
管楽器 **kangakki** wind instrument
歓迎 **kangei** welcome
感激する **kangeki suru** be moved
看護 **kango** nursing
看護婦 **kangofu** nurse
かに **kani** crab
患者 **kanja** patient
漢字 **kanji** Chinese character
感じ **kanji** sense
肝心(の) **kanjin (no)** essential
感じる **kanjiru** feel
勘定 **kanjō** calculation
感情 **kanjō** emotion
勘定書き **kanjōgaki** check *(in restaurant etc)*
感覚 **kankaku** sense
関係 **kankei** connection
歓喜 **kanki** jubilation
換気 **kanki** ventilation
監禁 **kankin** confinement
缶切り **kankiri** can opener
観光 **kankō** sightseeing
観光案内所 **kankō annaisho** tourist (information) office
韓国 **Kankoku** (South) Korea
観光客 **kankōkyaku** tourist
観客 **kankyaku** audience
環境 **kankyō** environment

環境保護 **kankyō-hogo** environmental protection

環境汚染 **kankyō-osen** environmental pollution

甘味料 **kanmiryō** sweetener

カンニングをする **kanningu o suru** cheat in an exam

観音 **kannon** goddess of mercy

神主 **kannushi** Shinto priest

彼女 **kanojo** she ◊ girlfriend

可能(な) **kanō (na)** possible

可能性 **kanōsei** possibility

乾杯 **kanpai** toast ◊ cheers!

完ぺき(な) **kanpeki (na)** perfect

漢方薬 **kanpōyaku** Chinese herbal medicine

関連 **kanren** link

管理人 **kanrinin** caretaker

官僚 **kanryō** bureaucracy; bureaucrat

完了する **kanryō suru** accomplish

官僚的(な) **kanryōteki (na)** bureaucratic

関西 **Kansai** area around Osaka, Kyoto and Hyogo

観察 **kansatsu** observation

観察者 **kansatsusha** observer

歓声 **kansei** cheering

完成 **kansei** completion

感染 **kansen** infection

関節炎 **kansetsuen** arthritis

間接的(な) **kansetsuteki (na)** indirect

感謝 **kansha** gratitude

感心 **kanshin** admiration

関心 **kanshin** concern

関して **kan shite**: …に関して … **ni kan shite** in connection with

鑑賞 **kanshō** appreciation

干渉 **kanshō** meddling

感触 **kanshoku** touch

感傷的(な) **kanshōteki (na)** sentimental

看守 **kanshu** guard

慣習 **kanshū** convention

感想 **kansō** impressions

乾燥機 **kansōki** drier

観測 **kansoku** observation

簡素(な) **kanso (na)** plain

乾燥した **kansō shita** arid; dried

簡単(な) **kantan (na)** simple

観点 **kanten** point of view

関東 **Kantō** central eastern district of Tokyo, Kanagawa

監督 **kantoku** director; supervision

緩和 **kanwa** relief

寛容(な) **kan'yō (na)** tolerant

慣用的(な) **kan'yōteki (na)** idiomatic

加入する **kanyū suru** join

換算 **kanzan** conversion

関税 **kanzei** tariff

完全(な) **kanzen (na)** complete

肝臓 **kanzō** liver *in body*

缶詰(の) **kanzume (no)** canned

顔 **kao** face

顔色 **kaoiro** complexion

香り **kaori** scent

カーペット **kāpetto** carpet

かっぱ **kappa** water imp

活発(な) **kappatsu (na)** vigorous

カップ **kappu** cup

カップル **kappuru** couple

カプセル **kapuseru** capsule

から **kara** from; after; because

殻 **kara** husk

空揚げ **kara-age** deep-fried

辛い **karai** spicy

からかう **karakau** make fun of

辛口(の) **karakuchi (no)** dry *wine*

絡まる **karamaru** become entangled in

絡み付く **karamitsuku** wind *(of ivy etc)*

空(の) **kara (no)** blank

カラオケ **karaoke** karaoke

空っぽ(の) **karappo (no)** empty

カラー写真 **karā-shashin** color photograph

からし **karashi** (Japanese) mustard

からす **karasu** crow

空手 **karate** karate

彼 **kare** ◊ boyfriend

かれい **karei** flounder

カレンダー **karendā** calendar

彼の **kare no** his

彼ら **karera** they

枯れる **kareru** wither

彼氏 **kareshi** boyfriend

狩り **kari** hunt

借り **kari** debt

借りる **kariru** borrow; rent

過労 **karō** overwork

かろうじて **karōjite** barely

カロリー **karorī** calorie

過労死 **karōshi** death from overwork

狩る **karu** hunt

刈る **karu** mow

軽い **karui** light; idle *threat*

傘 **kasa** umbrella

火災 **kasai** fire

火災報知機 **kasai-hōchiki** fire alarm

重なる **kasanaru** overlap

重ねる **kasaneru** pile up; repeat

稼ぐ **kasegu** earn

家政婦 **kaseifu** housekeeper

下線を引く **kasen o hiku**

underline

仮説上(の) **kasetsujō (no)** hypothetical

カセットテープ **kasetto-tēpu** cassette tape

歌詞 **kashi** lyrics

菓子 **kashi** cake; candy

賢い **kashikoi** wise

かしこまりました **kashikomarimashita** *(acknowledging order, request etc)* yes, sir

かしら **kashira** I wonder

頭文字 **kashiramoji** initial letter

柏餅 **kashiwamochi** rice cake with sweetbean paste wrapped in an oak leaf

歌手 **kashu** singer

火葬 **kasō** cremation

仮装 **kasō** fancy dress

加速 **kasoku** acceleration

滑走路 **kassōro** runway

貸す **kasu** loan; rent (out)

かす **kasu** dregs; scum

かすか(な) **kasuka (na)** faint

かすみ **kasumi** haze

かすむ **kasumu** mist over

…方 **-kata** how to…

…方 … **kata** care of, c/o

型 **kata** model

肩 **kata** shoulder

形 **katachi** shape

肩書き **katagaki** title

片方 **katahō** one side; one of a pair

硬い、固い、堅い **katai** solid; stiff; tight *drawer, screw*

かたかな **katakana** the angular Japanese syllabary

堅苦しい **katakurushī** stiff *(in manner)*

固まり **katamari** lump

固まる **katamaru** harden

片道切符 **katamichi-kippu** one-way ticket

傾き **katamuki** slope

傾く **katamuku** lean

刀 **katana** samurai sword

語る **kataru** talk

かたつむり **katatsumuri** snail

偏らない **katayoranai** impartial

片付ける **katazukeru** tidy up

仮定 **katei** assumption

家庭 **katei** home

過程 **katei** process

家庭教師 **katei-kyōshi** (private) tutor

家庭的(な) **kateiteki (na)** domestic

カーテン **kāten** curtains

カトリック(の) **katorikku (no)** Roman Catholic

勝つ **katsu** win

活動 **katsudō** activity

活動的(な) **katsudōteki (na)** active

担ぐ **katsugu** carry; play tricks on

かつお **katsuo** bonito

かつら **katsura** wig

かつて **katsute** once; long ago

活躍する **katsuyaku suru** active

活用 **katsuyō** practical use

飼っている **katte iru** have, keep *pet*

勝手(な) **katte (na)** selfish; arbitrary

カット **katto** cut

買う **kau** buy

飼う **kau** raise *pet*

カウンター **kauntā** counter

皮 **kawa** pelt

川, 河 **kawa** river

革 **kawa** leather

川岸 **kawagishi** riverside

かわいがる **kawaigaru** fondle

かわいい **kawaī** cute

かわいそう(な) **kawaisō (na)** pitiful

乾いた **kawaita** dry

乾かす **kawakasu** dry

乾く **kawaku** dry

代わりに **kawari** substitute

代わりに **kawari ni** instead (of)

変わりやすい **kawariyasui** changeable

変わる **kawaru** change

代わる **kawaru** replace

為替相場 **kawase-sōba** exchange rate

かわす **kawasu** evade

変わった **kawatta** unusual

蚊帳 **kaya** mosquito net

火曜日 **kayōbi** Tuesday

通う **kayou** attend *school*; commute; frequent *place*

かゆい **kayui** itchy

かゆみ **kayumi** itch

火山 **kazan** volcano

飾り **kazari** decoration

飾る **kazaru** decorate

風 **kaze** wind

風邪 **kaze** cold

課税 **kazei** taxation

数えきれない **kazoekirenai** countless

数える **kazoeru** count

家族 **kazoku** family

数 **kazu** number

毛 **ke** hair *(single)*

…家 **-ke** family

けばけばしい **kebakebashī** gaudy

毛深い **kebukai** hairy

ケーブルカー **kēburu-kā** cable car

ケーブルテレビ **kēburu-terebi** cable TV

ケチャップ **kechappu**

ketchup

けち **kechi** miser

けち(な) **kechi (na)** miserly

怪我 **kega** injury

毛皮 **kegawa** fur; coat *(of animal)*

競馬 **keiba** the races

刑罰 **keibatsu** punishment

軽べつ **keibetsu** contempt

警備 **keibi** security guard

警備員 **keibi-in** security guard

経度 **keido** longitude

経営 **keiei** management

経営学 **keieigaku** management studies

経営者 **keiesha** manager

敬語 **keigo** honorific language

敬具 **keigu** kind regards, yours truly

経費 **keihi** expenses

警報 **keihō** alarm

敬意 **kei-i** respect

刑事 **keiji** detective

掲示 **keiji** notice

掲示板 **keijiban** bulletin board

経過 **keika** passage

軽快(な) **keikai (na)** nimble

計画 **keikaku** project

経験 **keiken** experience

敬けん(な) **keiken (na)** devout

計器 **keiki** gauge

景気 **keiki** economic conditions

けいこ **keiko** practice

傾向 **keikō** tendency

警告 **keikoku** warning

蛍光(の) **keikō (no)** fluorescent

刑務所 **keimusho** jail

経歴 **keireki** career history

けいれん **keiren** cramp

敬老の日 **Keirō no hi** Respect-for-the-Aged Day

計算 **keisan** calculation

警察 **keisatsu** police

警察庁 **Keisatsuchō** National Police Agency

警察官 **keisatsukan** officer

警察署 **keisatsusho** police station

形成外科 **keisei-geka** plastic surgery

形跡 **keiseki** traces

傾斜 **keisha** slant

形式 **keishiki** formality

軽食 **keishoku** refreshments

軽率(な) **keisotsu (na)** hasty

携帯電話 **keitai-denwa** cell phone

毛糸 **keito** wool

系統 **keitō** system

系統的に **keitōteki ni** systematically

契約 **keiyaku** contract

経由で **keiyu de** via

経済 **keizai** economy

経済学 **keizaigaku** economics

経済産業省 **Keizaisangyōshō**
Department of Economy, Trade
and Industry

経済的(な) **keizaiteki (na)**
economical

ケーキ **kēki** cake

結果 **kekka** result

血管 **kekkan** blood vessel

欠陥 **kekkan** defect

結婚 **kekkon** marriage

結構(な) **kekkō (na)**
sufficient; 結構です **kekkō
desu** no, thank you

結婚記念日 **kekkon-kinenbi**
wedding anniversary

結婚式 **kekkonshiki** wedding

結局 **kekkyoku** after all

獣 **kemono** beast

煙 **kemuri** smoke

毛虫 **kemushi** caterpillar

県 **ken** prefecture

券 **ken** ticket

件 **ken** matter

剣 **ken** sword

顕微鏡 **kenbikyō** microscope

見物 **kenbutsu** sightseeing

見物人 **kenbutsunin** sightseer

建築 **kenchiku** architecture

建築家 **kenchikuka** architect

剣道 **kendō** kendo

検閲 **ken'etsu** censorship

見学する **kengaku suru** tour

権威 **ken'i** authority

検事 **kenji** public prosecutor

堅実(な) **kenjitsu (na)**
reliable

けんか **kenka** argument

献血 **kenketsu** blood donation

献金 **kenkin** donation

健康 **kenkō** health

健康保険 **kenkō-hoken**
health insurance

建国記念日 **kenkoku-
kinenbi** National Foundation
Day

健康(な) **kenkō (na)** healthy

健康診断 **kenkō-shindan**
health check

健康診断書 **kenkō-
shindansho** medical
certificate

健康食品 **kenkō-shokuhin**
health food

健康的(な) **kenkōteki (na)**
healthy

謙虚 **kenkyo** modesty

謙虚(な) **kenkyo (na)** modest

研究 **kenkyū** research

研究所 **kenkyūjo** laboratory

研究者 **kenkyūsha** researcher

賢明(な) **kenmei (na)** wise

嫌悪 **ken'o** hatred

憲法 **kenpō** constitution POL

憲法記念日 **kenpō-kinenbi**
Constitution Day

権利 **kenri** rights

権力 **kenryoku** power

検査 **kensa** inspection

検札 **kensatsu** ticket inspection

検察官 **kensatsukan** public prosecutor

建設 **kensetsu** construction

建設的（な）**kensetsuteki (na)** constructive

検診 **kenshin** checkup

献身的（な）**kenshinteki (na)** devoted

謙そん **kenson** humility

検討 **kentō** investigation

見当 **kentō** guess; aim; direction

倹約 **ken'yaku** thrift

建造物 **kenzōbutsu** structure

潔白 **keppaku** innocence

けれど（も）**keredo(mo)** but

ける **keru** kick

けさ **kesa** this morning

消しゴム **keshigomu** eraser

消印 **keshi-in** postmark

景色 **keshiki** scenery

化粧 **keshō** make-up

化粧品 **keshōhin** cosmetics

化粧室 **keshōshitsu** powder room

傑作 **kessaku** masterpiece

欠席 **kesseki** absence

決心 **kesshin** resolution

決して…ない **kesshite... nai** never

決勝戦 **kesshōsen** final

消す **kesu** extinguish; erase; drown *sound*

ケース **kēsu** case

けた **keta** digit; beam; girder

ケータイ **kētai** cell phone

決着 **ketchaku** conclusion

血圧 **ketsuatsu** blood pressure

欠乏 **ketsubō** lack

血液型 **ketsuekigata** blood group

決議 **ketsugi** resolution

決意 **ketsui** determination

結末 **ketsumatsu** conclusion

決裂 **ketsuretsu** breakdown; rupture

結論 **ketsuron** conclusion

決定 **kettei** decision

決定戦 **ketteisen** decider

決定的（な）**ketteiteki (na)** decisive

欠点 **ketten** flaw

血統 **kettō** pedigree

険しい **kewashī** steep

削る **kezuru** whittle; sharpen

木 **ki** tree

気 **ki** mood; feeling; will

キー **kī** key COMPUT, MUS

気圧 **kiatsu** air pressure

気晴らし **kibarashi** pastime

厳しい **kibishī** strict; severe *weather*; inhospitable *climate*

規模 **kibo** scale

希望 **kibō** wish

気分 **kibun** frame of mind

基地 **kichi** base MIL

気違い **kichigai** insane

きちんと **kichin to** properly

機長 **kichō** captain *(of aircraft)*

貴重品 **kichōhin** valuables

きちょうめん（な）
  kichōmen (na) methodical

貴重（な）**kichō (na)** valuable

軌道 **kidō** orbit

気取った **kidotta** pretentious

消える **kieru** disappear

寄付 **kifu** donation

飢餓 **kiga** starvation

着替え **kigae** change of
  clothes

着替える **kigaeru** change
  clothes

気軽（な）**kigaru (na)**
  lighthearted

喜劇 **kigeki** comedy

機嫌 **kigen** mood

起源 **kigen** origin

期限 **kigen** deadline

期限切れ **kigengire** expiry

記号 **kigō** symbol

器具 **kigu** appliance;
  instrument

企業 **kigyō** enterprise

規範 **kihan** model

基本 **kihon** foundation

基本的（な）**kihonteki (na)**
  fundamental

キーホルダー **kī-horudā**
  key ring

黄色 **ki-iro** yellow

記事 **kiji** article

生地 **kiji** dough; material

基準 **kijun** standard

機会 **kikai** opportunity

機械 **kikai** machine

機械工 **kikaikō** mechanic

機械（の）**kikai (no)**
  mechanical

機械的（な）**kikaiteki (na)**
  mechanical

規格 **kikaku** standard

企画 **kikaku** plan

期間 **kikan** duration; period

機関 **kikan** institution

器官 **kikan** organ ANAT

帰還 **kikan** return

気管支炎 **kikanshien**
  bronchitis

危険 **kiken** danger

危機 **kiki** crisis

効き目 **kikime** effect

基金 **kikin** fund

危機的（な）**kikiteki (na)**
  critical

聞き取る **kikitoru** catch
  (words)

きっかけ **kikkake** opportunity

きっかりに **kikkari ni**
  promptly

キック **kikku** kick

気候 **kikō** climate

聞こえない **kikoenai**
  inaudible

聞こえる **kikoeru** hear
◊ audible

帰国 **kikoku** return to one's
own country

着込む **kikomu** wrap up
warmly

菊 **kiku** chrysanthemum

聞く **kiku** listen to; ask

効く **kiku** take effect

気まぐれ(な) **kimagure
(na)** fickle

決まり **kimari** rule

決まり文句 **kimarimonku**
cliché

決まった **kimatta** fixed

決まっていない **kimatte
inai** undecided

気まずい **kimazui**
embarrassing

決める **kimeru** decide

君 **kimi** you (familiar)

気味 **kimi** feeling; a touch of

君が代 **Kimigayo** Kimigayo
(Japanese national anthem)

君の **kimi (no)** your
(familiar)

君達 **kimitachi** you (plural
familiar)

君達(の) **kimitachi (no)** your
(plural familiar)

機密 **kimitsu** secret

気持ち **kimochi** feeling

着物 **kimono** kimono

気難しい **kimuzukashī**
choosy

金 **kin** gold

勤勉(な) **kinben (na)**
industrious

緊張 **kinchō** tension

近代化 **kindaika**
modernization

近代的(な) **kindaiteki (na)**
modern

禁煙 **kin'en** no smoking

記念 **kinen** commemoration

記念日 **kinenbi** anniversary

記念碑 **kinenhi** memorial;
monument

記念品 **kinenhin** memento

禁煙席 **kin'en-seki** no
smoking seats

金額 **kingaku** amount

近眼(の) **kingan (no)**
shortsighted

金魚 **kingyo** goldfish

金色(の) **kin'iro (no)** golden

禁じられた **kinjirareta**
forbidden

禁じる **kinjiru** forbid

近所 **kinjo** vicinity

近畿 **Kinki** area around Osaka,
Kyoto and Hyogo

金庫 **kinko** safe

近郊 **kinkō** environs

均衡 **kinkō** balance

緊急着陸 **kinkyū-chakuriku**
emergency landing

緊急(な) **kinkyū (na)** urgent

金めっき **kinmekki** gilt

勤務中である **kinmuchū de aru** be on duty

勤務時間 **kinmu-jikan** office hours

筋肉 **kinniku** muscle

機能 **kinō** function

昨日 **kinō** yesterday

気の毒（な） **kinodoku（な）** unfortunate

きのこ **kinoko** mushroom

緊迫 **kinpaku** tension

金髪（の） **kinpatsu（no）** fair *hair*

禁止 **kinshi** prohibition

近視（の） **kinshi（no）** near-sighted

均等に **kintō ni** evenly

絹 **kinu** silk

金曜日 **kin'yōbi** Friday

金融（の） **kin'yū（no）** monetary

金属 **kinzoku** metal

記憶 **kioku** memory

記憶力 **kiokuryoku** memory

気温 **kion** temperature

キオスク **kiosuku** kiosk

気をつける **ki o tsukeru** take care

きっぱりと **kippari to** clearly; flatly *refuse*

切符 **kippu** ticket

切符売場 **kippu-uriba** ticket office

嫌い **kirai** dislike

きらきら光る **kirakira hikaru** twinkle

気楽（な） **kiraku（na）** easygoing

嫌う **kirau** dislike

…切れ **-kire** countword for *slices of bread, meat, cakes etc*

きれい（な） **kirei（na）** pretty; clean

キレる **kireru** lose self-control

亀裂 **kiretsu** crack

霧 **kiri** fog; mist

切り上げる **kiriageru** revalue; round up *figure*; cut short

切り離す **kirihanasu** isolate

切り替える **kirikaeru** switch

きりん **kirin** giraffe

切り抜く **kirinuku** cut out

切り落とす **kiriotosu** lop off

キリスト **Kirisuto** Christ

キリスト教 **Kirisutokyō** Christianity

切り倒す **kiritaosu** chop down

切り取る **kiritoru** cut off

規律 **kiritsu** discipline

起立 **kiritsu** all stand!

切り詰める **kiritsumeru** cut back

キログラム **kiroguramu** kilogram

記録 **kiroku** record(s); reading

(from meter etc)

キロメーター **kiromētā** kilometer

切る **kiru** cut; switch off; shuffle *cards*

着る **kiru** wear; put on

気さく(な) **kisaku (na)** friendly

規制 **kisei** regulation

既製(の) **kisei (no)** ready-made

奇跡 **kiseki** miracle

着せる **kiseru** dress; help dress

季節 **kisetsu** season

記者 **kisha** reporter

岸 **kishi** shore

きしむ **kishimu** creak; squeak

気質 **kishitsu** disposition

気性 **kishō** temperament

気象(の) **kishō (no)** meteorological

基礎 **kiso** basis

起訴 **kiso** prosecution JUR

規則 **kisoku** rule

規則的(な) **kisokuteki (na)** regular

基礎的(な) **kisoteki (na)** basic

喫茶店 **kissaten** coffee shop

キス **kisu** kiss

北 **kita** north

北アメリカ **Kita-Amerika** North America

北朝鮮 **Kita-Chōsen** North Korea

鍛える **kitaeru** train

期待 **kitai** expectation(s)

気体 **kitai** gas

期待はずれ **kitaihazure** disappointment

帰宅する **kitaku suru** return home

汚い **kitanai** dirty

きっちり **kitchiri** tightly; punctually; exactly

起点 **kiten** starting point

気転, 機転 **kiten** tact; quickwittedness

喫煙 **kitsuen** smoking

きつい **kitsui** demanding; tough; tight

きつね **kitsune** fox

切手 **kitte** stamp

きっと **kitto** no doubt

きわどい **kiwadoi** risky

きわめて **kiwamete** extremely

器用(な) **kiyō (na)** deft

刻む **kizamu** cut; carve; chop

兆し **kizashi** hint; symptom

気絶する **kizetsu suru** faint

寄贈 **kizō** donation

傷 **kizu** damage; wound

傷跡 **kizuato** scar

気づかって **kizukatte** caring

気付け **kizuke** c/o, care of

気づく **kizuku** become aware of

きずな **kizuna** bond

傷つける **kizutsukeru** wound

傷つく **kizutsuku** get hurt

子 **ko** child

故 **ko** the late; deceased

…個 **-ko** *countword for small objects*

香 **kō** incense

考案する **kōan suru** devise

交番 **kōban** police box

小人 **kobito** dwarf

こぼれる **koboreru** be spilled

こぼす **kobosu** spill

こぶ **kobu** bump; hump

後部(の) **kōbu (no)** rear

こぶし **kobushi** fist

好物 **kōbutsu** favorite (food)

鉱物 **kōbutsu** mineral

紅茶 **kōcha** (black) tea

コーチ **kōchi** coach

こちら **kochira** this *(polite)* ◊ this way ◊ this one; this person

校長 **kōchō** principal SCHOOL

好調(な) **kōchō (na)** in good condition

広大(な) **kōdai (na)** vast

古代(の) **kodai (no)** ancient

こだま **kodama** echo

こだわらない **kodawaranai** easy-going

こだわる **kodawaru** be obsessive

鼓動 **kodō** beat; throb (of heart)

コード **kōdo** cable; cord

高度 **kōdo** altitude

行動 **kōdō** behavior

孤独(な) **kodoku (na)** lonely

子供 **kodomo** child

子供の日 **kodomo no hi** Children's Day

高度(な) **kōdo (na)** sophisticated

声 **koe** voice

小枝 **koeda** twig

光栄 **kōei** honor

公園 **kōen** park

後援 **kōen** patronage

公演 **kōen** performance

越える **koeru** exceed, surpass

越えて **koete** beyond

坑夫 **kōfu** miner

幸福 **kōfuku** happiness

降伏 **kōfuku** surrender

興奮 **kōfun** excitement

郊外 **kōgai** suburbs

公害 **kōgai** environmental pollution

戸外で **kogai de** in the open air

工学 **kōgaku** engineering

小柄(の) **kogara (no)** undersized

焦がす **kogasu** burn; scorch

小型(の) **kogata (no)** compact

攻撃 **kōgeki** attack

攻撃的(な) **kōgekiteki (na)** aggressive

高原 **kōgen** plateau

焦げる **kogeru** burn; scorch

抗議 **kōgi** protest

講義 **kōgi** lecture

こぎれい(な) **kogirei (na)** neat

小切手 **kogitte** check FIN

皇后 **kōgō** empress

凍えた **kogoeta** frozen

こぐ **kogu** row

工業 **kōgyō** industry

鉱業 **kōgyō** mining

工業(の) **kōgyō (no)** industrial

後輩 **kōhai** junior

荒廃して **kōhai shite** in ruins

後半 **kōhan** second half

小春日和 **koharu-biyori** Indian summer

公平(な) **kōhei (na)** fair

コーヒー **kōhī** coffee

子羊 **kohitsuji** lamb

公報 **kōhō** official report

広報活動 **kōhō-katsudō** PR, public relations

候補者 **kōhosha** candidate

公表 **kōhyō** public announcement

好評 **kōhyō** rave review

こい **koi** carp

恋 **koi** romantic love

濃い **koi** thick; dense; dark

行為 **kōi** act

好意 **kōi** goodwill

恋人 **koibito** lover

コイン **koin** coin

こいのぼり **koinobori** carp streamers

コインランドリー **koin-randorī** laundromat

子犬 **koinu** puppy

恋しがる **koishigaru** pine for

恋しい **koishī** beloved ◊ miss

更衣室 **kōishitsu** changing room

好意的(な) **kōiteki (na)** favorable

孤児 **koji** orphan

工事 **kōji** construction

こじき **kojiki** beggar

故人 **kojin** the deceased

個人 **kojin** individual

個人的(な) **kojinteki (na)** personal

控除 **kōjo** deduction

工場 **kōjō** factory

硬貨 **kōka** coin

降下 **kōka** descent

効果 **kōka** effect

後悔 **kōkai** regret

公開(の) **kōkai (no)** public

交換 **kōkan** exchange

高価(な) **kōka (na)** expensive

交換留学 **kōkan-ryūgaku** (academic) exchange

こけ **koke** moss

光景 **kōkei** spectacle

後継者 **kōkeisha** successor

貢献 **kōken** contribution

高血圧 **kōketsuatsu** high blood pressure

後期 **kōki** second semester; latter half

高気圧 **kōkiatsu** high pressure

好奇心 **kōkishin** curiosity

国家 **kokka** nation

国歌 **kokka** national anthem

国会 **Kokkai** the Diet; national assembly

国会議員 **Kokkai-gi-in** Diet member

国家(の) **kokka (no)** national

国旗 **kokki** national flag

コック **kokku** cook

国境 **kokkyō** border

ここ **koko** here

航行 **kōkō** navigation

高校 **kōkō** high school

ココア **kokoa** cocoa

心地悪い **kokochiwarui** uncomfortable

心地よい **kokochiyoi** pleasant

考古学 **kōkogaku** archeology

広告 **kōkoku** advertisement

公告 **kōkoku** notice

広告代理店 **kōkoku-dairiten** advertising agency

個々(の) **koko (no)** individual

九日 **kokonoka** the 9th; nine days

九つ **kokonotsu** nine

心 **kokoro** mind; heart

心細い **kokorobosoi** downhearted

試み **kokoromi** attempt

試みる **kokoromiru** attempt

快く **kokoroyoku** gladly

志 **kokorozashi** ambition

志さす **kokorozasu** aspire to

心付け **kokorozuke** gratuity

心強い **kokorozuyoi** reassuring

高校生 **kōkōsei** high school student

航空 **kōkū** aviation

黒板 **kokuban** blackboard

航空便 **kōkūbin** airmail

国土 **kokudo** land

国道 **kokudō** national route

航空会社 **kōkū-gaisha** airline

国語 **kokugo** national language; Japanese

告白 **kokuhaku** confession

告発 **kokuhatsu** accusation

刻印 **kokuin** carved seal

黒人 **kokujin** black (person)

国民 **kokumin** the people

国民総生産 **kokumin-sōseisan** GNP, gross national product

穀物 **kokumotsu** grain

国内(の) **kokunai (no)** domestic

国王 kokuō king

国連 Kokuren UN

国立公園 kokuritsu-kōen national park

国立(の) kokuritsu(no) national

国際 kokusai international

国際電話 kokusai-denwa international call

国際連合 Kokusai-rengō United Nations

国際的(な) kokusaiteki (na) international

国籍 kokuseki nationality

顧客 kokyaku client

故郷 kokyō hometown

皇居 Kōkyo Imperial Palace

公共(の) kōkyō (no) public

呼吸 kokyū breathing

高級(な) kōkyū (na) high-quality

こま koma counter; piece

細かい komakai detailed

困る komaru be in trouble

コマーシャル komāsharu ad

困った komatta troubled

米 kome rice (uncooked)

コメント komento comment

込み合った komiatta crowded

小道 komichi lane; path

項目 kōmoku item

顧問 komon adviser

込む komu be crowded

小麦 komugi wheat

小麦粉 komugiko flour

公務員 kōmuin civil servant

こうむる kōmuru incur; suffer

巧妙(な) kōmyō (na) ingenious

コミュニケーション komyunikēshon communication

粉 kona powder

構内 kōnai on campus

今晩 konban this evening

こんばんは konbanwa good evening

コンビニ konbini convenience store

こんぶ konbu kelp

昆虫 konchū insect

今度 kondo this time; next time

コンドーム kondōmu condom

こねる koneru knead

今月 kongetsu this month

混合 kongō mixture

後任者 kōninsha successor

根気 konki perseverance

コンクリート konkurīto concrete

根拠 konkyo reason; cause; basis (of argument)

こんなに konna ni to this extent

こんにちは **konnichiwa** hello

この **kono** this

このあいだ **kono aida** the other day

好ましい **konomashī** pleasant

好み **konomi** preference

好む **konomu** like

このよう（な）**kono yō (na)** such

コンパ **konpa** party

根本的（な）**konponteki (na)** basic

コンピューター **konpyūtā** computer

混乱 **konran** confusion

コンサルタント **konsarutanto** consultant

コンサート **konsāto** concert

コンセント **konsento** outlet

今週 **konshū** this week

コンタクトレンズ **kontakuto-renzu** contact lens

コンテスト **kontesuto** contest

コントロール **kontorōru** control

今夜 **kon'ya** tonight

婚約 **kon'yaku** engagement

婚約者 **kon'yakusha** fiancé(e)

購入 **kōnyū** purchasing

混雑する **konzatsu suru** be crowded

コピー **kopī** photocopy; copy

コピー機 **kopī-ki** photocopier

コップ **koppu** glass

凍らせる **kōraseru** freeze

コーラス **kōrasu** chorus

これ **kore** this; this one

高齢者 **kōreisha** senior citizen

これから **kore kara** from now on

これら **korera** these

氷 **kōri** ice

孤立 **koritsu** isolation

公立（の）**kōritsu (no)** public

頃 **koro** time ◊ when

転ぶ **korobu** fall over

転がる **korogaru** roll

殺す **korosu** kill

こる **koru** become stiff; be absorbed in

凍る **kōru** freeze

コルク **koruku** cork

考慮 **kōryo** consideration

綱領 **kōryō** summary

交流 **kōryū** alternating current

耕作 **kōsaku** cultivation

降参 **kōsan** surrender

交差点 **kōsaten** junction

個性 **kosei** individuality; personality

構成 **kōsei** composition; structure

後世 **kōsei** posterity

抗生物質 **kōsei-busshitsu** antibiotic

公正（な）**kōsei (na)** unbiased

厚生省 **Kōseishō** Ministry of Health and Welfare

鉱石 **kōseki** ore

後者 **kōsha** the latter

校舎 **kōsha** school building

腰 **koshi** hip; waist

孔子 **Kōshi** Confucius

公使 **kōshi** envoy

講師 **kōshi** lecturer

腰掛ける **koshikakeru** sit

こし器 **koshiki** strainer

公式 **kōshiki** formula

行進 **kōshin** march

更新 **kōshin** renewal

香辛料 **kōshinryō** spice

個室 **koshitsu** private room

こしょう **koshō** pepper

故障 **koshō** breakdown

交渉 **kōshō** negotiation

公衆電話 **kōshū-denwa** pay phone

…こそ **-koso** (intensifier): これこそぼくが見たものだ **kore-koso boku ga mita mono da** this is the very one that I saw

構想 **kōsō** idea

高層ビル **kōsō-biru** high rise

高速道路 **kōsoku-dōro** expressway

骨折 **kossetsu** fracture

こっそり **kossori** stealthily

こす **kosu** filter, strain

越す **kosu** exceed

コース **kōsu** course

香水 **kōsui** perfume

こする **kosuru** rub; scrape

答え **kotae** answer

答える **kotaeru** answer

応える **kotaeru** affect

後退 **kōtai** retreat

交替 **kōtai** alternation

こたつ **kotatsu** heated table with quilt cover

こっち **kotchi** this; this one

皇帝 **kōtei** emperor

肯定する **kōtei suru** answer in the affirmative

公的(な) **kōteki (na)** official

古典 **koten** classic

鋼鉄 **kōtetsu** steel

事、こと **koto** affair; thing

琴 **koto** Japanese stringed instrument

コート **kōto** court SPORTS

言葉 **kotoba** language; word

高等学校 **kōtōgakkō** senior high school

異なる **kotonaru** differ

口頭(の) **kōtō (no)** oral

今年 **kotoshi** this year

断る **kotowaru** refuse

ことわざ **kotowaza** proverb

こつ **kotsu** knack

交通 **kōtsū** traffic

交通費 **kōtsūhi** travel expenses

こつこつ **kotsukotsu**
untiringly

こってりした **kotteri shita**
thick; rich

骨とう品 **kottōhin** antique

コットン **kotton** cotton

幸運, 好運 **kōun** good
fortune

小売業者 **kouri-gyōsha**
retailer

怖がる **kowagaru** be afraid

怖い **kowai** scary

壊れる **kowareru** break

壊す **kowasu** break

小屋 **koya** hut

雇用 **koyō** employment

こよみ **koyomi** calendar

雇用者 **koyōsha** employer

小指 **koyubi** little finger;
little toe

口座 **kōza** account

講座 **kōza** course

鉱山 **kōzan** mine

小銭 **kozeni** small change

公然(の) **kōzen (no)** public

構造 **kōzō** structure

洪水 **kōzui** flood

小遣い **kozukai** allowance

小包 **kozutsumi** parcel

区 **ku** ward *(of city)*

配る **kubaru** distribute

区別 **kubetsu** distinction

首 **kubi** neck

口 **kuchi** mouth

口紅 **kuchibeni** lipstick

唇 **kuchibiru** lip

口笛 **kuchibue** whistle

口げんか **kuchigenka** row

空調 **kūchō** air-conditioning

管 **kuda** tube

砕ける **kudakeru** be smashed

くだけた **kudaketa** informal;
plain; easy

果物 **kudamono** fruit

くだらない **kudaranai**
trashy; worthless

下さい **kudasai** please

下さる **kudasaru** give
(polite); be kind enough to do

下す **kudasu** hand down;
lower

くどい **kudoi** tedious

口説く **kudoku** make
advances

工夫 **kufū** means; device

空腹 **kūfuku** hunger

九月 **kugatsu** September

くぎ **kugi** nail; spike

空軍 **kūgun** air force

クイズ **kuizu** quiz

クイズ番組 **kuizu-bangumi**
quiz program

くじ **kuji** raffle

くじ引き **kujibiki** drawing
lots

鯨 **kujira** whale

苦情 **kujō** complaint

駆除する **kujo suru** exterminate

茎 **kuki** stem

空気 **kūki** air

クッキー **kukkī** cookie

空港 **kūkō** airport

空虚 **kūkyo** emptiness

くま **kuma** bear

組 **kumi** class; team

組合 **kumiai** association

組み合わせ **kumiawase** combination

組み合わせる **kumiawaseru** combine

組み立てる **kumitateru** put together

くも **kumo** spider

雲 **kumo** cloud

曇り **kumori** cloudy weather

曇る **kumoru** cloud over; mist up

組む **kumu** team up; assemble; fold *arms*; cross *legs*

…君 **-kun** Mr; Ms *(to address younger people)*

宮内庁 **Kunaichō** Imperial Household Agency

国 **kuni** country

訓練 **kunren** training

倉 **kura** storehouse

比べる **kuraberu** compare

クラブ **kurabu** club

暗がり **kuragari** gloom

くらげ **kurage** jellyfish

…くらい **-kurai** approximately ◊ at least

位 **kurai** rank; throne

暗い **kurai** dark

クラクション **kurakushon** horn AUTO

暮し **kurashi** living

クラシック（な）**kurashikku (na)** classical

クラス **kurasu** class

暮らす **kurasu** live

クラッチ **kuratchi** clutch AUTO

クレジットカード **kurejitto-kādo** credit card

くれる **kureru** give; do *(for me)*

暮れる **kureru** get dark; come to an end; be lost in

クレヨン **kureyon** crayon

くり **kuri** chestnut

繰り返し **kurikaeshi** repetition

繰り返す **kurikaesu** repeat

クリーム **kurīmu** cream

クリームソーダ **kurīmu sōda** soda

クリーニング店 **kurīninguten** laundry

クリップ **kurippu** clip

クリスマス **Kurisumasu** Christmas

苦労 **kurō** toil

黒い **kuroi** black

黒字で **kuroji de** in the black

クローク **kurōku** cloakroom

クロスカントリー (スキー) **kurosu-kantorī (sukī)** cross-country (skiing)

苦労する **kurō suru** struggle

来る **kuru** come

くるくる回る **kurukuru mawaru** whirl

車 **kuruma** car; vehicle

車いす **kurumaisu** wheelchair

くるみ **kurumi** walnut

くるむ **kurumu** wrap; tuck in *(in bed)*

苦しい **kurushī** agonizing

苦しめる **kurushimeru** distress

苦しみ **kurushimi** suffering

苦しむ **kurushimu** suffer

狂った **kurutta** crazy

草 **kusa** grass

くさい **kusai** smelly

鎖 **kusari** chain

腐る **kusaru** decay

癖 **kuse** habit

くしゃみ **kushami** sneeze

くし **kushi** comb

空想 **kūsō** fantasy

クッション **kusshon** cushion

くすぐる **kusuguru** tickle

くすぐったい **kusuguttai** ticklish

薬 **kusuri** medicine

くたびれる **kutabireru** be worn out

靴 **kutsu** shoe

苦痛 **kutsū** pain

覆す **kutsugaesu** demolish

靴ひも **kutsuhimo** shoelace

屈辱 **kutsujoku** humiliation

屈辱的 (な) **kutsujokuteki (na)** humiliating

くつろぐ **kutsurogu** relax

靴下 **kutsushita** sock

靴屋 **kutsuya** shoestore

靴墨 **kutsuzumi** shoe polish

くっつける **kuttsukeru** knit together

くっつく **kuttsuku** adhere

加える **kuwaeru** add

詳しい **kuwashī** detailed

区役所 **kuyakusho** ward office

悔やむ **kuyamu** regret

悔しい **kuyashī** regrettable

くず **kuzu** crumb; trash

崩れる **kuzureru** collapse

崩す **kuzusu** change *money*; destroy

キャベツ **kyabetsu** cabbage

客観的 (な) **kyakkanteki (na)** objective

客 **kyaku** customer; guest

脚本 **kyakuhon** script

客船 **kyakusen** cruise liner

客室 **kyakushitsu** room; cabin

キャンパス **kyanpasu** campus

キャンプ **kyanpu** camp

キャンプ場 **kyanpujō** campsite

キャリア **kyaria** career

今日 **kyō** today

競売 **kyōbai** auction

共謀する **kyōbō suru** conspire

強調 **kyōchō** emphasis

鏡台 **kyōdai** dressing table

巨大(な) **kyodai (na)** enormous

兄弟姉妹 **kyōdai-shimai** brothers and sisters

共同(の) **kyōdō (no)** joint

恐怖 **kyōfu** terror

狂言 **kyōgen** Noh comedy

協議 **kyōgi** consultation; conference

競技 **kyōgi** athletics competition

競技場 **kyōgijō** stadium; field

脅迫 **kyōhaku** threat

拒否 **kyohi** refusal

脅威 **kyōi** menace

教育 **kyōiku** education

巨人 **kyojin** giant

狂人 **kyōjin** maniac

教授 **kyōju** professor

居住者 **kyojūsha** resident

許可 **kyoka** permission

協会 **kyōkai** association

境界 **kyōkai** boundary

教会 **kyōkai** church

共感 **kyōkan** sympathy

許可証 **kyokashō** permit

教科書 **kyōkasho** textbook

狂気 **kyōki** insanity

強固(な) **kyōko (na)** strong; stubborn

局 **kyoku** bureau

曲 **kyoku** musical composition

極度の疲労 **kyokudo no hirō** exhaustion

極端 **kyokutan** extreme

極端(な) **kyokutan (na)** extreme

極東 **Kyokutō** Far East

供給 **kyōkyū** supply

興味 **kyōmi** interest

去年 **kyonen** last year

強烈(な) **kyōretsu (na)** forceful

距離 **kyori** distance

協力 **kyōryoku** cooperation

強力(な) **kyōryoku (na)** powerful

共産主義 **kyōsan-shugi** communism

強勢 **kyōsei** emphasis

強制的(な) **kyōseiteki (na)** compulsory

教師 **kyōshi** teacher

教室 **kyōshitsu** classroom

競争 **kyōsō** competition

競走 **kyōsō** race

協定 **kyōtei** pact

京都 **Kyōto** Kyoto

共通(の) **kyōtsū (no)** shared

共和国 **kyōwakoku** republic

許容 **kyoyō** permission

教養のある **kyōyō no aru** cultured

拒絶 **kyozetsu** rejection

九 **kyū** nine

球 **kyū** sphere; ball

旧 **kyū** old; former

宮殿 **kyūden** palace

休日 **kyūjitsu** holiday

救助 **kyūjo** rescue

九十 **kyūjū** ninety

休暇 **kyūka** vacation

休憩 **kyūkei** rest

休憩時間 **kyūkei-jikan** intermission

急行 **kyūkō** fast train

急行列車 **kyūkō-ressha** express train

窮屈(な) **kyūkutsu (na)** narrow; formal

救急車 **kyūkyūsha** ambulance

救命ボート **kyūmei-bōto** lifeboat

急(な) **kyū (na)** urgent

急に **kyū ni** suddenly

きゅうり **kyūri** cucumber

給料 **kyūryō** salary

旧姓 **kyūsei** maiden name
◇ née

休戦 **kyūsen** truce

休職 **kyūshoku** leave of absence

給食 **kyūshoku** school meals

九州 **Kyūshū** Kyushu

休息 **kyūsoku** respite

急速に **kyūsoku ni** rapidly

急用 **kyūyō** urgent business

M

間 **ma** interval; pause

まあ **mā** well!

まばたきする **mabataki suru** blink

幻 **maboroshi** vision REL

まぶしい **mabushī** dazzling

まぶた **mabuta** eyelid

町 **machi** town

待合室 **machiaishitsu** waiting room

待ち合わせる **machiawaseru** arrange to meet

間違える **machigaeru** be mistaken

間違えて **machigaete** by mistake

間違い **machigai** mistake

間違った **machigatta** wrong

まだ **mada** still; not yet

…まで … **made** until

…までに …**made ni** by

窓 **mado** window

窓ガラス **madogarasu** windowpane

窓口 **madoguchi** teller's window

前 **mae** front ◊ before; ago

前払い **maebarai** advance payment

前書き **maegaki** foreword

前もって **maemotte** beforehand

前向き(な) **maemuki (na)** positive; facing the front

前に **mae ni** previously; forward; in front

前売り **maeuri** advance sale; booking

マフラー **mafurā** muffler AUTO; scarf

曲がる **magaru** curve; turn

曲げる **mageru** bend; compromise

紛らわしい **magirawashī** confusing

孫 **mago** grandchild

まぐれ(の) **magure (no)** lucky

まぐろ **maguro** tuna

麻ひ **mahi** paralysis

魔法 **mahō** magic

魔法瓶 **mahōbin** vacuum flask

…まい **-mai** (negative suffix) not

…枚 **-mai** countword for flat items

毎… **mai-** every

毎朝 **maiasa** every morning

毎晩 **maiban** every evening

迷子 **maigo** lost child

毎回 **maikai** every time

マイク **maiku** microphone

マイナス **mainasu** minus

毎日 **mainichi** every day

参る **mairu** surrender; visit temple, grave; H go; H come

毎週 **maishū** every week

埋葬 **maisō** burial

毎年 **maitoshi** every year

毎月 **maitsuki** every month

麻雀 **mājan** mah-jong

まじめ(な) **majime (na)** earnest

混じる **majiru** be mixed

魔女 **majo** witch

任せる **makaseru** entrust

負かす **makasu** defeat

負け **make** defeat

負ける **makeru** lose

巻き **maki** reel; roll

巻き戻す **makimodosu** rewind

巻き物 **makimono** scroll

巻き付ける **makitsukeru** wind

真っ赤(な) **makka (na)** crimson; downright lie

真っ暗(な) **makkura (na)**
pitch dark

真っ黒(な) **makkura (na)**
jet-black

誠に **makoto ni** really

まく **maku** scatter

幕 **maku** act; curtain THEAT

巻く **maku** coil

枕 **makura** pillow

まま **mama** like that

ママ **mama** mom

まあまあ **māmā** so-so

まま母 **mama-haha**
stepmother

マーマレード **māmarēdo**
marmalade

豆 **mame** bean

豆まき **mamemaki** bean
scattering *(at the Setsubun
festival)*

まもなく **mamonaku** soon

守る **mamoru** protect; meet
deadline

万 **man** ten thousand

学ぶ **manabu** learn

万引き **manbiki** shoplifter;
shoplifting

満潮 **manchō** high tide

まね **mane** imitation

マネージャー **manējā**
manager

招き猫 **manekineko**
beckoning cat *(small figure
seen in shops and restaurants
to invite customers in)*

招く **maneku** invite

まねる **maneru** imitate

漫画 **manga** comic; cartoon

満月 **mangetsu** full moon

間に合う **ma ni au** be in time;
be suitable

満員 **man'in** full

満期 **manki** maturity

真ん中 **mannaka** middle

万年筆 **mannenhitsu**
(fountain) pen

慢性(の) **mansei (no)** chronic

マンション **manshon**
condominium

免れる **manugareru** escape
from; be excepted from

漫才 **manzai** comic double act

満足 **manzoku** satisfaction

マラソン **marason** marathon

まれ(な) **mare (na)** rare

丸 **maru** circle ◊ entire *(day)*
◊ *(suffix for names of ships)*

まるで **marude** completely

丸い **marui** round

丸める **marumeru** roll up

まさか **masaka** surely not!

まさに **masa ni** exactly

摩擦 **masatsu** friction

マッサージ **massāji** massage

真っ青(の) **massao (no)**
pale

真っ白(な) **masshiro (na)**
pure white

マッシュルーム **masshurūmu** mushroom

真っすぐ **massugu** straight

ます **masu** square *(in board game)*; trout; box seat *(for sumo)*

…ます -**masu** *(polite verbal suffix)*: 私が行きます **watashi ga ikimasu** I'm going

増す **masu** increase

麻酔 **masui** anesthetic

マスカラ **masukara** mascara

マスコミ **masukomi** the media

マスク **masuku** mask

ますます **masumasu** more and more

マスメディア **masumedia** mass media

また **mata** again; またね **mata ne** see you!

または **mata wa** or

抹茶 **matcha** powdered green tea

マッチ **matchi** match

的 **mato** target

まとまる **matomaru** be concluded

まとめる **matomeru** conclude

まとも(な) **matomo (na)** honest; decent

松 **matsu** pine

待つ **matsu** wait

松葉杖 **matsubazue** crutch

まつげ **matsuge** (eye)lash

祭り **matsuri** festival

まったく **mattaku** completely; honestly!

マットレス **mattoresu** mattress

回り **mawari** circumference ◊ via

回り道 **mawarimichi** detour

回る **mawaru** rotate

回す **mawasu** pass around

麻薬 **mayaku** drug

真夜中 **mayonaka** midnight

マヨネーズ **mayonēzu** mayonnaise

迷う **mayou** be lost

まゆ **mayu** eyebrow

混ざる、交ざる **mazaru** mix

混ぜ合わせる **mazeawaseru** combine

混ぜる **mazeru** mix

まず **mazu** first of all

まずい **mazui** tasteless

貧しい **mazushī** poor

目 **me** eye

芽 **me** sprout

めちゃくちゃ(な) **mechakucha (na)** disorganized

目玉焼き **medamayaki** fried egg

メダル **medaru** medal

目立たない **medatanai** inconspicuous

目立って **medatsu** striking

女神 **megami** goddess

眼鏡 **megane** (eye)glasses

眼鏡屋 **meganeya** optician

恵まれている **megumarete iru** be blessed with

目薬 **megusuri** (eye)drops

めい **mei** niece

名 **mei** renowned ◊ *(countword for people)*: 三名 **sanmei** three people

名案 **meian** brainwave

名簿 **meibo** list of names

名物 **meibutsu** famous (local) product

明白(な) **meihaku (na)** clear

明治時代 **Meiji-jidai** Meiji period (1868-1912)

名人 **meijin** master; expert

明確(な) **meikaku (na)** precise

名門(の) **meimon (no)** prestigious

命令 **meirei** command

明朗(な) **meirō (na)** bright

名作 **meisaku** masterpiece

名声 **meisei** fame

名刺 **meishi** (business) card

迷信 **meishin** superstition

名所 **meisho** famous place

めい想 **meisō** meditation

迷惑 **meiwaku** inconvenience

名誉 **meiyo** credit; honor

名誉棄損 **meiyo-kison** defamation

メークアップ **mēku-appu** make-up

めくる **mekuru** turn over

めまい **memai** dizziness

メモ **memo** memo

メモ帳 **memochō** notepad

めん **men** noodles

面 **men** mask; face; aspect

綿 **men** cotton

メンバー **menbā** member

面倒 **mendō** nuisance

面倒くさい **mendōkusai** annoying

免疫 **men'eki** immunity

免除 **menjo** exemption

面会 **menkai** interview; meeting

面会時間 **menkai-jikan** visiting hours

免許 **menkyo** license

免許証 **menkyoshō** license; certificate

綿密(な) **menmitsu (na)** detailed; scrupulous

面積 **menseki** area

面接 **mensetsu** interview

メニュー **menyū** menu

免税品 **menzeihin** duty-free goods

免税(の) **menzei (no)** duty-free

メロディー **merodī** melody; tune

メロン **meron** melon

メール **mēru** email

めし **meshi** rice; food; meal *(familiar)*

召し上がる **meshiagaru** *(polite)* eat; drink

メッセージ **messēji** message

雌 **mesu** female

メーター **mētā** meter

メートル **mētoru** meter

めったに…ない **metta ni … nai** rarely

目覚まし時計 **mezamashi-dokei** alarm clock

めざす **mezasu** aim at

めずらしい **mezurashī** rare

実 **mi** fruit; nut

身 **mi** body

未… **mi-** not yet

見合い **miai** arranged marriage meeting

未亡人 **mibōjin** widow

身分 **mibun** status

身分証明書 **mibun-shōmeisho** identity card

身ぶり **miburi** gesture

道 **michi** road; way

導く **michibiku** guide

未知(の) **michi (no)** unknown

満ちる **michiru** be full; come in *(tide)*

満ち潮 **michishio** incoming tide

乱れる **midareru** be disordered; be corrupt

見出し **midashi** headline

乱す **midasu** disrupt

緑色(の) **midori-iro (no)** green

見える **mieru** show; be seen

磨く **migaku** polish

右 **migi** right

右利き(の) **migikiki (no)** right-handed

見事(な) **migoto (na)** splendid

見苦しい **migurushī** unsightly

見本 **mihon** pattern; sample

見本市 **mihon'ichi** trade fair

短い **mijikai** short

みじめ(な) **mijime (na)** miserable

未熟(な) **mijuku (na)** immature

見かけ **mikake** appearance

見かける **mikakeru** catch sight of

味覚 **mikaku** taste *(sense)*

みかん **mikan** mandarin orange

未完成(の) **mikansei (no)** incomplete

味方 **mikata** ally

見方 **mikata** viewpoint

幹 **miki** trunk

ミキサー **mikisā** blender

三日 **mikka** three days; the 3rd

見込み **mikomi** likelihood

見込みなし **mikominashi** no-hoper

見込む **mikomu** anticipate

未婚(の) **mikon (no)** unmarried

みこし **mikoshi** ceremonial palanquin

見舞い **mimai** visit *(to sick person)*

…未満で … **miman de** less than

耳 **mimi** ear

身元 **mimoto** identity

皆 **mina** all

南 **minami** south

源 **minamoto** source

見直す **minaosu** overhaul

見習い **minarai** apprentice

身なり **minari** appearance; clothes

皆さん **minasan** ladies and gentlemen

みなす **minasu** consider

港 **minato** port

港町 **minatomachi** seaport

峰 **mine** peak

ミネラルウォーター **mineraru-wōtā** mineral water

民芸品 **mingeihin** folkcraft

醜い **minikui** ugly

身につける **mi ni tsukeru** put on; acquire

民間(の) **minkan (no)** private *industry*; civil *(not military)*

皆 **minna** everyone

見逃す **minogasu** overlook

実る **minoru** bear fruit

民宿 **minshuku** Japanese B&B

民主主義 **minshu-shugi** democracy

民主的(な) **minshuteki (na)** democratic

ミント **minto** mint

民謡 **min'yō** folk music

民族 **minzoku** people

見覚え **mioboe** recollection; recognition

見送る **miokuru** see off; pass up

見下ろす **miorosu** overlook

見落とす **miotosu** miss, overlook

未来 **mirai** future

ミリ(メートル) **miri(mētoru)** millimeter

味りん **mirin** sweet sake

見る **miru** look; watch; see

…みる **-miru** try to; 説得して みる **settoku shite miru** try to persuade

ミルク **miruku** milk

魅力 **miryoku** attraction

魅力的(な) **miryokuteki (na)** attractive

岬 **misaki** cape

店 **mise** store

未成年(の) **miseinen (no)** underage

見せかけ **misekake** pretense

見せる **miseru** show

ミシン **mishin** sewing machine

見知らぬ人 **mishiranu hito** stranger

みそ **miso** soybean paste

みそ汁 **miso shiru** miso soup

ミス **misu** mistake; unmarried woman

みすぼらしい **misuborashī** scruffy; seedy

未遂 **misui** failed attempt

ミステリー **misuterī** mystery

見捨てる **misuteru** abandon

…みたい **-mitai** like; 夢みたい **yume-mitai** like a dream

満たす **mitasu** satisfy

見たところ **mita tokoro** on the face of it

未定 **mitei** undecided

認める **mitomeru** acknowledge

見通し **mitōshi** outlook

ミツバチ **mitsubachi** bee

密売 **mitsubai** illicit sale

密度 **mitsudo** density

見つかる **mitsukaru** be found

見つける **mitsukeru** find

見つめる **mitsumeru** stare at

見積もり **mitsumori** estimate

見積もる **mitsumoru** estimate

密輸 **mitsuyu** smuggling

みっともない **mittomonai** shameful

三つ **mittsu** three

見失う **miushinau** lose sight of

見分ける **miwakeru** identify

魅惑 **miwaku** fascination; charm

魅惑的(な) **miwakuteki (na)** charming

見渡す **miwatasu** survey

みやげ **miyage** souvenir

都 **miyako** capital city

溝 **mizo** ditch; drain *(under street)*

みぞれ **mizore** sleet

水 **mizu** water

水着 **mizugi** swimsuit

湖 **mizūmi** lake

みずみずしい **mizumizushī** juicy

水っぽい **mizuppoi** watery

水差し **mizusashi** carafe

水たまり **mizutamari** puddle

水割り **mizuwari** whiskey and water

…も … **mo** also; …も…も **... mo ...** both ... and...; …も…もない **... mo ... mo nai** neither ... nor ...

喪 **mo** mourning

もう **mō** already; still; more ◊ another

もち **mochi** rice cake

持ち上げる **mochiageru** raise

持ちこたえる **mochikotaeru** endure

持ち物 **mochimono** belongings

持ち主 **mochinushi** owner

もちろん **mochiron** of course

盲腸炎 **mōchōen** appendicitis

喪中である **mochū de aru** be in mourning

モデム **modemu** modem

モデル **moderu** model

戻る **modoru** return

戻す **modosu** put back

燃える **moeru** burn

毛布 **mōfu** blanket

喪服 **mofuku** mourning (clothes)

模擬(の) **mogi (no)** mock

潜る **moguru** dive

模範 **mohan** model

文字 **moji** character (in writing); letter

文字どおり(の) **mojidōri (no)** literal

もうかる **mōkaru** be profitable

模型(の) **mokei (no)** model

設ける **mōkeru** set up

儲ける **mōkeru** profit

目撃者 **mokugekisha** eyewitness

目標 **mokuhyō** target

目次 **mokuji** table of contents

目録 **mokuroku** inventory; catalogue

木製(の) **mokusei (no)** wooden

目的 **mokuteki** purpose

目的地 **mokutekichi** destination

木曜日 **mokuyōbi** Thursday

木材 **mokuzai** wood

木綿 **momen** cotton

もめる **momeru** have a dispute

もみじ **momiji** Japanese maple

もみ消す **momikesu** cover up

もも **momo** thigh

桃 **momo** peach

盲目(の) **mōmoku (no)** blind

もむ **momu** rub

門 **mon** gate

文部科学省 **monbukagakushō** MEXT (Ministry of Education, Culture, Sports, Science and Technology)

問題 **mondai** problem

門限 **mongen** curfew

文句 **monku** phrase; complaint

文盲(の) **monmō (no)**

illiterate

物，もの **mono** thing

者 もの **mono** person

物語 **monogatari** story

ものまね **monomane** impression

物置 **mono-oki** storeroom; shed

物差し **monosashi** ruler

もの静か(な) **monoshizuka (na)** quiet

ものすごい **monosugoi** awesome

もっぱら **moppara** entirely

漏らす **morasu** divulge

森 **mori** forest

盛り上がり **moriagari** climax

もろい **moroi** fragile

漏る **moru** leak

もし **moshi** if

申し上げる **mōshiageru** *polite form of iu* say

申し出 **mōshide** offer

もしかしたら **moshikashitara** maybe

申込用紙 **mōshikomi-yōshi** application form

申し込む **mōshikomu**

apply for

もしもし **moshimoshi** hello TEL

申す **mōsu** H say; …と申しますが … **to mōshimasu ga** this is TEL

もうすぐ **mōsugu** straight away

モーター **mōtā** motor

もたらす **motarasu** bring; produce

もたれる **motareru** lean on

もてなす **motenasu** entertain

もてる **moteru** be popular

元 **moto** origin

元… **moto-** ex-

基 **moto** foundation

求める **motomeru** ask for

もともと **motomoto** originally

もと(の) **moto (no)** original

基づく **motozuku** rest on

もつ **motsu** hold out *(of supplies)*; keep *(of food, milk)*

持つ **motsu** have; hold

もつれる **motsureru** get tangled up

もったいない **mottainai** wasteful

持って行く **motte iku** take away

持っている **motte iru** have

持ってくる **motte kuru** bring

もっと **motto** more

最も **mottomo** most

モヤシ **moyashi** bean sprouts

燃やす **moyasu** burn

模様 **moyō** pattern

模様入り（の）**moyō-iri (no)** patterned

催し **moyōshi** meeting

模造品 **mozōhin** imitation

無… **mu-** non-; un-

無茶（な）**mucha (na)** reckless

むち **muchi** whip

無知（な）**muchi (na)** ignorant

夢中である **muchū de aru** be hooked on; be engrossed in

無駄 **muda** useless; unnecessary

無駄足 **muda-ashi** wildgoose chase

無駄（な）**muda (na)** wasteful

無鉛（の）**muen (no)** unleaded

無害（な）**mugai (na)** harmless

無限 **mugen** infinity

麦 **mugi** barley; wheat

麦茶 **mugicha** barley tea

麦わら **mugiwara** straw

無言（の）**mugon (no)** mute

無表情（な）**muhyōjō (na)** impassive

六日 **muika** six days; the 6th

無意識に **muishiki ni** mechanically; unintentionally

むいていない **muite inai** incompetent

無邪気（な）**mujaki (na)** innocent

無人（の）**mujin (no)** uninhabited; unmanned

無地（の）**muji (no)** plain

無条件（の）**mujōken (no)** unconditional

矛盾 **mujun** contradiction

迎えに行く **mukae ni iku** pick up

迎えに来る **mukae ni kuru** come for

向かい風 **mukaikaze** headwind

むかむかさせる **mukamuka saseru** nauseate

無関係（な）**mukankei (na)** irrelevant

無関心（な）**mukanshin (na)** indifferent

昔 **mukashi** long ago

ムカつく **mukatsuku** be mad

向かう **mukau** head for

向ける **mukeru** point towards

向き **muki** direction

無期限（の）**mukigen (no)** indefinite

無傷（の）**mukizu (no)** unscathed

婿 **muko** bridegroom

むこうみず（な）**mukōmizu (na)** foolhardy

無効（な）**mukō (na)** invalid

向こうに **mukō ni** beyond

向うずね mukōzune shin

むく muku peel

向く muku face

むくんだ mukunda swollen

無給(の) mukyū (no) unpaid

むなしい munashī empty; futile

胸 mune chest; bosom

胸やけ muneyake heartburn

無能(な) munō (na) incapable

村 mura village

紫色(の) murasaki-iro (no) violet; purple

群れ mure herd; flock

無理 muri impossible

無理やり muriyari forcibly

ムール貝 mūrugai mussel

無類(の) murui (no) incomparable

無料 muryō free of charge

無力(な) muryoku (na) powerless

無制限(の) museigen (no) unlimited

無責任(な) musekinin (na) irresponsible

無線 musen radio

虫 mushi bug

無視 mushi disregard

蒸し暑い mushiatsui humid

虫歯 mushiba bad tooth

虫眼鏡 mushimegane magnifying glass

無神経(な) mushinkei (na) insensitive

むしろ mushiro rather

虫刺され mushisasare sting; bite

虫よけ mushiyoke (insect) repellent

蒸す musu steam

結ぶ musubu tie up

息子 musuko son

娘 musume daughter

無数(の) musū (no) countless

無敵(の) muteki (no) invincible

むっとする mutto suru be annoyed

六つ muttsu six

無罪 muzai innocence

難しい muzukashī difficult

脈拍 myakuhaku pulse

名字 myōji family name

妙(な) myō (na) peculiar

明日 myōnichi tomorrow

ミュージカル myūjikaru musical

N

…な **-na** ◊ *(forms negative imperative)*: 忘れるな **wasureru-na** don't forget ◊ *(for emphasis)*: きれいだな **kirei da na** it's beautiful, isn't it!

な **na** *(forms adjectives)*: 憶病（な）**okubyō (na)** cowardly

名 **na** name

なべ **nabe** pot

なだめる **nadameru** soothe

なだれ **nadare** avalanche

なでる **naderu** caress

など **nado** et cetera

苗 **nae** seedling

名札 **nafuda** nametag

長引く **nagabiku** be prolonged

長靴 **nagagutsu** boots

長い **nagai** long

眺め **nagame** view

眺める **nagameru** gaze at

長持ちする **nagamochi suru** last

…ながら **-nagara** *(linking two actions)* while; 歩きながら食べる **arukinagara taberu** eat while walking

流れ **nagare** flow

流れ星 **nagareboshi** shooting star

流れる **nagareru** flow *(of current, traffic)*; run *(of river, paint)*

長さ **nagasa** length

流し **nagashi** sink

長袖（の）**nagasode (no)** long-sleeved

流す **nagasu** flush away

嘆く **nageku** sigh; lament

投げる **nageru** throw

名残 **nagori** remains

なごやか（な）**nagoyaka (na)** peaceful

殴る **naguru** hit

慰め **nagusame** consolation

慰める **nagusameru** console

…ない **-nai** *(negative suffix)* not; 私は行かない **watashi wa ikanai** I won't go

無い、ない **nai** there is / are not; do not have

内部 **naibu** inside

ナイフ **naifu** knife

内科医 **naikai** physician

内閣 **naikaku** cabinet POL

内密（の）**naimitsu (no)** undercover

内線 **naisen** extension TEL

内心（の）**naishin (no)** inward

内緒(の) naisho (no) secret

ナイトクラブ naitokurabu nightclub

内容 naiyō content

内臓 naizō internal organs

なじむ najimu become familiar with

なじる najiru rebuke

中 naka inside

仲 naka relationship

半ば nakaba half; middle

仲間 nakama group; comrade

中身, 中味 nakami contents

なかなか nakanaka very

仲直りさせる nakanaori saseru reconcile

中庭 nakaniwa courtyard

…なければならない -nakereba naranai must

泣き叫ぶ nakisakebu bawl

仲人 nakōdo go-between

泣く naku cry

鳴く naku roar; chirp; quack

なくなる nakunaru run out; go (of pain etc)

亡くなる nakunaru pass away

なくす nakusu lose

生ビール namabīru draft (beer)

名前 namae (given) name

生放送 namahōsō live broadcast

生意気(な) namaiki (na) impertinent

怠け者 namakemono layabout

怠ける namakeru laze around

生(の) nama (no) live broadcast; raw

なまり namari accent

鉛 namari lead

なめらか(な) nameraka (na) smooth

なめる nameru lick

波 nami wave (in sea)

涙 namida tear

並はずれた namihazureta extraordinary

並(の) nami (no) average

七 nana seven

斜め(の) naname (no) diagonal

七つ nanatsu seven

ナンバー nanbā number

ナンバープレート nanbāpurēto license plate

南米 Nanbei South America

南部(の) nanbu (no) southern

なんで nande why

何でも nan demo whatever

何度も nando mo many times

何 nani what

何か nani ka something; anything

何も nani mo nothing; anything

軟弱(な) **nanjaku (na)** weak; soft

何時 **nanji** what time

何回も **nankai mo** time and again

軟こう **nankō** ointment

南極 **Nankyoku** South Pole

難民 **nanmin** refugee

何人 **nannin** how many people

何(の) **nan (no)** what

…なので … **na node** as; so

七日 **nanoka** seven days; the 7th

難破 **nanpa** shipwreck

南西部(の) **nanseibu (no)** southwestern

ナンセンス **nansensu** nonsense

何て **nante** what; how

南東部(の) **nantōbu (no)** southeastern

何とか **nantoka** somehow; something or other

何となく **nantonaku** somehow or other

何曜日 **nan'yōbi** what day

直る **naoru** be repaired

治る **naoru** be healed

直す **naosu** repair

治す **naosu** heal

ナプキン **napukin** napkin

…なら … **nara** if

並べる **naraberu** lay out

並ぶ **narabu** line up

慣らす **narasu** familiarize

鳴らす **narasu** beep; honk; ring

習う **narau** learn

なれなれしい **narenareshī** familiar

慣れる **nareru** get accustomed to

鳴り響く **narihibiku** go off

成り立っている **naritatte iru** be composed of

なる **naru** become

鳴る **naru** sound; crash; ring

なるべく **narubeku** as … as possible

なるほど **naruhodo** I see!

情けない **nasakenai** pitiful

なさる **nasaru** polite form of **suru**

なし **nashi** pear

なし(で) **nashi (de)** without

なす **nasu** eggplant

夏 **natsu** summer

懐かしい **natsukashī** nostalgic ◊ miss

夏休み **natsuyasumi** summer vacation

納豆 **nattō** fermented soybeans

納得する **nattoku suru** consent

縄 **nawa** rope

悩み **nayami** worry

悩む **nayamu** get worried

なぜ **naze** why

なぞ **nazo** enigma

名づける **nazukeru** name

ね **ne** *(for emphasis)*: きれい
だね *kirei da ne* it's beautiful,
isn't it!

根 **ne** root

値 **ne** price

ねえ **nē** hey

値上がりする **neagari suru**
go up in price

ねばねばした **nebaneba
shita** sticky

粘り強い **nebarizuyoi**
persistent

値引き **nebiki** discount

寝坊する **nebō suru** sleep
late

寝袋 **nebukuro** sleeping bag

値段 **nedan** price

願い **negai** desire

願う **negau** ask for

ねぎ **negi** leek

値切る **negiru** haggle

ねじ **neji** screw

ねじる **nejiru** twist

寝かせる **nekaseru** lay down

ネックレス **nekkuresu**
necklace

熱狂的 (な) **nekkyōteki (na)**
fanatical

猫 **neko** cat

ネクタイ **nekutai** necktie

寝巻き **nemaki** nightshirt

眠い **nemui** drowsy

眠れない **nemurenai** have a
restless night ◊ sleepless

眠る **nemuru** fall asleep

粘土 **nendo** clay

年度 **nendo** (academic / fiscal)
year

ねーねー **nēnē** hey

年賀状 **nengajō** New Year's
card

年号 **nengō** era name

念入り (な) **nen'iri (na)**
careful

年間 **nenkan** year

年金 **nenkin** pension

年末 **nenmatsu** year end

年配 (の) **nenpai (no)** elderly

年齢 **nenrei** age

燃料 **nenryō** fuel

…年生 **-nensei** -grade student

ねんざ **nenza** sprain

ねらい **nerai** aim

ねらう **nerau** aim

寝る **neru** go to sleep

寝る時間 **nerujikan** bedtime

値下げした **nesage shita**
reduced (in price)

熱射病 **nesshabyō** heatstroke

熱心 (な) **nesshin (na)**
enthusiastic

寝過ごす **nesugosu**
oversleep

寝たきり (の) **netakiri (no)**
bedridden

ねたみ **netami** envy	逃げ出す **nigedasu** run off
熱中する **netchū suru** be enthusiastic about	逃げる **nigeru** escape
熱 **netsu** heat; fever	握り **nigiri** grip
熱意 **netsui** enthusiasm	にぎやか(な) **nigiyaka (na)** lively
熱情 **netsujō** passion	濁る **nigoru** not be clear *(of water etc)*
根付け **netsuke** netsuke *(small carved toggle)*	日本 **Nihon** Japan
熱烈(な) **netsuretsu (na)** ardent	日本晴れ **Nihonbare** very fine cloudless day
熱帯地方 **nettai-chihō** tropics	日本風 **nihonfū** Japanese style
熱帯(の) **nettai (no)** tropical	日本語 **Nihongo** Japanese *(language)*
ネットワーク **nettowāku** network	日本人 **Nihonjin** Japanese *(person)*
値打ち **neuchi** value	日本海 **Nihonkai** Sea of Japan
ねずみ **nezumi** mouse	日本列島 **Nihon-rettō** the Japanese Islands
…に … **ni** at; in; to; by; on; for ◊ and ◊ *(forms adverbs)*: 段階的に **dankaiteki ni** gradually	日本製 **Nihonsei** made in Japan
二 **ni** two	虹 **niji** rainbow
似合う **niau** suit	にじむ **nijimu** run *(of color)*; spread
二倍 **nibai** double	二次的(な) **nijiteki (na)** secondary
鈍い **nibui** dull	二十 **nijū** twenty
日没 **nichibotsu** sunset	二重(の) **nijū (no)** double
日時 **nichiji** date and time	二回 **nikai** twice
日常(の) **nichijō (no)** everyday	二階 **nikai** second floor
日曜日 **nichiyōbi** Sunday	にきび **nikibi** pimple
煮える **nieru** boil; be boiled	日記 **nikki** diary
苦い **nigai** bitter	日光 **nikkō** sunshine
逃がす **nigasu** set free	にっこり笑う **nikkori warau** grin
苦手である **nigate de aru** be bad at	
二月 **nigatsu** February	

日光浴する **nikkōyoku suru** sunbathe

ニックネーム **nikkunēmu** nickname

肉 **niku** meat

…にくい **-nikui** difficult to…; 食べにくい *tabenikui* difficult to eat

憎む **nikumu** hate

憎しみ **nikushimi** hatred

肉体 **nikutai** body

肉屋 **nikuya** butcher

にもかかわらず **ni mo kakawarazu** form despite

荷物 **nimotsu** luggage

…人 **-nin** (countword for people)

人間 **ningen** human (being)

人間らしい **ningenrashī** human

人形 **ningyō** doll

任意(の) **nin'i (no)** optional

にんじん **ninjin** carrot

人情 **ninjō** human feelings

人気 **ninki** popularity

任命 **ninmei** appointment

任務 **ninmu** assignment

にんにく **ninniku** garlic

認識 **ninshiki** awareness

妊娠 **ninshin** pregnancy

妊娠中絶 **ninshin-chūzetsu** abortion

忍耐 **nintai** endurance

認定された **nintei sareta** qualified

人数 **ninzū** number of people

におい **nioi** smell

におう **niou** smell

日本 **Nippon** Japan

にらむ **niramu** glare at

煮る **niru** boil

似る **niru** resemble

偽物 **nisemono** fake

偽(の) **nise (no)** fake

西 **nishi** west

にしん **nishin** herring

日射病 **nisshabyō** sunstroke

日中 **nitchū** by day

似ている **nite iru** resemble

二等 **nitō** second class

日程 **nittei** daily schedule

庭 **niwa** garden

…には …**niwa** concerning

にわか雨 **niwaka-ame** scattered showers

にわとり **niwatori** chicken

荷造り **nizukuri** packing

…の …**no** of; from; with; at; on ◊ (forms adjectives): 文法 *bunpō no* grammatical

能 **Nō** Noh play

脳 **nō** brain

延ばす **nobasu** delay

伸ばす **nobasu** lengthen

述べる **noberu** state

延びる **nobiru** be postponed

伸びる **nobiru** stretch

上る **noboru** go up

登る **noboru** climb

昇る **noboru** rise

後に **nochi ni** later on

…ので **...node** because

のど **nodo** throat

のどあめ **nodoame** throat lozenge

逃れる **nogareru** escape

逃す **nogasu** miss out on; set free

農業 **nōgyō** agriculture

野原 **nohara** field

農場 **nōjō** farm

農家 **nōka** farmhouse

ノックする **nokku suru** knock

のこぎり **nokogiri** saw

残り **nokori** remainder

残り物 **nokorimono** leftovers

残る **nokoru** remain

残す **nokosu** leave

…のみ **-nomi** form only

飲み込む **nomikomu** swallow

飲物 **nomimono** drink

農民 **nōmin** peasant

のみ屋 **nomiya** bookie; bar

飲む **nomu** drink; consume

のんびりした **nonbiri shita** laidback

…のに **-noni** although; if only; in order to

のんき(な) **nonki (na)** happy-go-lucky

のり **nori** paste *(adhesive)*; sheet of seaweed

乗り場 **noriba** stand *(taxi)*; stop *(bus)*

乗り出す **noridasu** set out

乗り換え **norikae** transfer

乗り換える **norikaeru** transfer

乗り越える **norikoeru** surmount

乗員組員 **norikumi-in** crew

乗り物 **norimono** vehicle

能率的に **nōritsuteki ni** efficiently

のろい **noroi** sluggish ◊ curse

のろう **norou** curse

乗る **noru** board; get in *(to car)*; ride

載る **noru** be on top of; be printed

能力 **nōryoku** ability

乗せる **noseru** carry; pick up *(in car)*

載せる **noseru** put; print

ノート **nōto** notebook

乗っ取り **nottori** hijack

乗っ取り犯 **nottorihan** hijacker

乗っ取る **nottoru** hijack; take over *company*

除いて **nozoite** except for

除く **nozoku** exclude

望ましい **nozomashī** desirable

望み **nozomi** wish

望む **nozomu** wish

縫う **nū** sew

脱ぐ **nugu** take off *clothes*

抜け出す **nukedasu** slip out

抜ける **nukeru** fall out; come off; be missing

抜く **nuku** take out *tooth*; draw *gun, knife*; pluck

沼地 **numachi** swamp

布 **nuno** cloth

ぬらす **nurasu** soak

ぬれた **nureta** wet

塗る **nuru** spread; paint

ぬるい **nurui** lukewarm

盗む **nusumu** steal

尿 **nyō** urine

入学式 **nyūgakushiki** admission ceremony

入院 **nyūin** hospitalization

入場 **nyūjō** admission

入場券 **nyūjōken** pass; platform ticket

入場無料 **nyūjō-muryō** admission free

入場料 **nyūjōryō** entrance fee

入国 **nyūkoku** entry (to country)

入力 **nyūryoku** input

ニュース **nyūsu** news

O

を **o** (direct object particle): 映画を見に行く **eiga o mi ni iku** go to see a movie

お **o** (honorific): お友達 **otomodachi** your friend

尾 **o** tail

王 **ō** king

おば **oba** aunt

オーバー **ōba** overcoat

おばさん **obasan** aunt

おばあさん **obāsan** grandmother

欧米 **ōbei** the West; Europe and the US

お弁当 **obentō** lunch box

おび **obi** obi (kimono sash)

おびえる **obieru** be frightened

脅かす **obiyakasu** menace

応募 **ōbo** application

覚える **oboeru** memorize

お盆 **Obon** Obon (Buddhist festival in August)

横柄(な) **ōhō (na)** domineering

おぼれる **oboreru** be drowned

お坊さん **obōsan** Buddhist priest

応募者 **ōbosha** applicant

オーブン **ōbun** oven

お茶 **ocha** Japanese tea

落ち着いた **ochisuita** calm

落ちる **ochiru** fall down; fail *exam*

落ち込む **ochikomu** sink

落ち着く **ochitsuku** calm down

お中元 **ochūgen** mid-year gift

お大事に **odaiji ni** take care *(said to sb who is ill)*

横断する **ōdan suru** go across

穏やか(な) **odayaka (na)** calm

踊り **odori** dance

大通り **ōdōri** main street

驚かす **odorokasu** surprise

驚き **odoroki** surprise

驚く **odoroku** be surprised

踊る **odoru** dance

脅し **odoshi** intimidation

脅す **odosu** intimidate

応援 **ōen** support

終える **oeru** finish

オーエル, O L **ōeru** female clerical employee (based on *Office Lady*)

往復 **ōfuku** round trip

往復切符 **ōfuku-kippu** round trip ticket

拝む **ogamu** pray

お元気で **ogenki de** all

the best!

(お)元気ですか **(o) genki desu ka** how are you?

大げさ **ōgesa** exaggeration

扇 **ōgi** (folding) fan

補う **oginau** supplement

大声 **ōgoe** shout

おごる **ogoru** treat

大幅に **ōhaba ni** greatly

お箸 **ohashi** chopsticks

おはよう(ございます) **ohayō (gozaimasu)** good morning

横柄(な) **ōhei (na)** arrogant

大広間 **ōhiroma** hall

お昼 **ohiru** lunch

お冷や **ohiya** iced water

おい **oi** nephew ◊ hey!

多い **ōi** many

追い出す **oidasu** throw out

追い払う **oiharau** repel

追いかける **oikakeru** chase

追い風 **oikaze** tailwind

追い越す **oikosu** overtake

オイル **oiru** oil

お医者さん **oishasan** doctor

おいしい **oishī** delicious

おいしそう(な) **oishisō (na)** appetizing

大急ぎ **ōisogi** urgency

追いつく **oitsuku** catch up

お祝い **oiwai** celebration

お邪魔します **ojama shimasu** excuse me for

disturbing you

おじ oji uncle

王子 ōji prince

おじぎ ojigi bow *(greeting)*

応じる ōjiru respond

おじさん ojisan uncle

おじいさん ojīsan grandfather

王女 ōjo princess

お嬢さん ojōsan daughter; ma'am

丘 oka hill

おかえりなさい okaerinasai welcome home

おかげで okage de thanks to

おおかみ ōkami wolf

お金 okane money

お金持ち(の) okanemochi (no) rich

お勘定 okanjō check

お母さん okāsan mother

お菓子 okashi confectionery

おかしい okashī humorous; odd

冒す okasu brave *danger*

犯す okasu commit

侵す okasu invade

おかわり okawari refill

おかず okazu side dishes

オーケストラ ōkesutora orchestra

大きい ōkī big; loud

置き場 okiba storage space

置きに oki ni every other: 一日置きに ichinichi oki ni

every other day

お気に入り oki ni iri favorite

起きる okiru get up

大きさ ōkisa size

行う okonau do

行われる okonawareru take place

お好み焼き okonomiyaki Japanese savory pancake

怒りっぽい okorippoi bad-tempered

怒る okoru get angry

起こる okoru happen; arise

起こす okosu rouse

…お断り …okotowari please do not ...

奥 oku back *(of room, drawer)*

億 oku hundred million

置く oku put

臆病(な) okubyō (na) cowardly

屋外(の) okugai (no) outdoor

屋内(の) okunai (no) indoor

多く(の) ōku (no) many

大蔵大臣 Ōkura-daijin Minister of Finance

遅らせる okuraseru make late

大蔵省 Ōkurashō Department of Finance

遅れる okureru lag behind; lose *(of clock)*

送り出す okuridasu see out

送りがな **okurigana** *syllabary letters added to Chinese characters to show inflection*

贈り物 **okurimono** gift

贈る **okuru** present

送る **okuru** send; see off *(at airport etc)*

奥さん **okusan** wife; ma'am

憶測 **okusoku** speculation

お悔やみ **okuyami** condolences

奥行き **okuyuki** depth

お経 **okyō** Buddhist sutra

お待ちください **omachi kudasai** please wait

お前 **omae** you *(familiar)*

おまけ **omake** extra; free gift

おまけに **omake ni** on top of that

お守り **omamori** lucky charm

お待たせしました **omatase shimashita** sorry to keep you waiting

お祭り **omatsuri** festival

お巡りさん **omawarisan** cop

おめでとう **omedetō** congratulations

お目にかかる **ome ni kakaru** *(polite)* see *person*

お見合い **omiai** meeting to discuss an arranged marriage

おみくじ **omikuji** *written oracle received at shrine*

大みそか **Ōmisoka** New Year's Eve

お土産 **omiyage** souvenir

おもちゃ **omocha** toy

重い **omoi** heavy

思い出す **omoidasu** recollect

思い出 **omoide** recollection

思い切り **omoikiri** with all one's might

思い切って…する **omoikitte ... suru** dare

思い込む **omoikomu** have the impression that

思いとどまらせる **omoi-todomaraseru** dissuade

思いつき **omoitsuki** plan

思いつく **omoitsuku** hit on a plan

思いやり **omoiyari** empathy

大文字 **ōmoji** capital letter

主(な) **omo (na)** main

主に **omo ni** mainly

重さ **omosa** weight

おもしろい **omoshiroi** interesting

重たい **omotai** heavy

表 **omote** front

表向きは **omotemuki wa** officially

おもてなし **omotenashi** hospitality

思う **omou** think

思わず **omowazu**

involuntarily

大麦 **ōmugi** barley

オムレツ **omuretsu** omelet

おむすび **omusubi** rice ball

おむつ **omutsu** diaper

恩 **on** debt of gratitude

オーナー **ōnā** owner

同じ **onaji** the same

おなか **onaka** stomach

おんぶ **onbu** piggyback

御中 **onchū** form to *(on envelope)*; Messrs

温度 **ondo** temperature

温度計 **ondokei** thermometer

おんどり **ondori** cockerel

尾根 **one** ridge

お願い **onegai** request

お願いします **onegai shimasu** please

お姉さん **onēsan** elder sister

恩返しする **ongaeshi suru** repay

音楽 **ongaku** music

音楽家 **ongakuka** musician

音楽(の) **ongaku (no)** musical

鬼 **oni** devil

おにぎり **onigiri** rice ball

お兄さん **onīsan** elder brother

恩人 **onjin** benefactor

穏健(な) **onken (na)** moderate

女 **onna** woman

女らしい **onnarashī** feminine

おの **ono** ax

音符 **onpu** note MUS

オンライン(の) **onrain (no)** on-line

温泉 **onsen** hot spring

恩知らず **onshirazu** ingratitude

温室 **onshitsu** greenhouse

温室効果 **onshitsu-kōka** greenhouse effect

オンス **onsu** ounce

オンザロック **on-za-rokku** on the rocks ◊ whiskey and water

オペラ **opera** opera

往来 **ōrai** traffic

オランダ **Oranda** Holland

おれ **ore** *(familiar, used by men)* I

お礼 **orei** bow; thanks

オレンジ **orenji** orange

オレンジ色 **orenji-iro** orange

オレンジジュース **orenji-jūsu** orange juice

折れる **oreru** break

おり **ori** cage; occasion

折り紙 **origami** origami

オリジナル **orijinaru** original *painting etc*

折り返し(で) **orikaeshi (de)** by return

折り返す **orikaesu** turn back *edges, sheets*

折り目 **orime** crease *(in pants)*; fold

織物 **orimono** textile

オリンピック **Orinpikku** Olympics

降りる，下りる **oriru** descend; get off

折りたたむ **oritatamu** fold (up)

愚か(な) **oroka (na)** stupid

下ろす **orosu** let down *hair, blinds*

降ろす **orosu** drop (off) *(from car)*; lower

折る **oru** break; fold

織る **oru** weave

オルガン **orugan** organ MUS

横領 **ōryō** misappropriation

抑える **osaeru** restrain; repress

大さじ **ōsaji** tablespoon

お先にどうぞ **osaki ni dōzo** after you

王様 **ōsama** king

収まる **osamaru** subside

納まる **osamaru** fit in

治める **osameru** govern

納める **osameru** settle *debts*

お産 **osan** confinement MED

幼い **osanai** very young; infantile

大騒ぎ **ōsawagi** scene

(argument); uproar

おせち料理 **osechi-ryōri** traditional New Year food

お歳暮 **oseibo** year-end gift

お世辞 **oseji** flattery

おせっかいな人 **osekkai na hito** busybody

汚染 **osen** pollution

応接室 **ōsetsushitsu** room for visitors

お世話になりました **osewa ni narimashita** thanks for your help

おしゃべり **oshaberi** gossip; chat

おしゃべり(な) **oshaberi (na)** talkative

おしゃぶり **oshaburi** pacifier

おしゃれ(な) **oshare (na)** stylish

お絞り **oshibori** small damp towel

教える **oshieru** teach

惜しい **oshī** regrettable; precious

押し入れ **oshi-ire** storage space

押し入る **oshi-iru** break into

おしまい **oshimai** end

押しのける **oshinokeru** elbow out of the way

お尻 **oshiri** butt

押し倒す **oshitaosu**

overpower

汚職 **oshoku** corruption

押収 **ōshū** seizure

遅い **osoi** late; slow

大掃除 **ōsōji** spring-cleaning

お粗末(な) **osomatsu (na)** poor; inferior

おそらく **osoraku** probably

恐れ **osore** fear

恐れいります **osore irimasu** *(polite)* thank you

恐れる **osoreru** fear

おそろい(の) **osoroi (no)** matching

恐ろしい **osoroshī** terrifying

襲う **osou** attack; break *(of storm)*

おっしゃる **ossharu** *(polite)* say

雄 **osu** male *(animal)*

押す **osu** push

オーストラリア **Ōsutoraria** Australia

オーストリア **Ōsutoria** Austria

お互いに **otagai ni** each other

応対する **ōtai suru** deal with customers

お宅 **otaku** nerd; fanatic

お誕生日おめでとう **otanjōbi omedetō** happy birthday!

王手 **ōte** checkmate

お手洗い **otearai** rest room

お手伝い **otetsudai** maid

音 **oto** sound

オートバイ **ōtobai** motorcycle

おとぎ話 **otogibanashi** fairy tale

男 **otoko** man

男の子 **otoko no ko** boy

男らしい **otokorashī** manly

お徳用 **otokuyō** economy size

大人 **otona** adult

おとなしい **otonashī** meek

衰える **otoroeru** weaken; ebb away

劣る **otoru** be inferior

お父さん **otōsan** father

落し穴 **otoshiana** pitfall

落し物 **otoshimono** lost property

お年寄り **otoshiyori** old person

落とす **otosu** drop

弟 **otōto** younger brother

おととい **ototoi** the day before yesterday

おととし **ototoshi** year before last

劣った **ototta** inferior

お釣り **otsuri** change

夫 **otto** husband

追う **ou** chase

負う **ou** bear *responsibility,
debt;* carry on one's back
覆う **ōu** cover; envelop
大売り出し **ōuridashi**
clearance sale
おわび **owabi** apology
終わり **owari** end
終わる **owaru** end
親 **oya** parent; dealer *(in card
games)*
公(の) **ōyake (no)** public
親子 **oyako** parent and child
おやすみ(なさい) **oyasumi
(nasai)** good night

親指 **oyayubi** thumb
及び **oyobi** and; as well as
及ぶ **oyobu** extend to
泳ぐ **oyogu** swim
大喜び **ōyorokobi** delight
およそ **oyoso** approximately
大ざっぱ(な) **ōzappa (na)**
broad
大皿 **ōzara** platter
大勢(の) **ōzei (no)** many
大関 **ōzeki** sumo champion
オゾン **ozon** ozone
オゾン層 **ozonsō** ozone
layer

P

パー **pā** par *(in golf)*
バブ **pabu** pub
パチンコ **pachinko** Japanese
pinball
パイ **pai** pie
パイナップル **painappuru**
pineapple
パイプ **paipu** pipe
パジャマ **pajama** pajamas
パック **pakku** carton; pack
パーマ **pāma** perm
パン **pan** bread
パンフレット **panfuretto**
pamphlet
パニック **panikku** panic
パンク **panku** blow-out

(of tire)
パンティー **pantī** panties
パンツ **pantsu** underpants
パン屋 **pan'ya** bakery
パパ **papa** dad
パーセント **pāsento** percent
パソコン **pasokon** personal
computer
パス **pasu** pass SPORTS
パスポート **pasupōto**
passport
パターン **patān** pattern
パーティー **pātī** party
パート **pāto** part MUS; part-
time job
パトカー **patokā** patrol car

パートナー **pātonā** partner
(in particular activity)

パズル **pazuru** puzzle

ペア **pea** pair

ペダル **pedaru** pedal

ページ **pēji** page

ぺこぺこする **pekopeko
suru** kowtow (to); be empty
(stomach)

ペン **pen** pen

ペンダント **pendanto**
pendant

ペンフレンド **pen-furendo**
pen friend

ペンキ **penki** paint

ペンキ塗りたて **penki-
nuritate** wet paint

ペンキ屋 **penkiya** painter
(decorator)

ペーパーバック **pēpābakku**
paperback

ペパーミント **pepāminto**
peppermint

ぺらぺら（の）**perapera
(no)** fluent

ペース **pēsu** pace

ペット **petto** pet

ペットボトル **petto-botoru**
plastic bottle

ピアノ **piano** piano

ぴかぴか（の）**pikapika (no)**
sparkling

ピーク **pīku** peak, high point

ピクニック **pikunikku** picnic

ピクルス **pikurusu** pickles

ピーマン **pīman** pepper

ピン **pin** pin

ピーナッツ **pīnattsu** peanut

ピンチ **pinchi** difficult situation

ピンク色 **pinku-iro** pink

ピンポン **pinpon** ping-pong
◊ used to indicate a correct
answer

ピント **pinto** focus

ピザ **piza** pizza

ポケット **poketto** pocket

ポンプ **ponpu** pump

ポップス **poppusu** pop;
pop song

ポスター **posutā** poster

ポスト **posuto** mailbox

ポテトチップス **poteto-
chippusu** potato chips

ポテトフライ **poteto-furai**
French fries

ポット **potto** pot; thermos

プライバシー **puraibashī**
privacy

プライド **puraido** pride

プラス **purasu** plus (sign)

プラスチック製（の）
purasuchikkusei (no) made
of plastic

プレー **purē** play SPORTS

プレゼント **purezento**
present

プリンター **purintā**
printer

プリント **purinto** print

プロ **puro** professional

プログラム **puroguramu**

program

プロポーズ **puropōzu**
proposal

プール **pūru** (swimming) pool;
pool *(game)*

R

ラベル **raberu** label

ラブレター **raburetā** love
letter

ライバル **raibaru** rival

ライフル **raifuru** rifle

来月 **raigetsu** next month

来客 **raikyaku** guest; visitor

来年 **rainen** next year

来日 **rainichi** visiting Japan

ライオン **raion** lion

来週 **raishū** next week

ライス **raisu** rice *(cooked)*

ライター **raitā** lighter

ラジオ **rajio** radio

ラケット **raketto** racket; bat

楽観的(な) **rakkanteki (na)**
optimistic

楽 **raku** comfortable; easy

落第する **rakudai suru** fail
an exam

落書き **rakugaki** graffiti

楽勝 **rakushō** walkover

落胆した **rakutan shita**
dejected

ラーメン **rāmen** Chinese

noodles

らん **ran** orchid

欄 **ran** box *(on form)*; column
(of text)

乱暴 **ranbō** violence

ランチ **ranchi** lunch; launch
(boat)

ランク **ranku** rank

乱用 **ran'yō** abuse

乱雑(な) **ranzatsu (na)**
disorderly

ラップ **rappu** clingfilm; lap
(in athletics); rap MUS

ラッシュアワー **rasshu-
awā** rush hour

ラテンアメリカ **Raten-
Amerika** Latin America

レバー **rebā** lever; liver
(food)

レベル **reberu** level

例 **rei** example

礼 **rei** etiquette; thanks; fee;
bow

零 **rei** zero

霊 **rei** spirit *(of dead person)*

冷房 **reibō** air conditioning

例外 **reigai** exception

例外的(な) **reigaiteki (na)** exceptional

礼儀 **reigi** courtesy

礼儀正しい **reigi-tadashī** polite

礼拝 **reihai** worship

零下 **reika** below zero

冷血(の) **reiketsu (no)** cold-blooded

礼金 **reikin** key money *(deposit on apartment)*

冷酷(な) **reikoku (na)** cold-blooded

例年(の) **reinen (no)** annual

レインコート **reinkōto** raincoat

冷静(な) **reisei (na)** cool; level-headed

冷淡(な) **reitan (na)** cool, icy *welcome*

冷凍庫 **reitōko** freezer

冷凍(の) **reitō (no)** frozen

冷凍食品 **reitō-shokuhin** (deep-)frozen food

冷蔵庫 **reizōko** refrigerator

レジ **reji** checkout

歴史 **rekishi** history

レコード **rekōdo** record MUS

レモン **remon** lemon

レモンティー **remon-tī**

lemon tea

恋愛 **ren'ai** love

れんが **renga** brick

連合 **rengō** union

レンジ **renji** stove; gas range

連盟 **renmei** league

連邦 **renpō** federation

連絡 **renraku** contact

連絡先 **renrakusaki** contact details

練習 **renshū** practice

レンタカー **renta-kā** rental car

レントゲン **rentogen** X-ray

連続 **renzoku** series

レンズ **renzu** lens

レポート **repōto** report

レシピ **reshipi** recipe

レシート **reshīto** receipt

列車 **ressha** train

レッスン **ressun** lesson

レース **rēsu** lace; race

レストラン **resutoran** restaurant

レタス **retasu** lettuce

レート **rēto** rate

列 **retsu** column; row; line

劣等感 **rettōkan** inferiority complex

レーザー **rēzā** laser

リビングルーム **ribingu-rūmu** living room

リボン **ribon** ribbon

リーダー **rīdā** leader

リードする **rīdo suru** lead
race
利益 **rieki** benefit; profit
理解 **rikai** understanding
離婚 **rikon** divorce
利口(な) **rikō (na)** clever
陸 **riku** land
陸軍 **rikugun** army
理屈 **rikutsu** reason
リキュール **rikyūru** liqueur
リモコン **rimokon** remote
control
りんご **ringo** apple
林檎ジュース **ringo-jūsu**
apple juice
臨時(の) **rinji (no)** temporary
倫理的(な) **rinriteki (na)**
ethical
隣接する **rinsetsu suru**
border on
臨床(の) **rinshō (no)** clinical
リンス **rinsu** conditioner
立派(な) **rippa (na)**
admirable
立方体 **rippōtai** cube
履歴書 **rirekisho** résumé
離陸 **ririku** takeoff
理論 **riron** theory
理論的(な) **rironteki (na)**
theoretical
理性 **risei** rationality
理性的(な) **riseiteki (na)**
rational
利子 **rishi** interest

理想 **risō** ideal
理想的(な) **risōteki (na)**
ideal
立証 **risshō** proof
リスク **risuku** risk
リスト **risuto** list
利点 **riten** advantage
率 **ritsu** rate
リットル **rittoru** liter
利用 **riyō** use
理由 **riyū** reason
リズム **rizumu** rhythm
ろうあ(の) **rōa (no)** deaf-
and-dumb
ロビー **robī** lobby; lounge *(in
hotel, airport)*
ロボット **robotto** robot
ロブスター **robusutā** lobster
労働 **rōdō** labor
労働組合 **rōdō-kumiai** labor
union
労働者 **rōdōsha** laborer
浪費 **rōhi** waste
老人 **rōjin** elderly person
老人ホーム **rōjin-hōmu**
nursing home
廊下 **rōka** corridor
ロケット **roketto** locket;
rocket
ロッカー **rokkā** locker
ろっ骨 **rokkotsu** rib
ロック **rokku** rock MUS.
六 **roku** six
録画 **rokuga** video recording

六月 rokugatsu June

録音 rokuon recording

ローマ字 rōmaji Roman script

ロマンチック（な） romanchikku (na) romantic

路面電車 romen-densha streetcar

論 ron theory

ローン rōn bank loan

論文 ronbun paper (academic)

老年 rōnen old age

浪人 rōnin student who will resit college entrance examinations

論じる ronjiru discuss

論理 ronri logic

論理的（な） ronriteki (na) logical

論争 ronsō dispute

ロープ rōpu rope

ロシア Roshia Russia

ローション rōshon lotion

露出 roshutsu exposure

ろうそく rōsoku candle

ロースト rōsuto roast

露天風呂 roten-buro open-air hot spa

ルビー rubī ruby

類似した ruiji shita similar

ルームサービス rūmu-sābisu room service

ルール rūru rule

留守番電話 rusuban-denwa answerphone

留守である rusu de aru be out

ルート rūto route

略 ryaku abbreviation

略奪する ryakudatsu suru loot

略語 ryakugo abbreviation

量 ryō amount

寮 ryō dormitory

漁 ryō fishing

猟 ryō hunting

領土 ryōdo territory

両替 ryōgae money changing

両側 ryōgawa both sides

両方（の） ryōhō (no) both

領域 ryōiki domain

領事 ryōji consul

領事館 ryōjikan consulate

領海 ryōkai territorial waters

旅館 ryokan Japanese-style inn

旅券 ryoken passport

料金 ryōkin fee

料金表 ryōkinhyō price list

料金所 ryōkinjo toll booth

旅行 ryokō trip

旅行代理店 ryokō-dairiten tour operator

旅行会社 ryokō-gaisha tour operator

旅行保険 ryokō-hoken travel insurance

旅行者 **ryokōsha** traveler

緑茶 **ryokucha** green tea

料理 **ryōri** cooking; cuisine

良性(の) **ryōsei (no)** benign

漁師 **ryōshi** fisherman

猟師 **ryōshi** hunter

良心 **ryōshin** conscience

両親 **ryōshin** parents

領収書 **ryōshūsho** receipt

両手 **ryōte** both hands

竜 **ryū** dragon

留学 **ryūgaku** study abroad

留学生 **ryūgakusei** overseas student

リュックサック **ryukkusakku** rucksack

流行 **ryūkō** epidemic; fashion

リューマチ **ryūmachi** rheumatism

流出する **ryūshutsu suru** drain away

流通 **ryūtsū** distribution

流産 **ryūzan** miscarriage

S

…さ **-sa** *(familiar emphatic particle used mostly by men):* もう、いいさ **mō īsa** that's enough

差 **sa** difference

さあ **sā** well; right

さば **saba** mackerel

砂漠 **sabaku** desert

差別 **sabetsu** discrimination

さび **sabi** rust

さびれた **sabireta** bleak; deserted

さびる **sabiru** rust

寂しい **sabishī** lonely

サービス **sābisu** service

サービスエリア **sābisu-eria** service area

さびた **sabita** rusty

さぼる **saboru** skip *class*

定める **sadameru** decide

茶道 **sadō** tea ceremony

…さえ … **sae** even

さえぎる **saegiru** obstruct

下がる **sagaru** come down *(in price etc)*

探す, 捜す **sagasu** search for

下げる **sageru** reduce; bow *head*

詐欺 **sagi** scam

詐欺師 **sagishi** trickster

探り出す **saguridasu** dig up *information*

さぐる **saguru** spy on; grope for

作業 **sagyō** work

左派 **saha** left POL

際 **sai** occasion

才 **sai** ability; years old

…歳 **-sai** years old

最悪(の) **saiaku (no)** worst

栽培 **saibai** cultivation

裁判 **saiban** trial

裁判官 **saibankan** judge

裁判所 **saibansho** courthouse

細胞 **saibō** cell BIOL

最中 **saichū** middle

最大限 **saidaigen** maximum

最大(の) **saidai (no)** maximum

祭壇 **saidan** altar

サイドブレーキ **saidoburēki** parking brake

財布 **saifu** wallet

災害 **saigai** disaster

再現する **saigen suru** reconstruct *crime*; reproduce *atmosphere*

最後(の) **saigo (no)** final

祭日 **saijitsu** (national) holiday

再開 **saikai** renewal

債券 **saiken** bond FIN

債権者 **saikensha** creditor

細菌 **saikin** bacteria

最近 **saikin** recently

最高(の) **saikō (no)** best

再婚する **saikon suru** remarry

さいころ **saikoro** dice

最高裁判所 **Saikō-saibansho** Supreme Court

サイクリング **saikuringu** cycling

採掘 **saikutsu** extraction *(of coal, oil)*

サイン **sain** autograph

災難 **sainan** disaster

才能 **sainō** talent

サイレン **sairen** siren

再利用する **sairiyō suru** reuse

再三(の) **saisan (no)** repeated

再生 **saisei** playback; reproduction

最新(の) **saishin (no)** latest

細心(の) **saishin (no)** meticulous

最初 **saisho** first

菜食主義(の) **saishoku-shugi (no)** vegetarian

菜食主義者 **saishoku-shugisha** vegetarian

最初に **saisho ni** first

最終電車 **saishū densha** last train

最終(の) **saishū (no)** final

最終的(な) **saishūteki (na)** final

最低(の) **saitei (no)** lousy; lowest

最適(な) **saiteki (na)**
optimum

採点 **saiten** score

幸い **saiwai** happiness

幸いにも **saiwai ni mo**
happily

採用 **saiyō** adoption (of plan)

サイズ **saizu** size

さじ **saji** spoon

坂 **saka** slope; hill

酒場 **sakaba** bar

栄える **sakaeru** thrive

境 **sakai** border

魚 **sakana** fish

魚屋 **sakanaya** fishmonger

盛ん(な) **sakan (na)**
flourishing

さかのぼる **sakanoboru** date
back ◊ retroactive

逆らう **sakarau** go against;
disobey

盛りにある **sakari ni aru** be
in one's prime

逆さま(の) **sakasama (no)**
topsy-turvy

サーカス **sākasu** circus

酒屋 **sakaya** liquor store

酒 **sake** liquor

さけ **sake** salmon

叫ぶ **sakebu** yell

裂け目 **sakeme** split

避けられない **sakerarenai**
inevitable

避ける **sakeru** avoid

裂ける **sakeru** split

先 **saki** tip ◊ ahead

先駆け **sakigake** pioneer

先(の) **saki (no)** former;
future

作家 **sakka** writer

サッカー **sakkā** soccer

さっき **sakki** a little while ago

殺菌する **sakkin suru**
sterilize

作曲 **sakkyoku** composition
MUS

作曲家 **sakkyokuka**
composer

策 **saku** plan

咲く **saku** bloom

裂く **saku** rip

作文 **sakubun** essay

削減 **sakugen** cutback

作品 **sakuhin** work (of art,
literature)

索引 **sakuin** index (of book)

昨日 **sakujitsu** yesterday

削除 **sakujo** deletion

昨年 **sakunen** last year

桜 **sakura** cherry blossom

さくらんぼ **sakuranbo**
cherry (fruit)

策略 **sakuryaku** set-up

作成 **sakusei** make

作戦 **sakusen** tactics

作者 **sakusha** author

昨夜 **sakuya** last night

砂丘 **sakyū** sand dune

…様 -sama Mr / Mrs / Ms *(in addresses)*

冷ます **samasu** cool down

覚ます **samasu** wake up

妨げる **samatageru** prevent; obstruct

様々(な) **samazama (na)** various

さめ **same** shark

冷める **sameru** cool down

覚める **sameru** wake up

サミット **samitto** summit

寒い **samui** cold

寒気 **samuke** chill *(illness)*

侍 **samurai** samurai

寒さ **samusa** cold

酸 **san** acid

…さん -san Mr; Mrs; Ms

…山 -san Mount

三 **san** three

三倍(の) **sanbai (no)** treble

サンダル **sandaru** sandal

サンド **sando** sand; sandwich

産婦人科 **sanfujinka** obstetrics and gynecology

三月 **sangatsu** March

参議院 **sangi-in** House of Councilors

さんご **sango** coral

サングラス **sangurasu** sunglasses

産業 **sangyō** industry

参加 **sanka** participation

三角形 **sankakkei** triangle

三角(の) **sankaku (no)** triangular

参加者 **sankasha** participant

参考 **sankō** reference

三脚 **sankyaku** tripod

産休 **sankyū** maternity leave

さんま **sanma** saury

山脈 **sanmyaku** range *(of mountains)*

散歩 **sanpo** stroll

サンプル **sanpuru** sample

賛成 **sansei** approval

酸素 **sanso** oxygen

算数 **sansū** arithmetic

さっぱりした **sappari shita** clean; neat ◊ feel refreshed

皿 **sara** dish

サラダ **sarada** salad

再来年 **sarainen** the year after next

再来週 **saraishū** the week after next

さらに **sara ni** in addition

サラリーマン **sararīman** white-collar worker

去る **saru** leave

猿 **saru** monkey

支える **sasaeru** support

捧げる **sasageru** lift up; devote

ささい(な) **sasai (na)** trivial

ささやく **sasayaku** whisper

…させる ... **saseru** allow; make (someone do something)

差し上げる **sashiageru**
(polite) give

差し当たり **sashiatari** for
the moment

差出人 **sashidashinin** sender

差し出す **sashidasu** hold out

挿絵 **sashie** illustration

差し込む **sashikomu** insert

さしみ **sashimi** sashimi

査証 **sashō** visa

誘う **sasou** invite; entice

早速 **sassoku** immediately

刺す **sasu** bite; sting; stab

指す **sasu** point

さす **sasu** insert; put up
umbrella; wear *sword*

さすがに **sasuga ni** as
expected

さて **sate** right

悟り **satori** enlightenment

…冊 **-satsu** countword for
books

札 **satsu** paper money

撮影 **satsuei** shooting film,
photo

殺害 **satsugai** murder

殺人 **satsujin** murder

殺人犯 **satsujinhan** murderer

さつま芋 **satsuma-imo**
sweet potato

サウナ **sauna** sauna

騒がしい **sawagashī** noisy

騒ぎ **sawagi** commotion

騒ぐ **sawagu** make a racket

触る **sawaru** touch

さわやか(な) **sawayaka**
(na) refreshing

左翼 **sayoku** left-wing

さようなら **sayōnara**
goodbye

背 **se** back; spine *(of book)*;
height

背広 **sebiro** suit *(for men)*

背骨 **sebone** spine

世代 **sedai** generation

せい **sei** fault

性 **sei** gender

姓 **sei** family name

性別 **seibetsu** gender

西部 **seibu** west *(of a country)*

生物 **seibutsu** organism

生物学 **seibutsugaku**
biology

成長 **seichō** growth

静電気 **seidenki** static
(electricity)

制度 **seido** system

青銅 **seidō** bronze *(metal)*

精鋭(の) **seiei (no)** elite

政府 **seifu** government

征服 **seifuku** conquest

制服 **seifuku** uniform

制限 **seigen** limit

正義 **seigi** justice

製品 **seihin** product

正方形 **seihōkei** square
(shape)

政治 **seiji** politics

政治家 **seijika** politician

成人 **seijin** adult

成人の日 **Seijin no hi** Adult's Day

政治(の) **seiji (no)** political

政治的(な) **seijiteki (na)** political

誠実 **seijitsu** reliability; fidelity

誠実(な) **seijitsu (na)** reliable; faithful

正常 **seijō** normality

正常に **seijō ni** normally

成熟 **seijuku** maturity

正解 **seikai** correct answer

性格 **seikaku** character

正確(な) **seikaku (na)** accurate

生活 **seikatsu** life; livelihood

生活費 **seikatsuhi** living expenses; cost of living

生計 **seikei** livelihood

整形外科(の) **seikei-geka (no)** orthopedic

政権 **seiken** political power; administration

清潔(な) **seiketsu (na)** clean

生気 **seiki** liveliness

世紀 **seiki** century

正規(の) **seiki (no)** regular

成功 **seikō** success

性交 **seikō** (sexual) intercourse

請求 **seikyū** demand *(for payment, damages)*

請求書 **seikyūsho** invoice

声明 **seimei** statement

生命 **seimei** life

姓名 **seimei** full name

青年 **seinen** young person

生年月日 **seinen-gappi** date of birth

性能 **seinō** performance *(of machine)*

西暦 **Seireki** Western calendar

生理 **seiri** menstruation

整理する **seiri suru** arrange

成立する **seiritsu suru** come into being

精力 **seiryoku** energy

勢力 **seiryoku** power

精力的(な) **seiryokuteki (na)** energetic

制裁 **seisai** punishment

政策 **seisaku** policy

製作 **seisaku** production *(of movie etc)*

清算 **seisan** settlement *(of debts)*; liquidation

生産 **seisan** production

生産物 **seisanbutsu** product

生産性 **seisansei** productivity

生産者 **seisansha** producer

生産的(な) **seisanteki (na)** productive

成績 **seiseki** grade

正社員 **seishain** permanent employee

生死 **seishi** life and death

精子 **seishi** sperm

正式(の) **seishiki (no)** formal

精神 **seishin** soul

精神病 **seishinbyō** mental illness

精神科医 **seishinkai** psychiatrist

精神力 **seishinryoku** willpower

精神的(な) **seishinteki (na)** mental

制止する **seishi suru** restrain

静止する **seishi suru** stand still; freeze *video*

性質 **seishitsu** nature *(of person)*

聖書 **seisho** Bible

青少年 **seishōnen** youngsters

青春 **seishun** adolescence

生態学 **seitaigaku** ecology

生態系 **seitaikei** ecosystem

性的(な) **seiteki (na)** sexual

生徒 **seito** schoolchild

政党 **seitō** political party

正当(な) **seitō (na)** just; lawful

西洋 **Seiyō** the West

西洋人 **Seiyōjin** Westerner

西洋なし **seiyōnashi** pear

星座 **seiza** signs of the zodiac

正座 **seiza** *formal Japanese* *sitting position, kneeling, with* *legs tucked under*

せいぜい **seizei** at (the) most; as much as possible

整然とした **seizen to shita** in order

製造 **seizō** manufacture

生存 **seizon** survival

生存者 **seizonsha** survivor

世界 **sekai** world

世界市場 **sekai-shijō** global market

世界大戦 **sekaitaisen** world war

世界的(な) **sekaiteki (na)** worldwide

世間 **seken** society

世間話 **sekenbanashi** small talk

せき **seki** family register; cough; barrier

席 **seki** seat

せき払い **sekibarai** clearing the throat

赤道 **sekidō** equator

せき止め薬 **sekidomeyaku** cough medicine

赤外線(の) **sekigaisen (no)** infra-red

赤十字 **Sekijūji** Red Cross

責任 **sekinin** responsibility

責任者である **sekininsha de aru** be in charge

石炭 **sekitan** coal

関取 **sekitori** ranking sumo wrestler

せきつい **sekitsui** spine

石油 **sekiyu** oil

切開 **sekkai** incision

折角 **sekkaku** at great pains

設計 **sekkei** design

石けん **sekken** soap

接近 **sekkin** approach

セックス **sekkusu** sex

説教 **sekkyō** sermon

積極的(な) **sekkyokuteki (na)** positive

セクハラ **sekuhara** sexual harassment

セクシー(な) **sekushī (na)** sexy

狭い **semai** narrow; cramped

迫る **semaru** approach; compel

責める **semeru** blame; persecute

せめて **semete** at least

せみ **semi** cicada

千 **sen** thousand

線 **sen** line

栓 **sen** stopper

背中 **senaka** back *(of person)*

専売 **senbai** monopoly

選抜 **senbatsu** selection *(that / those chosen)*

せんべい **senbei** rice cracker

センチ **senchi** centimeter

船長 **senchō** captain

宣伝 **senden** publicity

宣言 **sengen** declaration

先月 **sengetsu** last month

戦後(の) **sengo (no)** postwar

繊維 **sen'i** fiber

船員 **sen'in** seaman

先日 **senjitsu** the other day

線香 **senkō** incense

専攻 **senkō** major *(academic)*; specialty

宣告 **senkoku** sentence JUR

選挙 **senkyo** election

洗面台 **senmendai** (wash)basin

洗面所 **senmenjo** bathroom

洗面器 **senmenki** washbowl

専門 **senmon** specialty

専門的(な) **senmonteki (na)** technical

専門用語 **senmon-yōgo** terminology

栓抜き **sennuki** bottle-opener; corkscrew

先輩 **senpai** *one's senior at school or work*

扇風機 **senpūki** fan *(electric)*

先例 **senrei** precedent

線路 **senro** railroad track

戦略 **senryaku** strategy

戦略的(な) **senryakuteki (na)** strategic

染料 **senryō** dye

占領 **senryō** occupation *(of country)*

繊細(な) **sensai (na)** delicate

先生 **sensei** teacher; doctor *(form of address)*

宣誓 **sensei** oath JUR

洗車 **sensha** car wash

先進(の) **senshin (no)** advanced

選手 **senshu** player

先週 **senshū** last week

選手権 **senshuken** championship *(title)*

選出 **senshutsu** election

戦争 **sensō** war

センス **sensu** good sense; taste

扇子 **sensu** fan *(handheld)*

潜水艦 **sensuikan** submarine

センター **sentā** center *(building)*

選択 **sentaku** choice

洗濯 **sentaku** laundry

洗濯機 **sentakuki** washing machine

洗濯物 **sentakumono** laundry

選択(の) **sentaku (no)** elective

選択肢 **sentakushi** alternative

セント **sento** cent

先頭 **sentō** head; leader

戦闘 **sentō** combat

銭湯 **sentō** public bath

洗剤 **senzai** detergent

潜在的(な) **senzaiteki (na)** latent; hidden; potential customer

戦前(の) **senzen (no)** prewar

先祖 **senzo** forefathers

背負う **seou** shoulder *burden*

せりふ **serifu** speech *(in play)*

セロテープ **serotēpu** Scotch tape

セール **sēru** sale *(at reduced price)*

セルフサービス **serufu-sābisu** self-service

セールスマン **sērusuman** salesman

せっせと働く **sesse to hataraku** work hard

摂氏 **sesshi** centigrade

接触 **sesshoku** contact

接する **sessuru** touch

セーター **sētā** sweater

接着する **setchaku suru** bond *(of glue)*

接着剤 **setchakuzai** adhesive

設置する **setchi suru** set up

瀬戸物 **setomono** ceramics

節 **setsu** occasion; clause; verse

設備 **setsubi** facilities

切望 **setsubō** longing

切断する **setsudan suru** amputate

説明 **setsumei** explanation

設立 **setsuritsu** foundation

節約 **setsuyaku** economizing

接続 **setsuzoku** connection

設定 **settei** setting

セット **setto** scenery; set *(in tennis)*

窃盗 **settō** theft

説得 **settoku** persuasion

世話 **sewa** care *(of baby etc)*

しゃべる **shaberu** talk

シャベル **shaberu** shovel

しゃぶしゃぶ **shabushabu** beef fondue

社長 **shachō** president *(of company)*

車道 **shadō** roadway

しゃがむ **shagamu** squat

社員 **shain** employee

社会 **shakai** society

社会学 **shakaigaku** sociology

社会(の) **shakai (no)** social

社会主義 **shakai-shugi** socialism

借金 **shakkin** debt

しゃっくり **shakkuri** hiccup

車庫 **shako** garage

借地人 **shakuchinin** tenant

尺八 **shakuhachi** bamboo flute

釈放 **shakuhō** release

釈明する **shakumei suru** defend

斜面 **shamen** slope

三味線 **shamisen** Japanese banjo

車内 **shanai** *inside of a train car*

シャンプー **shanpū** shampoo

しゃれ **share** joke

謝礼 **sharei** remuneration

しゃれた **shareta** stylish

車両 **sharyō** car *(of train)*

写生 **shasei** sketch

車線 **shasen** lane AUTO

斜線 **shasen** oblique

写真 **shashin** photo

車掌 **shashō** conductor

シャツ **shatsu** shirt

シャッター **shattā** shutter

シャワー **shawā** shower

謝罪 **shazai** apology

シェフ **shefu** chef

…し **-shi** and

死 **shi** death

四 **shi** four

詩 **shi** poetry

市 **shi** city

…氏 **... shi** *polite form of san* Mr; Ms

仕上がり **shiagari** finish *(of product)*

試合 **shiai** match

指圧 **shiatsu** finger pressure therapy

幸せ **shiawase** happiness

幸せ(な) **shiawase (na)** happy

芝生 **shibafu** lawn

芝居 **shibai** play

しばらく **shibaraku** for a while

縛る **shibaru** bind

しばしば **shibashiba** frequently

しびれる **shibireru** go numb; have pins and needles

志望 **shibō** wish

脂肪 **shibō** fat

死亡 **shibō** death

絞る **shiboru** press *grapes*; wring out

渋い **shibui** astringent; austere; tasteful

渋る **shiburu** hesitate

試着する **shichaku suru** try on *clothes*

七 **shichi** seven

七福神 **Shichi-fukujin** the Seven Deities of Good Luck

七月 **shichigatsu** July

七五三 **Shichigosan** Shichi-Go-San *(festival for children aged 3, 5, and 7)*

質屋 **shichiya** pawnbroker

市長 **shichō** mayor

視聴者 **shichōsha** audience

次第に **shidai ni** gradually

指導 **shidō** guidance

指導者 **shidōsha** mentor

支援 **shien** support

シーフード **shīfūdo** seafood

市外 **shigai** area beyond city limits

市外局番 **shigai-kyokuban** area code

紫外線(の) **shigaisen (no)** ultraviolet

志願者 **shigansha** volunteer

四月 **shigatsu** April

刺激 **shigeki** incentive; irritation MED

刺激的(な) **shigekiteki (na)** stimulating; electric *fig*

茂み **shigemi** bush

資源 **shigen** resources

茂る **shigeru** grow thickly

仕事 **shigoto** work

支配 **shihai** control

支配人 **shihainin** manager *(of restaurant, hotel etc)*

支配者 **shihaisha** ruler *(of state)*

支払い **shiharai** payment *(of bill)*

支払う **shiharau** pay

始発 **shihatsu** the first train

紙幣 **shihei** bank bill

司法権 **shihōken** jurisdiction

資本 **shihon** capital *(money)*

資本主義 **shihon-shugi** capitalism

指示 **shiji** instructions

支持 **shiji** support

詩人 **shijin** poet

市場 **shijō** market

しか **shika** deer

…しか **… shika** only

視界 **shikai** visual field

司会者 **shikaisha** master of ceremonies

仕掛け **shikake** device

資格 **shikaku** certificate

死角 **shikaku** blind spot

しかも **shikamo** besides

士官 **shikan** officer

しかる **shikaru** scold

しかし **shikashi** however

仕方 **shikata** method しかたがない **shikata ga nai** it can't be helped

死刑 **shikei** death penalty

試験 **shiken** examination

式 **shiki** ceremony; style

指揮 **shiki** command; conducting

四季 **shiki** the four seasons

敷布団 **shikibuton** bottom futon

式服 **shikifuku** ceremonial robe

敷居 **shiki-i** threshold

敷金 **shikikin** deposit

敷物 **shikimono** rug

資金 **shikin** fund

色彩 **shikisai** color

指揮者 **shikisha** conductor MUS

式典 **shikiten** ceremony

しっかり **shikkari** tight

しっかりした **shikkari shita** steady

湿気 **shikke** humidity

漆器 **shikki** lacquerware

四国 **Shikoku** Shikoku

敷く **shiku** lay *cable, carpet*

仕組み **shikumi** structure; arrangement

至急 **shikyū** urgently

支給する **shikyū suru** supply

しま **shima** stripe

島 **shima** island

姉妹 **shimai** sisters

姉妹都市 **shimai-toshi** twin town

閉まる **shimaru** shut

します **shimasu** (*polite present tense of* **suru**): 私がします **watashi ga shimasu** I'll do it

しまった **shimatta** damn!

閉まっている **shimatte iru** be on (*of lid, top*)

しまう **shimau** end; put away (*in closet*)

氏名 **shimei** full name

指名する **shimei suru** nominate

締め切り **shimekiri** deadline

湿っぽい **shimeppoi** damp

占める **shimeru** constitute; occupy

閉める **shimeru** shut

締める **shimeru** fasten

示す **shimesu** show

湿った **shimetta** damp

染み **shimi** stain

市民 **shimin** citizen

染み抜き **shiminuki** stain remover

霜 **shimo** frost

指紋 **shimon** fingerprint

しもやけ **shimoyake** frostbite

しん… **shin** core; wick

新… **shin-** new

竹刀 **shinai** bamboo sword

市内 **shinai** area within city limits

市内通話 **shinai-tsūwa** local call

品物 **shinamono** goods

新聞 **shinbun** (news)paper

身長 **shinchō** height

慎重(な) **shinchō (na)** prudent

寝台 **shindai** berth

寝台車 **shindaisha** sleeping car

診断 **shindan** diagnosis

神殿 **shinden** *main building of a shrine*

震度 **shindo** magnitude *(of quake)*

進度 **shindo** progress

震動 **shindō** tremor

振動 **shindō** vibration; swing

侵害 **shingai** violation

神学 **shingaku** theology

震源地 **shingenchi** epicenter

信号 **shingō** traffic signal

信号無視 **shingō-mushi** jaywalking

シングル **shinguru** single

信者 **shinja** believer

信じがたい **shinjigatai** farfetched

信心深い **shinjinbukai** pious

新人類 **shinjinrui** *pej* younger generation

信じられない **shinjirarenai** unbelievable

信じる **shinjiru** believe

真実 **shinjitsu** truth

真珠 **shinju** pearl

新幹線 **shinkansen** bullet train

神経 **shinkei** nerve

神経(の) **shinkei (no)** nervous

神経質(な) **shinkeishitsu (na)** high-strung

神経症 **shinkeishō** neurosis

真剣(な) **shinken (na)** serious

信仰 **shinkō** belief

進行中である **shinkōchū de aru** be under way

深刻(な) **shinkoku (na)** deep *trouble*; grave

真空 **shinkū** vacuum

新年 **Shinnen** New Year

侵入 **shinnyū** penetration

心配 **shinpai** worry

審判 **shinpan** referee; judgment

神秘的(な) **shinpiteki (na)** mystical

進歩 **shinpo** progress

進歩的(な) **shinpoteki (na)** progressive

新婦 **shinpu** bride

信頼 **shinrai** belief; trust

真理 **shinri** truth

心理 **shinri** state of mind

心理学 **shinrigaku** psychology

森林 **shinrin** woods

心理的(な) **shinriteki (na)** psychological

針路 **shinro** course (of ship, plane)

新郎 **shinrō** groom

侵略 **shinryaku** invasion

診療 **shinryō** medical treatment

診療所 **shinryōjo** clinic

審査 **shinsa** investigation

診察 **shinsatsu** examination (of patient)

診察料 **shinsatsuryō** medical fee

申請 **shinsei** application

神聖(な) **shinsei (na)** holy

申請書 **shinseisho** application form

親せき **shinseki** relative

新鮮(な) **shinsen (na)** fresh

親切 **shinsetsu** kindness

紳士 **shinshi** gentleman

寝室 **shinshitsu** bedroom

進出 **shinshutsu** forging ahead

身体 **shintai** body

身体障害者 **shintai-shōgaisha** the disabled

身体的(な) **shintaiteki (na)** physical

信託 **shintaku** trust FIN

進展 **shinten** breakthrough

親展 **shinten** confidential

神道 **Shintō** Shinto

死ぬ **shinu** die

神話 **shinwa** myth

信用 **shin'yō** trust

親友 **shin'yū** close friend

心臓 **shinzō** heart

心臓発作 **shinzō-hossa** heart attack

塩 **shio** salt

潮 **shio** tide

塩味(の) **shioaji (no)** salty

塩辛い **shiokarai** salty

しおれる **shioreru** wilt; be depressed

失敗 **shippai** failure

失敗した **shippai shita** unsuccessful

尻尾 **shippo** tail

湿布 **shippu** poultice

調べる **shiraberu** find out

白髪(の) **shiraga (no)** gray-haired

知らせ **shirase** news

知らせる **shiraseru** break news; keep posted

しり **shiri** butt

知り合い **shiriai** acquaintance

知り合う **shiriau** get to know

私立(の) **shiritsu (no)** private

市立(の) **shiritsu (no)** municipal

退ける **shirizokeru** dismiss; repel

白 **shiro** white

城 **shiro** castle

白い **shiroi** white

素人 **shirōto** amateur

白ワイン **shiro wain** white wine

汁 **shiru** soup; juice

知る **shiru** know

印 **shirushi** mark

資料 **shiryō** material

視力 **shiryoku** eyesight

示唆 **shisa** suggestion

資産 **shisan** assets

視察 **shisatsu** inspection

姿勢 **shisei** posture

視線 **shisen** gaze

施設 **shisetsu** establishment

支社 **shisha** branch office

死者 **shisha** dead person

四捨五入 **shisha-gonyū** rounding off to the nearest whole number

司書 **shisho** librarian

私書箱 **shishobako** PO Box

死傷者 **shishōsha** casualty

ししゅう **shishū** embroidery

思春期 **shishunki** puberty

支出 **shishutsu** expenditure

しそ **shiso** perilla *(plant)*

思想 **shisō** thought

子孫 **shison** descendant

湿疹 **shisshin** eczema

失神する **shisshin suru** faint

質素(な) **shisso (na)** plain; simple

システム **shisutemu** system COMPUT

下 **shita** bottom

舌 **shita** tongue

下書き **shitagaki** (rough) draft

したがって **shitagatte** accordingly

従う **shitagau** obey

下着 **shitagi** underwear

死体 **shitai** corpse

支度 **shitaku** arrangements

下町 **shitamachi** downtown

親しい **shitashī** close

したたる **shitataru** drip

慕う **shitau** adore

指定席 **shiteiseki** reserved seat

指定する **shitei suru** specify

私的(な) **shiteki (na)** personal

詩的(な) **shiteki (na)** poetic

指摘する **shiteki suru** point out

支店 **shiten** branch (of bank)

私鉄 **shitetsu** private railroad

シートベルト **shīto-beruto** seat belt

質 **shitsu** quality (of goods etc)

シーツ **shītsu** sheet

失望 **shitsubō** disappointment

湿度 **shitsudo** humidity

失業 **shitsugyō** unemployment

失業者 **shitsugyōsha** the unemployed

しつけ **shitsuke** upbringing

しつける **shitsukeru** train

しつこい **shitsukoi** insistent

質問 **shitsumon** question

室内(の) **shitsunai (no)** interior (of house)

失礼 **shitsurei** rudeness; 失礼します **shitsurei shimasu** excuse me

知っている **shitte iru** know

しっと **shitto** jealousy

しっと深い **shittobukai** jealous

しわ **shiwa** wrinkle

市役所 **shiyakusho** city hall

しよう **shiyō** let's

使用 **shiyō** use

使用法 **shiyōhō** directions (for use)

使用者 **shiyōsha** user

私有(の) **shiyū (no)** private

自然 **shizen** nature

自然保護区域 **shizen-hogo-kuiki** nature reserve

自然科学 **shizen-kagaku** natural science

自然(の) **shizen (no)** natural

静か(な) **shizuka (na)** quiet

滴 **shizuku** drop

静まる **shizumaru** calm down; drop (of wind)

沈める **shizumeru** sink ship

沈む **shizumu** sink

シーズン **shīzun** season (for tourism etc)

シーズンオフ **shīzun'ofu** off-season

ショー **shō** show

賞 **shō** prize

章 **shō** chapter

省 **shō** ministry

商売 **shōbai** business

処罰 **shobatsu** punishment

小便 **shōben** urine

消防車 **shōbōsha** fire truck

消防士 **shōbōshi** firefighter

消防署 **shōbōsho** fire department

勝負 **shōbu** match

処分 **shobun** disposal; punishment

承知する **shōchi suru** consent

所長 **shochō** director

象徴 **shōchō** symbol

象徴的(な) **shōchōteki (na)** symbolic

承諾 **shōdaku** acceptance

書道 **shodō** calligraphy

衝動 **shōdō** impulse

消毒(の) **shōdoku (no)** antiseptic

消毒剤 **shōdokuzai** antiseptic

衝動的(な) **shōdōteki (na)** impulsive

省エネ(の) **shō-ene (no)** energy-saving

しょうが **shōga** ginger

障害 **shōgai** barrier; disorder MED

生涯 **shōgai** lifetime

障害物 **shōgaibutsu** obstacle

小学校 **shōgakkō** elementary school

奨学金 **shōgakukin** scholarship

小学生 **shōgakusei** elementary school student

しょうがない **shō ga nai** it can't be helped

正月 **shōgatsu** New Year

衝撃 **shōgeki** impact

衝撃的(な) **shōgekiteki (na)** shocking

証言 **shōgen** testimony

将棋 **shōgi** Japanese chess

正午 **shōgo** noon

将軍 **shōgun** general MIL

商業 **shōgyō** commerce

商業的(な) **shōgyōteki (na)** commercial

消費 **shōhi** consumption

商品 **shōhin** goods

賞品 **shōhin** prize

消費者 **shōhisha** consumer

消費税 **shōhizei** consumption tax

初歩(の) **shoho (no)** elementary

処方せん **shohōsen** prescription

所持 **shoji** possession *(of gun, drugs)*

障子 **shōji** sliding paper door

正直 **shōjiki** honesty

正直(な) **shōjiki (na)** honest

処女 **shojo** virgin *(female)*; virginity *(female)*

少女 **shōjo** girl

症状 **shōjō** symptom

賞状 **shōjō** certificate of merit

消化 **shōka** digestion

紹介 **shōkai** introduction *(to person)*; presentation *(of product)*

消火器 **shōkaki** fire extinguisher

処刑 **shokei** execution *(of criminal)*

証券 **shōken** bonds; securities; stocks

初期 **shoki** infancy *(of state, institution)*

正気 **shōki** sanity

賞金 **shōkin** reward

食器 **shokki** tableware

ショック **shokku** shock

証拠 **shōko** evidence

職 **shoku** job

職場 **shokuba** workplace

植物 **shokubutsu** plant

食中毒 **shokuchūdoku** food poisoning

食堂 **shokudō** canteen

食堂車 **shokudōsha** dining car

職業 **shokugyō** profession

食費 **shokuhi** spending on food

食品 **shokuhin** food products

職員 **shokuin** personnel

食事 **shokuji** meal

植民地 **shokuminchi** colony

職務 **shokumu** duty

職人 **shokunin** craftsman

食料 **shokuryō** food

食生活 **shokuseikatsu** diet *(regular food)*

食卓 **shokutaku** dining table

食欲 **shokuyoku** appetite

消極的(な) **shōkyokuteki (na)** passive; negative

初級 **shokyū** elementary level

昇給 **shōkyū** raise *(in salary)*

署名 **shomei** signature

照明 **shōmei** lighting

証明 **shōmei** identification; proof

証明書 **shōmeisho** certificate

正面 **shōmen** front *(of building, book)*

書面で **shomen de** in writing

正面入り口 **shōmen-iriguchi** front entrance

賞味期限の日付け **shōmi-kigen no hizuke** expiration date

庶民 **shomin** the people, the masses

正味(の) **shōmi (no)** net weight, amount

消耗する **shōmō suru** consume

少年 **shōnen** boy

初日 **shonichi** première

小児科 **shōnika** pediatrics

小児科医 **shōnikai** pediatrician

承認 **shōnin** recognition *(of state, sb's achievements)*; approval

証人 **shōnin** witness

商人 **shōnin** merchant

ショッピングセンター **shoppingu-sentā** shopping mall

将来 **shōrai** future

奨励 **shōrei** encouragement

処理 **shori** treatment

勝利 **shōri** victory

勝利者 **shōrisha** victor

書類 **shorui** document

省略 **shōryaku** omission

少量 **shōryō** small quantity

書斎 **shosai** study

詳細 **shōsai** details

称賛 **shōsan** applause, praise

小説 **shōsetsu** novel

小説家 **shōsetsuka** novelist

勝者 **shōsha** winner

商社 **shōsha** trading company

昇進 **shōshin** promotion

初心者 **shoshinsha** beginner

少々 **shōshō** a bit

少数派である **shōsūha de aru** be in the minority

少数（の）**shōsū (no)** few

招待 **shōtai** invitation

正体 **shōtai** true character

招待状 **shōtaijō** invitation (card)

書店 **shoten** bookstore

焦点 **shōten** focus

商店 **shōten** store

所得 **shotoku** earnings

所得税 **shotokuzei** income tax

衝突 **shōtotsu** collision

ショーツ **shōtsu** briefs

昭和時代 **Shōwa-jidai** Showa period *(1926-1989)*

昭和天皇 **Shōwa-tennō** Emperor Hirohito

ショーウィンドウ **shō-windo** store window

賞与 **shōyo** bonus

しょうゆ **shōyu** soy sauce

所有 **shoyū** possession

所有物 **shoyūbutsu** possessions

所有者 **shoyūsha** owner

肖像画 **shōzōga** portrait

所属する **shozoku suru** belong to

種 **shu** species

州 **shū** state

週 **shū** week

守備 **shubi** defense; fielding SPORTS

秋分 **shūbun** autumnal equinox

秋分の日 **Shūbun no hi** Autumnal Equinox Day

主張 **shuchō** assertion

集中する **shūchū suru** concentrate

集中的（な）**shūchūteki (na)** intensive

主題 **shudai** topic

手段 **shudan** means

集団 **shūdan** group

終電 **shūden** last train of the day

修道院 **shūdōin** monastery

収益 **shūeki** proceeds

主婦 **shufu** housewife

修学旅行 **shūgaku ryokō** school trip

主義 **shugi** doctrine

衆議院 **Shūgi-in** House of Representatives

集合 **shūgō** gathering; assembly; set MATH

宗派 **shūha** sect

周辺 **shūhen** periphery

周囲 **shūi** perimeter

習字 **shūji** calligraphy

主人 **shujin** master; landlord

囚人 **shūjin** prisoner

手術 **shujutsu** operation MED

集会 **shūkai** rally POL

収穫 **shūkaku** harvest; catch (of fish)

習慣 **shūkan** habit

週間 **shūkan** week

週刊 **shūkan** weekly magazine

主観的(な) **shukanteki (na)** subjective

主権 **shuken** sovereignty

集金 **shūkin** bill collection

周期的(な) **shūkiteki (na)** periodic

出血 **shukketsu** hemorrhage

出勤する **shukkin suru** go off to work

出国 **shukkoku** leaving the country

宿題 **shukudai** homework

祝福 **shukufuku** blessing

宿泊する **shukuhaku suru** stay

祝日 **shukujitsu** holiday (one day)

縮小 **shukushō** decrease

宗教 **shūkyō** religion

週末 **shūmatsu** weekend

趣味 **shumi** hobby

春分 **shunbun** vernal equinox

春分の日 **Shunbun no hi** Vernal Equinox Day

…周年 **-shūnen** anniversary

瞬間 **shunkan** instant

収入 **shūnyū** income

出版 **shuppan** publishing

出版社 **shuppansha** publishing company

出発 **shuppatsu** departure

出発時刻 **shuppatsu-jikoku** departure time

出発ラウンジ **shuppatsu-raunji** departure lounge

出品物 **shuppinbutsu** exhibit

修理 **shūri** repair

修理工 **shūrikō** mechanic

修理工場 **shūri-kōjō** repair shop

種類 **shurui** sort

狩猟 **shuryō** hunting

終了 **shūryō** termination

主催者 **shusaisha** sponsor

主催する **shusai suru** sponsor

修正 **shūsei** revision; correction

修正液 **shūseieki** correcting fluid

収支 **shūshi** income and expenditure

修士課程 **shūshi-katei** master's course *(academic)*

首相 **shushō** prime minister

主食 **shushoku** staple diet

就職 **shūshoku** seeking employment

収集家 **shūshūka** collector

収集する **shūshū suru** collect *(as hobby)*

出産 **shussan** childbirth

出生証明書 **shussei-shōmeisho** birth certificate

出席 **shusseki** attendance

出席者 **shussekisha** those attending

出身である **shusshin de aru** originate from

出張 **shutchō** business trip

終点 **shūten** terminus

首都 **shuto** capital

取得 **shutoku** acquisition

習得する **shūtoku suru** master *skill etc*

しゅうとめ **shūtome** mother-in-law

主として **shu to shite** chiefly

出演 **shutsuen** appearance *(in movie etc)*

出願 **shutsugan** application

出場する **shutsujō suru** enter *(in competition)*; take part SPORTS

手話 **shuwa** sign language

手腕 **shuwan** prowess

しゅよう **shuyō** tumor

主要(な) **shuyō (na)** main

取材する **shuzai suru** collect *news*; gather *material*

種族 **shuzoku** tribe

そう **sō** so; yes; in that way
◊ seeming; うれしそうな 顔 *ureshisō na kao* a happy-looking face

層 **sō** layer

そば **soba** buckwheat noodles

相場 **sōba** market price

そばに **soba ni** beside

送別会 **sōbetsukai** farewell party

装備 **sōbi** equipment

そびえる **sobieru** tower over

祖母 **sobo** grandmother

素朴(な) **soboku (na)** unsophisticated

装置 **sōchi** device

そちら **sochira** there; you

そうだ **sō da** that's right; it seems that …

ソーダ **sōda** soda

壮大(な) **sōdai (na)** magnificent

相談 **sōdan** consultation

育てる **sodateru** bring up *child*

育つ **sodatsu** grow up

そで **sode** sleeve

騒動 **sōdō** tumult

疎遠になる **soen ni naru** drift apart

ソファ **sofa** sofa

祖父 **sofu** grandfather

祖父母 **sofubo** grandparents

ソフト **sofuto** software

双眼鏡 **sōgankyō** binoculars

争議 **sōgi** dispute *(industrial)*

葬儀場 **sōgijō** funeral home

相互(の) **sōgo (no)** mutual

総合的(な) **sōgōteki (na)** comprehensive

双方で **sōhō de** bilateral

相違 **sōi** disparity

そういう **sō iu** such a

掃除 **sōji** cleaning

掃除機 **sōjiki** vacuum cleaner

総会 **sōkai** general meeting

総計 **sōkei** total sum

ソケット **soketto** socket

送金 **sōkin** transfer *(of money)*

即金 **sokkin** cash

そっくりである **sokkuri de aru** be the spitting image of

そこ **soko** there

底 **soko** bottom; bed *(of sea, river)*

倉庫 **sōko** storehouse

損なう **sokonau** harm

そこに **soko ni** there

…足 **-soku** countword for *footwear*

速度 **sokudo** speed

速度計 **sokudokei** speedometer

側面 **sokumen** side; flank MIL

測量 **sokuryō** survey *(of building)*

促進 **sokushin** promotion

速達 **sokutatsu** express delivery

測定 **sokutei** measurement

即座に **sokuza ni** instantly

染まる **somaru** be dyed; be tainted

粗末(な) **somatsu (na)** low *quality*

染める **someru** dye

そもそも **somosomo** in the first place

背く **somuku** go against

損 **son** loss

備える **sonaeru** provide; be equipped with

供える **sonaeru** offer *(at an altar)*

備え付ける **sonaetsukeru** equip

遭難する **sōnan suru** meet with disaster

尊重 **sonchō** respect

損害 **songai** damage

尊敬 **sonkei** respect

そんな **sonna** such a

その **sono** that; those; the

そのまま **sono mama** like that

損失 **sonshitsu** loss

挿入 **sōnyū** insertion

存在 **sonzai** existence

騒音 **sōon** din

空 **sora** sky

そらす **sorasu** avert; bend

それ **sore** that one

それで **sore de** and then ◊ so what?

それでも **soredemo** nevertheless

それでは **sore dewa** in that case; goodbye

それ以来 **sore irai** ever since then

それじゃ **sore ja** well; goodbye

それから **sore kara** after that; since then

それなら **sore nara** in that case

それに加えて **sore ni kuwaete** in addition to that

それにもかかわらず **sore ni mo kakawarazu** nevertheless

それに応じて **sore ni ōjite** accordingly

それら **sorera** they; those

それらの **sorera no** their; those ◊ theirs

それる **soreru** stray

それとも **sore tomo** or

それぞれ **sorezore** each; respectively

それぞれ（の）**sorezore (no)** each ◊ respective

そり **sori** sleigh

総理大臣 **sōri-daijin** prime minister

創立 **sōritsu** founding

創立者 **sōritsusha** founder

そろばん **soroban** abacus

そろえる **soroeru** put in order

そろそろ **sorosoro** soon; slowly

そろう **sorou** be complete; be equal; gather

そる **soru** shave

操作 **sōsa** operation

捜査 **sōsa** investigation

創作 **sōsaku** creation

捜索 **sōsaku** hunt

ソーセージ **sōsēji** sausage

祖先 **sosen** ancestor

総選挙 **sōsenkyo** general

election

組織 **soshiki** organization

葬式 **sōshiki** funeral

送信する **sōshin suru** transmit

阻止する **soshi suru** stop

そして **soshite** and (then)

素質 **soshitsu** character

訴訟 **soshō** lawsuit

そう祖母 **sōsobo** great-grandmother

そう祖父 **sōsofu** great-grandfather

注ぐ **sosogu** pour; devote oneself to

そそのかす **sosonokasu** instigate

ソース **sōsu** sauce

そうすると **sō suru to** in that case

相対的(な) **sōtaiteki (na)** relative

そっち **sotchi** over there ◊ you (informal)

率直(な) **sotchoku (na)** candid

外 **soto** outside

外側 **sotogawa** outside

相当(な) **sōtō (na)** substantial; suitable

相当する **sōtō suru** correspond to; suit

卒業 **sotsugyō** graduation

卒業生 **sotsugyōsei** graduate

卒業式 **sotsugyōshiki** graduation ceremony

そっと **sotto** quietly

沿う **sou** go alongside

添う **sou** meet; accompany

粗雑(な) **sozatsu (na)** sloppy

想像 **sōzō** imagination

創造 **sōzō** creation

相続人 **sōzokunin** heir; heiress

相続する **sōzoku suru** inherit

巣 **su** nest

酢 **su** vinegar

吸う **sū** inhale; smoke

素晴らしい **subarashī** wonderful

素早い **subayai** nimble

素早く **subayaku** speedily

滑りやすい **suberiyasui** slippery

滑る **suberu** glide; slip

すべて(の) **subete (no)** all

スチュワーデス **suchuwādesu** flight attendant

スチュワード **suchuwādo** steward

すでに **sude ni** already

末 **sue** end; trifle; tip; future

末っ子 **suekko** youngest child

数学 **sūgaku** math

すがすがしい **sugasugashī** refreshing

姿 **sugata** image; shape

すっごく **suggoku** extremely

杉 **sugi** Japanese cedar

過ぎる **sugiru** pass by; go too far

…すぎる **...sugiru** too; ごはんが多すぎる **gohan ga ōsugiru** there is too much rice

すごい **sugoi** terrific

すごく **sugoku** extremely

過ごす **sugosu** pass the time

すぐ **sugu** right away

すぐに **sugu ni** immediately

優れた **sugureta** excellent

崇拝 **sūhai** worship

崇拝者 **sūhaisha** worshiper

垂直(の) **suichoku (no)** vertical

水田 **suiden** ricefield

水道 **suidō** water supply

水道水 **suidōsui** running water

水泳 **suiei** swimming

吸い殻 **suigara** cigarette butt

炊飯器 **suihanki** rice cooker

水平(の) **suihei (no)** horizontal

水平線 **suiheisen** horizon

水準 **suijun** level

スイカ **suika** water melon

吸い込む **suikomu** inhale

睡眠 **suimin** sleep

睡眠薬 **suimin'yaku** sleeping pill

推理 **suiri** inference

推薦 **suisen** recommendation

推薦状 **suisenjō** reference

推測 **suisoku** conjecture

スイス **Suisu** Switzerland

スイッチ **suitchi** switch

推定 **suitei** estimate

吸い取る **suitoru** absorb

水曜日 **suiyōbi** Wednesday

水族館 **suizokukan** aquarium

筋 **suji** tendon; gristle; plot

数字 **sūji** digit

スカーフ **sukāfu** headscarf

スカート **sukāto** skirt

スケッチ **suketchi** sketch

スケート **sukēto** skate; skating

すき **suki** plow; spade

スキー **sukī** ski; skiing

好きである **suki de aru** like

すき間 **sukima** gap

すきま風 **sukimakaze** draft

すきやき **sukiyaki** sukiyaki

すっかり **sukkari** completely

スコア **sukoa** score MUS, SPORTS

スコップ **sukoppu** scoop; spade

少し **sukoshi** a little

少しずつ **sukoshi zutsu** little by little

すく **suku** be hungry; be transparent; plow

救う **sukū** rescue

救い **sukui** rescue

少ない **sukunai** few

少なくとも **sukunaku tomo** at least

スキャンダル **sukyandaru** scandal

住まい **sumai** residence

すまない **sumanai** inexcusable

済ます **sumasu** finish

スマート(な) **sumāto (na)** stylish; slim

炭 **sumi** charcoal

隅 **sumi** corner

墨 **sumi** Chinese ink

墨絵 **sumie** ink painting

すみません **sumimasen** excuse me; thank you

相撲 **sumō** sumo

相撲取り **sumōtori** sumo wrestler

住む **sumu** reside

澄む **sumu** be clear

済む **sumu** be finished

砂 **suna** sand

素直(な) **sunao (na)** obedient

すなわち **sunawachi** namely

澄んだ **sunda** clear

すねる **suneru** sulk

スニーカー **sunīkā** sneakers

スパゲティ **supageti** spaghetti

スーパーマーケット **sūpāmāketto** supermarket

スペイン **Supein** Spain

スピード **supīdo** speed

スピーカー **supīkā** (loud)speaker

スポーツ **supōtsu** sport

スポーツクラブ **supōtsu-kurabu** health club

酸っぱい **suppai** sour

スープ **sūpu** soup

スプーン **supūn** spoon

スプレー **supurē** spray

スライド **suraido** slide PHOT

すれば **sureba**: …とすれば …*to sureba* supposing that

すり **suri** pickpocket

擦り切れる **surikireru** wear *(of carpet, fabric)*

擦り傷 **surikizu** abrasion

擦りむく **surimuku** chafe

スリッパ **surippa** slipper

する **suru** do; choose; cost

擦る **suru** rub; grind; chafe

刷る **suru** print

鋭い **surudoi** sharp

すると **suruto** and then

すし **sushi** sushi

すそ **suso** hem; foot *(of mountain)*

すす **susu** soot

すすぐ **susugu** rinse

勧める **susumeru** advise; offer

薦める **susumeru** recommend

進む **susumu** progress

すすり泣き **susurinaki** sob

すする **susuru** sip; slurp

スタイル **sutairu** style

スタジアム **sutajiamu** stadium

スタンド **sutando** stand; the bleachers; lamp

スタンプ **sutanpu** stamp; postmark

すたれる **sutareru** decline; be abolished

ステーキ **sutēki** steak

素敵(な) **suteki (na)** gorgeous

ステレオ **sutereo** stereo

捨てる **suteru** abandon

ストーブ **sutōbu** stove

ストッキング **sutokkingu** stocking

ストライキ **sutoraiki** strike

ストライク **sutoraiku** strike *(in baseball, bowling)*

ストレス **sutoresu** stress

ストレート(の) **sutorēto (no)** straight; black *tea*

ストロー **sutorō** straw

スーツ **sūtsu** suit

スーツケース **sūtsukēsu** suitcase

座る **suwaru** sit

すず **suzu** tin

鈴 **suzu** bell

すずめ **suzume** sparrow

すずめばち **suzumebachi** hornet

鈴虫 **suzumushi** cricket *(insect)*

涼しい **suzushī** cool

T

田 **ta** paddy field

他 **ta** other

束 **taba** bundle

タバコ **tabako** cigarette; tobacco

食べ物 **tabemono** food

食べる **taberu** eat

旅 **tabi** journey

足袋 **tabi** *traditional split-toed Japanese socks*

度々 **tabitabi** often; repeatedly

たぶん **tabun** maybe

立ち上がる **tachiagaru** rise

立場 **tachiba** standpoint

立ち止まる **tachidomaru** stop

立入禁止 **tachi-iri-kinshi** no admittance

立ち見席 **tachimiseki** standing room only *(in movie theater)*

立ち去る **tachisaru** leave

立ち寄る **tachiyoru** call by

ただ **tada** only

ただいま **tadaima** I'm home

ただし **tadashi** but

正しい **tadashī** correct

漂う **tadayou** drift

絶え間なく **taema naku** nonstop

耐える **taeru** withstand

絶えず **taezu** continuously

互いに **tagai ni** each other

多額(の) **tagaku (no)** a large sum of

耕す **tagayasu** plow

タイ **Tai** Thailand

たい **tai** sea bream

…たい **-tai** want; 行きたい *ikitai* want to go

対 **tai** versus; to; 三対一 *san tai ichi* three to one

体調 **taichō** condition *(of health)*

怠惰(な) **taida (na)** indolent

態度 **taido** attitude

台風 **taifū** typhoon

たいがい **taigai** mostly

待遇 **taigū** treatment

太平洋 **Taiheiyō** Pacific (Ocean)

大変 **taihen** very

大変(な) **taihen (na)** difficult

逮捕 **taiho** arrest

体育 **tai-iku** gymnastics

体育館 **tai-ikukan** gym

退院する **tai-in suru** leave hospital

体重 **taijū** weight

体重計 **taijūkei** scales

大会 **taikai** tournament; convention

体格 **taikaku** physique

体系 **taikei** system

体験 **taiken** experience

大気 **taiki** atmosphere

大気汚染 **taiki-osen** air pollution

太鼓 **taiko** drum

対抗する **taikō suru** oppose

退屈(な) **taikutsu (na)** boring

耐久性 **taikyūsei** endurance

タイマー **taimā** timer

怠慢 **taiman** negligence

滞納している **tainō shite iru** be in arrears

体温 **taion** (body) temperature

体温計 **taionkei** clinical thermometer

対応する **taiō suru** correspond (to); cope (with)

タイプ **taipu** type; sort

平ら(な) **taira (na)** flat

大陸 **tairiku** continent

対立 **tairitsu** confrontation

タイル **tairu** tile

大量 **tairyō** mass

体力 **tairyoku** strength

対策 **taisaku** measures

体制 **taisei** system; the Establishment

大勢 **taisei** general situation

大西洋 **Taiseiyō** Atlantic Ocean

対戦する **taisen suru** meet SPORTS

大切(な) **taisetsu (na)** important

退社する **taisha suru** retire

大使 **taishi** ambassador

大使館 **taishikan** embassy

たいした **taishita** big

対して **taishite** against; concerning

体質 **taishitsu** constitution (of person)

対称 **taishō** symmetry

対象 **taishō** target

対照 **taishō** contrast

大正時代 **Taishō-jidai** Taisho period (1912-1926)

退職 **taishoku** retirement

退職金 **taishokukin** golden handshake

対称的(な) **taishōteki (na)** symmetrical

対照的(な) **taishōteki (na)** contrasting

体臭 **taishū** body odor

大衆 **taishū** the masses

体操 **taisō** gymnastics

たいてい **taitei** most of the time

対等(の) **taitō (no)** equal

タイトル **taitoru** title

対話 **taiwa** dialog

台湾 **Taiwan** Taiwan

タイヤ **taiya** tire

太陽 **taiyō** sun

滞在 **taizai** stay

高い **takai** high; tall; expensive

高める **takameru** enhance

宝 **takara** treasure

宝くじ **takarakuji** lottery

高さ **takasa** height

竹 **take** bamboo

丈 **take** height

竹の子 **takenoko** bamboo shoot

滝 **taki** waterfall

たき火 **takibi** bonfire

卓球 **takkyū** table tennis

宅急便 **takkyūbin®** express home delivery service

たこ **tako** kite; octopus; callus

宅 **taku** house

炊く **taku** boil; cook

たくましい **takumashī** strong

巧み(な) **takumi (na)** skillful

たくらみ **takurami** scheme

たくらむ **takuramu** scheme

たくさん **takusan** a lot

タクシー **takushī** cab

タクシー乗り場 **takushī-noriba** cab stand

タクシー運転手 **takushī-**

untenshu cab driver
蓄える **takuwaeru** hoard
玉 **tama** ball; jewel
球 **tama** ball
卵 **tamago** egg
たまねぎ **tamanegi** onion
たまに **tama ni** occasionally
貯まる **tamaru** be saved up
魂 **tamashī** soul REL
たまたま **tamatama** by
  chance
ため息 **tameiki** sigh
ため(に) **tame (ni)** for (the
  sake of)
ためらう **tamerau** hesitate
貯める **tameru** save
試してみる **tameshite miru**
  try out
試す **tamesu** test
保つ **tamotsu** keep
棚 **tana** shelf
七夕 **Tanabata** Star Festival
田んぼ **tanbo** paddy field
探知する **tanchi suru** detect
単調(な) **tanchō (na)**
  monotonous
単独(の) **tandoku (no)**
  separate; alone
種 **tane** seed; cause; trick
単語 **tango** word
端午の節句 **tango no sekku**
  Boys' Festival
単位 **tan'i** unit
谷 **tani** valley

他人 **tanin** stranger
誕生 **tanjō** birth
誕生日 **tanjōbi** birthday
単純(な) **tanjun (na)** simple
単価 **tanka** unit cost
担架 **tanka** stretcher
短歌 **tanka** 31-syllable
  Japanese poem
探検 **tanken** exploration
探検家 **tankenka** explorer
短期大学 **tanki daigaku**
  junior college
短期間(の) **tankikan (no)**
  short-term
短気(な) **tanki (na)** short-
  tempered
タンク **tanku** tank
単に **tan ni** simply
頼み **tanomi** request
頼む **tanomu** request
楽しい **tanoshī** enjoyable
楽しませる **tanoshimaseru**
  amuse
楽しみ **tanoshimi**
  entertainment
楽しむ **tanoshimu** enjoy
たんぱく質 **tanpakushitsu**
  protein
タンポン **tanpon** tampon
炭酸入り(の) **tansan'iri (no)**
  carbonated
単身赴任 **tanshin-funin**
  *living away from one's family
  after a job transfer*

短所 **tansho** shortcoming

短縮する **tanshuku suru** shorten

たんす **tansu** chest of drawers

担当する **tantō suru** be in charge of

たぬき **tanuki** raccoon dog

倒れる **taoreru** fall down

タオル **taoru** towel

倒す **taosu** bring down

たっぷり（の）**tappuri (no)** abundant

たら **tara** cod

…たら **-tara** if; when; 雨が降ったら *ame ga futtara* if it rains; 駅に着いたら *eki ni tsuitara* when you get to the station

タラップ **tarappu** landing steps

垂らす **tarasu** let fall

タレント **tarento** celebrity

垂れる **tareru** hang; drip

足りる **tariru** suffice

たる **taru** barrel

たるむ **tarumu** sag

多量（の）**taryō (no)** a large quantity of

多才（の）**tasai (no)** versatile

確かめる **tashikameru** make certain

確か（な）**tashika (na)** certain

確かに **tashika ni** certainly

足し算 **tashizan** addition

MATH

多少 **tashō** a little

達成する **tassei suru** achieve

達する **tassuru** arrive at

足す **tasu** add

助かる **tasukaru** be helpful

助け **tasuke** help

助ける **tasukeru** help

多数（の）**tasū (no)** numerous

戦い, 闘い **tatakai** fight

戦う, 闘う **tatakau** fight

たたく **tataku** beat; tap; swat

畳 **tatami** mat

たたむ **tatamu** fold up

縦 **tate** length

盾 **tate** shield

縦書き **tategaki** writing in vertical lines

立てかける **tatekakeru** lean against

建て前 **tatemae** the public face you put on

建物 **tatemono** building

建て直す **tatenaosu** rebuild

立て直す **tatenaosu** revise; restore

建てる **tateru** build

立てる **tateru** stand

例えば **tatoeba** for example

たつ **tatsu** pass

立つ **tatsu** stand

発つ **tatsu** leave

達人 **tatsujin** master

竜巻 **tatsumaki** tornado

たった **tatta** only

田植え **taue** rice-planting

便り **tayori** news

頼る **tayoru** rely on

多様性 **tayōsei** diversity

尋ねる **tazuneru** ask

訪ねる **tazuneru** visit

手 **te** hand; move *(in board game)*

手当 **teate** allowance; medical treatment

早く **tebayaku** quickly

手引き **tebiki** guidebook

手袋 **tebukuro** glove

テーブル **tēburu** table

手帳 **techō** small notebook

手がかり **tegakari** clue; grip

手紙 **tegami** letter

手柄 **tegara** achievement

手軽(な) **tegaru (na)** easy

手ごろ(な) **tegoro (na)** handy

手配 **tehai** arrangements

手本 **tehon** model

提案書 **teiansho** proposal

堤防 **teibō** levee

停電 **teiden** power outage

程度 **teido** extent

定義 **teigi** definition

定員 **tei-in** capacity *(of elevator, vehicle)*

低下 **teika** decline

定価 **teika** list price

低カロリー(の) **tei-karorī**

(no) low-calorie

定期券 **teikiken** season ticket

定期的(な) **teikiteki (na)** regular

定期的に **teikiteki ni** periodically

抵抗 **teikō** resistance

帝国 **teikoku** empire

定刻 **teikoku** scheduled time

抵抗力 **teikō-ryoku** resistance

提供 **teikyō** offer; donation MED

定休日 **teikyūbi** closing day

ていねい語 **teineigo** polite word

ていねい(な) **teinei (na)** polite

定年 **teinen** retirement age

停留所 **teiryūjo** bus stop

訂正 **teisei** correction

停車禁止 **teisha-kinshi** no stopping

停止 **teishi** halt

低脂肪(の) **teishibō (no)** low-fat

定食 **teishoku** set menu

提出する **teishutsu suru** hand in

停滞している **teitai shite iru** be backed up

手品 **tejina** magic

手品師 **tejinashi** magician

手錠 **tejō** handcuffs

手順 **tejun** process

敵 **teki** enemy

適度(の) **tekido (no)** moderate

適合する **tekigō suru** suit

敵意 **teki-i** hostility

適応性 **tekiōsei** compatibility

適切(な) **tekisetsu (na)** appropriate

テキスト **tekisuto** text; textbook

適当(な) **tekitō (na)** suitable

適用する **tekiyō suru** apply

てこ **teko** lever

手首 **tekubi** wrist

テーマ **tēma** theme

手前 **temae** this side; front

点 **ten** point

天 **ten** heaven

店長 **tenchō** manager

天国 **tengoku** heaven

手荷物 **tenimotsu** (hand) luggage

店員 **ten'in** sales clerk

テニス **tenisu** tennis

展示 **tenji** display

天井 **tenjō** ceiling

添乗員 **tenjōin** tour conductor

添加物 **tenkabutsu** additive

展開する **tenkai suru** unfold

転換 **tenkan** convert

典型的(な) **tenkeiteki (na)** typical

点検する **tenken suru** check

天気 **tenki** weather

天気予報 **tenki-yohō** weather forecast

転校する **tenkō suru** change schools

点滅する **tenmetsu suru** blink (of light)

天文学 **tenmongaku** astronomy

天然 **tennen** nature

天然痘 **tennentō** smallpox

天皇 **tennō** emperor

天皇誕生日 **Tennō-tanjōbi** Emperor's Birthday

転覆する **tenpuku suru** overturn

てんぷら **tenpura** tempura (deep-fried food)

転落 **tenraku** fall

展覧会 **tenrankai** exhibition

天才 **tensai** genius

天災 **tensai** natural disaster

天使 **tenshi** angel

店主 **tenshu** shopkeeper

転送する **tensō suru** forward

点数 **tensū** point

点滴 **tenteki** drip MED

テント **tento** tent

転倒 **tentō** fall

店頭 **tentō** storefront

手拭い **tenugui** hand towel

鉄板 **teppan** iron plate; hot plate

鉄砲 **teppō** gun

テープ **tēpu** tape

テープレコーダー **tēpu-rekōdā** tape recorder

寺 **tera** temple

照らす **terasu** shine

テラス **terasu** terrace

テレビ **terebi** TV

テレビ番組 **terebi-bangumi** TV program

テロ **tero** terrorism

照る **teru** shine

手製(の) **tesei (no)** handmade

手仕事 **teshigoto** handiwork

手数 **tesū** inconvenience

手すり **tesuri** handrail

手数料 **tesūryō** handling fee

テスト **tesuto** test

鉄 **tetsu** iron

手伝い **tetsudai** helper

手伝う **tetsudau** help

鉄道 **tetsudō** railroad

哲学 **tetsugaku** philosophy

手続き **tetsuzuki** procedure

撤退 **tettai** withdrawal

徹底的(な) **tetteiteki (na)** thorough

…てはいけない **-te wa ikenai** must not

手渡す **tewatasu** hand over

手触り **tezawari** feel

手作り(の) **tezukuri (no)** handmade

ティー **tī** tee

ティーシャツ **tīshatsu** T-shirt

ティースプーン **tīspūn** teaspoon

ティッシュペーパー **tisshu-pēpā** tissue paper

…と … **to** and ◊ with

戸 **to** door

都 **to** capital city

塔 **tō** pagoda; tower

党 **tō** political party

…頭 **-tō** countword for large *animals*

当番 **tōban** duty; person on duty

飛ばす **tobasu** skip; let fly; blow *fuse*

飛び上がる **tobiagaru** spring

飛び出す **tobidasu** rush out

飛び跳ねる **tobihaneru** bounce

飛び込む, 跳び込む **tobikomu** dive; leap

扉 **tobira** (double) door

逃亡 **tōbō** escape

逃亡者 **tōbōsha** fugitive

乏しい **toboshī** meager

飛ぶ **tobu** blow *(of fuse)*; fly

跳ぶ **tobu** jump

東部 **tōbu** east

到着 **tōchaku** arrival

到着ロビー **tōchaku-robī** arrivals

到着予定時刻 **tōchaku-yotei-jikoku** estimated time of arrival

父ちゃん **tōchan** dad
土地 **tochi** land
統治 **tōchi** rule
途中 **tochū** midway
灯台 **tōdai** lighthouse
戸棚 **todana** closet
都道府県 **todōfuken**
　prefectures of Japan
届け出る **todokederu** notify
届ける **todokeru** report;
　send on
届く **todoku** reach
とどまる **todomaru** remain
とうふ **tōfu** bean curd
とがめる **togameru** find fault
とうがらし **tōgarashi** chili
　(pepper)
とがる **togaru** be pointed
とげ **toge** thorn
峠 **tōge** pass *(in mountains)*
陶芸 **tōgei** ceramics
遂げる **togeru** achieve
討議 **tōgi** debate
途切れなく **togirenaku**
　uninterrupted
研ぐ **togu** sharpen; wash *rice*
徒歩 **toho** walk
途方に暮れる **tohō ni**
　kureru be at a loss
投票 **tōhyō** voting
投票者 **tōhyōsha** voter
問い **toi** question
遠い **tōi** distant
問い合わせ **toiawase** inquiry

問い合わせる **toiawaseru**
　inquire
トイレ **toire** bathroom, toilet
トイレットペーパー
　toiretto-pēpā toilet paper
統一 **tōitsu** unification
当時 **tōji** at that time
冬至 **tōji** winter solstice
陶磁器 **tōjiki** ceramics
閉じ込める **tojikomeru**
　confine
閉じる **tojiru** close
当日 **tōjitsu** (on) that day
登場 **tōjō** entrance
搭乗 **tōjō** embarkation
搭乗券 **tōjōken** boarding pass
とか ... **toka** and so on;
　something like
十日 **tōka** ten days; the 10th
都会 **tokai** city
溶かす **tokasu** melt
時計 **tokei** clock
統計 **tōkei** statistics
時計屋 **tokeiya** watchmaker
溶ける **tokeru** melt ◊ soluble
凍結する **tōketsu suru** freeze
時 **toki** time; when
陶器 **tōki** pottery
冬季 **tōki** winter
時々 **tokidoki** sometimes
解き放す **tokihanasu** set free
時には **toki ni wa** sometimes
投棄する **tōki suru** throw
　away

投機する **tōki suru** speculate

特権 **tokken** privilege

特許 **tokkyo** patent

特急 **tokkyū** express train

床 **toko** bed

陶工 **tōkō** potter

床の間 **tokonoma** alcove

所 **tokoro** place

ところで **tokoro de** incidentally

所々 **tokoro dokoro** here and there

ところが **tokoro ga** but

床屋 **tokoya** barber

得 **toku** advantage; profit

解く **toku** solve

特売 **tokubai** sale *(reduced prices)*

特別(な) **tokubetsu (na)** special

特徴 **tokuchō** characteristic

特派員 **tokuhain** correspondent

得意(な) **tokui (na)** skillful

匿名(の) **tokumei (no)** anonymous

特に **toku ni** especially

遠くに **tōku ni** in the distance

特色 **tokushoku** characteristic

特殊(な) **tokushu (na)** special

特定(の) **tokutei (no)** particular

得点 **tokuten** score

特典 **tokuten** privilege

特有(の) **tokuyū (no)** characteristic

東京 **Tōkyō** Tokyo

当局 **tōkyoku** the authorities

等級 **tōkyū** grade

止まる **tomaru** stop

泊まる **tomaru** stay the night

留まる **tomaru** fasten

トマト **tomato** tomato

遠回り **tōmawari** detour

透明(の) **tōmei (no)** transparent

止める **tomeru** stop; turn off

泊める **tomeru** take in *person*

留める **tomeru** fasten

富 **tomi** wealth

…とも **-tomo** both ◊ -ever

友 **tomo** friend

友達 **tomodachi** friend

ともかく **tomokaku** anyhow

伴う **tomonau** be accompanied

共に **tomo ni** together with

とうもろこし **tōmorokoshi** corn

富む **tomu** be wealthy

トン **ton** ton

隣 **tonari** neighbor

とんぼ **tonbo** dragonfly

とんでもない **tondemonai** absolutely not! ◊ shocking

とにかく **tonikaku** anyhow

豚カツ **tonkatsu** breaded pork cutlet

トンネル **tonneru** tunnel

問屋 **ton'ya** wholesaler

糖尿病 **tōnyōbyō** diabetes

投入 **tōnyū** injection *(of capital)*

トップ **toppu** top

トップレベル（の） **toppureberu (no)** top-level

とら **tora** tiger

トラベラーズチェック **toraberāzu-chekku** traveler's check

トラブル **toraburu** trouble

捕らえる **toraeru** capture

トラック **torakku** racetrack; truck

トランク **toranku** trunk

トランプ **toranpu** playing cards

トレーナー **torēnā** sweatshirt; trainer

トレーニング **torēningu** workout

取れる **toreru** come off; be obtained

採れる **toreru** be extracted

鳥 **tori** bird

通り **tōri** street

…通り **-tōri** as 先生のいう通り **sensei no iu tōri** as your teacher says

とりあえず **toriaezu** for the time being

取り上げる **toriageru** pick up

取り扱い **toriatsukai** treatment

取り扱い注意 **toriatsukai-chūi** (handle) with care

取扱説明書 **toriatsukai-setsumeisho** instruction manual

取り出す **toridasu** take out

取柄 **torie** personal worth

鳥肌 **torihada** gooseflesh

取りはずす **torihazusu** detach

取り引き **torihiki** transaction

鳥居 **tori-i** gateway to Shinto shrine

取り入れる **tori-ireru** incorporate

取り替える **torikaeru** change

取り囲む **torikakomu** encircle

取り消し **torikeshi** cancelation

取り消す **torikesu** cancel

通り道 **tōrimichi** route

取り戻す **torimodosu** recover

鳥肉 **toriniku** chicken *(food)*

取り除く **torinozoku** remove

通り抜ける **tōrinukeru** pass through

取締役 **torishimariyaku** director

取り締まる **torishimaru**
clamp down on

通り過ぎる **tōrisugiru**
pass (by)

取り付ける **toritsukeru**
attach; install

登録 **tōroku** registration

討論 **tōron** debate

とる **toru** have *meal*

取る **toru** take

捕る **toru** catch *fish*

撮る **toru** take *photo*

通る **tōru** penetrate

倒産 **tōsan** bankruptcy

と殺 **tosatsu** slaughter

当選する **tōsen suru** win

年 **toshi** year; age

都市 **toshi** city

投資 **tōshi** investment

都市(の) **toshi (no)** urban

投資者 **tōshisha** investor

年下(の) **toshishita (no)**
junior

…として **… to shite** in the
form of

通して **tōshite** through

年上 **toshiue** elder

年寄り **toshiyori** elderly
person

図書 **tosho** books

図書館 **toshokan** library

とそ **toso** New Year spiced
sake

逃走 **tōsō** escape

逃走車 **tōsōsha** getaway car

闘争的(な) **tōsōteki (na)**
militant

とっさに **tossa ni** instantly

通す **tōsu** let pass; run through
details

トースト **tōsuto** toast

…とたん **… totan** just when

到達 **tōtatsu** attainment

とても **totemo** very

とうとう **tōtō** at last; after all

整える **totonoeru** prepare

突然(の) **totsuzen (no)**
sudden

とって **totte**: …にとって
… ni totte to; for; 私にとっ
て for me

取っ手 **totte** handle

当惑 **tōwaku** embarrassment

東洋 **Tōyō** Orient

東洋(の) **Tōyō (no)** Oriental

灯油 **tōyu** kerosene

遠ざかる **tōzakaru** go away;
drift apart

遠ざける **tōzakeru** shun

登山 **tozan** mountaineering

当座預金口座 **tōza-yokin-
kōza** checking account

当然(の) **tōzen (no)** natural

つば **tsuba** saliva; brim
(of hat)

つばき **tsubaki** camellia

つばめ **tsubame** swallow
(bird)

翼 **tsubasa** wing

つぼ **tsubo** urn

坪 **tsubo** *unit of area, 3.6 square yards*

つぼみ **tsubomi** bud

粒 **tsubu** grain; speck

つぶれる **tsubureru** be crushed; go bankrupt

つぶす **tsubusu** crush; kill time

つぶやく **tsubuyaku** mutter

土 **tsuchi** earth

通知票 **tsūchihyō** report card

通知する **tsūchi suru** inform

通帳 **tsūchō** bank book

つえ **tsue** cane; walking stick

告げる **tsugeru** inform

次(の) **tsugi (no)** next

都合 **tsugō** circumstances

つぐ **tsugu** join; pour; rank after

継ぐ **tsugu** inherit

償う **tsugunau** make amends

つい **tsui** just; by accident; in spite of oneself

対 **tsui** pair

ついでに **tsuide ni** by the way

追放 **tsuihō** expulsion

追加 **tsuika** addition

追加料金 **tsuika-ryōkin** surcharge

追求 **tsuikyū** pursuit

ツインベッド **tsuin-beddo** twin beds

ついに **tsui ni** at last

墜落 **tsuiraku** crash

ついさっき **tsui sakki** a few moments ago

追伸 **tsuishin** PS, postscript

ついたて **tsuitate** partition

ついて **tsuite** concerning; per

ついて行く **tsuite iku** follow

ついてくる **tsuite kuru** keep up

費やす **tsuiyasu** spend

通じる **tsūjiru** lead to; communicate

通常(の) **tsūjō (no)** normal

通貨 **tsūka** currency

仕える **tsukaeru** serve

使い **tsukai** errand

使い古した **tsukaifurushita** well-worn

使いすぎる **tsukaisugiru** overuse; overwork

使い捨て(の) **tsukaisute (no)** disposable

捕まえる **tsukamaeru** capture

つかむ **tsukamu** seize

通関手続 **tsūkan-tetsuzuki** customs formalities

疲れる **tsukareru** get tired

通過する **tsūka suru** pass through

使う **tsukau** use

付け合わせ **tsukeawase** fixings

つけ込む **tsukekomu** take advantage of

付け加える **tsukekuwaeru** add

漬物 **tsukemono** pickled vegetables

つけっぱなしにする **tsukeppanashi ni suru** leave on *computer etc*

つける **tsukeru** apply; add; strike *match*; switch on *light etc*

着ける **tsukeru** wear

付ける **tsukeru** attach

月 **tsuki** month; moon

つき **tsuki**: …につき … *ni tsuki* per

付き合い **tsukiai** companionship

突き当たり **tsukiatari** end (of street)

付き合う **tsukiau** go out with

通勤 **tsūkin** commuting to work

通勤者 **tsūkinsha** commuter

尽きる **tsukiru** be used up

突き刺す **tsukisasu** plunge

付き添い **tsukisoi** nurse; attendant

付き添う **tsukisou** accompany; attend

つきとめる **tsukitomeru** pinpoint

突っ込む **tsukkomu** shove in

通行 **tsūkō** traffic

通告 **tsūkoku** notice

通行人 **tsūkōnin** passer-by

通行料 **tsūkōryō** toll

つく **tsuku** tell *lie*; leave for; catch fire; strike *bell*

付く **tsuku** stick; be attached to; cost; be in luck

突く **tsuku** jab

着く **tsuku** arrive

机 **tsukue** desk

作り上げる **tsukuriageru** make out *list*

作り話 **tsukuribanashi** lie, story

作り出す **tsukuridasu** produce

作り付け（の）**tsukuritsuke (no)** built-in

繕う **tsukurou** mend

作る **tsukuru** make

造る **tsukuru** build

尽くす **tsukusu** exhaust

妻 **tsuma** wife

つまみ **tsumami** pinch; knob

つまらない **tsumaranai** uninteresting

つまり **tsumari** that is to say

詰まり **tsumari** blockage

詰まる **tsumaru** clog up

つま先 **tsumasaki** toe (of shoe)

つまようじ **tsumayōji** toothpick

つまずく **tsumazuku** stumble

つめ **tsume** fingernail; claw

詰め込む **tsumekomu** cram

詰める **tsumeru** squeeze up; pack

冷たい **tsumetai** cold

罪 **tsumi** sin

積み荷 **tsumini** cargo

つもり **tsumori** intention

摘む **tsumu** pick

積む **tsumu** load

綱 **tsuna** cable

ツナ **tsuna** tuna

つながり **tsunagari** link

つながる **tsunagaru** link up

つなぐ **tsunagu** connect

津波 **tsunami** tidal wave

常に **tsune ni** always

角 **tsuno** horn

つらい **tsurai** painful

貫く **tsuranuku** pierce

連れ合い **tsure** companion

連れる **tsureru** bring along

釣り **tsuri** fishing; change

釣り合い **tsuriai** balance

つり橋 **tsuribashi** suspension bridge

通路 **tsūro** aisle

つる **tsuru** crane *(bird)*

釣る **tsuru** catch *fish with rod*

通信 **tsūshin** communication

通信衛星 **tsūshin-eisei** communications satellite

通信社 **tsūshinsha** news agency

伝える **tsutaeru** convey

伝わる **tsutawaru** carry *(of sound)*; be communicated

勤める **tsutomeru** be employed

務める **tsutomeru** make efforts

勤め先 **tsutomesaki** place of employment

筒 **tsutsu** cylinder

つつく **tsutsuku** peck; criticize

つつましい **tsutsumashī** modest

包み **tsutsumi** bundle

包む **tsutsumu** wrap

慎む **tsutsushimu** be discreet

つや **tsuya** gloss

つや消し(の) **tsuyakeshi (no)** matt

通訳 **tsūyaku** interpretation; interpreter

強い **tsuyoi** strong

強さ **tsuyosa** strength

つゆ **tsuyu** soup; sauce; juice

梅雨 **tsuyu** rainy season

露 **tsuyu** dew

続ける **tsuzukeru** continue

続き **tsuzuki** continuation

続く **tsuzuku** continue

U

乳母車 **ubaguruma** baby carriage

奪う **ubau** rob; fascinate

家 **uchi** home; family ◊ I (familiar)

内 **uchi** inside ◊ between

打ち合わせ **uchiawase** prior arrangement; briefing

打ち合わせる **uchiawaseru** make a prior arrangement

内側 **uchigawa** inside

打ち消す **uchikesu** deny

打ち負かす **uchimakasu** defeat

内に **uchi ni** in ◊ while

家の **uchi no** (familiar) my

打ち解ける **uchitokeru** open up (of person)

うちわ **uchiwa** fan (round, made of paper)

内訳 **uchiwake** itemization

有頂天 **uchōten** ecstasy

宇宙 **uchū** universe

宇宙飛行士 **uchū-hikōshi** astronaut

宇宙人 **uchūjin** alien

宇宙船 **uchūsen** spacecraft

腕 **ude** arm

腕時計 **udedokei** wrist watch

腕組みをする **udegumi o suru** fold one's arms

うどん **udon** noodles

上 **ue** top ◊ above; 上に **ue ni** on; on top of; upstairs

飢え **ue** hunger

ウエディングドレス **uedingu-doresu** wedding dress

ウエイター **ueitā** waiter

ウエイトレス **ueitoresu** waitress

飢え死にする **uejini suru** starve to death

植木 **ueki** garden plant; potted plant

植木鉢 **uekibachi** flowerpot

植え込み **uekomi** shrubbery

植える **ueru** plant

飢える **ueru** starve

ウエスト **uesuto** waist

うがいをする **ugai o suru** gargle

動かす **ugokasu** move; drive TECH

動き **ugoki** movement

動く **ugoku** move; operate (of machine)

右派 **uha** right wing

ウイルス **uirusu** virus

ウイスキー **uisukī** whiskey

浮かぶ **ukabu** float
うかがう **ukagau** H call on
う回路 **ukairo** detour
受かる **ukaru** pass *exam*
受け入れる **ukeireru** accept
受ける **ukeru** take *exam, degree*; undergo *surgery*; accept
受取人 **uketorinin** addressee; recipient
受け取る **uketoru** accept; receive
受け継ぐ **uketsugu** inherit
受付 **uketsuke** reception, accept
受け付ける **uketsukeru** accept
雨季, 雨期 **uki** rainy season
浮世絵 **ukiyoe** wood block print
うっかり **ukkari** carelessly
浮く **uku** float
馬 **uma** horse
うまい **umai** delicious; skillful
生まれる **umareru** be born
生まれつき(の) **umaretsuki (no)** inborn
梅 **ume** (Japanese) plum
埋め合せ **umeawase** compensation
梅干し **umeboshi** pickled plum
うめく **umeku** groan
埋める **umeru** bury; fill in *hole*

梅酒 **umeshu** plum liquor
うみ **umi** pus
海 **umi** sea
海辺 **umibe** seaside
羽毛 **umō** feather
生む **umu** yield
産む **umu** bear *children*; lay *eggs*
うん **un** yes
運 **un** luck
うなぎ **unagi** eel
うなる **unaru** growl
うなずく **unazuku** nod
運賃 **unchin** fare
運動 **undō** campaign; exercise
運動場 **undōjō** playing field
運動会 **undōkai** sports meet
運営 **un'ei** management
運河 **unga** canal
うに **uni** sea urchin
うんこ **unko** shit
運行する **unkō suru** run *(of trains etc)*; orbit
運命 **unmei** destiny
運搬する **unpan suru** transport
運送 **unsō** haulage
運送業者 **unsō-gyōsha** movers
運送料 **unsōryō** freight
運転 **unten** driving
運転免許証 **unten-menkyoshō** driver's license
運転手 **untenshu** driver

うんざりした **unzari shita**
fed up

裏 **ura** back; bottom

裏返しに **uragaeshi ni**
inside out

裏切り **uragiri** betrayal

裏切る **uragiru** betray

裏口 **uraguchi** backdoor

恨み **urami** grudge

恨む **uramu** bear a grudge

占い師 **uranaishi** fortune
teller

うらやましい **urayamashī**
enviable ◊ envy

売れる **ureru** sell; be in
demand

熟れる **ureru** ripen

うれしい **ureshī** glad

売り上げ **uriage** takings

売り場 **uriba** department
(of store)

売り切れ **urikire** sold out

売り手 **urite** seller

うろうろする **urouro suru**
hang around

売る **uru** sell

ウール **ūru** wool

うるう年 **urūdoshi** leap year

うるさい **urusai** noisy;
annoying

漆 **urushi** lacquer

うさぎ **usagi** rabbit

牛 **ushi** cow; bull

失う **ushinau** lose

後ろ **ushiro** back (of car, bus)

うそ **uso** lie

うそつき **usotsuki** liar

薄暗い **usugurai** dim

薄い **usui** thin; pale

薄める **usumeru** dilute

薄っぺらい **usupperai**
superficial; flimsy

歌 **uta** song

疑い **utagai** doubt

疑い深い **utagaibukai**
skeptical

疑う **utagau** doubt

疑わしい **utagawashī**
doubtful

うたた寝 **utatane** doze

歌う **utau** sing

うとうとする **utouto suru**
doze off

打つ **utsu** hit; strike (of clock);
type

撃つ **utsu** shoot

うつ病 **utsubyō** depression
MED

美しい **utsukushī** beautiful

美しさ **utsukushisa** beauty

うつむく **utsumuku** hang
one's head

移り変わり **utsurikawari**
transition

うつりやすい **utsuriyasui**
contagious

うつろ（な）**utsuro (na)**
hollow

移る **utsuru** transfer

映る **utsuru** be reflected; be shown *(on a screen)*; suit

うつす **utsusu** transfer

映す **utsusu** project

写す **utsusu** take a photo; copy

訴え **uttae** lawsuit

訴える **uttaeru** bring an action against

うっとりする **uttori suru** go into a trance

うっとうしい **uttōshī** gloomy

上着 **uwagi** coat; jacket

浮気（な）**uwaki (na)** unfaithful

うわさ **uwasa** rumor

敬う **uyamau** respect

右翼 **uyoku** right wing

渦 **uzu** whirlpool; eddy

渦巻 **uzumaki** whirlpool

うずら **uzura** quail

W

わ **wa** bundle ◊ *familiar softening or emphasizing particle used mostly by women*

は **wa** *(subject particle)*: 私は アメリカ人です*watashi wa Amerikajin desu* I'm American

和 **wa** peace; harmony

和… **wa-** Japanese(-style) *(particle)*

輪 **wa** circle; ring

わび **wabi** apology

わび寂び **wabisabi** *restrained quiet beauty of stark simplicity*

わびしい **wabishī** lonely

話題 **wadai** topic

和服 **wafuku** Japanese clothes *(traditional)*

和風（の）**wafū (no)** Japanese(-style)

我が **waga** my; our

わがまま（な）**wagamama (na)** selfish

和菓子 **wagashi** Japanese candy or cake

輪ゴム **wagomu** rubber band

ワゴン車 **wagonsha** station wagon

ワイン **wain** wine

ワインリスト **wainrisuto** wine list

ワイパー **waipā** windshield wiper

わいろ **wairo** bribe

わいせつ（な）**waisetsu (na)** lewd

ワイシャツ **waishatsu** shirt

和歌 **waka** waka *(31-syllable poem)*

若鶏 **wakadori** chicken

若い **wakai** young

和解 **wakai** reconciliation

わかめ **wakame** seaweed

若者 **wakamono** youngster

別れ **wakare** farewell

別れる **wakareru** break up; leave

わかりにくい **wakarinikui** hard to understand

わかりやすい **wakariyasui** clear

わかる **wakaru** understand

沸かす **wakasu** boil; excite

訳，わけ **wake** reason; meaning

分け前 **wakemae** share

分ける **wakeru** divide

わき腹 **wakibara** flank

わき道 **wakimichi** side street

ワックス **wakkusu** wax

沸く **waku** boil; be enthusiastic

枠 **waku** frame

ワクチン **wakuchin** vaccine

惑星 **wakusei** planet

わくわくする **wakuwaku suru** exciting ◊ be thrilled

わめく **wameku** shout; scream

湾 **wan** bay; gulf

わな **wana** trap

ワンピース **wanpīsu** dress

わんわん **wanwan** doggie

わら **wara** straw

笑い **warai** laugh

笑い声 **waraigoe** laughter

笑う **warau** laugh

割れ目 **wareme** split

割れる **wareru** break

我々 **wareware** we

割合 **wariai** proportion

割り当て **wariate** quota

割り当てる **wariateru** allocate

割りばし **waribashi** disposable chopsticks

割引 **waribiki** discount

割り勘にする **warikan ni suru** go Dutch

割増料金 **warimashi-ryōkin** surcharge

わりに **wari ni** rather

割り算 **warizan** division MATH

割る **waru** divide MATH; break; split

悪賢い **warugashikoi** devious

悪い **warui** bad; evil

わさび **wasabi** Japanese horseradish

わし **washi** eagle

和紙 **washi** Japanese paper

和室 **washitsu** Japanese room

和食 **washoku** Japanese cuisine

忘れ物 **wasuremono** item
left behind

忘れっぽい **wasureppoi**
forgetful

忘れる **wasureru** forget

綿 **wata** cotton

私 **watakushi** I *(formal)*

渡る **wataru** cross

私 **watashi** I; me

私達 **watashitachi** we; us

渡す **watasu** hand over

わざと **wazato**
deliberately

わざとらしい **wazatorashī**
artificial

災い **wazawai** calamity

わざわざ **wazawaza**
expressly

わずか(な) **wazuka (na)**
slight

わずかに **wazuka ni** slightly

わずらわしい **wazurawashī**
annoying

ウェブサイト **webusaito**
web site

ウォッカ **wokka** vodka

Y

や **ya** *(particle linking nouns
used as examples)* and; or

矢 **ya** arrow

やばい **yabai** dangerous;
terrible

野蛮(な) **yaban (na)** savage

破れる **yabureru** be ripped;
be broken

敗れる **yabureru** be defeated

破る **yaburu** break; tear up

家賃 **yachin** rent

宿 **yado** inn

野外(の) **yagai (no)** outdoor

やがて **yagate** before long

やぎ **yagi** goat

やはり **yahari** after all

矢印 **yajirushi** arrow

やかましい **yakamashī**
noisy; fastidious

夜間 **yakan** night time

やけど **yakedo** burn

焼ける **yakeru** burn; roast
(of food)

焼き肉 **yakiniku** grilled meat

夜勤する **yakin suru** work
nights

やきとり **yakitori** grilled
chicken on a skewer

焼き尽くす **yakitsukusu**
burn down

やっかい(な) **yakkai (na)**
troublesome

薬局 **yakkyoku** drugstore

焼く **yaku** burn; roast; get a

tan

約 **yaku** roughly

訳 **yaku** translation

役 **yaku** part *(in play, movie)*

薬品 **yakuhin** medicine

役員会 **yakuinkai** board (of directors)

役目 **yakume** role

役人 **yakunin** public servant

役に立つ **yaku ni tatsu** be helpful

役者 **yakusha** actor

役所 **yakusho** government office

約束 **yakusoku** promise; appointment

訳す **yakusu** translate

役割 **yakuwari** role

やくざ **yakuza** gangster

薬剤師 **yakuzaishi** pharmacist

野球 **yakyū** baseball

山 **yama** mountain; guess

やめる **yameru** stop

辞める **yameru** quit

やみ **yami** darkness

やむ **yamu** stop

やむを得ない **yamuoenai** unavoidable

柳 **yanagi** willow tree

屋根 **yane** roof

家主 **yanushi** landlord; landlady

八百屋 **yaoya** greengrocer

やっぱり **yappari** after all

やれやれ **yareyare** thank God!

やり返す **yarikaesu** hit back

やり方 **yarikata** method

やりくりする **yarikuri suru** manage *(financially)*

やり直す **yarinaosu** redo

やり遂げる **yaritogeru** accomplish

やりとり **yaritori** give and take; exchange *(of letters)*

やる **yaru** play; do; give

やる気 **yaruki** energy; enthusiasm

野菜 **yasai** vegetable

やさしい **yasashī** easy

優しい **yasashī** kind; affectionate

野生(の) **yasei (no)** wild

やせる **yaseru** lose weight

やせた **yaseta** skinny

やし **yashi** palm (tree)

野心 **yashin** ambition *pej*

養う **yashinau** bring up; support

安い **yasui** cheap

…やすい **-yasui** easy to

休み **yasumi** rest; vacation

休み時間 **yasumi-jikan** recess *(at school)*

休む **yasumu** rest

安っぽい **yasuppoi** cheap-looking

やすり **yasuri** file

屋台 **yatai** street stall

野党 **yatō** opposition POL

雇う **yatou** employ

やつ **yatsu** fellow, guy

やっと **yatto** finally; barely

八つ **yattsu** eight

和らげる **yawarageru** soften; relieve

和らぐ **yawaragu** soften; moderate

柔らかい **yawarakai** soft

やや **yaya** somewhat

ややこしい **yayakoshii** tricky

よ **yo** (exclamatory particle): 行こうよ **ikō yo** come on, let's go!

夜 **yo** night

世 **yo** world

…よう **-yō** let's

用 **yō** business; use

洋… **yō-** Western(-style)

夜明け **yoake** dawn

曜日 **yōbi** day of the week

呼び出す **yobidasu** page (with pager)

予備校 **yobikō** prep school

呼び戻す **yobimodosu** call back

予防 **yobō** prevention

要望 **yōbō** demand

呼ぶ **yobu** call

余分(な) **yobun (na)** extra

余地 **yochi** room

幼稚園 **yōchien** kindergarten

容態 **yōdai** condition MED

よだれ掛け **yodarekake** bib

溶液 **yōeki** solution

洋服 **yōfuku** clothes (Western)

洋服ダンス **yōfuku-dansu** wardrobe

洋服屋 **yōfukuya** tailor

予言 **yogen** prediction

容疑 **yōgi** suspicion

容疑者 **yōgisha** suspect

用語 **yōgo** term

擁護 **yōgo** defense

汚れ **yogore** dirt

汚れる **yogoreru** stain

汚す **yogosu** make dirty

ヨーグルト **yōguruto** yoghurt

予報 **yohō** weather forecast

余程 **yohodo** very much

よい、良い、善い **yoi** good

酔い **yoi** drunkenness

用意 **yōi** preparations

容易(な) **yōi (na)** simple

幼児 **yōji** infant

用事 **yōji** business

用心 **yōjin** caution

用心棒 **yōjinbō** bodyguard

余暇 **yoka** leisure time

八日 **yōka** eight days; the 8th

予感 **yokan** premonition

余計(な) **yokei (na)** superfluous

用件 **yōken** business

よければ **yokereba** if you like

よける **yokeru** avoid

予期 **yoki** expectation

容器 **yōki** container

預金 **yokin** deposit

陽気(な) **yōki (na)** cheerful

四日 **yokka** four days; the 4th

欲求不満 **yokkyū-fuman** frustration

横 **yoko** side

横顔 **yokogao** profile *(of face)*

横切る **yokogiru** cross

予告 **yokoku** warning

ようこそ **yōkoso** welcome!

横綱 **yokozuna** grand champion

よく **yoku** often; well

欲 **yoku** appetite

翌朝 **yokuasa** the following morning

欲望 **yokubō** desire

翌日 **yokujitsu** the following day

良くない **yoku nai** not good

翌年 **yokunen** the following year

抑制 **yokusei** control

浴室 **yokushitsu** bathroom

翌週 **yokushū** the following week

浴槽 **yokusō** bathtub

要求 **yōkyū** demand

嫁 **yome** daughter-in-law

よみがえる **yomigaeru** come back to life

読み物 **yomimono** reading matter

読みにくい **yominikui** difficult to read

読みやすい **yomiyasui** easy to read

読む **yomu** read

四 **yon** four

よう(な) **yō (na)**: …のよう(な) ... **no yō (na)** such as

夜中 **yonaka** middle of the night

…ように … **yō ni** as

四十 **yonjū** forty

酔っ払った **yopparatta** drunk

酔っ払う **yopparau** get drunk

余程 **yoppodo** very much

よれよれ(の) **yoreyore (no)** shabby

喜ばす **yorokobasu** please

喜び **yorokobi** pleasure

喜ぶ **yorokobu** be pleased

喜んで **yorokonde** with pleasure

よろめく **yoromeku** stagger

ヨーロッパ **Yōroppa** Europe

よろしい **yoroshī** good

よろしく **yoroshiku** please do; はじめましてどうぞよろしくお願いします *hajimemashite, dōzo yoroshiku onegai shimasu* hello, how do you do?; 彼女によろしく *kanojo ni yoroshiku* give her my best wishes

よる **yoru** according to ◊ be based on

夜 **yoru** night

要領 **yōryō** main point

予算 **yosan** budget

要請 **yōsei** request

陽性(の) **yōsei (no)** positive *medical test*

よし **yoshi** OK; all right

養子 **yōshi** adopted child

用紙 **yōshi** form *(document)*

様式 **yōshiki** mode; pattern

洋室 **yōshitsu** Western-style room

養殖 **yōshoku** cultivation

よそ **yoso** other *(person, place)*; out-group

要素 **yōso** element

予想 **yosō** expectation

様子 **yōsu** appearance

要するに **yō suru ni** in short

予定 **yotei** plan

要点 **yōten** main point

与党 **yotō** ruling party

よって **yotte**: …によって …

ni yotte with; according to

ヨット **yotto** yacht

四つ **yottsu** four

酔う **you** get drunk; get sick

弱い **yowai** weak

弱める **yowameru** weaken

弱虫 **yowamushi** wimp

弱る **yowaru** weaken

弱さ **yowasa** weakness

弱々しい **yowayowashī** feeble

予約 **yoyaku** reservation

ようやく **yōyaku** finally; barely

要約 **yōyaku** summary

余裕 **yoyū** leeway

湯 **yu** hot water

優 **yū** grade A

ゆうべ **yūbe** last night

雄弁(な) **yūben (na)** eloquent

指 **yubi** finger

郵便 **yūbin** mail

郵便番号 **yūbin-bangō** zip code

郵便局 **yūbinkyoku** post office

指先 **yubisaki** fingertip

指輪 **yubiwa** ring

有望(な) **yūbō (na)** promising

雄大(な) **yūdai (na)** grand

油断する **yudan suru** be careless

ユダヤ(の) Yudaya (no) Jewish

ゆでる yuderu boil

湯豆腐 yudōfu hot bean curd

有毒(な) yūdoku (na) poisonous

有益(な) yūeki (na) beneficial

遊園地 yūenchi amusement park

裕福(な) yūfuku (na) wealthy

有害(な) yūgai (na) harmful

優雅(な) yūga (na) elegant

夕方 yūgata evening

湯気 yuge steam

夕暮れ yūgure twilight

夕飯 yūhan dinner

夕日 yūhi setting sun

遊歩道 yūhodō walk

遺言 yuigon will JUR

友人 yūjin friend

友情 yūjō friendship

優柔不断(の) yūjū-fudan (no) indecisive

床 yuka floor (of room)

誘拐 yūkai kidnapping

愉快(な) yukai (na) pleasant

夕刊 yūkan evening paper

勇敢(な) yūkan (na) brave

浴衣 yukata summer kimono

輸血 yuketsu blood transfusion

雪 yuki snow

行き yuki bound for

勇気 yūki courage

雪だるま yukidaruma snowman

ゆっくり yukkuri slowly; at leisure

有効期限 yūkō-kigen expiry date

有効(な) yūkō (na) valid

友好的(な) yūkōteki (na) friendly

行方不明である yukue-fumei de aru be missing

夢 yume dream

有名人 yūmeijin celebrity

有名(な) yūmei (na) famous

弓 yumi bow MUS

ユーモア yūmoa humor

ユニーク(な) yunīku (na) unique

有能(な) yūnō (na) capable

由来する yurai suru be derived from

揺れ yure shake

幽霊 yūrei ghost

揺れる yureru shake; sway

ゆり yuri lily

有利(な) yūri (na) advantageous

ユーロ yūro euro FIN

揺るがす yurugasu shake; shock

緩い yurui loose

緩める yurumeru loosen

許し **yurushi** forgiveness

許す **yurusu** allow; forgive

有料 **yūryō** fee

有力(な) **yūryoku (na)** powerful

優良(な) **yūryō (na)** high-grade

優勢(な) **yūsei (na)** superior; dominant

優先権 **yūsenken** right of way

優先(の) **yūsen (no)** preferential

融資 **yūshi** financing

優勝 **yūshō** first prize

夕食 **yūshoku** dinner

優秀(な) **yūshū (na)** brilliant

輸出 **yushutsu** export

輸出禁止 **yushutsu-kinshi** export ban

輸送 **yusō** transport

郵送 **yūsō** mailing

郵送料 **yūsōryō** postage

ユースホステル **yūsu-hosuteru** youth hostel

ゆする **yusuru** extort

豊か(な) **yutaka (na)** rich

Uターン **yū-tān** U-turn

ゆとり **yutori** space

ゆったりした **yuttari shita** leisurely; loose *clothes*

憂うつ(な) **yūutsu (na)** gloomy

誘惑 **yūwaku** temptation

有罪(の) **yūzai (no)** guilty JUR

譲る **yuzuru** yield; sell

Z

ざぶとん **zabuton** (floor) cushion

財団 **zaidan** foundation *(organization)*

在庫 **zaiko** stock

材木 **zaimoku** lumber

材料 **zairyō** ingredient

財産 **zaisan** assets

財政 **zaisei** finance

財政上(の) **zaiseijō (no)** financial

残高 **zandaka** balance *(of*

bank account)

残がい **zangai** wreckage

残業 **zangyō** overtime

残酷(な) **zankoku (na)** cruel

残念(な) **zannen (na)** unfortunate

残念ながら **zannen-nagara** unfortunately

残忍(な) **zannin (na)** brutal

暫定的(な) **zanteiteki (na)** provisional

ざらざらした **zarazara**

shita rough; gritty

座席 zaseki seat

ざ折する zasetsu suru fall through

雑誌 zasshi magazine

雑種 zasshu hybrid

雑草 zassō weed

雑談 zatsudan chat

雑音 zatsuon interference

ざっと zatto briefly

雑踏 zattō hustle and bustle

座禅 zazen Zen meditation

ぜ ze *(familiar exclamatory particle used mostly by men)*: やろうぜ *yarō ze* let's do it!

ぜひ zehi by all means

税 zei duty *(on goods)*

税引き後 zeibikigo after tax

税関 zeikan customs

税関審査 zeikan-shinsa customs inspection

税金 zeikin tax

税込み zeikomi including tax

税務署 zeimusho tax office

ぜいたく（な）zeitaku (na) luxurious

絶交する zekkō suru sever relations

禅 Zen Zen

善 zen good

全… zen- *(prefix)* the whole

前… zen- *(prefix)* previous

全部 zenbu all

前部 zenbu front

全部で zenbu de altogether

前代未聞（の）zendai-mimon (no) unheard-of

前後 zengo around

前半 zenhan first half

善意 zen'i goodwill

全員 zen'in everybody

全国 zenkoku entire country

前任者 zenninsha predecessor *(in job)*

全般的（な）zenpanteki (na) overall

前例 zenrei precedent

前略 zenryaku hi there *(at start of informal letters)*

全力 zenryoku with all one's might

前菜 zensai appetizer

前線 zensen weather front

前者 zensha the former

全身 zenshin the whole body

前進する zenshin suru advance

禅宗 Zenshū Zen Buddhism

ぜんそく zensoku asthma

全体 zentai whole

前提 zentei premise

前夜 zen'ya eve

全然 zenzen not at all

絶版で zeppan de out of print

ゼロ zero zero

絶望 zetsubō despair

絶望的（な）zetsubōteki (na) desperate

絶縁 **zetsuen** breaking off relations; insulation ELEC

絶滅 **zetsumetsu** extinction

絶対 **zettai** absolutely

絶対的(な) **zettaiteki (na)** absolute

ぞ **zo** *(exclamatory particle used by men)*: 無理だぞ **muri da zo** it's impossible!

象 **zō** elephant

像 **zō** statue

増大 **zōdai** increase

象牙 **zōge** ivory

増加 **zōka** increase

ぞうきん **zōkin** rag

俗語 **zokugo** slang

属する **zoku suru** belong

続々 **zokuzoku** successively

ぞくぞくする **zokuzoku suru** be excited; have the shivers

雑煮 **zōni** rice cake soup

存じる **zonjiru** H know; think

ぞんざい(な) **zonzai (na)** rude; slipshod

ぞうり **zōri** Japanese sandals

造船 **zōsen** shipbuilding

ぞっとさせる **zotto saseru** give the creeps

図 **zu** drawing

ズボン **zubon** pants

ずぶぬれ(の) **zubunure (no)** dripping wet

図太い **zubutoi** impudent

頭がい骨 **zugaikotsu** skull

図表 **zuhyō** chart

ずいぶん **zuibun** very

随筆 **zuihitsu** essay

図面 **zumen** plan *(drawing)*

頭脳 **zunō** brains

…づらい **-zurai** difficult to

ずらす **zurasu** shift; stagger *breaks etc*

ずれ **zure** difference; gap *(in the market)*

ずれる **zureru** be shifted; be postponed

ずるい **zurui** sly

ずさん(な) **zusan (na)** slipshod

…ずつ **-zutsu** each

頭痛 **zutsū** headache

ずっと **zutto** all the time

ずうずうしい **zūzūshī** fresh; nervy

English – Japanese

A

a, an *(no translation)*: *a cat* neko 猫

abandon suteru 捨てる; *person* misuteru 見捨てる; *plan* chūshi suru 中止する

abbreviation shōryakukei 省略形

ability nōryoku 能力

able *(skillful)* yūnō (na) 有能(な); *be ~ to ...* koto ga dekiru …ことができる

abolish haishi suru 廃止する

abortion ninshin-chūzetsu 妊娠中絶

about 1 *prep (concerning)* … ni tsuite (no) …について (の); *what's it ~?* *(book etc)* nani ni tsuite desu ka 何について ですか **2** *adv (roughly: number)* … gurai …ぐら い; *(time)* … goro …頃; *be ~ to ...* tokoro desu …と ころです

above 1 *prep* … no ue (ni) …の上(に); *(more than)* … ijō (de) …以上(で) **2** *adv* ue ni 上に

abroad *live* gaikoku de 外国

で; *go* gaikoku e 外国へ

abrupt *departure* totsuzen (no) 突然(の)

absent *adj (from school)* kesseki (no) 欠席(の); *(from work)* kekkin (no) 欠勤(の)

absent-minded bon'yari shita ぼんやりした

absolutely *(completely)* hontō ni 本当に

absorb kyūshū suru 吸収する

abstain *(from voting)* kiken suru 棄権する

abstract *adj* chūshōteki (na) 抽象的(な); *art* chūshōha (no) 抽象派(の)

absurd bakageta ばかげた

abuse *n (insults)* nonoshiri の のしり; *(of child)* gyakutai 虐待

academic 1 *n* gakusha 学者 **2** *adj* gakumonteki (na) 学問的(な)

academy gakkō 学校

accelerate 1 *v/i* kasoku suru 加速する **2** *v/t production* no supīdo o ageru …のスピ ードを上げる

accent *(when speaking)* namari なまり

acceptable konomashī 好ましい

acceptance shōdaku 承諾

access code COMPUT akusesu kōdo アクセスコード

accident jiko 事故; **by ~** gūzen ni 偶然に

accommodations shukuhaku-setsubi 宿泊設備

accompany ... ni tsuite iku ...について行く; MUS bansō o suru 伴奏をする

accomplice kyōhansha 共犯者

accomplish *task* kanryō suru 完了する

according: ~ to ... ni yoru to ...によると

account *n* kōza 口座; *(report)* hōkoku 報告

accountant kaikeishi 会計士

accounts kaikei 会計

accumulate 1 *v/t* tameru ためる **2** *v/i* tamaru たまる

accuracy seikakusa 正確さ

accurate seikaku (na) 正確(な)

accusation hinan 非難

accuse hinan suru 非難する; be ~d of ... JUR ... de kokuso sarete iru ...で告訴されている

ace *(cards, tennis)* ēsu エース

ache *v/i* itamu 痛む

achieve tassei suru 達成する

achievement tassei 達成; *(thing achieved)* gyōseki 業績

acid *n* san 酸

acknowledge mitomeru 認める

acknowledg(e)ment shōnin 承認

acquaintance *(person)* shirai 知り合い

acquire *knowledge* mi ni tsukeru 身に付ける; *property* shutoku suru 取得する

acrobat akurobatto アクロバット

across 1 *prep (on other side of)* ... no mukōgawa ni ...の向こう側に; *(to other side of)* ... o ōdan shite ...を横断して **2** *adv (to other side)* mukōgawa e 向こう側へ

act 1 *v/i* THEAT enjiru 演じる; **~ as** ... o shite tsutomeru ...として務める **2** *n (deed)* kōi 行為; *(of play)* maku 幕; *(in vaudeville)* dashimono 出し物

acting 1 *n* engi 演技 **2** *adj (temporary)* dairi (no) 代理(の)

action kōi 行為; *(in movie)* jiken 事件; **be out of ~** ugokanai 動かない

active katsudōteki (na) 活動的(な); GRAM nōdō (no) 能動(の)

activity katsudō 活動; *(economic etc)* ugoki 動き

actor haiyū 俳優

actress joyū 女優

actual jissai (no) 実際(の)

acupuncture harichiryō ハリ治療

acute *pain* hageshī 激しい

adapt 1 *v/t (for TV etc)* kyakushoku suru 脚色する; *machine* kaizō suru 改造する 2 *v/i (of person)* tekiō suru 適応する

adapter ELEC adaputā アダプター

add *v/t* gōkei suru 合計する; *sugar* kuwaeru 加える

addict *n* chūdokusha 中毒者

addiction *(to drugs etc)* chūdoku 中毒

addition tashizan 足し算; *(to list)* tsuika 追加

additional tsuika (no) 追加(の)

additive tenkabutsu 添加物

address 1 *n* jūsho 住所; *form of ~* keishō 敬称 2 *v/t letter* … ni atena o kaku …に宛名を書く

address book adoresuchō アドレス帳

adequate jūbun (na) 十分(な)

adhesive setchakuzai 接着剤

adjourn *v/i (of court)* kyūtei suru 休廷する; *(of meeting)* kyūkai suru 休会する

adjust *v/t* chōsetsu suru 調節する

administration *(of company)* keiei 経営; *(of country)* gyōsei 行政

administrative keiei (no) 経営(の); *(in government)* gyōsei (no) 行政(の)

admiration kanshin 感心

admire kanshin suru 感心する

admirer sūhaisha 崇拝者

admission *(confession)* kokuhaku 告白; *~ free* nyūjō-muryō 入場無料

admit *(to a place)* nyūjō saseru 入場させる; *(to hospital)* nyūin saseru 入院させる; *(confess)* jihaku suru 自白する

adolescent *n* jūdai 十代

adopt *child* yōshi ni suru 養子にする; *plan* saiyō suru 採用する

adult 1 *n* otona 大人 2 *adj* otona (no) 大人(の)

adultery furin 不倫

advance *(money)* maekin 前金; *(in science etc)* shinpo 進

歩; MIL shingun 進軍; in ~ maemotte 前もって

advanced country senshin (no) 先進(の); level jōkyū (no) 上級(の)

adventure bōken 冒険

advertise kōkoku suru 広告する

advertisement kōkoku 広告

advice adobaisu アドバイス

advisable nozomashī 望ましい

advise person ... ni chūkoku suru ...に忠告する; ~ X to ... X ni ...suru yō susumeru Xに...するよう勧める

adviser sōdan'yaku 相談役; (to company) komon 顧問

aerobics earobikusu エアロビクス

affair (matter) koto こと; (business) shigoto 仕事; (love) jōji 情事

affect MED okasu 冒す; (influence, concern) ... ni eikyō o oyobosu ...に影響を及ぼす

affection aijō 愛情

affectionate yasashī 優しい

afford (financially) suru yoyū ga aru する余裕がある

afraid: be ~ kowagaru 怖がる; be ~ of ... o kowagaru ...を

怖がる

Africa Afurika アフリカ

African 1 adj Afurika (no) アフリカ(の) 2 n Afurikajin アフリカ人

after 1 prep (in order) ... no tsugi ni ...の次に; (in position) ... no ushiro ni ...の後ろに; (in time) ... no ato de ...の後で; ~ all kekkyoku 結局; it's ten ~ two niji juppun sugi desu 二時十分過ぎです 2 adv ato ni 後で

afternoon gogo 午後

aftershave afuta-shēbu アフターシェーブ

afterward ato de 後で

again mō ichido もう一度

against (lean etc ~ person) ... ni yorikakatte ...に寄り掛かって; (~ thing) ... ni tatekakete ...に立て掛けて; America ~ Brazil SPORTS Amerika tai Burajiru アメリカ対ブラジル

age n nenrei 年齢; (era) jidai 時代

agency dairiten 代理店

agenda gidai 議題

agent dairinin 代理人

aggressive kōgekiteki (na) 攻撃的(な)

agitated dōyō shita 動揺した

ago: 2 days ~ futsuka-mae 二

日前; **long** ~ zutto mae ni ず
っと前に

agony kumon 苦もん

agree v/i sansei suru 賛成す
る; (of figures) itchi suru 一
致する

agreement dōi 同意;
(contract) keiyaku 契約

agriculture nōgyō 農業

ahead: be ~ of … ni katte iru
…に勝っている

Aids eizu エイズ

aim 1 n nerai ねらい;
(objective) mokuteki 目的
2 v/i nerau ねらう; ~ **to
do** … suru tsumori de aru
…するつもりである

air n kūki 空気; **by ~** travel
hikōki de 飛行機で; **send**
kōkūbin de 航空便で

air-conditioned eakon-tsuki
(no) エアコン付き(の)

airline kōkū-gaisha 航空会社

airplane hikōki 飛行機

airport kūkō 空港

aisle seat tsūrogawa no seki 通
路側の席

alarm n keihō 警報

alarm clock mezamashi-dokei
目覚まし時計

album arubamu アルバム

alcohol arukōru アルコール;
(alcoholic drink) sake 酒

alcoholic 1 n arukōru-chūdoku-

kanja アルコール中毒患者
2 adj arukōru-iri (no) アルコ
ール入り(の)

alert adj yōjin-bukai 用心深い

alibi aribai アリバイ

alien (n gaikokujin 外国人;
(from space) uchūjin 宇宙人

alike adj: **be ~** nite iru 似
ている

alimony rikon-teate 離婚手当

alive: be ~ ikite iru 生きて
いる

all 1 adj subete (no) すべて
(の); ~ **the time** zutto ずっ
と **2** pron zenbu 全部, mina
皆; ~ **of us** watashitachi wa
mina 私達は皆; **that's ~,
thanks** kore dake desu これ
だけです **3** adv: **not at ~**
zenzen 全然; **two ~** (in score)
ni-tai-ni no dōten 二対二
の同点

allergic: be ~ to … … ni
arerugī ga aru …にアレルギ
ーがある

allergy arerugī アレルギー

almond āmondo アーモンド

allegation shuchō 主張; JUR
mōshitate 申し立て

alleviate keigen suru 軽減
する

alliance dōmei 同盟

alligator arigētā アリゲー
ター

allow yurusu 許す; *(of person in authority)* kyoka suru 許可する

allowance *(money)* teate 手当; *(to child)* kozukai 小遣い

all-wheel drive zenrin-kudō 全輪駆動

ally *n* mikata 味方

almost hotondo ほとんど ◇ *(negative consequences)* ayauku あやうく; *he was ~ killed* kare wa ayauku korosareru tokoro datta 彼はあやうく殺されるところだった

alone hitori de ひとりで

along 1 *prep (moving forward)* tōtte 通って; *(situated beside)* … ni sotte …に沿って **2** *adv: ~ with* … to issho ni …と一緒に

aloud koe o dashite 声を出して

alphabet arufabetto アルファベット

already sude ni すでに

alright: *that's ~ (doesn't matter)* sore de kamaimasen それで構いません; *(after thank you)* dō itashimashite どう致しまして; *(quite good)* nakanaka ī desu なかなかいいです; *I'm ~ (not hurt)* daijōbu 大丈夫

also … mo …も

alter *v/t* kaeru 変える

alteration henkō 変更; *(to clothes)* sunpō-naoshi 寸法直し

alternate 2 *adj* hitotsu-oki (no) 一つ置きの(の); *plan* kawari (no) 代わり(の)

alternative *n* kawari no hōhō 代わりの方法; *(choice)* sentakushi 選択肢 **2** *adj* kawari (no) 代わり(の)

alternatively sono kawari ni その代わりに

although … no ni …のに

altitude *(of plane)* kōdo 高度; *(of mountain)* hyōkō 標高; *(of city)* kaibatsu 海抜

altogether *(completely)* mattaku まったく; *(in all)* zenbu de 全部で

aluminum aruminiumu アルミニウム

always itsumo いつも

amateur *n* shirōto 素人; SPORTS amachua アマチュア

amaze gyōten saseru 仰天させる

amazement gyōten 仰天

amazing odoroku beki 驚くべき; *(very good)* subarashī 素晴らしい

ambassador taishi 大使

ambiguous aimai (na) あい まい(な)

ambition yume 夢

ambitious yashinteki (na) 野 心的(な); *plan* ōgakari (na) 大がかり(な)

ambulance kyūkyūsha 救 急車

amendment shūsei 修正

amends: *make* ~ tsugunau 償う

America Amerika アメリカ

American 1 *adj* Amerika (no) アメリカ(の) **2** *n* Amerikajin アメリカ人

ammunition dan'yaku 弾薬

amnesty onsha 恩赦

among(st) ... ni kakomarete …に囲まれて

amount ryō 量; *(of money)* gaku 額

♦**amount to** sōkei ... ni naru 総計…になる

amplifier anpu アンプ

amputate setsudan suru 切 断する

amuse *(make laugh etc)* warawaseru 笑わせる; *(entertain)* tanoshimaseru 楽 しませる

amusement *(merriment)* tanoshimi 楽しみ; *(entertainment)* kibarashi 気 晴らし

amusing omoshiroi おも しろい

analysis bunseki 分析

analyze bunseki suru 分析 する

anarchy muchitsujo 無秩序

anatomy kaibōgaku 解剖学

ancestor sosen 祖先

ancient *adj* kodai (no) 古代(の)

and ◊ *(with nouns)* ... to …と ◊ *(with verbs)* shi し ◊ *(with adjectives)* ...te …て ◊ *(and then)* soshite そして ◊ *(two things at the same time)* ...tari ...tari; *we ate − talked* tabetari hanashitari shita 食べたり話 したりした

anemic: *be − MED* hinketsu de aru 貧血である

anesthetic *n* masui 麻酔

anger *n* ikari 怒り

angle *n* kakudo 角度

angry okotta 怒った; *get −* okoru 怒る

animal dōbutsu 動物

animated cartoon anime-eiga アニメ映画

animosity teki-i 敵意

ankle ashikubi 足首

annex *n (building)* bekkan 別館

anniversary kinenbi 記念日; *wedding −* kekkon-kinenbi 結 婚記念日

announce happyō suru 発
表する

announcement happyō 発
表; *(at airport)* anaunsu アナ
ウンス

announcer RADIO, TV anaunsā
アナウンサー

annoy iraira saseru いらいら
させる; **be ~ed** mutto suru
むっとする

annual *adj (once a year)* reinen
(no) 例年(の); *(of a year)*
ichinenkan (no) 一年間(の)

anonymous tokumei (no) 匿
名(の)

another 1 *adj (different)* betsu
(no) 別(の); *(additional
thing)* mō hitotsu (no) もう一
つ(の); *(person)* mō
hitori (no) もう一人(の)
2 *pron (different one)* hoka no
mono 他のもの; *(additional
one)* mō hitotsu もう一つ;
(person) mō hitori もう一人;
one ~ o-tagai ni お互いに

answer 1 *n (to letter)* henji 返
事; *(to problem)* kaiketsu 解
決; *(to question)* kotae 答え **2**
v/t … ni henji o suru …に返
事をする

answerphone rusuban-denwa
留守番電話

ant ari あり

antenna TV antena アンテナ

antibiotic *n* kōsei-busshitsu 抗
生物質

anticipate yosō suru 予想する

antidote gedokuzai 解毒剤

antique dealer kottōya 骨
とう屋

antisocial hanshakaiteki (na)
反社会的(な)

antivirus program uirusu-
chekkā ウイルスチェッカー

anxiety shinpai 心配

anxious shinpai shite 心配
して

any 1 *adj* ◊ *(usually not
translated)*: *is there ~ bread?*
pan wa arimasu ka パンはあ
りますか; ◊ *(with abstracts)*
nanika 何か; *is there ~
improvement?* nanika kaizen
saremashita ka 何か改善さ
れましたか ◊ *(emphatic)*:
haven't you ~ idea (at all)?
zenzen omoi-atarimasen ka 全
然思い当たりませんか
2 *pron* ◊ *(usually not
translated)*: *do you have ~?*
motte imasu ka 持ってい
ますか

anybody dareka 誰か; *(with
negatives)* dare mo 誰も; *(in
statements, emphatic)* dare
demo 誰でも

anyhow *(regardless)* tonikaku
とにかく

anyone → *anybody*

anything nanika 何か; *(with negatives)* nani mo 何も; *(in statements, emphatic)* nan demo 何でも

anyway → *anyhow*

anywhere dokoka de どこか で; *(with negatives)* doko ni mo どこにも; *(in statements, emphatic)* doko demo ど こでも

apart hanarete 離れて; *live ~* bekkyo shite iru 別居し ている

apartment apāto アパート

apartment block apāto ア パート

apologize ayamaru 謝る

apology shazai 謝罪

apparently rashī らしい

appeal n *(charm)* miryoku 魅 力; *(for funds etc)* apīru アピ ール; JUR jōso 上訴

appear arawareru 現れる; *(of new product)* tōjō suru 登場 する; *(look, seem)* … no yō ni mieru …のように見える

appearance *(look)* gaiken 外見

appendicitis mōchōen 盲腸炎

appetite shokuyoku 食欲; *fig* yoku 欲

applaud v/i hakushu suru 拍 手する

applause hakushu 拍手

apple ringo りんご

appliance kigu 器具; *(household)* denka-seihin 電 化製品

applicant ōbosha 応募者

application *(for job etc)* ōbo 応 募; *(for university)* shutsugan 出願

apply 1 v/t tekiyō suru 適用す る 2 v/i *(of rule)* tekiyō sareru 適用される

♦ apply for *job* … ni ōbo suru …に応募する; *passport* shinsei suru 申請する; *university* … ni shutsugan suru …に出願する

appoint *(to position)* ninmei suru 任命する

appointment *(meeting)* yakusoku 約束; *(at hairdresser etc)* yoyaku 予約; *(to position)* ninmei 任命

appreciate 1 v/t *(value)* hyōka suru 評価する; *(be grateful for)* arigataku omou ありがた く思う 2 v/i FIN neagari suru 値上がりする

apprehensive shinpai shite iru 心配している

apprentice minarai 見習い

approach n sekkin 接近; *(offer etc)* apurōchi アプロー チ 2 v/t … ni chikazuku …に 近づく

appropriate *adj* tekisetsu (na) 適切(な)

approve 1 *v/i* sansei suru 賛成する **2** *v/t* ... ni sansei suru ...に賛成する

approximate *adj* ōyoso (no) おおよそ(の)

apricot anzu あんず

April shigatsu 四月

aquarium suizokukan 水族館

Arab 1 *adj* Arabu (no) アラブ(の) **2** *n* Arabujin アラブ人

archeologist kōkogakusha 考古学者

archeology kōkogaku 考古学

architect kenchikuka 建築家

architecture kenchiku 建築

archives kōbunsho-hozonjo 公文書保存所

area *(region)* chi-iki 地域; *(part)* han'i 範囲; *(of activity)* bun'ya 分野; *(square meters etc)* menseki 面積

area code TEL shigai-kyokuban 市外局番

argue *v/i* kenka suru けんかする; *(reason)* giron suru 議論する

argument kenka けんか; *(reasoning)* giron 議論

arise *(of situation)* okoru おこる

arithmetic sansū 算数

arm *n* ude 腕; *(of chair)*

hijikake ひじ掛け

armchair hijikake-isu ひじ掛け椅子

armed busō shita 武装した

armed forces guntai 軍隊

armed robbery busō-gōtō 武装強盗

aroma kaori 香り

arms *(weapons)* buki 武器

army rikugun 陸軍

around 1 *prep (in circle)* ... no mawari ni ...の回りに; *(roughly)* oyoso ... およそ...; *(with time)* ... goro ...ごろ **2** *adv (in the area)* chikaku ni 近くに; *(encircling)* mawari ni 回りに; *walk* ~ burabura aruku ぶらぶら歩く

arouse yobiokosu 呼び起こす; *(sexually)* shigeki suru 刺激する

arrange *(put in order)* seiton suru 整とんする; *furniture* haichi suru 配置する; *flowers* ikeru 生ける; *meeting* junbi suru 準備する; *time, place* kimeru 決める

arrangement *(plan)* yotei 予定; *(agreement)* yakusoku 約束; *(of furniture etc)* haichi 配置; *(of flowers)* ikebana 生け花

arrest 1 *n* taiho 逮捕 **2** *v/t* taiho suru 逮捕する

arrival tōchaku 到着; **~s** *(at airport)* tōchaku-robī 到着ロビー

arrive tsuku 着く

arrogance gōman 傲慢

arrogant gōman (na) 傲慢 (な)

art geijutsu 芸術

artery MED dōmyaku 動脈

art gallery bijutsukan 美術館; *(private)* garō 画廊

article buppin 物品; *(in newspaper)* kiji 記事

artificial jinkō (no) 人工の); *(not sincere)* wazato rashī わざとらしい

artist gaka 画家

artistic geijutsuteki (na) 芸術的(な)

as 1 *conj (while)* (shi)nagara (し)ながら ◊ *(because)* ... no de ...ので ◊ *(like)* ... yō ni ...ように; **~ usual** itsumo no yō ni いつものように **2** *adv* onaji kurai 同じくらい; **~ high** ... to onaji kurai takai ...と同じくらい高い **3** *prep (in capacity of)* ... to shite ...として; *(when)* ... no toki ni ...のときに

ashamed hazukashī 恥ずかしい; **be ~ of** ... o hazukashiku omou ...を恥ずかしく思う

ashore: go ~ jōriku suru 上陸する

ashtray haizara 灰皿

Asia Ajia アジア

Asian 1 *adj* Ajia (no) アジア (の) **2** *n* Ajiajin アジア人

aside waki ni わきに; **~ from** ... o nozoite ...を除いて

ask 1 *v/t (put question to)* kiku 聞く; *(inquire)* tazuneru 尋ねる; *(invite)* shōtai suru 招待する; *favor* tanomu 頼む; **~ a question** shitsumon suru 質問する **2** *v/i* tazuneru 尋ねる

◆**ask for** motomeru 求める; *person* yobidasu 呼び出す

◆**ask out** sasou 誘う

asleep: be ~ nemutte iru 眠っている; **fall ~** nemuru 眠る

aspect *(angle)* men 面

aspirin asupirin アスピリン

assassinate ansatsu suru 暗殺する

assault *n* bōkō 暴行

assemble 1 *v/t parts* kumitateru 組み立てる **2** *v/i (of people)* atsumaru 集まる

assembly *(of parts)* kumitate 組み立て; POL gikai 議会

assertive *person* gōin (na) 強引(な)

assess *situation* satei suru 査定する; *value* hyōka suru 評価する

asset FIN shisan 資産; fig zaisan 財産

assignment (task, study) kadai 課題

assist joryoku suru 助力する

assistant joshu 助手; (of minister etc) hosakan 補佐官

associate 1 v/t: be ~ed with (organization) … to kankei shite iru …と関係している **2** v/i: ~ with … to kōsai suru …と交際する **3** n dōryō 同僚

association kyōkai 協会; in ~ with … to kyōdō shite …と共同して

assume (suppose) … to kangaeru …と考える

assumption katei 仮定

assurance hoshō 保証; (confidence) kakushin 確信

assure (reassure) … ni hoshō suru …に保証する

asthma zensoku ぜんそく

astonish: be ~ed odoroku 驚く

astonishing odoroku hodo (no) 驚くほど(の)

astonishment odoroki 驚き

astrology senseijutsu 占星術

astronaut uchū-hikōshi 宇宙飛行士

astronomical tenmongaku (no) 天文学(の)

asylum POL hinansho 避難所

at ◊ (place) (with verbs of being) … ni …に; (with verbs of activity) … de …で; ~ Joe's Jō no tokoro de ジョーのところで ◊: ~ 10 dollars jū doru de 十ドルで ◊: ~ 5 o'clock goji ni 五時に; ◊: be good ~ … ga tokui de aru …が得意である

atheist mushinron-ja 無神論者

athlete supōtsu-senshu スポーツ選手

athletics undō-kyōgi 運動競技

Atlantic n Taiseiyō 大西洋

ATM (= automated teller machine) ATM (always in rōmaji)

atmosphere taiki 大気; (ambiance) fun'iki 雰囲気

atomic energy genshiryoku 原子力

atrocity zangyaku-kōi 残虐行為

attach toritsukeru 取り付ける

attachment (to e-mail) tenpu fairu 添付ファイル

attack 1 n shūgeki 襲撃; MIL kōgeki 攻撃; (verbal) hinan 非難 **2** v/t osou 襲う; MIL kōgeki suru 攻撃する; (verbally) hinan suru 非難する

attempt 1 *n* kokoromi 試み
2 *v/t* kokoromiru 試みる

attend ... ni shusseki suru
...に出席する

attendance shusseki 出席

attention chūi 注意; **pay ~**
chūi o harau 注意を払う

attitude taido 態度

attorney bengoshi 弁護士

attract hikitsukeru 引き付ける

attraction (*charm*) miryoku 魅
力; (*of city*) yobimono 呼び物

attractive miryokuteki (na) 魅
力的(な)

audible kikoeru 聞こえる

audience chōshū 聴衆; (*in
theater etc*) kankyaku 観客;
(*of TV program*) shichōsha
視聴者

audiovisual shichōkaku (no)
視聴覚(の)

audition *n* ōdishon オーディ
ション

auditor kaikei-kansakan 会計
監査人

August hachigatsu 八月

aunt (*own*) o-ba おば; (*sb
else's*) o-basan おばさん

Australia Ōsutoraria オース
トラリア

Australian *n* Ōsutoraria
(no) オーストラリア(の)
2 *n* Ōsutorariajin オースト
ラリア人

authentic honmono (no) 本
物(の)

author sakusha 作者; (*of text*)
chosha 著者

authority (*of officials*) kengen
権限; (*of parent, teacher*)
ken'i 権威; **the authorities**
tōkyoku 当局

authorize ninka suru 認可する

auto *n* jidōsha 自動車

autobiography jijoden 自
叙伝

automate jidōka suru 自動
化する

automatic *adj* jidō (no) 自
動(の)

automatically jidōteki ni 自
動的に

automobile jidōsha 自動車

available *service* riyō dekiru 利
用できる; *book* te ni irerareru
手に入れられる

avenue ōdōri 大通り

average 1 *adj* heikinteki (na)
平均的(な); (*ordinary*) nami
(no) 並(の) **2** *n* heikin 平均

avoid sakeru 避ける

awake *adj* me ga samete 目
が覚めて

award 1 *n* (*prize*) shō 賞 **2** *v/t*
ataeru 与える

aware: **be ~ of** ... ni ki ga
tsuite iru ...に気が付い
ている

awareness ninshiki 認識; *(knowledge)* ishiki 意識

away: **be ~** *(traveling etc)* rusu ni suru 留守にする; *run ~* hashirisaru 走り去る; *it's 2 miles ~* ni-mairu hanarete iru 二マイル離れている

awesome *infml (terrific)* monosugoi ものすごい

awful hidoi ひどい

awkward *(clumsy)* gikochinai ぎこちない; *(difficult)* yakkai (na) やっかい(な); *(embarrassing)* kimazui 気まずい

ax 1 *n* ono おの **2** *v/t project etc* haishi suru 廃止する

B

baby *n* akanbō 赤ん坊
baby-sitter bebīshittā ベビーシッター
bachelor dokushin no otoko 独身の男
back 1 *n (of person)* senaka 背中; *(of bus etc)* ushiro 後ろ; *(of paper etc)* ura 裏; SPORTS bakku ~ バック; *in ~* ura ni 裏に **2** *adj ushiro (no)* 後ろ(の); *~ road* uramichi 裏道 **3** *adv*: *please move ~* ushiro ni sagatte kudasai 後ろに下がって下さい; *I'm ~* tadaima ただいま **4** *v/t (support)* shien suru 支援する; *car* bakku saseru バックさせる
♦ **back down** jōho suru 譲歩する
♦ **back up 1** *v/t (support)* shien

suru 支援する; *file* bakku-appu バックアップ **2** *v/i (in car)* bakku suru バックする
backdate sakanobotte yūkō ni suru さかのぼって有効にする
backer kōensha 後援者
background haikei 背景; *(of person)* keireki 経歴
backing *(support)* shien 支援; MUS bansō 伴奏
backpacker bakku-pakkā バックパッカー
backward 1 *adj child* chieokure (no) 知恵遅れ(の); *society* okureta 遅れた(の) **2** *adv* ushiro ni 後ろに
bacon bēkon ベーコン
bacteria saikin 細菌
bad warui 悪い; *weather etc*

bar

hidoi ひどい; *mistake* ōki (na) 大き(な); *(rotten)* kusatta 腐った; *it's not ~* waruku nai 悪くない

badge badji バッジ

badly waruku 悪く; *work* heta ni 下手に; *damaged* hidoku ひどく; *(very much)* totemo とても

baffle: *be ~d* konwaku suru 困惑する

bag *(paper)* fukuro 袋; *(for traveling)* kaban かばん

baggage tenimotsu 手荷物

bake v/t yaku 焼く

bakery panya パン屋

balance 1 *n* tsurai 釣り合い; *(of bank account)* zandaka 残高 **2** v/... no tsurai o toru …の釣り合いを取る **3** v/i *(of accounts)* chōjiri ga au 帳尻が合う

balance sheet taishaku-taishōhyō 貸借対照表

balcony *(of house)* beranda ベランダ; *(in theater)* nikai-sajiki 二階桟敷

bald hageta はげた

ball bōru ボール

ballet barē バレエ

balloon *(child's)* fūsen 風船

ballot *n* mukimei-tōhyō 無記名投票

ballpoint (pen) bōrupen ボー

ルペン

bamboo take 竹

bamboo shoots takenoko 竹の子

ban 1 *n* kinshi 禁止 **2** v/t kinshi suru 禁止する

banana banana バナナ

band gakudan 楽団; *(pop)* bando バンド

bandage *n* hōtai 包帯

Band-Aid® bando-eido バンドエイド

bang 1 *n (noise)* batan to iu oto ばたんという音; *(blow)* kyōda 強打 **2** v/t *door* batan to shimeru ばたんと閉める

bank¹ *(of river)* dote 土手

bank² *n* FIN ginkō 銀行

bank account ginkō-kōza 銀行口座

bankrupt *adj person* hasan shita 破産した; *company* tōsan shita 倒産した

bank statement kōzashūshi-hōkokusho 口座収支報告書

banner ōdanmaku 横断幕

banquet enkai 宴会

baptize … ni senrei o hodokosu …に洗礼を施す

bar¹ *(iron)* bō 棒; *(for drinks)* sakaba 酒場; *(counter)* kauntā カウンター; *a chocolate ~* itachoko ichimai 板チョコ一枚

bar² v/t shimedasu 締め出す

barbecue 1 n bābekyū バーベキュー **2** v/t bābekyū ni suru バーベキューにする

barbed wire yūshi-tessen 有刺鉄線

barber tokoya 床屋

bare adj arms hadaka (no) 裸(の)

barefoot: be ~ hadashi de aru 裸足である

barely karōjite かろうじて

bargain 1 n (deal) torihiki 取り引き; (good buy) yasui kaimono 安い買物 **2** v/i nebiki no kōshō o suru 値引きの交渉をする

bark v/i hoeru ほえる

barracks MIL heisha 兵舎

barrel taru る

barricade n barikēdo バリケード

barrier saku さく; (cultural) shōgai 障害

base 1 n (bottom) soko 底; (center) honkyochi 本拠地; MIL kichi 基地 **2** v/t motozukaseru 基づかせる; be ~d in (in city) honkyochi ni suru 本拠地にする

baseball yakyū 野球; (ball) yakyū no bōru 野球のボール

baseball cap yakyūbō 野球帽

basement chika 地下; (of store) chikai 地階

basic kihonteki (na) 基本的(な); (rudimentary) kisoteki (na) 基礎的(な)

basically kihonteki ni 基本的に

basics: the ~ kisoteki na koto 基礎的なこと

basis kiso 基礎; (of argument) konkyo 根拠

basket kago かご

basketball basukettobōru バスケットボール

bass n (part) basu バス; (singer) basu-kashu バス歌手; (instrument) bēsu ベース

bat¹ n (baseball) batto バット

bat² (animal) kōmori こうもり

bath furo 風呂; have a ~ furo ni hairu 風呂に入る

bathrobe basurōbu バスローブ

bathroom yokushitsu 浴室; (for washing hands) senmenjo 洗面所; (toilet) toire トイレ

bathtub yokusō 浴槽

battery denchi 電池; AUTO batterī バッテリー

battle n tatakai 戦い

be ◊ desu です; I'm 15 watashi wa jūgo-sai desu 私は十五歳です ◊ (location: of animate beings) imasu います; (of objects) arimasu あります;

was she there? kanojo wa soko ni imashita ka 彼女はそこにいましたか; *there is / are (of animate beings)* imasu います; *(of objects)* arimasu あります ◊ *(imperatives)* ... te ...て; *~ careful* ki o tsukete 気をつけて ◊ *I've never been to Japan* watashi wa Nihon ni itta koto ga arimasen 私は日本に行ったことがありません

beach hamabe 浜辺

beam 1 *n (in ceiling etc)* hari はり **2** *v/i (smile)* egao ni naru 笑顔になる

bean mame 豆

beansprouts moyashi もやし

bear *v/t weight* sasaeru 支える; *cost* futan suru 負担する; *(tolerate)* gaman suru 我慢する

bearable taerareru 耐えられる

beard hige ひげ

beat 1 *n (of heart)* kodō 鼓動; *(of music)* bīto ビート **2** *v/i (of heart)* kodō suru 鼓動する **3** *v/t (in competition)* makasu 負かす; *(hit)* butsu ぶつ

beating *(physical)* bōkō 暴行

beautiful utsukushī 美しい; *meal etc* subarashī 素晴らしい

beauty utsukushisa 美しさ

because ... kara ...から; *~ of* ... no tame ni ...のために; *(referring to sth negative)* ... no sei de ...のせいで

become ... ni naru ...になる

bed beddo ベッド; *(of flowers)* kadan 花壇; *(of sea)* soko 底; *go to ~* neru 寝る

bedroom shinshitsu 寝室

bee mitsubachi ミツバチ

beef *n* gyūniku 牛肉

beer bīru ビール

beetle kabutomushi かぶと虫

before 1 *prep* ... no mae ni ...の前に **2** *adv* mae ni mae ni; *the week ~* isshūkan mae 一週間前 **3** *conj* ... (suru) mae ni ... (する)前に

beforehand maemotte 前もって

beg *v/i* monogoi suru 物ごいする

beggar kojiki こじき

begin 1 *v/i* hajimaru 始まる **2** *v/t* hajimeru 始める

beginner shoshinsha 初心者

beginning hajime 初め; *(origin)* hajimari 初まり

behalf: *in ~ of* ... ni kawatte ...に代わって

behave *v/i* furumau ふるまう; *~ (oneself)* gyōgi yoku suru 行儀良くする

behavior kōdō 行動

behind 1 prep (in position) …
no ushiro ni …の後ろに; (in
race etc) … yori okurete …よ
り遅れて **2** adv (at the back)
ushiro ni 後ろに; **stay** ato ni
あとに

being sonzai 存在; (creature)
ikimono 生き物

belief shinrai 信頼; (religious)
shinkō 信仰

believe shinjiru 信じる

◆**believe in** REL shinkō suru 信
仰する

bell beru ベル

bellhop bōi ボーイ

belly hara 腹; (fat stomach)
onaka おなか

◆**belong to** … no mono de aru
…のものである

belongings mochimono 持
ち物

below 1 prep … no shita ni
…の下に; (amount) … ika ni
…以下に **2** adv shita ni 下
に; **10 degrees** … reika jūdo
零下十度

belt beruto ベルト

bend 1 n kābu カーブ **2** v/t
mageru 曲げる **3** v/i magaru
曲がる

◆**bend down** karada o
kagamuru からだをかがめる

beneath 1 prep … no shita ni
…の下に **2** adv shita ni 下に

beneficial yūeki (na) 有益
(な)

benefit 1 n rieki 利益 **2** v/t
… no yaku ni tatsu …の役
に立つ **3** v/i rieki o eru 利益
を得る

beside … no soba ni …の
そばに

besides 1 adv sono ue そのう
え **2** prep (apart from) … no
hoka ni …のほかに

best 1 adj mottomo yoi 最も
よい **2** adv mottomo yoku 最
もよく **3** n: **do one's ~** saizen
o tsukusu 最善を尽くす; **the
~ (thing)** saikō no mono 最高
のもの; **all the ~!** ogenki de
お元気で

best before date shōmi-
kigen賞味期限

best man shinrō-tsukisoinin 新
郎付添人

bet 1 n kake 賭け **2** v/i (on
horse etc) kakeru 賭ける

betray uragiru 裏切る

better 1 adj motto yoi もっと
よい; **get ~** umaku naru う
まくなる; (in health) kaifuku
suru 回復する **2** adv motto
yoku もっとよく; **I'd really
~ not** yamete oita hō ga ī やめ
ておいた方がいい

better-off … yori kane ga aru
…より金がある

between prep … no aida ni …の間に

beware: **~ of** chūi suru 注意する

beyond 1 prep … o koete …を越えて **2** adv mukō ni 向こうに

bias(s)ed henken ni motozuita 偏見に基づいた

Bible seisho 聖書

bicycle n jitensha 自転車

bid n (at auction) tsukene 付け値

big adj ōkī 大きい; **~ brother** ani 兄; **~ sister** ane 姉

bike jitensha 自転車

bill n (money) shihei 紙幣; (for electricity etc) seikyūsho 請求書; Br (in restaurant) o-kanjō お勘定

billboard kōkokuban 広告板

billfold satsuire 札入れ

billion jū-oku 十億

bind v/t (connect) musubi-tsukeru 結び付ける; (tie) shibaru 縛る

binoculars sōgankyō 双眼鏡

biography denki 伝記

biological seibutsugaku-jō (no) 生物学上(の)

biology seibutsugaku 生物学

biotechnology baiotekunorojī バイオテクノロジー

bird tori 鳥

birth tanjō 誕生; (labor) shussan 出産; **date of ~** seinen-gappi 生年月日

birth certificate shussei-shōmeisho 出生証明書

birth control hinin 避妊

birthday tanjōbi 誕生日; **happy ~!** o-tanjōbi o-medetō お誕生日おめでとう

bit n (of a whole) kakera かけら; (part, section) bubun 部分; **a ~** (a little) sukoshi 少し

bitch n mesuinu 雌犬; infml (woman) ama あま

bite 1 n kamikizu かみ傷; (of mosquito) mushisasare 虫刺され **2** v/t kamu かむ; (of mosquito) sasu 刺す

bitter taste nigai 苦い

black 1 adj kuroi 黒い; person kokujin (no) 黒人(の); coffee burakku (no) ブラック(の) **2** n (color) kuro 黒

black belt kuro-obi 黒帯

blackboard kokuban 黒板

black box burakku-bokkusu ブラックボックス

black eye aoaza 青あざ

blackmail n yusuri ゆすり

black market yamishijō やみ市場

blackout ELEC teiden 停電; MED ishiki-sōshitsu 意識喪失

blade (of knife) ha 刃

blame 1 *n* hinan 非難; *(responsibility)* sekinin 責任 **2** *v/t* ... no sei ni suru ...のせいにする

blank 1 *adj page* hakushi (no) 白紙 (の); *tape* kara (no) から(の) **2** *n (empty space)* yohaku 余白

blanket *n* mōfu 毛布

blast *n* bakuhatsu 爆発

blatant zūzūshī ずうずうしい

blaze *n (fire)* kaji 火事

bleach *n* burīchi ブリーチ

bleak *countryside* sabireta さびれた; *future* kurai 暗い

bleed *v/i* shukketsu suru 出血する

blend *n* burendo ブレンド

bless shukufuku suru 祝福する

blessing REL shukufuku suru 祝福 する

blind 1 *adj* mōmoku (no) 盲目 (の) **2** *n: the* ~ mōjin 盲人

blink *v/i (of person)* mabataki suru まばたきする

blister *n* mizubukure 水ぶくれ

blizzard fubuki 吹雪

bloc POL ken 圏

block 1 *n* katamari かたまり; *(in town)* burokku ブロック **2** *v/t* fusagu ふさぐ

blockage tsumari 詰まり

blog buroggu ブログ

blond *adj* kinpatsu (no) 金髪(の)

blonde *n (woman)* kinpatsu no josei 金髪の女性

blood chi 血

blood group ketsuekigata 血液型

blood pressure ketsuatsu 血圧

blood test ketsueki-kensa 血液検査

blood transfusion yuketsu 輸血

bloom 1 *n* hana 花 **2** *v/i* hana ga saku 花が咲く

blossom *n* hana 花; ~ *viewing* hanami 花見

blouse burausu ブラウス

blow¹ *n* ōda 殴打; *fig* dageki 打撃

blow² **1** *v/t whistle* fuku 吹く; ~ *one's nose* hana o kamu 鼻をかむ **2** *v/i (of wind)* fuku 吹く; *(of whistle)* naru 鳴る; *(of tire)* panku suru パンクする

♦ **blow up** *v/t (with explosives)* bakuha suru 爆破する; *balloon* fukuramasu 膨らます; *photo* hikinobasu 引き伸ばす

blow-dry *n* burō-dorai ブロードライ

blue *adj* aoi 青い

blueberry burūberī ブルー
ベリー

blue-collar worker nikutai-
rōdōsha 肉体労働者

blues MUS burūsu ブルース

bluff 1 n *(deception)* hattari は
ったり **2** v/i hattari o kikaseru
はったりをきかせる

blunt adj nibui 鈍い

bluntly speak bukkirabō ni ぶ
っきらぼうに

blush v/i sekimen suru 赤
面する

blusher hōbeni ほお紅

BO *(body odor)* taishū 体臭

board 1 n ita 板; *(for game)*
bōdo ボード; *(for notices)*
keijiban 掲示板; *(committee)*
i-inkai 委員会; **on** ... ni
notte ...に乗って **2** v/t plane
etc ... ni noru ...に乗る

board game bōdo-gēmu ボー
ドゲーム

boarding card tōjōken 搭
乗券

boarding school kishuku-
gakkō 寄宿学校

board meeting jūyaku-kaigi
重役会議

boast v/i jiman suru 自慢する

boat fune 船; *(small, for
leisure)* bōto ボート

body karada 体; *(dead)* shitai
死体

bodyguard bodīgādo ボディ
ーガード

body odor taishū 体臭

boil v/t liquid futtō saseru 沸
騰させる; eggs etc yuderu
ゆでる

boiled rice *(on plate)* raisu ラ
イス; *(in bowl)* gohan ご飯

boiler boirā ボイラー

bold 1 adj daitan (na) 大胆
(な) **2** n *(print)* futoji 太字

bolt 1 n boruto ボルト; *(on
door)* kannuki かんぬき **2** v/t
(fix) boruto de shimeru ボルト
で締める; door ... ni kannuki
o kakeru ...にかんぬきを
掛ける

bomb 1 n bakudan 爆弾 **2** v/t
bakuha suru 爆破する

bomber bakugekiki 爆撃機;
(terrorist) bakugeki-hannin 爆
撃犯人

bond 1 n *(tie)* kizuna きずな; FIN
saiken 債券

bone n hone 骨

bonus *(money)* bōnasu ボーナ
ス; *(extra)* omake おまけ

boo 1 n būingu ブーイング
2 v/t yajiru やじる

book 1 n hon 本 **2** v/t *(reserve)*
yoyaku suru 予約する

bookcase hondana 本棚

bookkeeper bokigakari 簿
記係

booklet shōsasshi 小冊子

bookstore hon'ya 本屋

boom n būmu ブーム

boost v/t production fuyasu 増やす

boot n būtsu ブーツ

booth (market) baiten 売店; (in restaurant) shikiriseki 仕切り席

border n (between countries) kokkyō 国境; (edge) heri

bore[1] v/t hole akeru あける

bore[2] 1 n (person) taikutsu na hito 退屈な人 2 v/t taikutsu saseru 退屈させる

bored unzari shita うんざりした

boredom taikutsu 退屈

boring taikutsu (na) 退屈(な)

born: be ~ umareru 生まれる

borrow kariru 借りる

boss jōshi 上司

botanical shokubutsu (no) 植物(の)

both 1 adj & pron ryōhō (no) 両方(の); ~ of them (things) ryōhō tomo 両方とも; (people) futari tomo 二人とも 2 adv: ~ my mother and I haha mo watashi mo 母も私も

bother 1 n mendō 面倒; it's no ~ zenzen kamaimasen 全然かまいません 2 v/t (disturb) ...

ni meiwaku o kakeru …に迷惑をかける; person working … no jama o suru …の邪魔をする 3 v/i don't ~! yamete やめて

bottle n bin びん; (for baby) honyūbin ほ乳びん

bottled water botoru-iri mineraru-wōta ボトル入りミネラルウォーター

bottleneck n (in road) kyū ni semaku natte iru michi 急に狭くなっている道

bottle-opener sennuki 栓抜き

bottom 1 adj mottomo shita (no) 最も下(の) 2 n (underside) ura 裏; (on the inside) soko 底; (of hill) fumoto ふもと; (of pile) shita 下; (buttocks) shiri 尻
♦ **bottom out** soko o tsuku 底をつく

bottom line (outcome) kekka 結果; (the real issue) hondai 本題

bounce v/i (of ball) hazumu 弾む; SPORTS baundo suru バウンドする; (of check) fuwatari de modoru 不渡りで戻る

bouncer yōjinbō 用心棒

bound: be ~ to do ... (sure to) kitto ... suru きっと …する

boundary kyōkai 境界

bouquet hanataba 花束; (of

break

wine) kaori 香り

bourbon bābon バーボン

bout MED hossa 発作; (*boxing*) ichishiai 一試合

bow¹ **1** n (as greeting) o-jigi お じぎ **2** v/i o-jigi o suru おじ ぎをする

bow² (knot) chōmusubi 蝶結び

bowels chō 腸

bowl hachi 鉢; (for rice) chawan 茶わん; (for Japanese soup) o-wan おわん; (for cooking, salad) bōru ボール

bowling bōringu ボーリング

bow tie chōnekutai 蝶ネ クタイ

box¹ n hako 箱; (on form) ran 欄

boxer bokusā ボクサー

boxing bokushingu ボク シング

boxing match bokushingu no shiai ボクシングの試合

box office kippu-uriba 切符 売り場

boy otoko no ko 男の子; (son) musuko 息子

boycott n boikotto ボイコ ット

boyfriend bōifurendo ボーイ フレンド

bracelet buresuretto ブレス レット

bracket udeki 腕木; (in text) kakko かっこ

brag v/i hora o fuku ほら を吹く

braid n (in hair) o-sagegami お さげ髪; (trim) mōru モール

brain n nō 脳

brains (mind) zunō 頭脳

brainwashing sennō 洗脳

brake 1 n burēki ブレーキ **2** v/i burēki o kakeru ブレーキ をかける

branch n (of tree) eda 枝; (of bank) shiten 支店

brand n burando ブランド

brand name burando-mei ブ ランド名

brand-new ma-atarashī 真 新しい

brandy burandē ブランデー

brassiere burajā ブラジャー

brat pej gaki がき

brave adj yūkan (na) 勇敢 (な)

bravery yūkan 勇敢

breach (violation) ihan 違反

breach of contract JUR keiyaku-furikō 契約不履行

bread n pan パン

breadth haba 幅; (of knowledge) hirosa 広さ

break 1 n hason 破損; (in bone) kossetsu 骨折; (rest) yasumi 休み; (in relationship) reikyaku-kikan 冷却期間 **2** v/t device kowasu 壊す; stick

oru 折る; *arm* kossetsu suru
骨折する; *china* waru 割る;
promise yaburu 破る **3** *v/i*
(of device) kowareru 壊れる;
(of china) wareru 割れる; *(of
stick)* oreru 折れる

♦ **break down 1** *v/i (of vehicle)*
koshō suru 故障する; *(of
talks)* shippai ni owaru 失
敗に終わる; *(in tears)*
nakikuzureru 泣き崩れ
る **2** *v/t door* uchikowasu 打
ち壊す

♦ **break even** COMM sontoku
nashi ni owaru 損得なしに
終わる

♦ **break up 1** *v/t (into parts)*
bunkai suru 分解する **2** *v/i
(of ice)* wareru 割れる; *(of
couple)* wakareru 別れる

breakdown *(of vehicle)* koshō
故障; *(of talks)* ketsuretsu 決
裂; *(nervous ~)* noirōze ノイ
ローゼ; *(of figures)* uchiwake
内訳

breakfast *n* asagohan 朝ご
はん

break-in oshikomi-gōtō 押し
込み強盗

breakthrough *(in talks)* shinten
進展; *(in science)* hiyakuteki-
hatten 飛躍的発展

breakup *(of partnership)* hatan
破たん

breast mune 胸

breastfeed *v/t* bonyū de
sodateru 母乳で育てる

breath hitoiki ひと息

breathe *v/i* iki o suru 息
をする

breathtaking iki o nomu yō
(na) 息を飲むよう(な)

breed 1 *n* hinshu 品種 **2** *v/t*
hanshoku saseru 繁殖させる

breeze soyokaze そよ風

brew *v/t beer* jōzō suru 醸造す
る; *tea* ireru 入れる

bribe 1 *n* wairo わいろ **2** *v/t*
baishū suru 買収する

bribery oshoku 汚職

brick renga れんが

bride hanayome 花嫁

bridegroom hanamuko 花婿

bridesmaid hanayome-
tsukisoinin 花嫁付添人

bridge *n* hashi 橋; *(of ship)*
burijji ブリッジ

brief *adj* mijikai 短い

briefcase burīfukēsu ブリー
フケース

briefing uchiawase 打ち合せ

briefly sukoshi no aida 少し
の間; *(in few words)* kantan
ni 簡単に

briefs *(for women)* shōtsu シ
ョーツ; *(for men)* burīfu ブ
リーフ

bright *color* akarui 明る
い; *(sunny)* hareta 晴れ

た; *(intelligent)* rikō (na) 利口 (な)

brilliant *sunshine* hikarikagayaku 光り輝く; *idea* subarashī 素晴らしい; *(very intelligent)* yūshū (na) 優秀 (な)

bring *object* motte kuru 持って くる; *person* tsurete kuru 連れてくる; *peace, happiness* motarasu もたらす

♦ **bring back** *(return)* kaesu 返す; *(re-introduce)* fukkatsu saseru 復活させる; *memories* omoidasaseru 思い出させる

♦ **bring down** *fence* taosu 倒す; *government* datō suru 打倒 する; *price* sageru 下げる

♦ **bring out** *video, CD* rirīsu suru リリースする; *new product* happyō suru 発表 する

♦ **bring up** *child* sodateru 育て る; *subject* mochidasu 持ち出 す; *(vomit)* haku 吐く

Britain Eikoku 英国

British 1 *adj* Eikoku (no) 英 国(の) **2** *n: the ~* Eikokujin 英国人

broad *adj* hiroi 広い; *(general)* ōzappa (na) 大ざっぱ(な)

broadcast 1 *n* hōsō 放送 **2** *v/t* hōsō suru 放送する

broadcasting hōsō 放送

broadminded kokoro no hiroi 心の広い

broccoli burokkori ブロッ コリ

brochure panfuretto パンフ レット

broil *v/t* yakiami de yaku 焼き 網で焼く

broiler *n (on stove)* yakiami 焼き網; *(chicken)* wakadori 若鶏

broke *infml* kinketsu (no) 金 欠(の); *(long term)* ichimon-nashi (no) 一文なし(の)

broken *adj* kowareta 壊れた; *glass* wareta 割れた; *neck* kossetsu shita 骨折した

broken-hearted kanashimi ni kureta 悲しみにくれた

bronchitis kikanshien 気 管支炎

brooch burōchi ブローチ

broth *(soup)* sūpu スープ

brothel baishun'yado 売春宿

brother *(own, elder)* ani 兄; *(somebody else's, elder)* o-nīsan お兄さん; *(own, younger)* otōto 弟; *(somebody else's, younger)* otōtosan 弟さん

brother-in-law *(own, elder)* giri no ani 義理の兄; *(somebody else's, elder)* giri no o-nīsan 義理のお兄さん; *(own, younger)* giri no otōto

義理の弟; *(somebody else's, younger)* giri no otōtosan 義理の弟さん

brown *adj* chairo (no) 茶色 (の); *(tanned)* hi ni yaketa 日に焼けた

browse *(in store)* busshoku suru 物色する; *(on Web)* burauzu suru ブラウズする

bruise *n* dabokushō 打撲症

brunette burunetto ブルネット

brush 1 *n* burashi ブラシ; *(for paint)* fude 筆 **2** *v/t* burashi o kakeru ブラシをかける

brutal zannin (na) 残忍(な)

brutality zanninsa 残忍さ

bubble *n* awa 泡

bubble gum fūsengamu 風船ガム

buck *n infml (dollar)* doru ドル

bucket *n* baketsu バケツ

buckle[1] *n* bakkuru バックル

buckle[2] *v/i (of metal)* yugamu ゆがむ

Buddha Budda 仏陀; **Great ~** daibutsu 大仏

Buddhism Bukkyō 仏教

Buddhist 1 *n* Bukkyōto 仏教徒 **2** *adj* Bukkyō (no) 仏教(の)

Buddhist altar butsudan 仏壇

Buddhist monk bōzu 坊主

buddy *infml* aibō 相棒

budget *n* yosan 予算; *(of a family)* kakei 家計

buffalo baffarō バッファロー

bug *n (insect)* mushi 虫; *(virus)* baikin ばい菌; *(device)* tōchōki 盗聴器; COMPUT bagu バグ

buggy *(for baby)* ubaguruma 乳母車

build 1 *n (of person)* taikaku 体格 **2** *v/t* tateru 建てる

♦**build up 1** *v/t strength* tsukeru つける; *relationship* kizukiageru 築き上げる **2** *v/i* masu 増す

builder kenchiku-gyōsha 建築業者

building kensetsu 建設; *(house etc)* tatemono 建物

building site kensetsu-genba 建設現場

build-up chikuseki 蓄積; *(publicity)* senden 宣伝

built-up area jūtakugai 住宅街

bulb *(of plant)* kyūkon 球根; *(light)* denkyū 電球

bulge 1 *n* fukurami 膨らみ **2** *v/i (of pocket)* fukureru 膨れる

bulk daibubun 大部分; **in ~** tairyō ni 大量に

bulky kasabatta かさばった

bulldozer burudōza ブルドーザー

bullet tama 弾

bulletin kōhō 公報

bulletin board keijiban 掲示板

bullet-proof bōdan (no) 防弾(の)

bullet train shinkansen 新幹線

bull's-eye mato no chūshin 的の中心

bully 1 n (child) ijimekko いじめっ子 2 v/t ijimeru いじめる

bum 1 n (hobo) furōsha 浮浪者 2 adj (useless) yaku ni tatanai 役に立たない

bump 1 n (swelling) kobu こぶ; (in road) dansa 段差 2 v/t butsukeru ぶつける

bumper n AUTO banpā バンパー

bunch (of people) gurūpu グループ; a ~ of flowers hanataba 花束; a whole ~ of takusan no たくさんの

bungle v/t shikujiru しくじる

bunk shindai 寝台

burden n omoni 重荷; fig futan 負担

bureau (furniture) tansu たんす; (government department) kyoku 局; (office) ka 課

bureaucracy (red tape) kanryō-shugi 官僚主義; (system) kanryō 官僚

bureaucrat kanryō 官僚

bureaucratic kanryōteki (na) 官僚的(な)

burger hanbāgā ハンバーガー

burglar gōtō 強盗

burglar alarm tōnan-hōchiki 盗難報知機

burglarize gōtō suru 強盗する

burglary gōtō 強盗

burial maisō 埋葬

burn 1 n (on finger etc) yakedo やけど 2 v/t moyasu 燃やす; toast, meat kogasu 焦がす; finger, tongue etc yakedo suru やけどする 3 v/i moeru 燃える; (of house) yakeru 焼ける

♦ **burn down** 1 v/t yakitsukusu 焼き尽くす 2 v/i zenshō suru 全焼する

burp 1 n geppu げっぷ 2 v/i geppu suru げっぷする

burst 1 n (in pipe) haretsu 破裂 2 adj tire haretsu shita 破裂した 3 v/t balloon haretsu saseru 破裂させる 4 v/i (of balloon, tire) haretsu suru 破裂する; ~ out laughing kyū ni waraidasu 急に笑い出す

bury person maisō suru 埋葬する

bus n basu バス

bush shigemi 茂み

business (trade) shōbai 商売;

(company) kaisha 会社; *(work)* shigoto 仕事; *(affair, matter)* koto 事; **on ~** shigoto de 仕事で

business card meishi 名刺

business class bijinesu-kurasu ビジネスクラス

business hours eigyō-jikan 営業時間

businessman jitsugyōka 実業家

business meeting kaigō 会合

business school keieigaku-daigakuin 経営学大学院

business studies keieigaku 経営学

business suit sūtsu スーツ

business trip shutchō 出張

businesswoman josei-jitsugyōka 女性実業家

bus station basu-tāminaru バスターミナル

bus stop basutei バス停

bust n *(of woman)* basuto バ

スト

busy adj isogashī 忙しい; *street* nigiyaka (na) にぎやか(な); TEL hanashichū (no) 話中(の)

but conj kedo けど

butcher n nikuya 肉屋

butter n batā バター

butterfly *(insect)* chō ちょう

buttocks shiri 尻

button n botan ボタン

buy v/t kau 買う

buyer kaite 買い手

buzzer buzā ブザー

by prep ◊ *(agency)* ... ni ...に ◊ *(near, next to)* ... no soba ni ...のそばに ◊ *(mode of transport)* ... de ...で; **~ train** densha de 電車で ◊ *(no later than)* ... made ni ...までに◊: **~ oneself** hitori de ひとりで

bye(-bye) baibai バイバイ

by-product fukusanbutsu 副産物

C

cab *(taxi)* takushī タクシー

cabbage kyabetsu キャベツ

cab driver takushī doraibā タクシードライバー

cabin *(ship)* kyakushitsu 客室

cabin crew kyakushitsu-gakari

客室係

cabinet todana 戸棚; POL naikaku 内閣

cable ELEC kōdo コード; **~ *(TV)*** kēburu-terebi ケーブルテレビ

cab stand takushī noriba タクシー乗り場

café kafe カフェ

cafeteria kafeteria カフェテリア

caffeine kafein カフェイン

cage (for bird) kago かご; (for lion) ori おり

cake n kēki ケーキ

calculate (work out) mitsumoru 見積もる; (in math) keisan suru 計算する

calculation keisan 計算

calculator dentaku 電卓

calendar karendā カレンダー

calf (young cow) koushi 子牛

call 1 n TEL denwa 電話; (shout) koe 声; (demand) yōkyū 要求 **2** v/t (on phone) ... ni denwa o suru ...に電話をする; (shout) yobu 呼ぶ **3** v/i (on phone) denwa o kakeru 電話をかける; (shout) yobu 呼ぶ; (visit) tachiyoru 立ち寄る

♦**call back 1** v/t TEL ... ni orikaeshi denwa suru ...に折り返し電話する **2** v/i TEL denwa o kakenaosu 電話をかけ直す; (visit) ato de mata tachiyoru あとでまた立ち寄る

♦**call for** (collect) tori ni tachiyoru 取りに立ち寄る;

(demand) yōkyū suru 要求する; (require) hitsuyō to suru 必要とする

♦**call in** (summon) yobi-ireru 呼び入れる

♦**call on** (urge) ... ni yōkyū suru ...に要求する; (visit) hōmon suru 訪問する

caller TEL denwa o kaketa hito 電話をかけた人; (visitor) hōmonsha 訪問者

calligraphy shodō 書道

calm adj sea odayaka (na) 穏やか(な); person ochitsuita 落ち着いた

♦**calm down 1** v/t shizumeru 静める **2** v/i (of sea, wind) shizuka ni naru 静かになる; (of person) ochitsuku 落ち着く

calorie karorī カロリー

Cambodia Kanbojia カンボジア

camcorder bideo-kamera ビデオカメラ

camera kamera カメラ

cameraman kameraman カメラマン

camouflage n kamufurāju カムフラージュ

camp 1 n kyanpu キャンプ **2** v/i kyanpu suru キャンプする

campaign n undō 運動

camper kyanpu o suru hito キャンプをする人; *(vehicle)* kyanpingu-kā キャンピングカー

campsite kyanpu-jō キャンプ場

campus kōnai 構内, kyanpasu キャンパス

can[1] *(ability)* … koto ga dekiru …ことができる
◊ *(request, permission)* … te mo ī desu ka …てもいいですか; ~ *I borrow the car?* kuruma o karite mo ī desu ka 車を借りてもいいですか *(prohibition)*: ~*not* … te wa ikenai …てはいけない
◊ *(offer)*: ~ *I help you?* nanika o-tetsudai shimashō ka 何かお手伝いしましょうか

can[2] *n (for drinks)* kan 缶

Canada Kanada カナダ

Canadian 1 *adj* Kanada (no) カナダ(の) **2** *n* Kanadajin カナダ人

canal *(waterway)* unga 運河

cancel torikesu 取り消す

cancellation torikeshi 取り消し

cancer gan がん

candid sotchoku (na) 率直 (な)

candidacy rikkōho 立候補

candidate kōhosha 候補者;

(in exam) jukensha 受験者

candle rōsoku ろうそく

candor sotchokusa 率直さ

candy kyandī キャンディー

canned *fruit* kanzume (no) 缶詰(の)

cannot → **can**[1]

can opener kankiri 缶切り

canteen *(in factory)* shokudō 食堂

canyon kyōkoku 峡谷

cap *(hat)* bōshi 帽子; *(of bottle)* futa ふた

capability nōryoku 能力; MIL senryoku 戦力

capable *(efficient)* yūnō (na) 有能(な)

capacity *(of container)* yōseki 容積; *(of elevator)* tei-in 定員; *(of engine)* haikiryō 排気量

capital *n (of country)* shuto 首都; *(letter)* ōmoji 大文字; *(money)* shihon 資本

capitalism shihon-shugi 資本主義

capitalist *adj* shihon-shugi (no) 資本主義(の)

capital punishment shikei 死刑

capsize *v/i* hikkurikaeru ひっくり返る

capsule kapuseru カプセル

captain *n (of ship)* senchō 船長; *(of aircraft)* kichō 機

長; *(of team)* kyaputen キャプテン

caption *n* setsumeibun 説明文

captivate miryō suru 魅了する

captivity toraware no mi とらわれの身

capture *v/t person, animal* tsukamaeru 捕まえる

car kuruma 車; *(of train)* sharyō 車両; *by ~* kuruma de 車で

carbohydrate tansuika-butsu 炭水化物

carbon monoxide issanka-tanso 一酸化炭素

carbureter, carburetor kyaburetā キャブレター

card kādo カード; *(post~)* hagaki 葉書; *(business ~)* meishi 名刺; *(playing ~)* toranpu トランプ

cardboard bōrugami ボール紙

cardigan kādigan カーディガン

care 1 *n (of baby, pet)* sewa 世話; *(of elderly)* kaigo 介護; *(of sick)* kango 看護; *(medical ~)* iryō 医療; *(worry)* nayami 悩み; *take ~* ki o tsukeru 気をつける; *take ~!* ki o tsukete 気をつけて **2** *v/i* ~ *ki ni kakeru* 気にかける; *I couldn't ~ less* zenzen ki ni

shinai 全然気にしない

♦ **care about** ... ni kanshin ga aru …に関心がある

career *(profession)* shokugyō 職業; *(path through life)* kyaria キャリア

careful chūibukai 注意深い; *(thorough)* nen'iri (na) 念入り(な); *(be)* ~! ki o tsukete 気をつけて

careless fuchūi (na) 不注意(な)

caretaker kanrinin 管理人

cargo tsumini 積み荷

caricature *n* fūshi-manga 風刺漫画

caring *adj* omoiyari no aru 思いやりのある

carousel *(at airport)* enkei-beruto-konbeyā 円形ベルトコンベヤー

carp koi コイ

carpet kāpetto カーペット

car rental renta-kā レンタカー

carrier *(company)* un'yu-gyōsha 運輸業者; *(of disease)* hokinsha 保菌者

carrot ninjin にんじん

carry 1 *v/t (in hand)* mochihakobu 持ち運ぶ; *(from one place to another)* hakobu 運ぶ **2** *v/i (of sound)* tsutawaru 伝わる

♦ **carry out** *survey* okonau

行う; *orders* jikkō suru 実
行する

cart niguruma 荷車

cartel karuteru カルテル

carton *(storage)* hako 箱; *(for
eggs etc)* pakku パック

cartoon manga 漫画; *(on TV)*
anime アニメ

cartridge kātoridji カート
リッジ

carve *meat* kiriwakeru 切り
分ける; *wood* chōkoku suru
彫刻する

car wash sensha 洗車

case[1] *(container)* kēsu ケース;
(of wine) hitohako ひと箱

case[2] *n (instance)* rei 例;
(situation) ba-ai 場合; *(for
police etc)* jiken 事件; **in any
~** tonikaku とにかく

cash 1 *n* genkin 現金 2 *v/t
check* genkinka suru 現金化
する

cash desk reji レジ

cash flow kyasshu-furō キャ
ッシュフロー

cashier *n (in store etc)*
rejigakari レジ係

cash register rejisutā レジ
スター

casino kajino カジノ

casket *(coffin)* hitsugi ひつぎ

cassette kasetto カセット

cassette player kasetto-

pureiyā カセットプレイヤー

cast 1 *n (of play)* shutsuensha
出演者 2 *v/t doubt*
nagekakeru 投げかける

castle shiro 城

casual *(chance)* nanigenai 何
気ない; *(offhand)* mutonchaku
(na) むとんちゃく(な); *(not
formal)* kajuaru (na) カジュ
アル(な)

casualty shishōsha 死傷者

cat neko 猫

catalog *n* katarogu カタログ

catastrophe daisaigai 大災害

catch 1 *n* hokyū 捕球; *(of fish)*
shūkaku 収穫; *(locking device)*
tomegane 留め金 2 *v/t ball*
tsukamaeru 捕まえる; *bus ...*
ni noru …に乗る; *fish with
net* toru 捕る; *(hear)* kikitoru
聞き取る; **~ (a) cold** kaze o
hiku 風邪を引く

◆**catch up** *v/i* oitsuku 追
いつく

◆**catch up on** ... no okure o
torimodosu …の遅れを取り
戻す

catcher *(in baseball)* kyatchā
キャッチャー

catching *disease* densensei
(no) 伝染性(の)

category burui 部類

Catholic 1 *adj* Katorikku
(no) カトリック(の) 2 *n*

Katorikku-kyōto カトリック教徒

cattle ushi 牛

cauliflower karifurawā カリフラワー

cause 1 *n* gen'in 原因; *(grounds)* konkyo 根拠 2 *v/t* hikiokosu 引き起こす

caution *n* yōjin 用心

cautious shinchō (na) 慎重(な)

cave hora-ana 洞穴

caviar kyabia キャビア

cavity mushiba 虫歯

CD (= *compact disc*) shī-dī CD

cease *v/i* owaru 終わる

cease-fire teisen 停戦

ceiling tenjō 天井; *(limit)* saikō-gendo 最高限度

celebrate *v/t* & *v/t* iwau 祝う

celebration o-iwai お祝い

celebrity yūmeijin 有名人

celery serori セロリ

cell *(for prisoner)* dokubō 独房; BIOL saibō 細胞

cello chero チェロ

cell(ular) phone keitai-denwa 携帯電話

cemetery bochi 墓地

censor *v/t* ken'etsu suru 検閲する

censorship ken'etsu 検閲

cent sento セント

centennial *n* hyakushūnen 百周年

center *n* chūshin 中心; *(building)* sentā センター; *(region)* chūshin 中心

central chūshin (no) 中心(の); *location* chūshinbu de benri (na) 中心部で便利(な); *(main)* chūshinteki (na) 中心的(な)

central heating sentoraru-hītingu セントラル・ヒーティング

centralize chūō ni atsumeru 中央に集める

century seiki 世紀

CEO (= *Chief Executive Officer*) saikō-sekininsha 最高責任者

cereal *(grain)* kokumotsu 穀物; *(breakfast ~)* shiriaru シリアル

ceremony *(event)* shikiten 式典; *(ritual)* gishiki 儀式

certain kakushin shite iru 確信している; *(particular)* aru ある

certainly *(definitely)* tashika ni 確かに; *(of course)* mochiron もちろん; ~ *not!* tondemonai とんでもない

certainty *(confidence)* kakushin 確信; *(inevitability)* kakujitsusei 確実性

certificate *(qualification)*
shikaku 資格; *(official paper)*
shōmeisho 証明書

certify shōmei suru 証明する

Cesarean *n* teiō-sekkai 帝
王切開

CFC (= chlorofluorocarbon)
furongasu フロンガス

chain *n* kusari 鎖; *(hotels)* chēn
チェーン

chain reaction rensa-hannō
連鎖反応

chair *n* isu いす

chairman gichō 議長

chairwoman gichō 議長

challenge 1 *n (difficulty)*
nandai 難題; *(competition)*
chōsen 挑戦 2 *v/t (to race)*
mōshikomu 申し込む;
(question) igi o tonaeru 異議
を唱える

challenging yarigai no aru や
りがいのある

champagne shanpan シャ
ンパン

champion *n* SPORTS chanpion
チャンピオン

championship senshuken-
taikai 選手権大会; *(title)*
senshuken 選手権

chance *(possibility)* kanōsei 可
能性; *(opportunity)* kikai 機会

change 1 *n (to plan)* henkō
変更; *(in condition)* henka

変化; *(coins)* kozeni 小銭;
(from purchase) o-tsuri お釣
り 2 *v/t (alter)* kaeru 変え
る; *bank bill* kuzusu くずす;
(replace) torikaeru 取り替え
る; *trains* norikaeru 乗り換
える; *clothes* kigaeru 着替え
る 3 *v/i* kawaru 変わる; *(put
on different clothes)* kigaeru 着
替える; *(take different train)*
norikaeru 乗り換える

channel RADIO, TV channeru
チャンネル; *(waterway)*
suiro 水路

chant *n* kakegoe 掛け声

chaos daikonran 大混乱

chaotic muchitsujo (no) 無秩
序(の)

chapter shō 章

character *(nature)* seikaku 性
格; *(person)* hito 人; *(in book)*
tōjō-jinbutsu 登場人物; *(in
writing)* moji 文字; **Chinese ~**
kanji 漢字

characteristic *n* tokushoku
特色

charbroiled sumibiyaki (no)
炭火焼き(の)

charge 1 *n (fee)* ryōkin 料
金; JUR yōgi 容疑 2 *v/t sum
seikyū suru 請求する; *(put
on account)* kādo de harau カ
ードで払う; JUR kiso suru 起
訴する; *battery* jūden suru 充

電する

charge account tsuke つけ

charge card kado カード

charitable *institution* jizen-katsudō (no) 慈善活動(の)

charity jizen-dantai 慈善団体

charm 1 *n (quality)* miryoku 魅力 **2** *v/t (delight)* uttori saseru うっとりさせる

charming miryokuteki (na) 魅力的(な)

chart *(diagram)* zuhyō 図表; NAUT kaizu 海図

charter *v/t* chātā suru チャーターする

chase 1 *n* tsuiseki 追跡 **2** *v/t* oikakeru 追いかける

chat 1 *n* o-shaberi おしゃべり **2** *v/i* o-shaberi suru おしゃべりする

chatter *v/i* pechakucha to shaberu ぺちゃくちゃとしゃべる; *(of teeth)* katakata naru かたかた鳴る

chatterbox o-shaberi おしゃべり

chauffeur *n* tenshu 運転手

chauvinist *(male ~)* danson-johi no hito 男尊女卑の人

cheap *adj* yasui 安い; *(mean)* kechi (na) けち(な)

cheat 1 *n* ikasamashi いかさま師 **2** *v/t (in exam)* kanningu o suru カンニングをする;

(in cards etc) ikasama o suru いかさまをする

check¹ **1** *adj shirt* chekku (no) チェック(の) **2** *n* chekku チェック

check² *n* FIN kogitte 小切手; *(in restaurant etc)* kanjōgaki 勘定書き; **~ please** o-kanjō o-negai お勘定お願い

check³ **1** *n (to verify sth)* kensa 検査 **2** *v/t (verify)* kakunin suru 確認する; *machinery* tenken suru 点検する **3** *v/i* shiraberu 調べる

♦**check in** *(at hotel etc)* chekku-in suru チェックインする

♦**check out 1** *v/i (of hotel)* chekku-auto suru チェックアウトする **2** *v/t restaurant etc ...* ni itte miru …に行ってみる

checkbook kogitte-chō 小切手帳

check-in (counter) chekku-in (kauntā) チェックイン(カウンター)

checking account tōza-yokin-kōza 当座預金口座

check-in time chekku-in no jikan チェックインの時間

checklist chekku-risuto チェックリスト

checkmark chekku no shirushi

チェックの印

checkout reji レジ

checkpoint MIL kenmonjo 検問所; (race) chekku-pointo チェックポイント

checkroom (for coats) kurōku クローク; (for baggage) tenimotsu-azukarisho 手荷物預かり所

checkup MED kenkō-shindan 健康診断

cheek hō ほお

cheer 1 n kansei 歓声; ~s! (toast) kanpai 乾杯 2 v/t seien suru 声援する 3 v/i kansei o ageru 歓声を上げる

♦**cheer up** 1 v/i genki o dasu 元気を出す; ~! genki dashite 元気出して 2 v/t genki zukeru 元気づける

cheerful kigen no ī 機嫌のいい

cheerleader chiarīdā チアリーダー

cheese chīzu チーズ

chef shefu シェフ; (Japanese cuisine) itamae 板前

chemical 1 adj kagaku (no) 化学(の) 2 n kagaku-yakuhin 化学薬品

chemist kagakusha 化学者

chemistry kagaku 化学; fig aishō 相性

chemotherapy kagaku-ryōhō 化学療法

cherry sakuranbo さくらんぼ; (tree) sakura no ki 桜の木

cherry blossom sakura 桜

chess chesu チェス

chessboard chesu-ban チェス盤

chest mune 胸; (box) shūnōbako 収納箱

chestnut kuri くり; (tree) kuri no ki くりの木

chew v/t kamu かむ; (of rats etc) kajiru かじる

chewing gum chūingamu チューインガム

chicken n niwatori にわとり; (food) toriniku とり肉

chicken pox mizubōsō 水ぼうそう

chief adj omo (na) 主(な)

chiefly shu to shite 主として

child kodomo 子供

childhood kodomo no koro 子供の頃

childish pej kodomojimita 子供じみた

chili (pepper) tōgarashi とうがらし

chilly hadazamui 肌寒い

chimney entotsu 煙突

chin ago あご

China Chūgoku 中国

Chinese 1 adj Chūgoku (no) 中国(の); ~ character

kanji 漢字 2 n (language)

Chūgokugo 中国語; (person)
Chūgokujin 中国人

chip 1 n (fragment) kakera か
けら; (damage) kaketa tokoro
欠けたところ; (in gambling)
chippu チップ; COMPUT
maikuro-chippu マイクロ
チップ; ~s potetochippu ポ
テトチップ 2 v/t (damage)
kaku 欠く

chiropractor kairopurakutā カ
イロプラクター

chlorine enso 塩素

chocolate chokorēto チョコ
レート

choice n sentaku 選択

choir gasshōdan 合唱団

choke 1 n AUTO chōku チョ
ーク 2 v/i iki ga tsumaru 息
が詰まる

cholesterol koresuterōru コレ
ステロール

choose v/t & v/i erabu 選ぶ

chop 1 n (meat) choppu チョ
ップ 2 v/t wood waru 割る;
vegetables kiru 切る

chopsticks hashi はし;
disposable ~ waribashi わ
りばし; ~ *rest* hashioki は
し置き

chore zatsuyō 雑用

choreography furitsuke 振
り付け

chorus kurikaeshi 繰り返し;
(singers) gasshōdan 合唱団

christen senrei suru 洗礼する

Christian 1 n Kirisuto-kyōto
キリスト教徒 2 adj
Kirisutokyō (no) キリスト
教(の)

Christmas Kurisumasu ク
リスマス; *Merry ~!* Merī-
Kurisumasu メリークリ
スマス

Christmas card Kurisumasu-
kādo クリスマスカード

Christmas Day Kurisumasu
クリスマス

Christmas Eve Kurisumasu-
ibu クリスマスイブ

Christmas present
Kurisumasu-purezento クリス
マスプレゼント

Christmas tree Kurisumasu-
tsurī クリスマスツリー

chrome kuromu クロム

chronic mansei (no) 慢性(の)

chronological nendaijun (no)
年代順(の)

church kyōkai 教会

CIA shī-ai-ē シーアイエー

cigar hamaki 葉巻き

cigarette tabako たばこ

cinema eigakai 映画界; Br
(building) eigakan 映画館

cinnamon shinamon シナ
モン

circle 1 *n* en 円; *(group)* nakama 仲間 **2** *v/i (of plane)* senkai suru 旋回する

circular *adj* enkei (no) 円形(の)

circulate *v/t memo* kairan suru 回覧する

circulation BIOL junkan 循環; *(of paper)* hakkō-busū 発行部数

circumstances jijō 事情; *(financial)* keizai-jōtai 経済状態

circus sākasu サーカス

citizen shimin 市民

citizenship shiminken 市民権

city toshi 都市

civil *(not military)* minkan (no) 民間(の); *(polite)* reigitadashī 礼儀正しい

civil engineer doboku-gishi 土木技師

civilian *n* minkanjin 民間人

civilization bunmei 文明

civil servant kōmuin 公務員

civil war naisen 内戦

claim 1 *n (request)* seikyū 請求; *(right)* kenri 権利; *(assertion)* shuchō 主張 **2** *v/t (ask for)* seikyū suru 請求する; *(assert)* shuchō suru 主張する

clamp *n (fastener)* kuranpu クランプ

clandestine himitsu (no) 秘密(の)

clap *v/i* hakushu suru 拍手する

clarify hakkiri saseru はっきりさせる

clarity meiryōsa 明りょうさ

clash 1 *n* shōtotsu 衝突; *(of personalities)* fuitchi 不一致 **2** *v/i (of colors)* awanai 合わない

clasp 1 *n* tomegu 留め具 **2** *v/t (in hand)* nigirishimeru 握りしめる

class *n (lesson)* jugyō 授業; *(students)* kurasu クラス; *(category)* burui 部類; *(social)* kaikyū 階級

classic 1 *adj (typical)* tenkeiteki (na) 典型的(な); *(definitive)* ichiryū (no) 一流(の) **2** *n* meisaku 名作

classical *music* kurashikku (no) クラシック(の)

classified *information* kimitsu (no) 機密(の)

classified ad kōmokubetsu-kōkoku 項目別広告

classify *(categorize)* bunrui suru 分類する

classroom kyōshitsu 教室

clause *(in agreement)* jōkō 条項; GRAM setsu 節

claustrophobia heishokyōfushō 閉所恐怖症

claw n tsume つめ

clean 1 adj kirei (na) きれい
(な) **2** v/t kirei ni suru きれ
いにする; teeth migaku 磨
く; house sōji suru 掃除す
る; hands arau 洗う; clothes
kurīningu suru クリーニン
グする

cleaning woman sōjifu 掃
除婦

cleanser senganryō 洗顔料

clear 1 adj voice hakkiri
shita はっきりした; (to
understand) wakariyasui わか
りやすい; (obvious) akiraka
(na) 明らか(な); weather
hareta 晴れた; water sunda 澄
んだ; skin kenkō-sō 健康そ
う **2** v/t roads etc
torinozoku 取り除く; (acquit)
yōgi o harasu 容疑を晴らす
3 v/i (of sky) hareru 晴れる

♦ **clear up 1** v/i katazuke o suru
片付けをする; (of weather)
hare-agaru 晴れ上がる **2** v/t
(tidy) katazukeru 片付ける

clearance (space) yutori ゆ
とり; (authorization) kyoka
許可

clearly (with clarity) hakkiri
to はっきりと; (evidently)
akiraka ni 明らかに

clench fist kobushi o

nigirishimeru こぶしを握
り締める

clerk jimuin 事務員; (in store)
ten'in 店員

clever rikō (na) 利口(な);
idea umai うまい

client kokyaku 顧客; (of
lawyer etc) irainin 依頼人

climate kikō 気候

climax n kuraimakkusu クラ
イマックス

climb 1 n (up mountain) tozan
登山 **2** v/i ... ni noboru ···に
登る **3** v/i noboru 登る; (up
mountain) tozan suru 登山
する

climber tozansha 登山者

clingfilm rappu ラップ

clinic shinryōjo 診療所

clip¹ n (fastener) kurippu ク
リップ

clip² **1** n (extract) kurippu ク
リップ **2** v/t hair karikomu
刈り込む

clipping (from newspaper)
kirinuki 切り抜き

clock tokei 時計

clockwise tokeimawari 時
計回り

close¹ **1** adj friend shitashī 親
しい; resemblance nite iru 似
ている **2** adv sugu soba す
ぐそば

close² **1** v/t shimeru 閉める;

business yameru やめる; *factory* heisa suru 閉鎖する **2** *v/i* (*of door, store*) shimaru 閉まる; (*of eyes*) tojiru 閉じる; (*of store*) heiten suru 閉店する

closed *store* shimatta 閉まった; *eyes* tojita 閉じた

closely *listen* chūibukaku 注意深く; *cooperate* missetsu shite 密接して

closet *n* todana 戸棚

closing time (*of store*) heiten-jikan 閉店時間; (*of museum*) heikan-jikan 閉館時間

clot *n* (*of blood*) katamari 固まり

cloth (*fabric*) nuno 布; (*for kitchen*) fukin ふきん; (*for cleaning etc*) zōkin ぞうきん

clothes fuku 服

cloud *n* kumo 雲

cloudy kumotta 曇った

club *n* (*weapon*) konbō こん棒; (*golf iron*) gorufu-kurabu ゴルフクラブ; (*organization*) kurabu クラブ

clue tegakari 手がかり

clumsy *person* bukiyō (na) 不器用 (な)

clutch 1 *n* AUTO kuratchi クラッチ **2** *v/t* shikkari nigiru しっかり握る

coach 1 *n* (*trainer*) kōchi コー

coal sekitan 石炭

coalition renritsu 連立

coarse kime no arai きめの粗い; (*vulgar*) gehin (na) 下品 (な)

coast *n* kaigan 海岸

coastal engan (no) 沿岸 (の)

coastguard engan-keibitai 沿岸警備隊

coastline kaigansen 海岸線

coat 1 *n* uwagi 上着; (*over~*) ōbā オーバー **2** *v/t* (*cover*) ōu 覆う

coathanger hangā ハンガー

coating ōi 覆い

coax settoku suru 説得する

cocaine kokain コカイン

cock *n* (*chicken*) ondori おんどり

cockpit kokkupitto コックピット

cockroach gokiburi ごきぶり

coconut kokonattsu ココナッツ

code *n* angō 暗号

co-educational danjo-kyōgaku (no) 男女共学 (の)

coexistence kyōzon 共存

coffee kōhī コーヒー

coffee break kōhī-bureiku コーヒーブレイク

coffee maker kōhī-mēkā コーヒーメーカー

coffee shop kissaten 喫茶店

coffin hitsugi ひつぎ

cog ha 歯

coherent suji no tōtta 筋の通った

coin n kōka 硬貨

coincide dōji ni okoru 同時に起こる

coincidence gūzen 偶然

Coke® koka-kōra コカコーラ

cold 1 adj tsumetai 冷たい; weather, day, room samui 寒い; 2 n samusa 寒さ; **I have a ~** kaze o hīte iru 風邪をひいている

collaborate kyōryoku suru 協力する

collaboration kyōryoku 協力

collapse kuzureru 崩れる; (of person) taoreru 倒れる

collar eri 襟

colleague dōryō 同僚

collect 1 v/t person mukae ni iku 迎えにいく; tickets tori ni iku 取りにいく; (as hobby) shūshū suru 収集する; (gather) atsumeru 集める 2 adv: **call** ~ ... ni korekutokōru o kakeru …にコレクトコールをかける

collection korekushon コレクション

collective kyōdō (no) 共同(の)

collector shūshūka 収集家

college daigaku 大学

collision shōtotsu 衝突

colonial adj shokuminchi (no) 植民地(の)

colony shokuminchi 植民地

color n iro 色

color-blind shikikaku-ijō (no) 色覚異常(の)

colorful shikisai ni tonda 色彩に富んだ

color photograph karāshashin カラー写真

column (architectural) enchū 円柱; (of text) ran 欄; (newspaper feature) koramu コラム

columnist koramunisuto コラムニスト

comb 1 n kushi くし **2** v/t tokasu とかす

combat 1 n sentō 戦闘 **2** v/t ... to tatakau …と闘う

combination kumiawase 組み合わせ

combine v/t kumiawaseru 組み合わせる

come (toward speaker) kuru 来る; (toward listener) iku 行く

♦**come back** modotte kuru 戻ってくる

♦**come down** v/i oriru 降りる; (in price, amount etc) sagaru 下がる

♦ come in hairu 入る; ~! dōzo どうぞ

♦ come off (of handle etc) toreru とれる

♦ come on (progress) shinpo suru 進歩する; ~! sā, hayaku さあ早く; (in disbelief) masaka まさか

♦ come out (of person) dete kuru 出てくる; (of sun) deru 出る; (of stain) ochiru 落ちる

comedian komedian コメディアン

comedy kigeki 喜劇

comfort 1 n kaitekisa 快適さ; (consolation) nagusame 慰め 2 v/t nagusameru 慰める

comfortable chair suwarigokochi no yoi 座り心地のよい; house, room igokochi no yoi 居心地のよい

comic 1 n (to read) manga 漫画 2 adj kigeki (no) 喜劇(の)

comma konma コンマ

command 1 n meirei 命令 2 v/t meirei suru 命令する

commander shireikan 司令官

commemorate kinen suru 記念する

comment 1 n komento コメント 2 v/t iken o noberu 意見を述べる

commentary jikkyō-hōsō 実況放送

commentator kaisetsusha 解説者

commercial 1 adj shōgyō (no) 商業(の) 2 n (ad) komāsharu コマーシャル

commission 1 n (payment) buai 歩合 2 v/t (for a job) irai suru 依頼する

commit crime okasu 犯す; ~ oneself yakusoku suru 約束する

commitment (in professional relationship) sekininkan 責任感; (in personal relationship) kenshin 献身; (responsibility) sekinin 責任

committee i-inkai 委員会

commodity shōhin 商品

common (not rare) arifureta ありふれた; (shared) kyōtsū (no) 共通(の)

common sense jōshiki 常識

communicate 1 v/i (have contact) renraku o toru 連絡をとる 2 v/t tsutaeru 伝える

communications tsūshin-shudan 通信手段

communicative person hanashizuki (na) 話好き(な)

communism kyōsan-shugi 共産主義

communist adj kyōsan-shugi (no) 共産主義(の)

community shakai 社会

commute v/i tsūkin suru 通勤する

companion aite 相手

company COMM kaisha 会社; *(companionship)* tsukiai 付き合い; *(guests)* raikyaku 来客

company car shayō-sha 社用車

comparatively hikakuteki 比較的

compare v/t hikaku suru 比較する; **~ X with Y** X o Y to kuraberu X を Y と比べる

comparison hikaku 比較

compassion dōjō 同情

compatible *people* ki ga au 気が合う; *blood types* tekigō shite iru 適合している

compel kyōsei suru 強制する

compensate 1 v/t *(with money)* hoshō suru 補償する 2 v/i: **~ for** umeawaseru 埋め合わせる

compensation *(money)* hoshōkin 補償金; *(reward)* hōshū 報酬

compete kyōsō suru 競争する

competent *person* yūnō (na) 有能(な); *work* deki no ī できのいい

competition kyōsō 競争; SPORTS shiai 試合

competitive kyōsōshin ga tsuyoi 競争心が強い; *price* kyōgō dekiru 競合できる

competitor sankasha 参加者; COMM kyōsō-aite 競争相手

complain v/i fuhei o iu 不平を言う; *(to shop etc)* kujō o iu 苦情を言う

complaint *(grumble)* monku 文句; MED byōki 病気

complete 1 adj *(total)* kanzen (na) 完全(な); *(full)* zenbu (no) 全部(の); *(finished)* kansei shite 完成して 2 v/t *task* kansei suru 完成する

completely kanzen ni 完全に

completion kansei 完成

complex adj fukuzatsu (na) 複雑(な)

complicated fukuzatsu (na) 複雑(な)

compliment n homekotoba ほめ言葉

complimentary shōsan o hyōshita 賞賛を表した; *(free)* muryō (no) 無料(の)

comply: ~ with … … ni shitagau …に従う

component bubun 部分

compose v/t kōsei suru 構成する; MUS sakkyoku suru 作曲する

composer MUS sakkyokuka 作曲家

composure ochitsuki 落ち着き

comprise: *be ~d of...* ... de kōsei sarete iru …で構成されている

compromise n dakyō 妥協

compulsory kyōseiteki (na) 強制的(な); *subject* hisshū (no) 必修(の)

computer konpyūtā コンピューター

computer game konpyūtā-gēmu コンピューターゲーム

conceal kakusu 隠す

conceited omoiagatta 思い上った

concentrate shūchū suru 集中する

concentration shūchūryoku 集中力

concept gainen 概念

concern 1 n *(anxiety)* shinpai 心配; *(company)* jigyō 事業 **2** v/t *(involve)* ... ni kankei ga aru …に関係がある

concerned *(anxious)* shinpai shite iru 心配している

concert konsāto コンサート

concise kanketsu (na) 簡潔(な)

conclude v/t *(deduce)* ketsuron o kudasu 結論を下す; *(end)* oeru 終える

conclusion *(deduction)* ketsuron 結論; *(end)* ketsumatsu 結末

concrete n konkurīto コンクリート

concussion nōshintō 脳しんとう

condensation ketsuro 結露

condescending onkisegamashī 恩きせがましい

condition n *(state)* jōtai 状態; *(of health)* taichō 体調; *(requirement)* jōken 条件

conditioner *(for hair)* rinsu リンス

condolences o-kuyami お悔やみ

condom kondōmu コンドーム

conduct 1 n *(behavior)* okonai 行い **2** v/t *(carry out)* okonau 行う; ELEC dendō suru 伝導する; MUS shiki suru 指揮する

conductor MUS shikisha 指揮者; *(on train)* shashō 車掌

conference kaigi 会議

confess hakujō suru 白状する; *(to the police)* jihaku suru 自白する

confession kokuhaku 告白; *(to police)* jihaku 自白

confidence *(assurance)* jishin 自信; *(trust)* shinrai 信頼

confident *(self-assured)* jishin no aru 自信のある; *(convinced)* kakushin shite 確信して

confidential himitsu (no) 秘密(の)

confirm *v/t* kakunin suru 確認する

confirmation kakunin 確認

confiscate bosshū suru 没収する

conflict 1 *n (disagreement)* ronsō 論争; *(war)* arasoi 争い **2** *v/i (clash)* kachiau かちあう; *(of theories)* mujun suru 矛盾する

conform junnō suru 順応する; *(of product)* tekigō suru 適合する

confront ... ni tachimukau …に立ち向かう

confrontation taiketsu 対決

confuse *(muddle)* konran saseru 混乱させる

confusing magirawashī 紛らわしい

confusion konran 混乱

congestion *(on roads)* jūtai 渋滞; *(in nose)* hanazumari 鼻詰まり

congratulate ... ni o-medetō to iu …におめでとうと言う

congratulations o-iwai no

kotoba お祝いの言葉; ~ *on* ... o-medetō …おめでとう

congregation REL kaishū 会衆

congress kaigi 会議; *Congress (of US)* Gikai 議会

congressional Gikai (no) 議会(の)

congressman Kain-gi-in 下院議員

conjunctivitis ketsumakuen 結膜炎

con man ikasamashi いかさま師

connect tsunagu つなぐ; *(to power supply)* setsuzoku suru 接続する

connecting flight setsuzoku-bin 接続便

connection *(in wiring)* setsuzoku 接続; *(link)* kankei 関係

conquer seifuku suru 征服する

conscience ryōshin 良心

conscious *adj (aware)* ki ga tsuite iru 気がついている; MED ishiki no aru 意識のある

consciousness jikaku 自覚; MED ishiki 意識

consecutive renzoku (no) 連続(の)

consent 1 *n* dōi 同意 **2** *v/i* dōi suru 同意する

consequence kekka 結果

consequently sono kekka その結果

conservative adj hoshuteki (na) 保守的(な); *clothes* jimi (na) 地味(な)

consider *(regard)* ... to minasu ...とみなす; *(show regard for)* omoiyaru 思いやる; *(think about)* yoku kangaeru よく考える

considerable kanari (no) かなり(の)

considerate omoiyari no aru 思いやりのある

consideration *(thought)* jukkō 熟考; *(thoughtfulness)* omoiyari 思いやり; *(factor)* kōryo subeki ten 考慮すべき点

consignment COMM yusō-kamotsu 輸送貨物

♦consist of ... kara naru ...から成る

consistent ikkan shita 一貫した

consolation nagusame 慰め

console *v/t* nagusameru 慰める

conspicuous medatsu 目立つ

conspiracy inbō 陰謀

constant *(continuous)* taezu tsuzuku 絶えず続く

constipation benpi 便秘

constitution POL. kenpō 憲法

construction *(of building etc)* kensetsu 建設; *(building)* kenzōbutsu 建造物

construction industry kensetsu-gyōkai 建設業界

construction worker kensetsu-rōdōsha 建設労働者

constructive kensetsuteki (na) 建設的(な)

consul ryōji 領事

consulate ryōjikan 領事館

consult ... ni sōdan suru ...に相談する

consultancy *(company)* konsarutanto-gyō コンサルタント業; *(advice)* adobaisu アドバイス

consultant konsarutanto コンサルタント

consumer shōhisha 消費者

consumption shōhi 消費; *(of energy)* shōhiryō 消費量

contact 1 *n (person)* tsute つて; *(communication)* renraku 連絡; *(physical)* sesshoku 接触 2 *v/t* ... ni renraku suru ...に連絡する

contact lens kontakuto-renzu コンタクトレンズ

contagious densensei (no) 伝染性(の)

contain *laughter* osaeru 抑える; *it ~ed my camera* sono

naka ni watashi no kamera ga haitte ita その中に私のカメラが入っていた

container iremono 入れ物; COMM kontena コンテナ

contamination osen 汚染

contemporary 1 adj gendai (no) 現代(の) **2** n dōjidai no hito 同時代の人

contempt keibetsu 軽べつ

contender SPORTS senshu 選手; (against champion) chōsensha 挑戦者

content[1] n naiyō 内容

content[2] adj manzoku de 満足で

contentment manzoku 満足

contents nakami 中身

contest[1] n (competition) kontesuto コンテスト; (for power) arasoi 争い

contest[2] v/t leadership etc arasou 争う

contestant kyōsōsha 競争者; (in competition) shutsujōsha 出場者

context bunmyaku 文脈

continent n tairiku 大陸

continual taema nai 絶え間ない

continue 1 v/t tsuzukeru 続ける **2** v/i tsuzuku 続く

continuous taema nai 絶え間ない

contraception hinin 避妊

contraceptive n hinin-gu 避妊具; (pill) hinin'yaku 避妊薬

contract n keiyaku 契約

contractor ukeoinin 請負人

contradict statement hitei suru 否定する; person hanron suru 反論する

contrary 1 adj hantai (no) 反対(の); ~ to ... ... ni hanshite ...に反して **2** n: on the ~ soredokoroka それどころか

contrast 1 n chigai 違い **2** v/t taihi suru 対比する

contribute v/t money kifu suru 寄付する; time teikyō suru 提供する

control 1 n (of organization) shihai 支配 **2** v/t (govern) shihai suru 支配する; class kontorōru suru コントロールする; (restrict) kisei suru 規制する; (regulate) kanri suru 管理する; ~ oneself jisei suru 自制する

control panel kontorōru-paneru コントロールパネル

control tower kōkū-kanseitō 航空管制塔

controversial ronsō no mato ni natte iru 論争の的になっている

convalescence kaifukuki 回復期

convenience benri 便利

convenience store konbini コンビニ

convenient *location* benri (na) 便利 (な)

convention *(tradition)* kanshū 慣習; *(conference)* taikai 大会

convention center kaigijō 会議場

conventional *person* kata ni hamatta 型にはまった

conversation kaiwa 会話

conversion henkan 変換; *(of measurement)* kanzan 換算

convert 1 *n* tenkōsha 転向者 **2** *v/t* kaeru 変える; *measurement* kanzan suru 換算する

convertible *n (car)* ōpun-kā オープンカー

convict 1 *n* jukeisha 受刑者 **2** *v/t* JUR yūzai-hanketsu o kudasu 有罪判決を下す

conviction JUR yūzai-hanketsu 有罪判決; *(belief)* kakushin 確信

convince kakushin saseru 確信させる

convincing settokuryoku no aru 説得力のある

cook 1 *n* ryōrinin 料理人 **2** *v/t & v/i* ryōri suru 料理する

cookbook ryōri no hon 料理の本

cookie kukkī クッキー

cooking *(food)* ryōri 料理

cool 1 *adj weather* suzushī 涼しい; *drink* tsumetai 冷たい; *(calm)* reisei (na) 冷静 (な); *(unfriendly)* reitan (na) 冷淡 (な); *infml (great)* kakko ī かっこいい **2** *v/i (of food)* sameru さめる; *(of tempers)* ochitsuku 落ち着く

cooperate kyōryoku suru 協力する

cooperative *adj (helpful)* kyōryokuteki (na) 協力的 (な)

coordinate *activities* chōsei suru 調整する

coordination *(of activities)* chōsei 調整

cop *infml* o-mawarisan お巡りさん

cope taiō suru 対応する

copier *(machine)* kopīki コピー機

copilot fuku-sōjūshi 副操縦士

copper *n (metal)* dō 銅

copy 1 *n (duplicate)* fukusei 複製; *(photo~)* kopī コピー; *(of book)* issatsu 一冊; *(of record, CD)* ichimai 一枚 **2** *v/t (imitate)* maneru まねる; *painting* fukusei suru 複製する

る; *(on photocopier, computer)* kopī suru コピーする

copyright n chosaku-ken 著作権

cord *(string)* himo ひも; *(cable)* kōdo コード

cordless phone kōdoresu-denwa コードレス電話

core 1 n *(of fruit)* shin しん 2 *adj* issue jūyō (na) 重要(な)

cork korukusen コルク栓; *(material)* koruku コルク

corkscrew sennuki 栓抜き

corn tōmorokoshi とうもろこし

corner n *(of page, room)* sumi 隅; *(of table, street)* kado 角; *(bend: on road)* magarikado 曲り角; *(in soccer)* kōnā kikku コーナーキック

corporal punishment taibatsu 体罰

corporate COMM kigyō (no) 企業(の)

corpse shitai 死体

corral n kakoi 囲い

correct 1 *adj* tadashī 正しい 2 *v/t* naosu 直す

correspondence *(letters)* tegami 手紙; *(exchange of letters)* buntsū 文通

correspondent *(reporter)* kisha 記者; *(abroad)* tokuhain 特派員

corridor rōka 廊下

corroborate urazukeru 裏付ける

corrosion fushoku 腐食

corrupt *adj* fuhai shita 腐敗した; COMPUT mojibake suru 文字化けする

corruption oshoku 汚職

cosmetics keshōhin 化粧品

cosmetic surgery biyō-seikei 美容整形

cost 1 n hiyō 費用; ~s kosuto コスト 2 *v/t* kakaru かかる; *how much does it ~?* ikura desu ka いくらですか

cost of living seikatsuhi 生活費

cot *(folding)* oritatami-shiki beddo 折りたたみ式ベッド

cotton 1 n wata 綿 2 *adj* men (no) 綿(の)

couch n nagaisu 長いす

cough 1 n seki せき 2 *v/i* seki o suru せきをする

could: *~ you help me?* tetsudatte itadakemasu ka 手伝って頂けますか; *this ~ be our bus* kore ga watashitachi no basu kamo shiremasen これが私達のバスかもしれません

council *(assembly)* gikai 議会

councilor gi-in 議員

counselor (*adviser*) kaunserā
カウンセラー; JUR bengonin
弁護人

count 1 *v/i* (*to ten etc*) kazu
o kazoeru 数を数える;
(*calculate*) keisan suru 計算
する; (*be important*) jūyō de
aru 重要である **2** *v/t* (~ *up*)
kazoeru 数える; (*include*)
kazu ni ireru 数に入れる

♦**count on** ate ni suru 当て
にする

countdown byōyomi 秒読み

counter (*in shop, café*) kauntā
カウンター; (*in game*) koma
こま

counteract chūwa suru 中
和する

counterfeit *adj* gizō (no) 偽
造(の)

counterpart (*person*) sōtō suru
hito 相当する人

counterproductive gyakukōka
(no) 逆効果(の)

countless kazoekirenai 数え
きれない

country kuni 国; (*not town*)
inaka 田舎

countryside inaka 田舎

coup POL kūdetā クーデター

couple (*married*) fūfu 夫
婦; (*romantically involved*)
kappuru カップル; (*two
people*) futarigumi 二人組;

just a ~ sukoshi dake 少し
だけ; *a* ~ *of* ni, san no 二、
三の

courage yūki 勇気

courier kūrie クーリエ; (*with
tourists*) tenjōin 添乗員;
motorcycle ~ baiku-bin バ
イク便

course *n* (*lessons, for sports*)
kōsu コース; (*part of meal*)
ippin 一品; (*of ship, plane*)
shinro 針路; *of* ~ mochiron
もちろん

court *n* JUR hōtei 法廷; SPORTS
kōto コート

courthouse saibansho 裁判所

courtroom hōtei 法廷

cousin itoko いとこ

cover 1 *n* (*protective*) kabā カ
バー; (*of book, magazine*)
hyōshi 表紙; (*for bed*) beddokabā ベッドカバー **2** *v/t*
ōu 覆う; (*hide*) kakusu 隠す;
(*of insurance*) ... ni hoken o
kakeru …に保険をかける

♦**cover up** *v/t* ōu 覆う; *fig*
momikesu もみ消す

coverage (*media*) hōdō 報道

covert hisoka (na) ひそか
(な)

coverup (*of crime etc*)
momikeshi もみ消し

cow *n* ushi 牛

coward okubyō-mono おく

びょう者

cowboy kaubōi カウボーイ

cozy igokochi no yoi 居心地
のよい

crab n kani かに

crack 1 n hibi ひび **2** v/t
cup hibi o ireru ひびを入れ
る; nut waru 割る; (solve)
kaiketsu suru 解決する

♦crack down on kibishiku
torishimaru 厳しく取り
締まる

cracker (to eat) kurakkā クラ
ッカー

craft (skill) gijutsu 技術;
(trade) shokugyō 職業

craftsman shokunin 職人

cramped room semai 狭い

cramps keiren けいれん

crane n (machine) kurēn クレ
ーン; (bird) tsuru つる

crash 1 n (noise) gachan to
iu oto がちゃんという
音; (accident) shōtotsu 衝突;
(plane ~) tsuiraku 墜落; COMM
tōsan 倒産; COMPUT kurasshu
クラッシュ **2** v/i (of car)
shōtotsu suru 衝突する; (of
plane) tsuiraku suru 墜落す
る; (of market) bōraku suru 暴
落する; COMPUT kurasshu suru
クラッシュする

crash helmet herumetto ヘ
ルメット

crater (of volcano) funkakō
噴火口

craving tsuyoi yokkyū 強
い欲求

crawl 1 n (swimming) kurōru
クロール **2** v/i (on floor) hau
はう; (move slowly) noronoro
susumu のろのろ進む

crayon kureyon クレヨン

crazy adj ki ga kurutta 気が
狂った; be ~ about ... ni
netchū shite iru …に熱中し
ている

cream 1 n (for skin, coffee)
kurīmu クリーム **2** adj
kurīmu-iro (no) クリーム
色(の)

crease (n) shiwa しわ;
(deliberate) orime 折り目

create v/t hikiokosu 引き起こ
す; jobs tsukuru 作る

creative sōzōsei ga aru 創造
性がある

creature (animal) ikimono
生き物

credible shin'yō dekiru 信用
できる; candidate etc shinrai
dekiru 信頼できる

credit n FIN tsuke つけ; (use of
~ cards) kurejitto クレジッ
ト; (honor) meiyo 名誉

credit card kurejitto-kādo ク
レジットカード

creditor saikensha 債権者

creek ogawa 小川

creep 1 *n pej* kobiru yatsu こ
びるやつ **2** *v/i* shinobiyoru
忍び寄る

cremation kasō 火葬

crew *n (of ship, plane)*
norikumi-in 乗組員

crime hanzai 犯罪

criminal 1 *n* hanzaisha 犯罪者
2 *adj* hanzai (no) 犯罪(の);
(shameful) keshikaran けし
からん

crisis kiki 危機

crisp *adj air* sawayaka (na)
さわやか(な); *lettuce*
shakishaki shita しゃきしゃ
きした; *shirt* paritto shita ぱ
りっとした

criterion kijun 基準

critic hyōronka 評論家

critical *(criticizing)* hihanteki
(na) 批判的(な); *(serious)*
kikiteki (na) 危機的(な);
moment etc jūdai (na) 重大
(な); MED jūtai (no) 重体(の)

criticism hihan 批判

criticize *v/t* hihan suru 批
判する

crook *n (dishonest)* akutō 悪党

crooked *(not straight)* magatta
曲がった; *business* fusei (na)
不正(な)

crop 1 *n* shūkaku 収穫
2 *v/t hair* karikomu 刈り込む;

photo hashi o kiriotosu 端を切
り落とす

cross 1 *adj (angry)* okotte
iru 怒っている **2** *n (X)*
batsu(jirushi) ばつ (印);
(Christian) jūjika 十字架 **3** *v/t
& v/i (go across)* wataru 渡る

♦ **cross out** kesu 消す

cross-examine hantai-jinmon
o okonau 反対尋問を行う

crosswalk ōdan-hodō 横
断歩道

crossword kurosuwādo-pazuru
クロスワードパズル

crouch *v/i* kagamu かがむ

crowd *n* gunshū 群衆; *(at
sports event)* kankyaku 観
客; *(in department store etc)*
hitogomi 人込み

crowded konda 込んだ

crucial jūdai (na) 重大(な)

crude *adj (vulgar)* gehin (na)
下品(な); *(unsophisticated)*
sozatsu (na) 粗雑(な)

cruel zankoku(na) 残酷(な)

cruelty gyakutai-kōi 虐待行為

cruise liner kyakusen 客船

crumb kuzu くず

crumble *v/i* kuzureru 崩れる;
fig hōkai suru 崩壊する

crusade *n fig* undō 運動

crush *v/t* oshitsubusu 押し
つぶす

crust *(on bread)* kawa 皮

crutch *(for walking)*
matsubazue 松葉杖

cry *v/i (weep)* naku 泣く

cub ko子

cube *(shape)* rippōtai 立方体

cucumber kyūri きゅうり

cuddle 1 *n* hōyō 抱擁 2 *v/t*
dakishimeru 抱き締める

cue *n (for actor, pool)* kyū キ
ュー

cuff *n (of shirt)* kafusu カフス;
(of pants) orikaeshi 折り返し

culinary ryōri (no) 料理(の)

culmination chōten 頂点

culprit hannin 犯人

cult *(sect)* shūha 宗派

cultivate *land* kōsaku suru 耕
作する

cultivated *person* kyōyō no aru
教養のある

cultural *(of the arts)*
geijutsuteki (na) 芸術的
(な); *(of a country's identity)*
bunkateki (na) 文化的(な)

culture *n* geijutsu 芸術; *(of a
country)* bunka 文化

cunning 1 *n* warugashikosa
悪賢さ 2 *adj* warugashikoi
悪賢い

cup *n* kappu カップ; *a ~
of tea* ippai no ocha 一杯
のお茶

cupboard todana 戸棚

curator kanchō 館長

curb 1 *n (of street)* fuchi-ishi
縁石 2 *v/t* yokusei suru 抑
制する

cure MED 1 *n* chiryōhō 治療法
2 *v/t* chiryō suru 治療する

curiosity kōkishin 好奇心

curious kōkishin no tsuyoi 好
奇心の強い; *(strange)* kimyō
(na) 奇妙(な)

currency *(money)* tsūka 通貨;
foreign ~ gaika 外貨

current 1 *n (in river)* nagare 流
れ; *(in sea)* kairyū 海流; ELEC
denryū 電流 2 *adj (present)*
genzai (no) 現在(の)

current affairs jiji-mondai 時
事問題

currently ima no tokoro 今の
ところ

curriculum karikyuramu カリ
キュラム

curse *n (spell)* noroi のろい

cursor kāsoru カーソル

curtain kāten カーテン; THEAT
maku 幕

curve 1 *n* kābu カーブ 2 *v/i*
magaru 曲がる

cushion *n* kusshon クッシ
ョン

custody *(of children)* yōikuken
養育権; *in ~* JUR kōryū sarete
拘留されて

custom *(tradition)* kanshū
慣習

customer kyaku 客
customs zeikan 税関
customs officer zeikanri 税関官吏
cut 1 n (with knife) kirikuchi 切り口; (injury) kirikizu 切り傷; (of garment, hair) katto カット; (reduction) sakugen 削減 **2** v/t kiru 切る; (reduce) sakugen suru 削減する; **get one's hair ~** kami o kitte morau 髪を切ってもらう
♦ **cut back** v/i (in costs) kiritsumeru 切り詰める
♦ **cut down 1** v/t tree kiritaosu 切り倒す **2** v/i (in smoking etc) herasu 減らす

♦ **cut off** (with knife) kiritoru 切り取る; (isolate) koritsu saseru 孤立させる; TEL denwa o kiru 電話を切る
cute (pretty) kawaii かわいい; (sexually) suteki (na) 素敵(な)
cutting adj remark shinratsu (na) 辛らつ(な)
cycle 1 n (bicycle) jitensha 自転車 **2** v/i: **~ to work** jitensha de shigoto ni iku 自転車で仕事に行く
cyclist saikuringu suru hito サイクリングする人
cynic hinikuya 皮肉屋
cynical hiniku (na) 皮肉(な)

D

DA (= district attorney) chihō-kenji 地方検事
dad o-tōsan お父さん, papa パパ; (talking to outsiders about own father) chichi 父
daily 1 n (paper) nikkan-shi 日刊紙 **2** adj mainichi (no) 毎日(の)
dairy products nyūseihin 乳製品
dam n (for water) damu ダム
damage 1 n songai 損害; fig (to reputation) kizu 傷

2 v/t songai o ataeru 損害を与える
damages JUR songai-baishō 損害賠償
damn infml **1** interjection shimatta しまった **2** adj imaimashī いまいましい
damp room shimeppoi 湿っぽい; cloth shimetta 湿った
dance 1 n dansu ダンス; (event) dansu-pāti ダンスパーティー; **Japanese ~** Nihon-buyō 日本舞踊 **2** v/i

odoru 踊る

dancer odoru hito 踊る人;
(performer) dansā ダンサー

dancing dansu ダンス

danger kiken 危険

dangerous kiken (na) 危
険(な)

dare v/i omoikitte ... suru 思い
切って…する

daring adj daitan (na) 大胆
(な)

dark 1 n kuragari 暗がり
2 adj night kurai 暗い; *hair*
kuroppoi 黒っぽい; *color* koi
濃い; ~ *blue* kon 紺

darling n *(woman to man)* anata
あなた; *(man to woman)*
nē ねえ

dash 1 n *(punctuation)* dasshu
ダッシュ 2 v/i tosshin suru
突進する

data dēta データ

database dēta-bēsu データ
ベース

data protection dēta-hogo デ
ータ保護

date n hizuke 日付; *(romantic)*
dēto デート; *what's the ~
today?* kyō wa nannichi desu
ka 今日は何日ですか; *out
of ~ passport* kigengire de 期
限切れで

daughter *(own)* musume 娘;
(sb else's) o-jōsan お嬢さん,

musumesan 娘さん

daughter-in-law giri no
musume 義理の娘; *(sb else's)*
giri no musumesan 義理の
娘さん

dawn n yoake 夜明け

day hi 日; *(daytime)* hiruma 昼
間; *the ~ after* sono tsugi no
hi その次の日; *the other ~*
senjitsu 先日; *~ by ~* higoto ni
日ごとに ◊ *(with count word)*
nichi 日; *a ~* ichinichi 一日;
two ~s futsuka 二日; *three
~s* mikka 三日; *four ~s* yokka
四日; *five ~s* itsuka 五日;
six ~s muika 六日; *seven ~s*
nanoka 七日; *eight ~s* yōka
八日; *nine ~s* kokonoka 九
日; *ten ~s* tōka 十日

daylight hi no hikari 日の光

daytrip higaeri-ryokō 日帰
り旅行

dazed *(by blow)* bon'yari shite
ぼんやりして

dazzle v/t *(of light)* ... no me
o kuramaseru …の目をく
らませる

dead 1 adj shinda 死んだ;
battery kirete iru 切れている;
phone tsūjinai 通じない
2 n: *the ~* shinda hito 死
んだ人

dead end *(street)* ikidomari 行
きどまり

deadline saishū-kigen 最終期限; *(for submissions)* shimekiri 締め切り

deadlock *n* ikizumari 行き詰まり

deaf mimi ga kikoenai 耳が聞こえない

deaf-and-dumb rōa (no) ろうあ(の)

deafening mimi o tsunzaku yō (na) 耳をつんざくよう(な)

deal *n* torihiki 取り引き; *a good ~ (bargain)* toku na kaimono 得な買物; *a great ~ of* takusan (no) たくさん(の)

dealer COMM dīrā ディーラー; *(drugs)* mayaku-mitsubainin 麻薬密売人

dealings *(business)* kankei 関係

dear *adj (to a person)* shin'ai (na) 親愛(な); *Dear Sir* haikei 拝啓; *Dear Richard* richādo-sama リチャード様

death shi 死

death penalty shikei 死刑

death toll shibōsha-sū 死亡者数

debate 1 *n* tōgi 討議; POL tōron 討論 2 *v/t & v/i* tōron suru 討論する

debit *n* hikiotoshi 引き落とし

debris zangai 残がい

debt shakkin 借金

debtor fusaisha 負債者

decade jūnenkan 十年間

decaffeinated kafein o nuita カフェインを抜いた

decay 1 *n (process)* fuhai 腐敗 2 *v/i* kusaru 腐る; *(of teeth)* mushiba ni naru 虫歯になる

deceased: *the ~* kojin 故人

deceitful fushōjiki (na) 不正直(な)

deceive damasu だます

December jūnigatsu 十二月

decency reigi 礼儀

decent *person* mattō (na) まっとう(な); *price* kekkō (na) 結構(な)

deception gomakashi ごまかし

deceptive mikake to nakami no chigatta 見かけと中身の違った

decide *v/t & v/i* kimeru 決める

decipher kaidoku suru 解読する

decision kettei 決定

decision-maker ketteisha 決定者

decisive kippari shita きっぱりした; *(crucial)* ketteiteki (na) 決定的(な)

deck *(of ship)* dekki デッキ; *(of cards)* hitokumi 一組

declare dangen suru 断言す

る; *independence* sengen suru 宣言する; *(customs)* shinkoku suru 申告する

decline 1 *n (fall)* genshō 減少; *(in standards)* teika 低下 **2** *v/t invitation* kotowaru 断わる **3** *v/i (refuse)* kotowaru 断わる; *(decrease)* genshō suru 減少する; *(of health)* teika suru 低下する

decode kaidoku suru 解読する

décor interia インテリア

decorate *(with paint, paper)* naisō suru 内装する

decoy *n* otori おとり

decrease 1 *n (in number)* genshō 減少; *(in size)* shukushō 縮小 **2** *v/t number* genshō saseru 減少させる; *size* shukushō suru 縮小する **3** *v/i (of number)* genshō suru 減少する; *(of size)* shukushō suru 縮小する

dedicate *book etc* sasageru 捧げる

dedication *(to cause)* kenshin 献身

deduce suiron suru 推論する

deduct sashihiku 差し引く

deduction *(from salary)* kōjo 控除; *(conclusion)* suiron 推論

deed *n (act)* okonai 行い; JUR shōsho 証書

deep *water* fukai 深い; *voice* hikui 低い

deep freeze *n* reitōko 冷凍庫

deep-fry ageru 揚げる

deer shika しか

deface sokonau 損なう

defamation meiyo-kison 名誉棄損

defeat 1 *n* haiboku 敗北 **2** *v/t* makasu 負かす

defect *n* kekkan 欠陥

defective kekkan no aru 欠陥のある

defend mamoru 守る; *(justify)* shakumei suru 釈明する; JUR bengo suru 弁護する

defendant hikoku 被告

defense *n* bōei 防衛; SPORTS difensu ディフェンス; JUR bengo *(justification)* shakumei 釈明

defense lawyer hikoku-bengonin 被告弁護人

defiance hankō 反抗

defiant hankōteki (na) 反抗的 (な)

deficit akaji 赤字

define *word* teigi suru 定義する; *goal* akiraka ni suru 明らかにする

definite hakkiri to kimatta はっきりと決まった; *(certain)* kakujitsu (na) 確実 (な)

definitely tashika ni 確かに

definition teigi 定義; *(of objective)* setsumei 説明

deformity kikei 奇形

defraud ... kara damashitoru …からだまし取る

defrost *v/t food* kaitō suru 解凍する

defuse *bomb* shinkan o torinozoku 信管を取り除く; *situation* yawarageru 和らげる

defy mushi suru 無視する

degrading kutsujokuteki (na) 屈辱的(な)

degree do 度; *(university)* gakui 学位; *(amount)* teido 程度

dehydrated dassui-shōjō o okoshite 脱水症状を起こして

dejected rakutan shita 落胆した

delay 1 *n* okure 遅れ **2** *v/t* nobasu 延ばす; *be ~ed* okureru 遅れる

delegate 1 *n* daihyō 代表 **2** *v/t task* makaseru 任せる

delegation *(of task)* inin 委任; *(people)* daihyō-dan 代表団

delete sakujo suru 削除する; *(cross out)* kesu 消す

deli derikatessen デリカテッセン

deliberate 1 *adj* koi (no) 故意(の) **2** *v/i* jukkō suru 熟考する

deliberately waza to わざと

delicate *fabric* sensai (na) 繊細(な); *problem* derikēto (na) デリケート(な); *health* yowai 弱い

delicious oishī おいしい

delight *n* ōyorokobi 大喜び

delighted yorokonde iru 喜んでいる

delightful tanoshī 楽しい

deliver haitatsu suru 配達する; *message* todokeru 届ける

delivery haitatsu 配達; *(of baby)* shussan 出産

delusion sakkaku 錯覚

de luxe gōka (na) 豪華(な)

demand 1 *n* yōkyū 要求; COMM juyō 需要 **2** *v/t* yōkyū suru 要求する; *(require)* hitsuyō to suru 必要とする

demanding *job* kitsui きつい; *person* kimuzukashī 気難しい

democracy *(system)* minshu-shugi 民主主義

democrat minshu-shugisha 民主主義者; *Democrat* POL minshutō-in 民主党員

democratic minshuteki (na) 民主的(な)

demolish *building* torikowasu 取り壊す

demonstrate 1 *v/t* (prove) risshō suru 立証する; *machine* miseru 見せる 2 *v/i* (politically) demo o suru デモをする

demonstration (show) risshō 立証; (protest) demo デモ; (of machine) demonsutorēshon デモンストレーション

demonstrator (protester) demo-sankasha デモ参加者

demoralized yaru ki o nakusaseta やる気をなくさせた

denial (of rumor) hitei 否定; (of request) kyohi 拒否

denims jīnzu ジーンズ

denomination FIN gakumen 額面; REL shūha 宗派

dense (thick) koi 濃い; *foliage* missei shita 密生した; *crowd* misshū shita 密集した

dent 1 *n* hekomi へこみ 2 *v/t* hekomaseru へこませる

dental ha (no) 歯(の); *hospital* shika (no) 歯科(の)

dentist haisha 歯医者

dentures ireba 入れ歯

deny *rumor* hitei suru 否定する; *request* kyohi suru 拒否する

deodorant deodoranto デオドラント

department (of company) bu 部; ka 課; (of university) gakubu 学部, gakka 学科; (of government) shō 省; (of store) uriba 売り場

department store depāto デパート

departure shuppatsu 出発; (of train, bus) hassha 発車

departure lounge shuppatsu-raunji 出発ラウンジ

departure time shuppatsu-jikoku 出発時刻

depend: *that ~s* bāi ni yoru 場合による; *it ~s on the weather* tenki ni yoru 天気による

dependence izon 依存

dependent *n* fuyō-kazoku 扶養家族

deplorable nagekawashī 嘆かわしい

deport kyōsei-sōkan suru 強制送還する

deposit 1 *n* (in bank) yokin 預金; (on purchase) tetsukekin 手付け金 2 *v/t money* yokin suru 預金する

depressed *person* yū-utsu (na) 憂うつ(な)

depressing yū-utsu (na) 憂うつ(な)

depression MED utsubyō うつ病; (economic) fukyō 不況; (weather) teikiatsu 低気圧

deprive: ~ *X of Y* X kara Y o ubau XからYを奪う

deprived mazushī 貧しい

depth fukasa 深さ; *(of voice)* hikusa 低さ

deputy dairinin 代理人

derelict *adj* hōki sareta 放棄された

derive *v/t* eru 得る

derogatory keibetsuteki (na) 軽べつ的(な)

descend 1 *v/i* oriru 下りる **2** *v/t* oriru 降りる; *(of road)* kudari ni naru 下りになる

descendant shison 子孫

descent *(from hill)* gezan 下山; *(of plane)* kōka 降下; *(ancestry)* kakei 家系; *of Chinese* ~ chūgokukei no 中国系の

describe īarawasu 言い表す

description byōsha 描写; *(of criminal)* ninsō 人相

desert[1] *n* sabaku 砂漠

desert[2] **1** *v/t (abandon)* misuteru 見捨てる **2** *v/i (of soldier)* dassō suru 脱走する

deserted sabireta さびれた

deserter MIL dassōhei 脱走兵

deserve ... ni atai suru …に値する

design 1 *n* dezain デザイン; *(for building)* sekkei 設計 **2** *v/t* sekkei suru 設計する; *clothes* dezain suru デザインする

designer dezainā デザイナー; *(of building)* sekkeisha 設計者

designer clothes burando-mono ブランド物

desire *n (wish)* negai 願い; *(sexual)* yokubō 欲望

desk tsukue 机; *(in hotel)* furonto フロント

desktop publishing desukutoppu-paburisshingu デスクトップパブリッシング

despair *n* zetsubō 絶望

desperate *action* hisshi (no) 必死(の); *situation* zetsubōteki (na) 絶望的(な)

despise keibetsu suru 軽べつする

despite ... nimo kakawarazu …にもかかわらず

dessert dezāto デザート

destination mokutekichi 目的地

destiny unmei 運命

destitute konkyū (no) 困窮(の)

destroy hakai suru 破壊する

destruction hakai 破壊

detach torihazusu 取りはずす

detached *(objective)* reisei (na)

冷静(な)

detail n komakai ten 細かい
点; (information) shōsai 詳細

detailed komakai 細かい

detain hikitomeru 引き止め
る; (as prisoner) kōryū suru
拘留する

detainee POL. seijihan 政治犯

detect ... ni kizuku …に気
づく; (of device) tanchi suru
探知する

detective keiji 刑事

detention (prison) kōkin 拘禁

deter soshi suru 阻止する

detergent senzai 洗剤

deteriorate waruku naru 悪
くなる

determination ketsui 決意

determined kataku kesshin
shite 堅く決心して; effort
danko to shita 断固とした

deterrent n yokushiryoku 抑
止力

detest hidoku kirau ひど
く嫌う

devaluation FIN heika-kirisage
平価切り下げ

develop 1 v/t film genzō suru
現像する; land kaihatsu suru
開発する; business hatten
saseru 発展させる; (improve
on) shinten saseru 進展させ
る **2** v/i (grow) sodatsu 育
つ; (of business) hatten suru

developing country hatten-
tojōkoku 発展途上国

development (of film) genzō
現像; (of land) kaihatsu 開
発; (of business) hatten 発展;
(improving) shinten 進展

device (tool) dōgu 道具;
(gadget) sōchi 装置

devil akuma 悪魔

devise kōan suru 考案する

devote time etc ateru 充てる;
life sasageru 捧げる

devotion (to person) kenshin
献身; (to job) chūsei 忠誠

devour food musaborikū むさ
ぼり食う

diabetes tōnyōbyō 糖尿病

diagonal adj naname (no) 斜
め(の)

diagram zu 図

dial 1 n (of clock) moji-ban 文
字盤; (of meter) keiki-ban 計
器盤 **2** v/t number daiyaru suru
ダイヤルする

dialect hōgen 方言

dialog taiwa 対話

diameter chokkei 直径

diamond daiyamondo ダイ
ヤモンド

diaper o-shime おしめ

diarrhea geri 下痢

diary nikki 日記; (for
appointments) techō 手帳

dictator dokusaisha 独裁者

dictionary jisho 辞書

die shinu 死ぬ

diet 1 *n (regular food)* shokuseikatsu 食生活; *(for weight)* daietto ダイエット; *(for health)* shokuji-ryōhō 食事療法 2 *v/i* daietto suru ダイエットする

differ *(be different)* kotonaru 異なる

difference chigai 違い

different *(dissimilar)* chigau 違う; *(distinct)* betsu (no) 別(の)

difficult muzukashī 難しい

difficulty muzukashisa 難しさ

dig *v/t* horu 掘る

digest *v/t* shōka suru 消化する

digestion shōka 消化

digital dejitaru-shiki (no) デジタル式(の)

dignified dōdō to shita 堂々とした

dignity kihin 気品

dilapidated arehateta 荒れ果てた

dilemma jirenma ジレンマ

dilute *v/t* usumeru 薄める

dim 1 *adj light* usugurai 薄暗い; *outline* bon'yari shita ぼんやりした 2 *v/t: ~ the headlights* heddoraito o shita ni mukeru ヘッドライトを

下に向ける

dime jussento-kōka 十セント硬貨

dimension *(measurement)* sunpō 寸法

diminish *v/i* genshō suru 減少する

dine shokuji o suru 食事をする

diner *(person)* kyaku 客; *(restaurant)* shokudō 食堂

dining car shokudōsha 食堂車

dining room shokudō 食堂

dinner *(evening)* yūshoku 夕食; *(midday)* chūshoku 昼食

dinner jacket takishīdo タキシード

dinner party dinā-pātī ディナーパーティー

dip *n (food)* dippu ディップ; *(in road)* kubomi くぼみ

diploma sotsugyō-shōsho 卒業証書

diplomat gaikōkan 外交官

diplomatic gaikōkan (no) 外交官(の); *(tactful)* sotsu no nai そつのない

direct 1 *adj chokusetsu (no)* 直接(の); *flight* chokkō (no) 直行(の); *train* chokutsū (no) 直通(の); *person* sotchoku (na) 率直(な) 2 *v/t (to a place)* ... ni michi o oshieru

…に道を教える; *movie kantoku suru* 監督する

direction *hōkō* 方向; *~s (instructions) shiji* 指示; *(to a place) michi* 道; *(for use) shiyōhō* 使用法; *(for medicine) fukuyōhō* 服用法

director *(of company) torishimariyaku* 取締役; *(of movie) kantoku* 監督

directory *meibo* 名簿; TEL *denwachō* 電話帳

dirt *yogore* 汚れ

dirty *adj kitanai* 汚い

disabled *n: the ~ shintai-shōgaisha* 身体障害者

disadvantage *furi na koto* 不利なこと

disagree *iken ga awanai* 意見が合わない

disagreement *iken no sōi* 意見の相違; *(argument) kenka* けんか

disappear *kieru* 消える

disappearance *shissō* 失そう

disappoint *gakkari saseru* がっかりさせる

disappointed *gakkari shita* がっかりした

disappointment *shitsubō* 失望

disapproval *fusansei* 不賛成

disapprove *sansei shinai* 賛成しない

disaster *saigai* 災害

disastrous *hisan (na)* 悲惨(な)

discharge *v/t (from hospital) tai-in saseru* 退院させる; *(from army) jotai saseru* 除隊させる

disciple REL *deshi* 弟子

discipline *n kiritsu* 規律

disc jockey *dī-jē* DJ

disclosure *(of information) kōhyō* 公表

disco *disuko* ディスコ

disconnect *appliance torihazusu* 取りはずす; *supply tomeru* 止める

discount *n waribiki* 割引

discourage *(dissuade) … ni omoitodomaru yō ni iu* …に思いとどまるようにいう; *(dishearten) jishin o ushinawaseru* 自信を失わせる

discover *hakken suru* 発見する

discovery *hakken* 発見

discreet *person shinchō (na)* 慎重(な)

discrepancy *mujun* 矛盾

discretion *shinchōsa* 慎重さ

discrimination *sabetsu* 差別

discuss *hanashiau* 話し合う

discussion *hanashiai* 話し合い; *(in the press) giron* 議論

disease byōki 病気

disembark v/i (from plane) oriru 降りる; (from ship) gesen suru 下船する

disgrace n haji 恥

disgraceful hazubeki 恥ずべき

disguise n hensō 変装

disgust 1 n ken'o 嫌悪 **2** v/t mukatsukaseru むかつかせる

disgusting habit iya (na) いや (な); smell, food kimochi no warui 気持ちの悪い

dish (part of meal) ryōri 料理; (container) sara 皿

dishcloth shokki-araiyō kurosu 食器洗い用クロス

disheartened gakkari shita がっかりした

dishonest fushōjiki (na) 不正直(な)

dishonesty fushōjiki 不正直

dishonor n fumeiyo 不名誉

dishwasher sara-araiki 皿洗い機

dishwashing liquid senzai 洗剤

disinfectant shōdokuzai 消毒剤

disintegrate barabara ni naru ばらばらになる

disjointed matomari no nai まとまりのない

disk (shape) enban 円盤; COMPUT disuku ディスク

diskette furoppī-disuku フロッピーディスク

dislike v/t kirau 嫌う

dislocate shoulder dakkyū saseru 脱臼させる

disloyal uragirimono (no) 裏切り者(の)

dismal weather iya (na) いや(な); news kurai 暗い; person (sad) inki (na) 陰気(な)

dismantle machine bunkai suru 分解する

dismay n (alarm) tōwaku 当惑; (disappointment) shitsubō 失望

dismiss employee kaiko suru 解雇する

disobedience fufukujū 不服従

disobedient hankōteki (na) 反抗的(な)

disobey ... ni sakarau …に逆らう

disorder (untidiness) ranzatsu 乱雑; MED shōgai 障害

disorganized mechakucha (na) めちゃくちゃ(な); person keikakusei no nai 計画性のない

disoriented konran shita 混乱した

disown kandō suru 勘当する

dispatch *v/t (send)* hassō suru
発送する

dispensary *(in pharmacy)*
chōzaishitsu 調剤室

display 1 *n* tenji 展示; *(in store
window)* disupurē ディスプ
レー; COMPUT monitā モニタ
ー **2** *v/t emotion* miseru 見せ
る; *(at exhibition)* tenji suru 展
示する; *(for sale)* chinretsu
suru 陳列する

displeasure ikari 怒り

disposable tsukaisute (no) 使
い捨て(の)

disposal shobun 処分; *(of
pollutants)* haiki 廃棄

dispose: ~ *of* shimatsu suru
始末する

disposition *(nature)* kishitsu
気質

disproportionate futsuriai (na)
不つり合い(な)

disprove hanshō suru 反証
する

dispute 1 *n* ronsō 論争,
(between countries) funsō 紛
争; *(industrial)* sōgi 争議 **2** *v/t*
hanron suru 反論する

disqualify shikkaku to suru 失
格とする

disrespectful shitsurei (na) 失
礼(な)

disrupt *train service* midasu 乱
す; *meeting* jama suru 邪魔す

る; *(intentionally)* bōgai suru
妨害する

disruptive meiwaku (na) 迷
惑(な)

dissatisfaction fuman 不満

dissatisfied fuman (na) 不
満(な)

dissent *n* hantai 反対

dissident *n* iken no chigau hito
意見の違う人

dissolve 1 *v/t substance* tokasu
溶かす **2** *v/i (of substance)*
tokeru 溶ける

dissuade omoi-todomaraseru
思いとどまらせる

distance *n* kyori 距離; *in the
~* tōku ni 遠くに

distant tōi 遠い; *(aloof)*
yosoyososhi よそよそしい

distasteful fuyukai (na) 不愉
快(な)

distinct *(clear)* hakkiri shita は
っきりした; *(different)* betsu
(no) 別(の)

distinctive dokutoku (na) 独
特(な)

distinctly hakkiri to はっき
りと; *(decidedly)* utagai naku
疑いなく

distinguish: ~ *between X and
Y* X to Y no kubetsu o suru
XとYの区別をする

distinguished *(famous)* yūmei
(na) 有名(な); *(dignified)*

jōhin (na) 上品（な）

distort yugameru ゆがめる

distract person jama suru 邪魔する; attention sorasu そらす

distraught torimidashita 取り乱した

distress n kunō 苦悩; (physical pain) kutsū 苦痛

distribute kubaru 配る; COMM hanbai suru 販売する

distribution haifu 配布; COMM ryūtsū 流通

distributor COMM ryūtsū-gyōsha 流通業者

district chiku 地区

district attorney chihō-kenji 地方検事

distrust 1 n fushinkan 不信感 2 v/t shin'yō shinai 信用しない

disturb (interrupt) ... no jama o suru ...の邪魔をする; (upset) fuan ni saseru 不安にさせる

disturbance (interruption) jama 邪魔; ~s bōdō 暴動

disturbed (worried) shinpai (na) 心配（な）

disturbing dōyō saseru 動揺させる

ditch n mizo 溝

dive 1 n tobikomi 飛び込み; (underwater) daibingu ダイ

ビング 2 v/i tobikomu 飛び込む; (underwater) daibingu o suru ダイビングをする; (of plane) kyūkōka suru 急降下する

diver (off board) tobikomi no senshu 飛び込みの選手; (underwater) daibā ダイバー

diverge bunki suru 分岐する

diversify v/i COMM takaku-keiei suru 多角経営する

diversion (for traffic) ukairo う回路

divert traffic ukai saseru う回させる; attention sorasu そらす

divide wakeru 分ける; waru 割る

dividend FIN haitōkin 配当金

divine REL kami (no) 神（の）

division warizan 割り算; (splitting into parts) bunkatsu 分割; (of company) bu 部

divorce 1 n rikon 離婚 2 v/t ... to rikon suru ...と離婚する 3 v/i rikon suru 離婚する

divorced rikon shita 離婚した

dizzy: feel ~ memai ga suru めまいがする

do 1 v/t suru する; what are you ~ing tonight? kyō no yoru wa nani o suru no desu ka 今日の夜は何をするのですか; I don't know what to

~ dō shitara ī ka wakarimasen どうしたらいいか分かりません 2 v/i (be suitable, enough) ma ni au 間に合う; **well done!** o-medetō おめでとう; **how ~ you ~?** hajimemashite はじめまして

dock[1] 1 n NAUT dokku ドック 2 v/i (of ship) dokku ni hairu ドックに入る

dock[2] JUR hikokuseki 被告席

doctor n MED isha 医者; (form of address) sensei 先生

document n bunsho 文書

documentary n dokyumentarī ドキュメンタリー

documentation shorui 書類

dodge v/t blow yokeru よける; question hagurakasu はぐらかす

dog n inu 犬

dogma kyōgi 教義

do-it-yourself nichiyō-daiku 日曜大工

doll (toy) ningyō 人形

dollar doru ドル

dolphin iruka いるか

domestic adj chores katei (no) 家庭(の); policy kokunai (no) 国内(の)

domestic flight kokunaisen 国内線

dominant omo (na) 主(な); member yūsei (na) 優勢(な)

dominate shihai suru 支配する; landscape ... ni sobieru …にそびえる

donate money kifu suru 寄付する

donkey roba ろば

donor (of money) kizōsha 寄贈者

donut dōnattsu ドーナッツ

door to 戸, doa ドア; (double ~s) tobira 扉; (entrance) deiriguchi 出入口

doorbell buzā ブザー

doorman doaman ドアマン

dormitory ryō 寮

dose n ikkaibun 一回分

dot n ten 点; (in e-mail address) dotto ドット

dotted line tensen 点線

double 1 n (amount) nibai (二)倍; (person) sokkuri na hito そっくりな人 2 adj (twice as much) (ni)bai (no) (二)倍(の); whiskey daburu (no) ダブル(の) 3 adv bai (no) (二)倍(の) 4 v/t (ni)bai ni suru (二)倍にする 5 v/i (ni)bai ni naru (二)倍になる

double bed daburubeddo ダブルベッド

doublecheck v/t & v/i saitenken suru 再点検する

double click daburu kurikku suru ダブルクリックする

doublecross v/t … ni nimaijita o tsukau …に二枚舌を使う

double room daburu-rūmu ダブルルーム

doubles (in tennis) daburusu ダブルス

doubt 1 n utagai 疑い; (uncertainty) gimon 疑問 2 v/t utagau 疑う

doubtful remark utagawashī 疑わしい

doubtless utagai nai 疑いない

dough kiji 生地

dove hato はと

down 1 adv (downward) shita no hō e 下の方へ; $200 ~ (as deposit) nihyaku doru sokkin de 200ドル即金で; be ~ (of price, rate) sagatte iru 下がっている; (not working) sadō shite inai 作動していない 2 prep: run ~ the stairs kaidan o kakeoriru 階段を駆け降りる; walk ~ the street (along) michi o aruku 道を歩く

downfall botsuraku 没落; (of politician) shikkyaku 失脚

download COMPUT daunrōdo suru ダウンロードする

down payment atamakin 頭金

downpour doshaburi どしゃ降り

downscale adj yasui 安い

downstairs 1 adj kaika (no) 階下（の）2 adv kaika ni 階下に

downtown 1 adj hankagai (no) 繁華街（の）2 adv hankagai ni 繁華街に

downturn (in economy) kakō 下降

doze 1 n utatane うたたね 2 v/i utatane suru うたたねする

dozen dāsu ダース

draft n (of air) sukimakaze すきま風; (of document) shitagaki 下書き; MIL chōhei 徴兵; ~ (beer) namabīru 生ビール

drafty sukimakaze no hairu すきま風の入る

drag 1 v/t (pull) hikizuriru 引きずる; person hikizuridasu 引きずり出す 2 v/i (of time) noronoro susumu のろのろ進む; (of show) daradara nagabiku だらだら長引く

dragon ryū 竜

drain 1 n (pipe) haisuikan 排水管; (under street) mizo 溝 2 v/t water haisui suru 排水する; oil nuku 抜く

drama dorama ドラマ; (theater) engeki 演劇

dramatic engeki (no) 演劇（の）; (exciting) doramachikku (na) ドラマチック（な）

drapes kāten カーテン

drastic *(extreme)* kyokutan (na) 極端(な); *measures* bapponteki (na) 抜本的(な)

draw 1 *n (in lottery)* kujibiki く じ引き; *(attraction)* yobimono 呼び物 **2** *v/t picture* kaku か く; *gun* nuku 抜く; *(attract)* hikiyoseru 引き寄せる; *(lead)* hipparu 引っ張る; *(from bank account)* hikidasu 引き出す **3** *v/i e o kaku* 絵をかく

drawback ketten 欠点

drawer *(of desk etc)* hikidashi 引き出し

drawing suketchi スケッチ

dread *v/t* kowagaru 怖がる

dreadful hidoi ひどい

dream 1 *n* yume 夢 **2** *v/i* yume o miru 夢を見る

dreary inki (na) 陰気(な)

dress 1 *n (for woman)* wanpīsu ワンピース; *(clothing)* fukusō 服装 **2** *v/t person ... ni fuku o kiseru* ...に服を着せ る **3** *v/i (get ~ed)* fuku o kiru 服を着る

dresser *(dressing table)* kyōdai 鏡台; *(in kitchen)* shokkidana 食器棚

dressing *(for salad)* doresshingu ドレッシング; MED hōtai 包帯

dress rehearsal butai-geiko 舞台げいこ

dried *fruit etc* kansō shita 乾 燥した

drier *(machine)* kansōki 乾 燥機

drift *v/i (of snow)* fukidamaru 吹きだまる; *(of ship)* hyōryū suru 漂流する

drill 1 *n (tool)* doriru ドリル; *(exercise)* bōsai-kunren 防災 訓練 **2** *v/t hole ... ni ana o akeru* ...に穴をあける **3** *v/i (for oil)* horu 掘る

drink 1 *n* nomimono 飲物; *(alcoholic)* sake 酒; *a ~ of ... ... ippai* ...一杯; *go for a ~* nomi ni iku 飲みに行く **2** *v/t & v/i* nomu 飲む

drinkable inryōyō (no) 飲料 用(の)

drinking water inryōsui 飲 料水

drip *v/i* shitataru したたる

drive 1 *n (journey)* michinori 道のり; *(outing)* doraibu ド ライブ; *(energy)* yaruki やる 気; COMPUT doraibu ドライブ **2** *v/t vehicle* unten suru 運転 する; *(take in car)* nosete iku 乗せて行く; *(power)* ugokasu 動かす **3** *v/i* unten suru 運 転する

driver untenshu 運転手

driver's license unten-menkyoshō 運転免許証

driveway kuruma-mawashi 車回し

driving n unten 運転

driving lesson jidōsha-kyōshū 自動車教習

driving test unten-menkyo-shiken 運転免許試験

drizzle n kirisame 霧雨

droop v/i tareru 垂れる; (of plant) shioreru しおれる

drop 1 n (of rain) shizuku 滴; (small amount) shōryō 少量; (in price) teika 低下; (in number) genshō 減少 2 v/t object otosu 落とす; person from car orosu 降ろす; (give up) yameru やめる 3 v/i ochiru 落ちる; (decline) sagaru 下がる

dropout (school) chūto-taigakusha 中途退学者; (society) rakugosha 落伍者

drought kanbatsu 干ばつ

drown v/i oboreshinu おぼれ死ぬ

drowsy nemui 眠い

drug n MED kusuri 薬; (illegal) mayaku 麻薬

drug addict mayaku-jōyōsha 麻薬常用者

drug dealer mayaku-mitsubainin 麻薬密売人

druggist yakuzaishi 薬剤師

drugstore yakkyoku 薬局

drug trafficking mayaku-mitsubai 麻薬密売

drum n MUS doramu ドラム; (Japanese-style) taiko 太鼓; (container) doramu-kan ドラム缶

drunk 1 n nondakure 飲んだくれ 2 adj yopparatta 酔っ払った; **get ~** yopparau 酔っ払う

drunk driving inshu-unten 飲酒運転

dry 1 adj weather ame no furanai 雨の降らない; mouth kawaita 乾いた; wine karakuchi (no) 辛口 (の) 2 v/t kawakasu 乾かす 3 v/i kawaku 乾く

dry-cleaner doraikurīninguya ドライクリーニング屋

dry-cleaning doraikurīningu ドライクリーニング

dryer (machine) kansōki 乾燥機

due (owed) shiharawarerubeki 支払われるべき; be ~ (of train, baby etc) yotei de aru 予定である; **~ to** (because of) ... no tame ...のため

dull weather kumori (no) くもり (の); pain nibui 鈍い; (boring) taikutsu (na) 退屈 (な)

duly (as expected) todokōri

naku 滞りなく; *(properly)* seitō ni 正当に

dump 1 *n (for garbage)* gomi-suteba ごみ捨て場; *(unpleasant place)* usugitanai basho 薄汚い場所 **2** *v/t (deposit)* oku 置く; *(dispose of)* suteru 捨てる

dumpling dango だんご

dune sakyū 砂丘

dung fun ふん

duplex (apartment) mezonetto メゾネット

duration kikan 期間

during … no aida ni …の間に; *(throughout)* … no aida zutto …の間ずっと

dusk tasogare たそがれ

dust *n* hokori ほこり

duty gimu 義務; *(task)* shokumu 職務; *(on goods)* zei 税; **be on ~** kinmuchū de aru 勤務中である; **be off ~** hiban de aru 非番である

duty-free *adj* menzei (no) 免税(の)

DVD dībuidī DVD

dye *v/t* someru 染める

dying *person* shinikakatte iru 死にかかっている; *tradition* kiekakatte iru 消えかかっている

dynamic *person* katsudōteki (na) 活動的(な)

dynamite *n* dainamaito ダイナマイト

dynasty ōchō 王朝

dyslexia nandokushō 難読症

E

each 1 *adj* sorezore (no) それぞれ(の) **2** *adv & pron* sorezore それぞれ; **~ other** o-tagai ni お互いに

eager nesshin (na) 熱心(な)

eagle washi わし

ear mimi 耳

earache mimi no itami 耳の痛み

early 1 *adj* hayai 早い; *(ahead of time)* hayame (no) 早め

(の); **~ October** jūgatsu no hajime 十月の初め **2** *adv* hayaku 早く

earn kasegu 稼ぐ

earnings shotoku 所得

earphones iyahon イヤホン

earring iyaringu イヤリング

earth *(soil)* tsuchi 土, *(world)* chikyū 地球; **where on ~ ?** ittai doko (ni / de) … 一体どこ(に / で)

earthquake jishin 地震

east 1 *n* higashi 東; *(of a country)* tōbu 東部; *East (Orient)* Tōyō 東洋 **2** *adj coast* higashi (no) 東(の); *wind* higashi kara (no) 東から(の) **3** *adv* higashi ni 東に; *travel* higashi e 東へ

East China Sea Higashi-shinakai 東シナ海

Easter Fukkatsu-sai 復活祭

eastern tōbu (no) 東部(の); *(oriental)* tōyō (no) 東洋(の)

eastward higashi e 東へ

easy kantan (na) 簡単(な)

eat *v/t* & *v/i* taberu 食べる

eccentric 1 *adj* fūgawari (na) 風変わり(な) **2** *n* henjin 変人

echo *n* kodama こだま

eclipse *n (of sun)* nisshoku 日食; *(of moon)* gesshoku 月食

ecofriendly kankyō ni yasashii 環境にやさしい

ecological kankyō-hogo (no) 環境保護(の)

ecology seitaigaku 生態学

economic keizaigaku (no) 経済学(の)

economical keizaiteki (na) 経済的(な); *(thrifty)* tsumashii つましい

economics keizaigaku 経済学; *(financial aspects)*

keizaiteki-sokumen 経済的側面

economist keizai-gakusha 経済学者

♦**economize on** setsuyaku suru 節約する

economy keizai 経済; *(saving)* setsuyaku 節約

economy class ekonomī-kurasu エコノミークラス

ecosystem seitaikei 生態系

ecstasy uchōten 有頂天

eczema shisshin 湿疹

edge *n* hashi 端; *(of knife)* hasaki 刃先; *(of cliff)* fuchi ふち

edible taberareru 食べられる

edit *text* kōetsu suru 校閲する; *book* henshū suru 編集する

edition han 版

educate kyōiku suru 教育する

education kyōiku 教育

eel unagi うなぎ; *(marine)* anago あなご

effect *n* eikyō 影響; *take ~ (of medicine, drug)* kiku 効く

effective kōkateki (na) 効果的(な); *(striking)* inshōteki (na) 印象的(な)

efficiency nōryoku 能力

efficient *person* yūnō (na) 有能(な); *method* kōritsuteki (na) 効率的(な)

effort (struggle) kurō 苦労; (attempt) doryoku 努力

egg tamago 卵

eggcup yudetamago-tate ゆで卵立て

eggplant nasu なす

ego PSYCH ego エゴ; (self-esteem) jisonshin 自尊心

egocentric jiko-chūshinteki (na) 自己中心的(な)

either 1 adj dochira ka (no) どちらか(の) **2** pron dochira de mo どちらでも **3** adv: I won't go ~ watashi mo ikanai 私も行かない **4** conj: ~ ... or ... ka ... ka ...か...か; (in negative sentence) ... mo ... mo ...も...も

eject v/t cassette toridasu 取り出す; people tsuihō suru 追放する

elaborate adj design kotta 凝った

elastic n gomuhimo ゴムひも

elbow n hiji ひじ

elder adj toshiue (no) 年上(の); ~ **brother** ani 兄; ~ **sister** ane 姉

elderly nenpai (no) 年配(の)

eldest 1 adj ichiban toshiue (no) いちばん年上(の) **2** n sainen-chōsa 最年長者

elect v/t senkyo suru 選挙する

election senkyo 選挙

election campaign senkyo-undō 選挙運動

electric denki (no) 電気(の)

electric chair denki-isu 電気いす

electrician denki-gishi 電気技師

electrocute kandenshi saseru 感電死させる

electronic denshi-kōgaku (no) 電子工学(の)

electronics denshi-kōgaku 電子工学

elegant yūga (na) 優雅(な)

elementary (rudimentary) shoho (no) 初歩(の)

elementary school shōgakkō 小学校

elephant zō 象

elevator erebētā エレベーター

eligible shikaku no aru 資格のある

eliminate poverty etc nakusu なくす; (from inquiries) jogai suru 除外する; (from competition) haitai suru 敗退する

elite 1 n erīto エリート **2** adj erīto (no) エリート(の); troops seiei (no) 精鋭(の)

elk herajika へらじか

elm nire no ki にれの木

eloquent yūben (na) 雄弁(な)

elsewhere hoka no basho de wa 他の場所では

e-mail *n* mēru メール

e-mail address mēru adoresu メールアドレス

emancipation kaihō 解放

embargo *n* yushutsu-kinshi 輸出禁止

embark (*on ship*) jōsen suru 乗船する; (*on plane*) tōjō suru 搭乗する

♦embark on (*begin*) ... ni noridasu ...に乗り出す

embarrass (*put in awkward position*) komaraseru 困らせる; (*shame*) ... ni haji o kakaseru ...に恥をかかせる; (*make lose face*) ... no menboku o tsubusu ...の面目をつぶす

embarrassed: *I was ~* hazukashikatta 恥ずかしかった

embarrassing hazukashī 恥ずかしい

embarrassment (*shame*) haji 恥

embassy taishikan 大使館

embezzlement tsukaikomi 使い込み

embodiment keshin 化身

embrace 1 *n* hōyō 抱擁 **2** *v/t* (*hug*) dakishimeru 抱き締める

embryo BIOL hai 胚; (*fetus*) taiji 胎児

emerald (*stone*) emerarudo エメラルド

emerge (*appear*) arawareru 現れる

emergency kinkyū-jitai 緊急事態

emergency exit hijōguchi 非常口

emergency landing kinkyū-chakuriku 緊急着陸

emigrate ijū suru 移住する

eminent chomei (na) 著名(な)

emission (*gases*) haishutsu 排出

emotion kanjō 感情

emotional *problem* kanjōteki (na) 感情的(な); (*full of emotion*) kandōteki (na) 感動的(な)

emperor kōtei 皇帝; (*of Japan*) Tennō 天皇; *Emperor's Birthday* Tennō-Tanjōbi 天皇誕生日

emphasis kyōchō 強調

emphasize kyōchō suru 強調する

empire teikoku 帝国

employ yatou 雇う; *tool* riyō suru 利用する

employee jūgyōin 従業員

employer koyōsha 雇用者

empress jotei 女帝; *(of Japan)* kōgō 皇后

enable ... dekiru yō ni suru …できるようにする

enclose *(in letter)* dōfū suru 同封する; *area* kakomu 囲む

enclosure *(with letter)* dōfūbutsu 同封物

encore *n* ankōru アンコール

encounter *v/t person* ... ni deau …に出会う; *problem, resistance* ... ni chokumen suru …に直面する

encourage *person* hagemasu 励ます; *participation* shōrei suru 奨励する

encouragement hagemashi 励まし

encyclopedia hyakka-jiten 百科辞典

end 1 *n* hashi 端; *(conclusion)* owari 終わり; **in the ~** tsui ni ついに **2** *v/t* owaru 終える **3** *v/i* owaru 終わる

endangered species zetsumetsu-sunzen no shu 絶滅寸前の種

ending owari 終わり; GRAM gobi 語尾

endless owari no nai 終わりのない; *desert* hateshi no nai 果てしのない

endorse *check* ... ni uragaki o suru …に裏書きをする;

candidacy suisen suru 推薦する; *product* senden suru 宣伝する

end product saishū-seisanbutsu 最終生産物

endurance jikyūryoku 持久力; *(mental)* nintai 忍耐

endure 1 *v/t* taeshinobu 耐え忍ぶ; *(tolerate)* gaman suru 我慢する **2** *v/i* (last) mochikotaeru 持ちこたえる

end-user mattan-shōhisha 末端消費者

enemy teki 敵; *(in war)* tekigun 敵軍

energetic seiryokuteki (na) 精力的(な)

energy seiryoku 精力; *(electricity etc)* enerugī エネルギー

enforce jisshi suru 実施する

engaged *(to be married)* kon'yaku shite iru 婚約している; **get ~** kon'yaku suru 婚約する

engagement *(to be married)* kon'yaku 婚約

engagement ring kon'yaku-yubiwa 婚約指輪

engine enjin エンジン

engineer *n* gishi 技師; NAUT kikanshi 機関士; RAIL untenshi 運転士

engineering kōgaku 工学

English 1 adj Ingurando (no) イングランド(の) **2** n (language) Eigo 英語

Englishman Ingurandojin-dansei イングランド人男性

Englishwoman Ingurandojin-josei イングランド人女性

engrave horu 彫る

enigma nazo なぞ

enjoy tanoshimu 楽しむ; **~ oneself** tanoshī omoi o suru 楽しい思いをする; **~!** dōzo どうぞ

enjoyable tanoshī 楽しい

enjoyment tanoshimi 楽しみ

enlarge PHOT hikinobasu 引き伸ばす

enlist v/i MIL nyūtai suru 入隊する

enormous kyodai (na) 巨大(な); amount bakudai (na) 莫大(な); satisfaction taihen (na) 大変(な)

enough 1 adj jūbun (na) 十分(な) **2** pron jūbun 十分; will $50 be **~?** gojū doru de tarimasu ka 五十ドルで足りますか; I've had **~!** mō takusan もうたくさん

enroll v/i (for a course) tōroku suru 登録する

ensure kakujitsu ni suru 確実にする

enter 1 v/t room … ni hairu

…に入る; competition … ni shutsujō suru …に出場する; COMPUT nyūryoku suru 入力する **2** v/i hairu 入る

enterprise shinshu no kishō 進取の気性; (venture) jigyō 事業

entertain 1 v/t (amuse) tanoshimaseru 楽しませる **2** v/i (have guests) raikyaku o motenasu 来客をもてなす

entertainer entāteinā エンターテイナー

entertaining adj omoshiroi おもしろい

entertainment tanoshimi 楽しみ

enthusiasm netsui 熱意

enthusiast fan ファン

enthusiastic netchū shite iru 熱中している

entire zentai (no) 全体(の); **the ~ country** zenkoku 全国; **the ~ day** maru ichinichi まる一日

entirely mattaku 全く

entitle … ni kenri o ataeru …に権利を与える

entitled book … ni taitoru o tsukeru …にタイトルをつける

entrance n (doorway) iriguchi 入り口; (of house) genkan 玄関; (entering) tōjō 登場

entrance fee nyūjōryō 入場料

entry (way in) iriguchi 入り口; (for competition) sankasha 参加者; (item submitted) shuppinbutsu 出品物; (in diary) kinyū 記入

entry form shutsujō-mōshikomi-yōshi 出場申し込み用紙

envelope fūtō 封筒

envious urayamashige (na) うらやましげ(な); be ~ of netande iru ねたんでいる

environment kankyō 環境

environmentalist kankyō-hogo-ronsha 環境保護論者

environmentally friendly kankyō ni yasashī 環境に優しい

envision yosō suru 予想する

envy 1 n netami ねたみ 2 v/t … ga urayamashī …がうらやましい

epidemic ryūkō 流行

epilepsy tenkan てんかん

episode ejisōdo エピソード; (of TV series) ikkai 一回; (event) dekigoto 出来事

epoch jidai 時代

equal 1 adj amount hitoshī 等しい; opportunity byōdō (no) 平等(の) 2 n (person) dōtō no hito 同等の人

equality byōdō 平等

equally divide etc byōdō ni 平等に; guilty etc hitoshiku 等しく

equator sekidō 赤道

equipment (machinery) setsubi 設備; (tools) yōgu 用具

equivalent adj sōtō (no) 相当(の)

era jidai 時代

eradicate konzetsu suru 根絶する

erase kesu 消す

eraser keshigomu 消しゴム

erosion shinshoku 侵食

erotic erochikku (na) エロチック(な)

errand tsukai 使い

erratic behavior toppi (na) とっぴ(な)

error machigai 間違い

erupt (of volcano) funka suru 噴火する; (of violence) hassei suru 発生する

escalate dandan kakudai suru だんだん拡大する

escalator esukarētā エスカレーター

escape 1 n dassō 脱走; (of gas) more 漏れ 2 v/i dassō suru 脱走する; (of animal) nigeru 逃げる; (of gas) moreru 漏れる

escort 1 n dēto no aite デートの相手; (guard) goei 護衛

especially toku ni 特に

espionage supai-kōi スパイ行為

essential *adj* kanjin (no) 肝心(の)

establish *company* setsuritsu suru 設立する; *(create)* kakuritsu suru 確立する; *(determine)* kakutei suru 確定する

establishment *(shop etc)* shisetsu 施設

estate jisho 地所; *(of dead person)* zaisan 財産

esthetic biteki (na) 美的(な)

estimate 1 *n* mitsumori 見積り 2 *v/t* mitsumoru 見積もる

estuary irie 入り江

eternal eien (no) 永遠(の)

ethical rinriteki (na) 倫理的(な)

ethnic minzoku (no) 民族(の)

ethnic minority shōsū-minzoku 少数民族

Europe Yōroppa ヨーロッパ

European 1 *adj* Yōroppa (no) ヨーロッパ(の) 2 *n* Yōroppajin ヨーロッパ人

evacuate *v/t* hinan saseru 避難させる

evade *question* hagurakasu はぐらかす; *person* sakeru 避ける

evaluate hyōka suru 評価

する; *damage* satei suru 査定する

evangelist dendōshi 伝道師

evasive kaihiteki (na) 回避的(な)

even 1 *adj* *(regular)* kisokuteki (na) 規則的(な); *(level)* taira (na) 平ら(な); *number* gūsū (no) 偶数(の) 2 *adv* … de sae mo …でさえも; ~ *he said it was good* kare de sae mo sore wa yokatta to itta 彼でさえもそれはよかったと言った; ~ *bigger* sara ni ōkiku さらに大きく; *not* ~ … sae … nai …さえ…ない; ~ *so* tatoe sō demo そうだそうでも; *if* tatoe … demo たとえ…でも

evening ban 晩; *in the* ~ yūgata ni 夕方に; *this* ~ konban 今晩; *good* ~ konban wa こんばんは

evening class yakan-kōza 夜間講座

evening paper yūkan 夕刊

evenly *distribute* kintō ni 均等に

event dekigoto できごと; SPORTS shumoku 種目

eventually *(finally)* tsui ni ついに; *(in time)* sono uchi ni そのうちに

ever *adv* ◊ *(in if clause)* itsuka

いつか; *if I ~ see you again* moshi itsuka mata aetara もしいつかまた会えたら; ◊ *(up to now / then)* ima made で; *the worst movie ~ made* ima made tsukurareta saiaku no eiga ima まで作られた最悪の映画; *have you ~ been to Japan?* Nihon ni itta koto ga arimasu ka 日本に行ったことがありますか◊; *do you ~ see her now?* kanojo ni ima mo ite iru no 彼女に今も会っているの; *for ~* itsu made mo いつまでも; *~ since* sore irai それ以来

every subete (no) すべて(の); *~ week / month* maishū / maitsuki 毎週 / 毎月; *~ Sunday* mainichiyōbi 毎日曜日

everybody minna 皆

everyday *language* nichijō (no) 日常(の)

everyone minna 皆

everything zenbu 全部

everywhere doko demo どこでも

evict tachinokaseru 立ち退かせる

evidence shōko 証拠

evidently *(clearly)* akiraka ni 明らかに

evil 1 *adj* ja-aku (na) 邪悪(な)

2 *n* ja-aku 邪悪

evoke *image* yobiokosu 呼び起こす

evolution shinka 進化

evolve *v/i* shinka suru 進化する

ex- moto … 元…

exact *adj* seikaku (na) 正確(な)

exactly chōdo ちょうど

exaggerate 1 *v/t* kochō suru 誇張する **2** *v/i* ōgesa na īkata o suru 大げさな言い方をする

exam shiken 試験

examine chōsa suru 調査する; *patient* shinsatsu suru 診察する; SCHOOL shiken suru 試験する

example rei 例; *for ~* tatoeba 例えば

exceed *(be more than)* koeru 越える; *(go beyond)* kosu 越す

exceedingly kiwamete きわめて

excellence sugurete iru koto 優れていること

excellent sugureta 優れた

except … igai wa …以外は

exception reigai 例外

exceptional reigaiteki (na) 例外的(な)

excerpt bassui 抜粋

excess adj kajō (no) 過剰(の)

excess baggage chōka-tenimotsu 超過手荷物

exchange 1 n (of views) kōkan 交換; (between schools) kōkan-ryūgaku 交換留学; in ～ for … to hikikae ni …と引き換えに **2** v/t (in store) torikaeru 取り替える; addresses torikawasu 取り交わす

exchange rate kawase-sōba 為替相場

excited kōfun shita 興奮した

exciting wakuwaku suru わくわくする

exclamation point kantanfu 感嘆符

exclude nozoku 除く

exclusive hotel kōkyū (na) 高級(な); rights yui-itsu (no) 唯一(の)

excruciating pain taegatai 耐えがたい

excursion ensoku 遠足

excuse 1 n iwake 言い訳 **2** v/t (forgive) yurusu 許す; ～ me (to get attention) sumimasen すみません; (to get past) chotto sumimasen ちょっとすみません; (interrupting) shitsurei desu ga 失礼ですが

execute criminal shokei suru 処刑する; plan jikkō suru 実行する

execution (of criminal) shokei 処刑; (of plan) jikkō 実行

executive n jūyaku 重役

exemplary mohanteki (na) 模範的(な)

exercise 1 n undō 運動; SCHOOL renshū-mondai 練習問題 **2** v/i (do exercise) undō suru 運動する

exert authority kōshi suru 行使する; ～ oneself doryoku suru 努力する

exertion doryoku 努力

exhale hakidasu 吐き出す

exhaust 1 n (fumes) haikigasu 排気ガス; (pipe) haikikan 排気管 **2** v/t (use up) tsukaihatasu 使い果たす

exhausted (tired) tsukarekitta 疲れ切った

exhausting hidoku tsukareru ひどく疲れる

exhaustion kyokudo no hirō 極度の疲労

exhibition tenrankai 展覧会

exile n bōmei 亡命; (person) bōmeisha 亡命者

exist sonzai suru 存在する

existence sonzai 存在; (life) seikatsu 生活

existing genzai (no) 現在(の)

exit n deguchi 出口

exorbitant hōgai (na) 法外

(な)

exotic ekizochikku (na) エキ
ゾチック (な)

expand 1 v/t *market* hirogeru
広げる **2** v/i *(of business)*
kakuchō suru 拡張する; *(of
city)* kakudai suru 拡大す
る; *(of metal)* bōchō suru 膨
張する

expansion *(of business)*
kakuchō 拡張; *(of city)*
kakudai 拡大; *(of metal)*
bōchō 膨張

expect 1 v/t *person etc*
machiukeru 待ち受ける;
rain etc yosō suru 予想する;
(suppose) … to omou … と
思う; *(demand)* kitai suru
期待する **2** v/i: *I ~ so* sō
omoimasu そう思います

expectation *(anticipation)*
yosō 予想; *(hope)* kitai 期待;
~s (demands) kitai 期待

expedition tanken 探検

expel *person* tsuihō suru 追
放する

expenditure shishutsu 支出

expense *(cost)* hiyō 費用

expenses keihi 経費

expensive takai 高い

experience 1 n keiken 経験 2
v/t keiken suru 経験する

experienced jukuren shita 熟
練した

experiment 1 n jikken 実験 2
v/i jikken suru 実験する

expert 1 adj jukuren shita 熟練
した **2** n senmonka 専門家

expertise gijutsu 技術

expiration kigengire 期限
切れ

expiration date yūkō-kigen
有効期限

expire yūkō-kigen ga kireru
有効期限が切れる; *(of
contract)* shikkō to naru 失効
となる

explain v/t & v/i setsumei suru
説明する

explanation setsumei 説明

explode v/i *(of bomb)*
bakuhatsu suru 爆発する

exploit v/t *person* sakushu suru
搾取する

exploration tanken 探検

explore tanken suru 探検する

explosion bakuhatsu 爆発

exporter yushutsu-gyōsha 輸
出業者

expose *(uncover)* mukidashi ni
suru むき出しにする

express 1 adj *(fast)* kyūkō
(no) 急行 (の); *(explicit)*
meihaku (na) 明白 (な) **2** n
(train) kyūkō-ressha 急行列
車; *(bus)* kyūkō-basu 急行バ
ス **3** v/t *feelings* hyōgen suru
表現する

expression *(voiced)* hyōgen 表現; *(on face)* hyōjō 表情; *(phrase)* īmawashi 言い回し

expressway kōsoku-dōro 高速道路

expulsion *(from school)* taigaku-shobun 退学処分; *(of diplomat)* tsuihō 追放

extend 1 *v/t (make longer)* enchō suru 延長する 2 *v/i (of garden etc)* hirogaru 広がる

extension *(of visa)* enchō 延長; TEL naisen 内線

extensive kōhan'i ni watatta 広範囲にわたった

extent *(degree)* teido 程度

extension cable enchō-kōdo 延長コード

exterior 1 *adj* gaibu (no) 外部 (の) 2 *n (of building)* gaibu 外部; *(of person)* gaiken 外見

external gaibu (no) 外部(の)

extinct zetsumetsu shita 絶滅した

extinguish kesu 消す

extinguisher shōkaki 消火器

extortion yusuri ゆすり

extra 1 *n* omake おまけ 2 *adj* yobun (no) 余分(の); *be ~ (cost more)* warimashi-ryōkin ga iru 割増料金がいる

extract 1 *v/t* hikinuku 引き抜く; *oil* saikutsu suru 採掘する; *tooth* nuku 抜く; *information* muriyari kikidasu 無理やり聞き出す 2 *n* bassui 抜粋

extradition hikiwatashi 引き渡し

extraordinary namihazureta 並はずれた

extravagant *(with money)* zeitaku (na) ぜいたく(な)

extreme 1 *n* kyokutan 極端 2 *adj* kyokutan (na) 極端(な); *views* kageki (na) 過激(な)

extremely kiwamete きわめて

extremist *n* kagekiha 過激派

extrovert *n* gaikōteki na hito 外向的な人

eye *n* me 目

eyebrow mayu まゆ

eyelash matsuge まつげ

eyelid mabuta まぶた

eyeliner airainā アイライナー

eyeshadow aishadō アイシャドウ

eyesight shiryoku 視力

eyesore mezawari 目ざわり

eyewitness mokugekisha 目撃者

F

fabric kiji 生地

fabulous subarashī すばらしい

façade gaikan 外観; *(of person)* misekake 見せかけ

face 1 *n* kao 顔; **lose ~** menboku o ushinau 面目を失う **2** *v/t person* muku 向く

facilitate sokushin suru 促進する

facilities setsubi 設備

fact jijitsu 事実; **in ~** jissai wa 実際は

factor yōin 要因

factory kōjō 工場

fade *v/i (of color)* iro ga aseru 色があせる; *(of light)* kiete iku 消えていく

Fahrenheit kashi 華氏

fail 1 *v/i* shippai suru 失敗する **2** *v/t exam* ochiru 落ちる

failure shippai 失敗

faint 1 *adj* kasuka (na) かすか(な) **2** *v/i* ki o ushinau 気を失う

fair¹ *n (fun~)* yūenchi 遊園地; COMM mihon'ichi 見本市

fair² *adj hair* kinpatsu (no) 金髪(の); *(just)* kōhei (na) 公平(な)

fairly *treat* kōhei ni 公平に; *(quite)* kanari かなり

fairy tale *n* o-togibanashi おとぎ話

faith shinrai 信頼; REL shinkō 信仰

faithful seijitsu (na) 誠実(な)

fake 1 *n* nisemono 偽物 **2** *adj* nise (no) 偽(の)

fall¹ *n (autumn)* aki 秋

fall² 1 *v/i (of person)* tentō suru 転倒する; *(from being)* tenraku suru 転落する; *(of government)* hōkai suru 崩壊する; *(of prices)* teika suru 低下する **2** *n (of person)* tentō 転倒; *(from height)* tenraku 転落; *(of government)* hōkai 崩壊; *(in price)* teika 低下; *(of exchange rate)* geraku 下落

♦fall out *(of hair)* nukeru 抜ける; *(argue)* kenka suru けんかする

false uso (no) うそ(の); *(mistaken)* machigatta 間違った

false teeth ireba 入れ歯

fame meisei 名声

familiar *adj (intimate)* narenareshī なれなれしい

family kazoku 家族

family name sei 姓

family planning kazoku-keikaku 家族計画

famine kikin ききん

famous yūmei (na) 有名(な)

fan[1] n (supporter) fan ファン

fan[2] n (electric) senpūki 扇風機; (handheld) sensu 扇子

fanatic n mania マニア

fanatical nekkyōteki (na) 熱狂的(な)

fancy dress kasō 仮装

fang kiba きば

fantastic totemo subarashī とてもすばらしい

fantasy kūsō 空想

far adv tōku ni 遠くに; ~ away haruka tōku ni はるか遠くに; how ~ is it to …? … made dorekurai desu ka …までどれくらいですか; as ~ as I know watashi no shiru kagiri de wa 私の知る限りでは

fare (for travel) unchin 運賃

Far East Kyokutō 極東

farewell party sōbetsukai 送別会

farm n nōjō 農場

farmer nōjōshu 農場主

farsighted enshi (no) 遠視(の)

farther adv sara ni tōku ni さらに遠くに

farthest ichiban tōku ni 一番遠くに

fascinate v/t miryō suru 魅了する

fascinating miryokuteki (na) 魅力的(な)

fascination toriko ni naru koto とりこになること

fascism fashizumu ファシズム

fashion n fasshon ファッション; in ~ ryūkō shite 流行して

fashionable clothes ryūkō (no) 流行(の); person imafū (no) 今風(の)

fashion designer fasshon-dezainā ファッションデザイナー

fast 1 adj hayai 速い 2 adv hayaku 速く; ~ asleep gussuri nemutte ぐっすり眠って

fasten v/t shikkari shimeru しっかりしめる

fast food fāsutofūdo ファーストフード

fat 1 adj futotta 太った 2 n (on meat) aburami 脂身

fatal chimeiteki (na) 致命的(な); error ketteiteki (na) 決定的なこと

fatality shibō-jiko 死亡事故

fate unmei 運命

father n o-tōsan お父さん;

(talking to outsiders about one's own) chichi 父

father-in-law giri no chichi 義理の父; *(sb else's)* giri no o-tōsan 義理のお父さん; 父

fatigue *n* hirō 疲労

faucet jaguchi 蛇口

fault *n* sekinin 責任; *(in machine etc)* kekkan 欠陥; *it's your / my ~* anata / watashi no sei desu あなた/私のせいです

faulty kekkan no aru 欠陥のある

favor *(service)* tasuke 助け

favorable *reply etc* kōiteki (na) 好意的(な)

favorite *adj* ichiban suki (na) 一番好き(な)

fax 1 *n* fakkusu ファックス **2** *v/t* fakkusu de okuru ファックスで送る

fear 1 *n* osore 恐れ **2** *v/t* osoreru 恐れる

feasible kanō (na) 可能(な)

feather umō 羽毛

feature *n (on face)* kaodachi 顔立ち; *(of city etc)* tokuchō 特徴; *(in paper)* tokushū-kiji 特集記事; *(movie)* chōhen-eiga 長編映画

February nigatsu 二月

fed up *adj infml* unzari shite うんざりして

federal renpō (no) 連邦(の)

fee ryōkin 料金; *(of doctor)* shinsatsu-ryō 診察料; *(for membership)* kaihi 会費

feed *v/t* … ni tabemono o ageru …に食べ物をあげる; *animal* … ni esa o yaru …にえさをやる

feedback kansō 感想

feel 1 *v/t* … ni sawaru …に触る; *pleasure etc* oboeru 覚える; *pain* kanjiru 感じる; *(think)* … to omou …と思う **2** *v/i (of cloth etc)* kanjirareru 感じられる

feeling *(opinion)* kimochi 気持ち; *(emotion)* kanjō 感情; *(sensation)* kankaku 感覚

felony jūzai 重罪

felt-tip(ped) pen ferutopen フェルトペン

female 1 *adj* mesu (no) 雌(の); *person* josei (no) 女性(の) **2** *n* mesu 雌; *(person)* josei 女性

feminine *adj qualities* joseirashī 女性らしい

feminism feminizumu フェミニズム

feminist 1 *n* feminisuto フェミニスト **2** *adj group* feminisuto (no) フェミニスト(の); *ideas* danjo-dōken-shugi (no) 男女同権主義

fence saku さく

fender AUTO fendā フェンダー

fern shida シダ

ferocious *animal* dōmō（な）どう猛（な）; *attack* hageshī 激しい

ferry *n* ferī フェリー

fertile hiyoku (na) 肥よく（な）; *woman* ninshin-kanō (na) 妊娠可能（な）

fertility *(of soil)* hiyokusa 肥よくさ; *(of woman)* seishokuryoku 生殖力

fertilizer *(for soil)* hiryō 肥料

fervent *admirer* netsuretsu (na) 熱烈（な）

festival o-matsuri お祭り

festivities gyōji 行事

fetch *person* tsurete kaeru 連れてかえる; *thing* totte kuru 取ってくる

fetus taiji 胎児

feud *n* hanmoku 反目

fever netsu 熱

few 1 *adj (not many)* shōsū (no) 少数 (の); *a ~* ikutsuka (no) いくつか（の）; *quite a ~ (a lot)* kanari (no) かなり（の）**2** *pron (not many)* shōsū 少数; *a ~* ikutsuka 幾つか; *quite a ~ (a lot)* kanari かなり

fewer *adj* yori sukunai より少ない

fiancé kon'yakusha 婚約者

fiasco daishippai 大失敗

fiber sen'i 繊維

fiction *(novels)* shōsetsu 小説

fictitious kakū (no) 架空（の）

fidget *v/i* sowasowa suru そわそわする

field *n* nohara 野原; *(with crops)* hatake 畑; SPORTS kyōgijō 競技場; *(competitors in race)* kyōgisha 競技者; *(research etc)* bun'ya 分野

fierce *adj animal* dōmō (na) どう猛（な）; *storm* mōretsu (na) 猛烈（な）

fifty-fifty *adv* gobugobu ni 五分五分に

fig ichijiku いちじく

fight 1 *n* tatakai 戦い; *(argument)* kenka けんか**2** *v/t ... to tatakau ... と戦う**3** *v/i* tatakau 戦う; *(argue)* kenka suru けんかする

♦**fight for** ... no tame ni tatakau ...のために闘う

figure *n (digit)* sūji 数字; *(of person)* sutairu スタイル; *(shape)* katachi 形

file¹ *n also* COMPUT fairu ファイル; *v/t documents* fairu suru ファイルする

file² *n (tool)* yasuri やすり

file cabinet seiriyō kyabinetto 整理用キャビネット

fill v/t mitasu 満たす

♦fill in form kinyū suru 記入する; hole umeru 埋める

♦fill out v/t form kinyū suru 記入する

filling 1 n (in cake etc) nakami 中味; (in tooth) jūten 充てん 2 adj food onaka ga ippai ni naru おなかが一杯になる

film 1 n (for camera) firumu フィルム; (movie) eiga 映画 2 v/t satsuei suru 撮影する

film star eiga-sutā 映画スター

filter n firutā フィルター

filthy fuketsu (na) 不潔(な)

fin (of fish) hire ひれ

final 1 adj saigo (no) 最後(の); decision saishū (no) 最終(の) 2 n SPORTS kesshōsen 決勝戦

finalist kesshōsen-shutsujō-senshu 決勝戦出場選手

finalize saishū-kettei suru 最終決定する

finally saigo ni 最後に; (at last) tsui ni ついに

finance 1 n zaisei 財政 2 v/t yūshi suru 融資する

financial zaiseijō (no) 財政上(の)

financial year kaikei-nendo 会計年度

find v/t mitsukeru 見つける

♦find out 1 v/t (inquire) shiraberu 調べる; (discover) ... ga wakaru ...がわかる 2 v/i (inquire) shiraberu 調べる; (discover) wakaru わかる

fine¹ adj weather hare (no) 晴れ(の); wine subarashī 素晴らしい; distinction komakai 細かい; line hosoi 細い; how are you? - ~ o-genki desu ka – genki desu お気元ですか – 元気です

fine² n (penalty) bakkin 罰金

finger n yubi 指

fingernail tsume つめ

fingerprint n shimon 指紋

finish 1 v/t oeru 終える; ~ doing .... suru no o oeru ...するのを終える 2 v/i owaru 終わる 3 n (of race) gōru ゴール

finish line gōru ゴール

fir momi no ki もみの木

fire 1 n hi 火; (electric) hītā ヒーター; (blaze) kaji 火事; (bonfire etc) takibi たき火; be on ~ moete iru 燃えている 2 v/i (shoot) hassha suru 発射する 3 v/t infml (dismiss) kaiko suru 解雇する

fire alarm kasai-hōchiki 火災報知機

fire department shōbōsho 消防署

fire escape hijō-kaidan 非
常階段
fire extinguisher shōkaki
消火器
firefighter shōbōshi 消防士
fireplace danro 暖炉
fireworks hanabi 花火;
(display) hanabi no uchiage 花
火の打ち上げ
firm[1] *adj* grip antei shita 安定
した; *muscles* hikishimatta 引
き締まった
firm[2] *n* COMM kaisha 会社
first 1 *adj* dai-ichi (no) 第一
(の) **2** *n* ichiban 一番; *(of
month)* tsuitachi 一日 **3** *adv*
finish ichiban ni 一番に;
(beforehand) saisho ni 最初に;
at ~ hajime wa 初めは
first aid kyūkyū-shochi 救
急処置
first-aid kit kyūkyū-bako 救
急箱
first-class *adj (on boat etc)*
ittō (no) 一等(の); *(on bullet
train)* gurīnsha (no) グリーン
車(の); *(on airplane)* fāsuto
kurasu (no) ファーストクラ
ス(の); *(very good)* ichiryū
(no) 一流の
first floor ikkai 一階
firsthand *adj* chokusetsu (no)
直接(の)
firstly mazu saisho ni まず

first 最初に
first name namae 名前
fish 1 *n* sakana 魚 **2** *v/i* tsuri o
suru 釣りをする
fisherman ryōshi 漁師
fishing tsuri 釣り
fishing boat gyosen 漁船
fishing rod tsuri-zao 釣り
ざお
fishmonger sakanaya 魚屋
fist kobushi こぶし
fit[1] *n* MED hossa 発作
fit[2] *adj* chōshi ga yoi 調子が
よい; *(morally)* fusawashī ふ
さわしい
fit[3] *v/i (of clothes)* au 合う; *(of
piece of furniture etc)* hairu
入る
fitness *(physical)* kenkō 健康
fitness center fittonesu kurabu
フィットネスクラブ
fitted kitchen shisutemu
kitchin システムキッチン
fittings setsubi 設備
fix *v/t (attach)* toritsukeru 取り
付ける; *(repair)* shūri suru 修
理する; *meeting etc* tehai suru
手配する; *lunch* tsukuru 作
る; *boxing match etc* yaochō o
shikumu 八百長を仕組む
fixture *(in room)* setsubi 設備
flabby *muscles* tarunda た
るんだ
flag *n* hata 旗

flake n (of snow) ippen 一片

flamboyant person daitan (na) 大胆(な)

flame n honō ほのお

flammable kansei (no) 可燃性(の)

flash 1 n (of light) senkō せん光; PHOT furasshu フラッシュ 2 v/i (of light) patto hikaru ぱっとひかる

flashback n furasshu-bakku フラッシュバック

flashlight n kaichū-dentō 懐中電灯

flask mahōbin 魔法びん

flat adj surface taira (na) 平ら(な); beer ki no nuketa 気の抜けた; battery kireta 切れた; tire panku shita パンクした; shoes hiru no nai ヒールのない

flatter v/t ... ni o-seji o iu …にお世辞を言う

flattery o-seji お世辞

flavor n fūmi 風味

flawless kanpeki (na) 完璧(な)

flea nomi のみ

flee v/i nigeru 逃げる

fleet n NAUT kansen 艦船

flesh niku 肉

flexible jūnan (na) 柔軟(な)

flicker v/i chirachira suru ちらちらする

flies (on pants) zubon no chakku ズボンのチャック

flight bin 便; (flying) hikō 飛行

flight number binmei 便名

flight path hikō-keiro 飛行経路

flimsy structure chachi (na) ちゃち(な); material usui 薄い; excuse o-somatsu (na) お粗末(な)

fling v/t hōridasu ほうり出す

flipper (for swimming) ashihire 足ひれ

flirt 1 v/i kobiru こびる 2 n (male) purei-bōi プレイボーイ; (female) purei-gāru プレイガール

float v/i uku 浮く

flock n (of sheep) mure 群れ

flood 1 n kōzui 洪水 2 v/t (of river) hanran saseru はんらんさせる

floodlight n furaddo-raito フラッドライト

floor n (of room) yuka 床; (story) kai 階

floorboard yukaita 床板

floppy (disk) furoppī-disuku フロッピーディスク

florist hanaya 花屋

flour komugiko 小麦粉

flourish v/i han'ei suru 繁栄する

flow 1 *v/i (of current)* nagareru 流れる; *(of work)* susumu 進む **2** *n* nagare 流れ

flowchart furōchāto フローチャート

flower *n* hana 花

flowerbed kadan 花壇

flowerpot uekibachi 植木鉢

flu infuruenza インフルエンザ

fluctuate *v/i* hendō suru 変動する

fluent *adj* ryūchō (na) 流ちょう (な)

fluid *n* ryūdōtai 流動体

fluorescent keikō (no) 蛍光 (の)

flush *v/t toilet* nagasu 流す

flute furūto フルート

fly[1] *n (insect)* hae ハエ

fly[2] *n (on pants)* chakku ズボンのチャック

fly[3] *v/i (of bird)* tobu 飛ぶ; *(in airplane)* hikōki de iku 飛行機で行く

flying *n* hikōki de ryokō suru koto 飛行機で旅行する事

foam *n (on liquid)* awa 泡

focus *n (of attention)* chūshin 中心; PHOT pinto ピント

fog kiri 霧

foggy *adj* kiri no tachikometa 霧の立ち込めた

fold *v/t paper etc* oritatamu 折りたたむ; ~ *one's arms*

udegumi o suru 腕組みをする

folder *(for documents)* fairu ファイル; COMPUT foruda フォルダ

foliage ha 葉

folk *(people)* hitobito 人々

folk music fōku-myūjikku オークミュージック

folk-song fōku-songu フォークソング; *(Japanese)* min'yō 民謡

follow 1 *v/t ato ni tsuite iku* 後について行く; *road ...* ni sotte iku …に沿って行く; *instructions ...* ni shitagau …に従う; *TV series* tsuzukete miru 続けて見る **2** *v/i* tsuite iku ついていく; *(logically)* ... to naru …となる

♦**follow up** *v/t letter* forō suru フォローする

following *adj* tsugi (no) 次 (の)

fond *(loving)* yasashī 優しい; *be ~ of* ... ga suki de aru …が好きである

food tabemono 食べ物

food poisoning shoku-chūdoku 食中毒

fool *n* baka 馬鹿

foolish baka (na) 馬鹿 (な)

foolproof machigaeyō no nai 間違えようのない

foot ashi 足; *(length)* fīto フィ

ート; *on* ~ aruite 歩いて

football amerikan-futtobōru アメリカンフットボール; *(soccer)* sakkā サッカー; *(ball)* bōru ボール

footbridge hodōkyō 歩道橋

footnote kyakuchū 脚注

footprint ashiato 足跡

for ◊ *(purpose, destination etc)*: *a train* ~ ...yuki no ressha ...行きの列車; *clothes* ~ *children* kodomo yō no fuku 子供用の服; *this is* ~ *you* kore wa anata ni desu これはあなたにです ◊ *(time)*: ~ *three days* / ~ *two hours* mikkakan / nijikan 三日間 / 二時間 ◊ *(instead of)*: *let me do that* ~ *you* watashi ni yarasete kudasai 私にやらせて下さい

forbid kinjiru 禁じる

force 1 *n (violence)* bōryoku 暴力; *(of explosion etc)* chikara 力; *the* ~*s* MIL. guntai 軍隊 2 *v/t door, lock* kojiakeru こじ開ける

forecast *n* yosō 予想; *(of weather)* yohō 予報

foreground zenkei 前景

forehead hitai 額

foreign affairs gaimu 外務

foreign currency gaikoku-tsūka 外国通貨

foreigner gaikokujin 外国人

foreign language gaikokugo 外国語

foreign policy gaikō-seisaku 外交政策

foresee yosō suru 予想する

forest mori 森

foretell yogen suru 予言する

forever eikyū ni 永久に

foreword maegaki 前書き

forfeit *v/t right* ushinau 失う

forge *v/t (counterfeit)* gizō suru 偽造する

forgery *(bank bill)* gizō 偽造; *(document)* gizō-bunsho 偽造文書

forget wasureru 忘れる

forgetful wasureppoi 忘れっぽい

forgive *v/t & v/i* yurusu 許す

forgiveness yurushi 許し

fork *n* fōku フォーク; *(in road)* bunkiten 分岐点

forklift (truck) fōkurifuto フォークリフト

form 1 *n (shape)* katachi 形; *(document)* yōshi 用紙 2 *v/t (in clay etc)* katachizukuru 形作る; *friendship* musubu 結ぶ; *opinion* matomeru まとめる 3 *v/i (take shape)* katachi ni naru 形になる

formal seishiki (no) 正式(の); ~ *clothes* seisō 正装

format 1 *v/t disk* fōmatto suru フォーマットする; *document* keishiki o totonoeru 形式を整える **2** *n (of paper etc)* saizu サイズ; *(of program)* teisai 体裁

former izen (no) 以前(の); *the ~* mae no mono 前のもの

formidable osoroshī 恐ろしい

formula kōshiki 公式; *(for baby)* konamiruku 粉ミルク

fortnight *Br* nishūkan 二週間

fortunate kōun (na) 幸運(な)

fortune kōun 好運; *(lot of money)* zaisan 財産

fortune-teller uranaishi 占い師

forward 1 *adv* mae ni 前に **2** *n sports* fowādo フォワード **3** *v/t letter* tensō suru 転送する

fossil kaseki 化石

foster child satogo 里子

foster parents sato-oya 里親

foul 1 *n sports* fauru ファウル **2** *adj smell* fuketsu (na) 不潔 (な); *weather* warui 悪い

found *v/t* sōritsu suru 創立する

foundation *(of theory etc)* kiso 基礎; *(organization)* zaidan 財団; *(setting up)* setsuritsu 設立

foundations *(of house)* dodai 土台

founder *n* sōritsusha 創立者

fountain funsui 噴水

fox *n* kitsune きつね

fracture 1 *n* kossetsu 骨折 **2** *v/t* kossetsu suru 骨折する

fragile kowareyasui 壊れやすい

fragment hahen 破片

fragrance ī kaori いい香り

frail moroi もろい

frank sotchoku (na) 率直 (な)

frantic hankyōran (no) 半狂乱(の)

fraud sagi 詐欺; *(person)* sagishi 詐欺師

freak 1 *n (event)* ijō 異常; *(animal etc)* kikei 奇形 **2** *adj storm etc* ijō 異常(な)

freckle sobakasu そばかす

free 1 *adj (at liberty)* jiyū 自由(な); *(no cost)* muryō (no) 無料(の); *room* aite iru 空いている **2** *v/t prisoners* kaihō suru 解放する

freedom jiyū 自由

freelance *adj* furī (no) フリー(の)

free speech genron no jiyū 言論の自由

freeway kōsoku-dōro 高速道路

freeze 1 *v/t* kōraseru 凍らせる; *wages* tōketsu suru 凍結する; *video* seishi suru 静止

frosty

する 2 v/i *(of water)* kōru 凍る; *(of weather)* hieru 冷える

freezer reitōko 冷凍庫

freight n kamotsu 貨物

French 1 adj Furansu (no) フランス(の) **2** n *(language)* Furansugo フランス語

French fries furenchi-furai フレンチフライ

frequency hindo 頻度; RADIO shūhasū 周波数

frequent adj hinpan (na) 頻繁(な)

frequently shibashiba しばしば

fresh *fruit etc* shinsen (na) 新鮮(な); *(cool)* sawayaka (na) さわやか(な); *(impertinent)* namaiki (na) 生意気(な)

freshman shinnyūsei 新入生

friction masatsu 摩擦; *(between people)* fuwa 不和

Friday kin'yōbi 金曜日

fridge reizōko 冷蔵庫

fried egg medamayaki 目玉焼き

friend tomodachi 友達

friendly adj *atmosphere* yūkōteki (na) 友好的(な); *person* hitonatsukoi 人なつこい

friendship yūjō 友情

fries furenchi-furai フレンチフライ

frighten v/t kowagaraseru 怖がらせる; *be ~ed* obieta おびえた

frill *(on dress etc)* furiru フリル; *(extra)* yokei na mono 余計な物

frog kaeru かえる

from ◇ *(in time):* ~ **9 to 5** *(o'clock)* kuji kara goji made 九時から五時まで; ~ **today** *(on)* kyō kara 今日から ◇ *(in space):* ~ **here to there** koko kara soko made ここからそこまで ◇ *(origin): a letter ~ Jo* jō kara no tegami ジョーからの手紙; *I am ~ New Jersey* watashi wa Nyūjājī no shusshin desu 私はニュージャージーの出身です

front 1 n *(of building)* shōmen 正面; *(of car)* zenbu 前部; *in ~* mae ni 前に; *(in a race)* rīdo shite リードして; *in ~ of ...* no mae no …の前の **2** adj *wheel, seat* mae (no) 前(の)

front door genkan 玄関

frontier kokkyō 国境

front page ichimen 一面

front row saizenretsu 最前列

frost shimo 霜

frostbite tōshō 凍傷

frosting aishingu アイシング

frosty *weather* shimo no orita 霜の降りた

frown v/i kao o shikameru 顔を
しかめる

frozen feet etc kogoeta 凍えた;
food reitō (no) 冷凍(の)

fruit furūtsu フルーツ

fruit juice furūtsu-jūsu フルー
ツジュース

frustrated sigh yokkyū-fuman
(no) 欲求不満(の)

frustrating iradatashī いらだ
たしい

fry v/t yaku 焼く; (stir~)
itameru 炒める; (deep~)
ageru 揚げる

fuel n nenryō 燃料

Fuji: Mt ~ Fujisan 富士山

fulfill v/t (carry out) hatasu
果たす; (satisfy) mitasu 満
たす

full ippai (no) いっぱい(の);
schedule isogashī 忙しい

full moon mangetsu 満月

full-time adj job seishain (no)
正社員(の); teaching jōkin
(no) 常勤(の); student seiki
(no) 正規(の)

fully booked manpai ni 満杯に;
understand jūbun ni 十分に

fumes (from car) haikigasu
排気ガス; (from chemicals,
machine) gasu ガス

fun tanoshimi 楽しみ; have ~!
tanoshinde ne 楽しんでね;
make ~ of karakau からかう

function 1 n (of machine) kinō
機能; (of employee) yakuwari
役割 2 v/i hataraku 働く

fund n shikin 資金

fundamental kihonteki (na) 基
本的(な)

funeral sōshiki 葬式

funny okashī (na) おかし(な);
(odd) hen (na) へん(な)

fur kegawa 毛皮

furious (angry) gekido shite 激
怒して

furniture kagu 家具

further 1 adj (additional) sore
ijō (no) それ以上(の); (more
distant) sara ni susunda さら
に進んだ 2 adv walk, drive
motto saki ni もっと先に; 2
miles ~ (on) sara ni ni-mairu
さらに二マイル

furthest 1 adj ichiban tōku (no)
一番遠く(の) 2 adv ichiban
tōku ni 一番遠くに

fury (anger) gekido 激怒

fuse ELEC **1** n hyūzu ヒュー
ズ 2 v/i hyūzu ga tobu ヒュー
ズが飛ぶ

fuss n hitosawagi 一騒ぎ

fussy person urusai うるさい

futile muda (na) 無駄(な)

future n (of person) shōrai 将
来; (of humanity, earth) mirai
未来; in ~ kore kara saki こ
れから先

G

gadget kigu 器具
gain *v/t (acquire)* eru 得る
gale *n* kyōfū 強風
gallery *(art)* bijutsukan 美術館; *(shop)* garō 画廊
gallon garon ガロン
gallstone tanseki 胆石
gambler bakuchiuchi ばくち打ち
gambling gyanburu ギャンブル
game *n* SPORTS shiai 試合; *(child's)* asobi 遊び; *(in tennis)* gēmu ゲーム
gang ichimi 一味
gangster yakuza やくざ
gangway tarappu タラップ
gap sukima すきま; *(in time)* hedatari 隔たり
♦gape at pokan to kuchi o akete ... ni mitoreru ぽかんと口を開けて…に見とれる
garage shako 車庫; garēji ガレージ; *(repairs)* shūri-kōjō 修理工場
garbage gomi ごみ; *(nonsense)* tawagoto たわごと
garbage can gomi-baketsu ごみバケツ
garden niwa 庭; *Japanese ~*

Nihon-teien 日本庭園
garland *n* hanawa 花輪
garlic ninniku にんにく
gas *n* kitai 気体; *(gasoline)* gasorin ガソリン
gasp *v/i* iki o nomu 息をのむ
gas station gasorin-sutando ガソリンスタンド
gate mon 門; *(at airport)* gēto ゲート
gather *v/t* atsumeru 集める
gay 1 *n* homo ホモ 2 *adj* homo (no) ホモ(の)
♦gaze at jitto mitsumeru じっと見つめる
gear *n* gia ギア; *(equipment)* sōbi 装備
geisha geisha 芸者
gel *(hair)* jeru ジェル; *(shower)* bodīsōpu ボディーソープ
gender sei 性
gene idenshi 遺伝子
general 1 *n (in army)* shōgun 将軍 2 *adj* ippanteki (na) 一般的(な)
generalize ippanka suru 一般化する
generally ippanteki ni 一般的に

generate *(create)* umidasu 生み出す; ~ *electricity* hatsuden suru 発電する

generation sedai 世代

generator hatsudenki 発電機

generosity kimae no yosa 気前のよさ

generous kimae no yoi 気前のよい; *portion etc* takusan (no) たくさん(の)

genetic idenshi (no) 遺伝子(の)

genetic fingerprint idenshi-shimon 遺伝子指紋

genetics idenshigaku 遺伝学

genitals seiki 性器

genius tensai 天才

gentle yasashii 優しい

gentleman shinshi 紳士

gents *(toilet)* danseiyō toire 男性用トイレ

genuine shōshin-shōmei (no) 正真正銘(の)

geographical chiriteki (na) 地理的(な)

geography chirigaku 地理学

geological chishitsugaku (no) 地質学(の)

geology chishitsugaku 地質学

geometry kikagaku 幾何学

germ baikin ばい菌

gesture *n* miburi 身ぶり; *(of friendship)* shirushi 印

get *v/t (obtain)* te ni ireru 手に入れる; *(fetch)* totte kuru 取ってくる; *letter* uketoru 受け取る; *bus etc* … ni noru …に乗る ◊ *(become)* … ni naru …になる; ~ *nervous* shinkeishitsu ni naru 神経質になる ◊ *(causative)*: ~ *X repaired* X o shūri shite morau Xを修理してもらう; ~ *X to do Y* X ni Y saseru XにYさせる; ~ *one's hair cut* … no kami o kitte morau …の髪を切ってもらう ◊ *have got* motte iru 持っている ◊ *have got to (must)*: *I have got to study* benkyō shinakereba naranai 勉強しなければならない

♦ **get on** *(to train etc)* noru 乗る; *(be friendly)* umaku yatte iku うまくやっていく; *(progress)* susumu 進む

♦ **get out 1** *v/i (of car etc)* deru 出る; ~! dete ike 出て行け **2** *v/t nail etc* torinozoku 取り除く

♦ **get up** *v/i (in morning)* okiru 起きる; *(from chair)* tachiagaru 立ち上がる

gherkin kyūri no pikurusu きゅうりのピクルス

ghetto hinmingai 貧民街

ghost yūrei 幽霊

giant n kyojin 巨人

gift okurimono 贈り物

giftwrap okurimono o no hōsō o suru 贈り物用の包装をする

gigantic kyodai (na) 巨大(な)

giggle v/i kusukusu warau くすくす笑う

gin jin ジン

ginger (spice) shōga しょうが

giraffe kirin きりん

girl onna no ko 女の子

girlfriend kanojo 彼女; (of girl) onna-tomodachi 女友達

gist yōten 要点

give ataeru 与える; (from viewpoint of giver) ageru あげる; (from viewpoint of receiver) kureru くれる; present okuru 贈る

♦**give away** hito ni ageru 人にあげる; (betray) barasu ばらす

♦**give in** v/i (surrender) kōsan suru 降参する 2 v/t homework dasu 出す

♦**give up** v/t smoking etc yameru やめる 2 v/i (stop trying) akirameru あきらめる

glacier hyōga 氷河

glad ureshī うれしい

gladly yorokonde 喜んで

glamor miryoku 魅力

glamorous miryokuteki (na)

glance v/i chiratto miru ちらっと見る

gland sen 腺

glare v/i (of light) giragira hikaru ぎらぎら光る

♦**glare at** niramu にらむ

glass garasu ガラス; (for drink) koppu コップ

glasses megane 眼鏡

glide v/i suberu 滑る

glimpse v/t chirari to hitome miru ちらりとひと目見る

glitter v/i pikapika hikaru ぴかぴか光る

gloat ninmari suru にんまりする

global zensekaiteki (na) 全世界的(な); (no exception) zentaiteki (na) 全体的(な)

global warming chikyū no ondanka 地球の温暖化

globe (the earth) chikyū 地球; (model) chikyūgi 地球儀

gloomy room kurai 暗い; mood yū-utsu (na) 憂うつ(な)

glorious subarashī すばらしい

glossary yōgoshū 用語集

glossy n (magazine) gurabia-zasshi グラビア雑誌

glove tebukuro 手袋

glow v/i (of light) kagayaku
輝く

glue n setchakuzai 接着剤

go v/i iku 行く; (leave: of train
etc) shuppatsu suru 出発する;
(of people) saru 去る; (work)
sadō suru 作動する; (become)
naru なる; (match: of colors
etc) au 合う; **I must be ~ing**
ikanakereba narimasen 行か
なければなりません; **let's
~!** ikō 行こう; **hamburger to
~** teikuauto no hanbāgā テイ
クアウトのハンバーガー;
be all gone sukkari nakunaru
すっかりなくなる; **be ~ing
to ...** (future) ... tsumori de aru
…つもりである

♦ **go back** modoru 戻る;
(date back) sakanoboru さか
のぼる

♦ **go down** (descend) oriru 降
りる; (of sun) shizumu 沈む;
(of swelling) hiku 引く

♦ **go in** naka ni hairu 中に入
る; (of sun) kumo ni kakureru
雲に隠れる; (fit: of part etc)
osamaru 納まる

♦ **go off** v/i (leave) tachisaru 立
ち去る; (of bomb) bakuhatsu
suru 爆発する; (of alarm)
narihibiku 鳴り響く

♦ **go on** (continue) tsuzukeru 続
ける; (happen) okoru 起こる

♦ **go out** (of person) dete iku
出て行く; (of light) kieru
消える

goal SPORTS gōru ゴー
ル; (point) tokuten 得点;
(objective) mokuhyō 目標

goalkeeper gōru-kīpā ゴール
キーパー

goat yagi やぎ

go-between chūkaisha 仲介
者; (for arranged marriage)
nakōdo 仲人

god kami 神

goddess megami 女神

godfather (in mafia) goddofāzā
ゴッドファーザー

gold 1 n kin 金 **2** adj kin (no)
金(の)

golden wedding kinkonshiki
金婚式

gold fish kingyo 金魚

goldsmith kinzaikushi 金
細工師

golf gorufu ゴルフ

golf club gorufu-kurabu ゴル
フクラブ

golf course gorufu-kōsu ゴル
フコース

gong dora どら; (in wrestling)
gongu ゴング

good yoi よい; food oishī お
いしい; **be ~ at ...** ... ga jōzu
de aru …が上手である

goodbye sayōnara さよう

なら

Good Friday Seikin'yōbi 聖金曜日

good-looking *woman* bijin (no) 美人(の); *man* hansamu (na) ハンサム(な)

good-natured kidate no yoi 気立てのよい

goods COMM shōhin 商品

goose gachō がちょう

gorgeous *weather* subarashī すばらしい; *dress* suteki (na) すてき(な)

gorilla gorira ゴリラ

Gospel Fukuinsho 福音書

gossip *n* uwasabanashi うわさ話; *(person)* oshaberi おしゃべり

government seifu 政府

governor chiji 知事

grab *v/t* tsukamu つかむ

graceful yūbi (na) 優美(な)

grade *n (quality)* tōkyū 等級; SCHOOL *(class)* gakunen 学年; *(in exam)* seiseki 成績

gradual jojo (no) 徐々(の)

graduate *n* sotsugyōsei 卒業生

graduation sotsugyōshiki 卒業式

graffiti rakugaki 落書き

grain tsubu 粒; *(in wood)* mokume 木目

gram guramu グラム

grammar bunpō 文法

grand *adj* sōdai (na) 壮大(な)

granddaughter mago-musume 孫娘; *(somebody else's)* o-magosan お孫さん

grandfather sofu 祖父; *(somebody else's)* o-jīsan おじいさん

grandmother sobo 祖母; *(somebody else's)* o-bāsan おばあさん

grandparents sofubo 祖父母; *(somebody else's)* o-jīsan, o-bāsan おじいさんおばあさん

grandson mago-musuko 孫息子; *(somebody else's)* o-magosan お孫さん

granite kakōgan 花こう岩

grant *n (money)* kōfukin 交付金; *(for university)* shōgakukin 奨学金

grape budō ぶどう

grapefruit gurēpufurūtsu グレープフルーツ

graph gurafu グラフ

graphics COMPUT seizuhō 製図法

grasp 1 *n (mental)* ha-aku 把握 **2** *v/t (mentally)* ha-aku suru 把握する; *(physically)* tsukamaeru つかまえる

grass kusa 草

grasshopper batta ばった

grate v/t carrots etc suriorosu すりおろす

grateful kansha shite iru 感謝している

gratitude kansha 感謝

grave n haka 墓

gravestone hakaishi 墓石

graveyard bochi 墓地

gravy gurēbī sōsu グレービーソース

gray adj hai-iro (no) 灰色(の)

graze v/t arm etc kasumeru かすめる

greasy aburappoi 脂っぽい; food aburakkoi 脂っこい

great mistake ōki (na) 大き(な); area hiroi 広い; amount bakudai (na) ばく大(な); composer idai (na) 偉大(な); infml (very good) subarashī すばらしい

Great Britain Eikoku 英国

greatly hijō ni 非常に

greed (for money) don'yoku どん欲

greedy (for money) don'yoku (na) どん欲(な); (for food) ijikitanai 意地きたない

green midori-iro (no) 緑色(の)

greenhouse gas onshitsu-kōkagasu 温室効果ガス

greet aisatsu suru あいさつする

greeting aisatsu あいさつ

gridlock (in traffic) kōtsū-jūtai 交通渋滞; (in city) kinō-mahi 機能まひ

grief kanashimi 悲しみ

grieve kanashimu 悲しむ

grim kibishī 厳しい

grin v/i nikkori warau にっこり笑う

grind v/t meat etc hiku ひく

grip v/t gyutto nigiru ぎゅっと握る

groan v/i umeku うめく

grocery store shokuryō-zakkaten 食料雑貨店

gross adj (vulgar) gehin (na) 下品(な); FIN zentai (no) 全体(の)

ground 1 n jimen 地面; (reason) konkyo 根拠; ELEC āsu アース **2** v/t ELEC āsu suru アースする

ground meat hikiniku ひき肉

groundwork kiso-junbi 基礎準備

group n gurūpu グループ

grow 1 v/i (of child) sodatsu 育つ; (of plants) haeru 生える; (of amount) zōka suru 増加する; (of business) hatten suru 発展する **2** v/t flowers saibai suru 栽培する

♦**grow up** (of person) seichō suru 成長する

growl v/i unaru うなる

grown-up n otona 大人

growth *(of person)* seichō 成長; *(of company)* hatten 発展; *(increase)* zōka 増加; MED shuyō しゅよう

grubby kitanai 汚い

grumble v/i butsubutsu fuhei o iu ぶつぶつ不平を言う

grunt v/i būbū iu ぶうぶう言う

guarantee 1 n hoshō 保証 2 v/t hoshō suru 保証する

guarantor hoshōnin 保証人

guard 1 n *(security ~)* gādoman ガードマン; MIL keibitai 警備隊; *(in prison)* kanshu 看守 2 v/t keibi suru 警備する

guardian JUR kōkennin 後見人

guerrilla gerira-hei ゲリラ兵

guess 1 n suisoku 推測 2 v/t & v/i suisoku suru 推測する

guesswork atezuppō あてずっぽう

guest kyaku 客

guidance shidō 指導

guide 1 n *(person)* gaido ガイ

ド; *(book)* gaido-bukku ガイドブック 2 v/t annai suru 案内する

guidelines shihyō 指標

guilt JUR yūzai 有罪; *(feeling)* zaiakukan 罪悪感

guilty JUR yūzai (no) 有罪(の); *feeling* yamashī やましい

guinea pig morumotto モルモット; *fig* jikkendai 実験台

guitar gitā ギター

gulf wan 湾

gum haguki 歯ぐき; *(chewing ~)* chūingu-gamu チューイングガム

gun jū 銃

gunman *(robber)* kenjū-gōtō けん銃強盗

gust n ichijin no kaze 一陣の風

gutter *(on sidewalk)* mizo 溝; *(on roof)* toi とい

guy infml yatsu やつ

gym *(sports club)* jimu ジム; SCHOOL tai-ikukan 体育館

gynecologist fujinka 婦人科

H

habit kuse 癖

habitat seisokuchi 生息地

hacker COMPUT hakkā ハッカー

haddock tara たら

haggle *(bargain)* negiru 値切る

hair kami no ke 髪の毛; *(single)* ke 毛

hairbrush heaburashi ヘア
ブラシ

haircut heakatto ヘアカット

hairdresser biyōshi 美容師;
(shop) biyōin 美容院

hairdrier headoraiyā ヘアド
ライヤー

hairstyle heasutairu ヘアス
タイル

half 1 *n* hanbun 半分; ~ *past
ten* jūji han 十時半; ~ *an
hour* sanjuppun 三十分 2 *adj
size* hanbun (no) 半分(の);
price hangaku (no) 半額(の)

half time *n* SPORTS hāfu-taimu
ハーフタイム

halfway *adv:* ~ *between the
two* sono futatsu no chūkan ni
その二つの中間に

hall hōru ホール; *(hallway)*
genkan 玄関

halo gokō 後光

halt 1 *v/i* tomaru 止まる 2 *v/t*
tomeru 止める

halve *v/t* hanbun ni suru 半分
にする

ham hamu ハム

hamburger hanbāgā ハンバ
ーガー

hammer *n* kanazuchi 金づち

hamper *v/t (obstruct)*
samatageru 妨げる

hamster hamusutā ハムス
ター

hand *n* te 手; *(of clock)* hari 針;
on the one ~, *on the other*
~ ippō dewa ... de, mō ippō
dewa ... da 一方では…で、
もう一方では…だ

♦**hand over** baton tewatasu 手
渡す; *hostage etc* hikiwatasu
引き渡す

hand baggage tenimotsu
手荷物

handcuffs tejō 手錠

handicap *n (disability)* shintai-
shōgai 身体障害; *fig* furi na
jōken 不利な条件

handicapped *(physically)*
shōgai no aru 障害のある

handkerchief hankachi ハ
ンカチ

handle 1 *n* totte 取っ手; *(on
door)* nobu ノブ 2 *v/t goods*
atsukau 扱う

handmade tesei (no) 手製
(の)

handshake akushu 握手

handsome hansamu (na) ハン
サム(な)

handwriting hisseki 筆跡

handwritten tegaki (no) 手
書き(の)

handy benri (na) 便利(な)

hang 1 *v/t picture* kakeru 掛け
る; *person* kōshukei ni suru 絞
首刑にする 2 *v/i (of dress,
hair)* kakaru 掛かる

♦hang up *v/i* TEL kiru 切る

hanger *(for clothes)* hangā ハンガー

hangover futsukayoi 二日酔い

haphazard detarame (na) でたらめ(な)

happen okoru 起こる

happily tanoshisō ni 楽しそうに; *(willingly)* yorokonde 喜んで; *(luckily)* saiwai ni mo 幸いにも

happiness shiawase 幸せ

happy shiawase (na) 幸せ(な)

harass ... ni iyagarase o suru …にいやがらせをする

harassment iyagarase いやがらせ; *sexual* ~ sekuhara セクハラ

harbor *n* minato 港

hard *material* katai 硬い; *(difficult)* muzukashī 難しい

hardback hādo kabā ハードカバー

hard-boiled *egg* katayude (no) 固ゆで(の)

hard currency kōkan-kanō-tsūka 交換可能通貨

hardliner kyōkōha 強硬派

hardly hotondo ... nai ほとんど…ない

hardship konnan 困難

hardware kanamonorui 金物

類; COMPUT hādowea ハードウェア

hard-working hatarakimono (no) 働き者(の)

harm 1 *n* gai 害 **2** *v/t* sokonau 損なう

harmful yūgai (na) 有害(な)

harmless mugai (na) 無害(な)

harmony hāmonī ハーモニー; *(relationship)* chōwa 調和

harp hāpu ハープ

harsh kibishī 厳しい

harvest *n* shūkaku 収穫

hash browns hasshu-buraun ハッシュブラウン

hasty keisotsu (na) 軽率(な)

hat bōshi 帽子

hate 1 *n* nikushimi 憎しみ **2** nikumu 憎む

have ◊ *(possess)* motte iru 持っている; *brother etc* ... ga iru …がいる **◊** *breakfast etc* toru とる **◊** *(requests)*: *can I ~ a cup of coffee?* kōhī o itadakemasu ka コーヒーをいただけますか◊; *~ (got) to (must)* ... shinakereba naranai …しなければならない; *you don't ~ to go* ikanakute mo ī desu 行かなくてもいいです **◊** *(causative)*: *~ X done* X shite morau X してもらう; *I'll ~ it repaired*

278

shūri shite morau 修理して
もらう

◆have on *(wear)* kite iru 着て
いる; *(have planned)* yotei ga
aru 予定がある

hawk taka たか

hay fever kafunshō 花粉症

hazard lights AUTO kiken-
keikoku-sōchi 危険警告装置

hazelnut hēzerunattsu ヘーゼ
ルナッツ

hazy *view* bon'yari shita ぼん
やりした; *memory* mōrō to
shita もうろうとした

he kare 彼; ~ *is American* kare
wa Amerikajin desu 彼はア
メリカ人です ◊ *(omission
of pronoun): where is ~? - ~
isn't here* kare wa doko? - inai
彼はどこ? - いない

head 1 *n* atama 頭; *(boss)* chō
長; *(of department)* buchō 部
長; *(of company)* shachō 社長
2 *v/t (lead)* hikīru 率いる

headache zutsū 頭痛

headhunter COMM heddohantā
ヘッドハンター

heading *(in list)* hyōdai 表題

headlight heddoraito ヘッド
ライト

headline midashi 見出し

head office honsha 本社

headphones heddohon ヘッ
ドホン

headquarters honbu 本部

heal 1 *v/t* naosu 治す 2 *v/i*
naoru 治る

health kenkō 健康; *your ~!*
kanpai 乾杯

health food store kenkō-
shokuhinten 健康食品店

health insurance kenkō-hoken
健康保険

health resort kenkō-rizōto 健
康リゾート

healthy kenkō (na) 健康(な);
lifestyle kenkōteki (na) 健康
的な

heap *n* tsumikasane 積み重ね

hear kikoeru 聞こえる

hearing chōkaku 聴覚

hearing aid hochōki 補聴器

heart shinzō 心臓; *(of city)*
chūshin 中心; *learn by ~* anki
suru暗記する

heart attack shinzō-hossa 心
臓発作

heartburn muneyake 胸やけ

hearts *(in cards)* hāto ハート

heat *n* netsu 熱

heated *pool* onsui (no) 温水
(の); *discussion* kōfun shita
興奮した

heater hītā ヒーター

heating danbō 暖房

heatwave neppa 熱波

heaven tengoku 天国

heavy omoi 重い; *coat* atsui 厚

い; *cold* hidoi ひどい; *rain* hageshī 激しい; *traffic* noroi のろい; *food* shitsukoi しつこい

hectic yatara isogashī やたら忙しい

hedgehog harinezumi はりねずみ

heel kakato かかと; *(of shoe)* hīru ヒール

height takasa 高さ; *(of person)* shinchō 身長; *(of plane)* kōdo 高度

heir sōzokunin 相続人

heiress sōzokunin 相続人

helicopter herikoputā ヘリコプター

hell jigoku 地獄

hello konnichiwa こんにちは; TEL moshimoshi もしもし

helmet herumetto ヘルメット

help 1 *n* tasuke 助け 2 *v/t* tasukeru 助ける; ~ *oneself (to food)* jiyū ni toru 自由に取る; *I can't ~ it* shō ga nai しょうがない

helpful yaku ni tatsu 役に立つ

helpless *(unable to cope)* muryoku (na) 無力(な)

hemisphere hankyū 半球

hemorrhage *n* shukketsu 出血

hepatitis kan'en 肝炎

her 1 *adj* kanojo no 彼女の 2 *pron* kanojo 彼女

herb kōsō 香草, hābu ハーブ

herb tea hābu-tī ハーブティー

here *live* koko ni ここに; ~ *eat* koko de ここで; *come* koko e ここへ; ~ *you are (giving sth)* hai, dōzo はい、どうぞ

hereditary *disease* idensei (no) 遺伝性(の)

heritage isan 遺産

hermit yosutebito 世捨て人

hero eiyū 英雄

heroin heroin ヘロイン

heroine hiroin ヒロイン

herpes MED herupesu ヘルペス

herring nishin にしん

hers kanojo no mono 彼女のもの

herself jishin 自身; *she* ~ kanojo jishin 彼女自身; *by* ~ jibun de 自分で; *(alone)* hitori de ひとりで

hesitate tamerau ためらう

hesitation tamerai ためらい

heterosexual *adj* isei-aisha 異性愛者

hi konnichiwa こんにちは

hiccup *n* shakkuri しゃっくり

hide 1 *v/t* kakusu 隠す 2 *v/i* kakureru 隠れる

hideaway kakurebasho 隠れ場所

hiding place kakurebasho 隠れ場所

hierarchy kaikyū-soshiki 階級組織

high adj takai 高い; wind tsuyoi 強い; quality kōkyū (na) 高級(な); (on drugs) hai (na) ハイ(な)

high jump haijanpu ハイジャンプ

high-level toppu-reberu (no) トップレベル(の)

highlight 1 n hairaito ハイライト **2** v/t (with pen) keikō-pen de kyōchō suru 蛍光ペンで強調する

highlighter (pen) keikō-pen 蛍光ペン

highly likely hijō ni 非常に; be ~ paid kōkyū o moratte iru 高給をもらっている

high point pīku ピーク

high school kōkō 高校

high society jōryū-shakai 上流社会

high-speed train kōsoku-ressha 高速列車

high tech n haiteku ハイテク

highway kansen-dōro 幹線道路

hijack v/t haijakku suru ハイジャックする

hijacker nottorihannin 乗っ取り犯人

hike n haikingu ハイキング

hilarious omoshiroi おもしろい

hill oka 丘; (slope) saka 坂

hilly oka no ōi 丘の多い

him kare 彼

himself jishin 自身; he ~ kare jishin 彼自身; by ~ jibun de 自分で; (alone) hitori de ひとりで

hinder samatageru 妨げる

hint (clue) hinto ヒント

hip koshi 腰

hippopotamus kaba かば

his 1 adj kare no 彼の **2** pron kare no mono 彼のもの

historian rekishika 歴史家

historic rekishiteki ni yūmei (na) 歴史的に有名(な)

historical rekishijō (no) 歴史上(の)

history rekishi 歴史

hit 1 v/t tataku たたく; ball utsu 打つ; (collide with) …ni butsukaru …にぶつかる **2** n (blow) dageki 打撃; MUS hitto ヒット; (success) daiseikō 大成功

hitchhike hitchihaiku suru ヒッチハイクする

hitman koroshiya 殺し屋

HIV hito-men'eki-fuzen-uirusu ヒト免疫不全ウィルス

HIV-positive eichi-ai-bui-yōsei (no) ＨＩＶ陽性(の)

hoarse shagaregoe (no) しゃ

がれ声(の)

hoax *n* itazura いたずら

hobby shumi 趣味

hog *n (pig)* buta 豚

hold 1 *v/t (in hands)* te ni motsu 手に持つ; *(in arms)* kakaeru 抱える; *(support)* sasaeru 支える; *passport* motte iru 持っている; *prisoner* kōryū suru 拘留する; *(contain)* ireru koto ga dekiru 入れることができる; **~ the line** TEL kirazu ni sono mama matsu 切らずにそのまま待つ 2 *n (in plane)* kamotsushitsu 貨物室; **catch ~ of** ... tsukamu つかむ

holdup *(robbery)* gōtō 強盗; *(delay)* okure 遅れ

hole ana 穴

holiday *(single day)* shukujitsu 祝日; *Br (period)* kyūka 休暇

hollow karappo (no) 空っぽ(の)

holy shinsei (na) 神聖(な)

home 1 *n* katei 家庭; *(native country)* kokoku 故国; *(area)* kokyō 故郷; *(for old people)* rōjin-hōmu 老人ホーム; **at ~** *(in my house)* ie de 家で; *(in my country)* jibun no kuni de 自分の国で 2 *adv* jitaku e 自宅へ; *(country)* kokoku e 故国へ; *(area)* kokyō e 故郷へ

homeless *adj* hōmuresu (no) ホームレス(の)

homemade jikasei (no) 自家製(の)

homeopathy homeopashī ホメオパシー

homesick: *be ~* hōmushikku ni naru ホームシックになる

home town kokyō 故郷

homicide satsujin 殺人

homosexual *n* dōsei-aisha 同性愛者

honest shōjiki (na) 正直(な)

honesty shōjiki 正直

honeymoon *n* hanemūn ハネムーン

honor 1 *n* meiyo 名誉 2 *v/t* uyamau 敬う

honorable rippa (na) 立派(な)

hood *(on head)* fūdo フード; AUTO bonnetto ボンネット

hook *(for clothes)* yōfuku-kake 洋服掛け; *(on dress)* hokku ホック; *(for fishing)* tsuribari 釣り針

hooligan fūrigan フーリガン

hope 1 *n* nozomi 望み 2 *v/i* kibō o motsu 希望を持つ 3 *v/t* tsumaranai mono desu ga つまらないものですが

hopeful kibō o motta 希望を持った; *(promising)* yūbō 有望(な)

hopefully kitai shite 期待し
て; *(I / we hope)* dekireba で
きれば

hopeless *position* zetsubōteki
(na) 絶望的(な); *(useless:
person)* dō shiyō mo nai どう
しようもない

horizon chiheisen 地平線; *(at
sea)* suiheisen 水平線

horizontal suihei (no) 水
平(の)

hormone horumon ホルモン

horoscope hoshiuranai 星
占い

horrible osoroshī 恐ろしい

horrifying osoroshī 恐ろしい

horror kyōfu 恐怖

horse uma 馬

horsepower bariki 馬力

horse race keiba 競馬

horticulture engei 園芸

hose *n* hōsu ホース

hospice hosupisu ホスピス

hospitable motenashi no yoi
もてなしのよい

hospital byōin 病院; *go into
the* ~ nyūin suru 入院する

hospitality motenashi もて
なし

host *n* (at party) shujin'yaku 主
人役; *(of TV show)* shikaisha
司会者

hostage hitojichi 人質

hostel *(youth ~)* yūsu-hosuteru

ユースホステル

hostess *(at party)* shujin'yaku
主人役; *(on airplane)*
suchuwādesu スチュワー
デス; *(in bar)* hosutesu ホ
ステス

hostility teki-i 敵意

hot *weather* atsui 暑い; *object*
atsui 熱い; *(spicy)* karai 辛い

hot dog hottodoggu ホット
ドッグ

hotel hoteru ホテル;
(Japanese-style) ryokan 旅館

hot spring onsen 温泉

hour jikan 時間

house *n* ie 家

housekeeper kaseifu 家政婦

House of Representatives
(Japanese) Shūgi-in 衆議院;
(in USA) Kain 下院

housewife shufu 主婦

housework kaji 家事

how dō yatte どうやって;
are you? o-genki desu ka お
元気ですか; ~ *about...?* ...
wa dō desu ka …はどうです
か; ~ *much?* dono kurai どの
くらい; ~ *much is it?* ikura
desu ka いくらですか; ~
many? ikutsu いくつ

however keredomo けれど
も; ~ *big they are* dore hodo
ōkikute mo どれほど大き
くても

howl v/i (of dog) tōboe suru 遠ぼえする

hug v/t dakishimeru 抱き締める

huge kyodai (na) 巨大(な)

human 1 n ningen 人間 2 adj ningen (no) 人間(の)

human being ningen 人間

humane ningenteki (na) 人間的(な)

humanitarian jindōteki (na) 人道的(な)

human resources jinzai 人材; (department) jinjibu 人事部

humble tsutsumashī つつましい; origin iyashī 卑しい; home shisso (na) 質素(な)

humid mushiatsui 蒸し暑い

humidity shikke 湿気

humiliate ... ni haji o kakaseru …に恥をかかせる

humor (comical) yūmoa ユーモア

hunch (idea) yokan 予感

hundred hyaku 百

hunger kūfuku 空腹

hungry onaka o sukaseta お腹をすかせた; I'm ~ onaka ga suita お腹がすいた

hunt 1 n kari 狩り; (for missing person) sōsaku 捜索 2 v/t

animal karu 狩る

hurricane harikēn ハリケーン

hurry 1 n ōisogi 大急ぎ; be in a ~ awatete iru あわてている 2 v/i isogu 急ぐ
♦**hurry up** v/i isogu 急ぐ; ~! isoide 急いで

hurt 1 v/i itamu 痛む 2 v/t itameru 痛める; (emotionally) kizutsukeru 傷つける

husband otto 夫
♦**hush up** scandal etc momikesu もみ消す

hut koya 小屋

hydraulic suiryoku (no) 水力(の); brake yuatsushiki (no) 油圧式(の)

hydroelectric suiryoku-hatsuden (no) 水力発電(の)

hygiene eisei 衛生

hygienic eiseiteki (na) 衛生的(な)

hymn sanbika 賛美歌

hyphen haifun ハイフン

hypocrite gizensha 偽善者

hypothermia teitai-onshō 低体温症

hysterical hisuterikku (na) ヒステリック(な); (very funny) hidoku omoshiroi ひどくおもしろい

I

I watashi 私; *(informal use by men)* boku ぼく; *(informal use by women)* atashi あたし *(omission of pronoun):* **~ don't understand** wakarimasen わかりません

ice kōri 氷

icebox reitōshitsu 冷凍室

ice cream aisukurīmu アイスクリーム

icon *(cultural)* gūzō 偶像; COMPUT aikon アイコン

icy *surface* kōri de ōwareta 氷で覆われた

idea kangae 考え

ideal *(perfect)* risōteki (na) 理想的(な)

identical mattaku onaji 全く同じ

identification mimoto-kakunin 身元確認; *(card)* mibun-shōmeisho 身分証明書

identify *person* miwakeru 見分ける

identity mimoto 身元

identity card mibun-shōmeisho 身分証明書

ideology ideorogī イデオロギー

idiot baka ばか

idle *adj (lazy)* namakemono (no) 怠け者(の)

idolize sūhai suru 崇拝する

if moshimo ... naraba もしも…ならば; *(whether or not)* ... ka dō ka …かどうか

ignition *(in car)* tenka-sōchi 点火装置; **~ key** igunisshon-kī イグニッションキー

ignorance muchi 無知

ignore mushi suru 無視する

ill guai no warui 具合の悪い; *(with specific illness)* byōki (no) 病気(の)

illegal ihan (no) 違反(の); *immigrant* fuhō (no) 不法(の)

illegible yomenai 読めない

illiterate monmō (no) 文盲(の)

illness byōki 病気

illogical fugōri (na) 不合理(な)

illusion gensō 幻想

illustration sashie 挿絵

image *(of politician, company)* imēji イメージ

imaginary sōzōjō (no) 想像上(の)

imagination sōzōryoku 想像力

imaginative sōzōryoku no

yutaka (na) 想像力の豊
か(な)
imagine sōzō suru 想像する
imitate maneru まねる
imitation mane まね; (sth
copied) mozōhin 模造品
immature mijuku (na) 未
熟(な)
immediate sugu (no) すぐ(の)
immediately sugusama す
ぐさま
immigrant n imin 移民
immigration ijū 移住
immoral fudōtoku (na) 不道
徳(な)
immortal fushi (no) 不死(の)
immunity men'eki 免疫;
diplomatic ~ gaikōkan-tokken
外交官特権
impact n (of crash) shōtotsu 衝
突; (effect) eikyō 影響
impartial kōhei (na) 公平(な)
impassable tōrenai 通れない
impatient ki no mijikai 気
の短い
impediment: speech ~ gengo-
shōgai 言語障害
imperial teikoku (no) 帝国
(の); Imperial Palace Kōkyo
皇居
impersonal ningenmi no nai
人間味のない
impetuous mōretsu (na) 猛
烈(な)

implement 1 n dōgu 道具 2
v/t measures etc jikkō suru 実
行する
implication imi 意味
imply imi suru 意味する
import 1 n yunyū 輸入 2 v/t
yunyū suru 輸入する
importance jūyōsei 重要性
important jūyō (na) 重要(な)
impossible fukanō (na) 不可
能(な)
impression inshō 印象
impressive inshōteki (na) 印
象的(な)
imprison keimusho ni ireru 刑
務所に入れる
improve 1 v/t kaizen suru 改
善する 2 v/i yoku naru よく
なる; (of skills) jōtatsu suru
上達する
improvement kaizen 改善; (in
skills) jōtatsu 上達
improvise sokkyō de
ensō suru 即興で演奏する
impulsive shōdōteki (na) 衝
動的(な)
in 1 prep (with verbs of being)
… ni …に; (with verbs of
activity) … de …で; ~ Japan
(live) Nihon ni 日本に; (work)
Nihon de 日本で◊ (time) …
ni …に; ~ 2000 nisen-nen ni
2000 年に; ~ two hours (from
now) nijikan go ni 二時間後

に; **~ August** hachigatsu ni 八
月に ◊ *(manner)* ... de …で;
~ English Eigo de 英語で
2 *adv (at home)* ie ni 家に

inability munō 無能

inaccessible ikizurai 行き
づらい

inadequate *supply* fujūbun
(na) 不十分(な)

inappropriate futekitō (na) 不
適切(な)

inaugural *speech* shūninshiki
(no) 就任式(の)

incentive shigeki 刺激

incessant taema no nai 絶え
間のない

inch *n* inchi インチ

incident jiken 事件

incidentally tokoro de と
ころで

incite *(to riot)* sendō suru 扇
動する

include ireru 入れる; *(of
price)* fukumu 含む

including *prep* fukumete含
めて

inclusive 1 *adj price* issaikomi
(no) 一切込み(の) 2 *prep*
fukumete含めて

incoherent tsujitsuma no
awanai つじつまの合わない

income shūnyū 収入

income tax shotokuzei 所得税

incoming *flight* tōchaku suru

到着する; *president* kōnin
(no) 後任(の)

incompatible *people* ai-
irenai 相い入れない; *systems*
gokansei no nai 互換性の
ない

incompetent munō (na) 無
能(な); *work* heta (na) 下
手(な)

incomprehensible rikai
dekinai 理解できない

inconsiderate omoiyari no nai
思いやりのない

inconsistent *argument* mujun
shita 矛盾した

inconvenient fuben (na) 不便
(な); *time* tsugō no warui 都
合の悪い

incorrect fuseikaku (na) 不
正確(な)

increase 1 *v/t* ageru 上げる;
amount fuyasu 増やす 2 *v/i*
agaru 上がる; *(amount)* fueru
増える 3 *n (in number)* zōka
増加; *(in amount)* zōryō 増量

incredible shinjirarenai 信じ
られない

incurable chiryō-fukanō (na)
治療不可能(な)

indecisive yūjū-fudan (no) 優
柔不断(の)

indeed *(in fact)* hontō ni 本
当に

indefinitely mukigen ni 無

期限に

independence dokuritsu 独立

Independence Day
Dokuritsu-kinenbi 独立記
念日

independent dokuritsu (no)
独立(の)

indicate v/t (show) shimesu
示す

indifferent mukanshin (na) 無
関心(な)

indigestion shōka-furyō 消
化不良

indignant fungai shita 憤
慨した

indirect link kansetsuteki (na)
間接的(な)

indiscriminate musabetsu (na)
無差別(な)

indispensable kakegae no nai
掛け替えのない

indistinct fumeiryō (na) 不明
りょう(な)

individual 1 n kojin 個人
2 adj koko (no) 個々(の);
(personal) kojin (no) 個人
(の)

individually koko ni 個々に

indoor okunai (no) 屋内(の)

indoors play okunai de 屋内で

industrial kōgyō (no) 工業(の)

industrial action sutoraiki ス
トライキ

industrial waste sangyō-

haikibutsu 産業廃棄物

industry kōgyō 工業

inefficient hinōritsuteki (na) 非
能率的(な)

inequality fubyōdō 不平等

inevitable sakerarenai 避け
られない

inexpensive yasui 安い

inexperienced keiken no nai
経験のない

infamous akumei no takai 悪
名の高い

infant yōji 幼児

infantry hoheitai 歩兵隊

infection kansen 感染

infectious disease kansen suru
感染する

inferior quality ototta 劣った

inferiority complex rettōkan
劣等感

infidelity futei 不貞

infiltrate v/t shinnyū saseru 侵
入させる

infinite mugen (no) 無限(の)

infinity mugen 無限

inflammable kanensei (no) 可
燃性(の)

inflammation MED enshō 炎症

inflation infure インフレ

inflexible yūzū no kikanai 融
通のきかない

influence 1 n eikyō 影響 **2** v/t
… ni eikyō o oyobosu …に影
響を及ぼす

influential eikyōryoku no aru 影響力のある

influenza infuruenza インフルエンザ

inform tsūchi suru 通知する

informal *talk* kudaketa くだけた; *dress* fudan (no) 普段(の)

informant jōhō-teikyōsha 情報提供者

information jōhō 情報

informer mikkokusha 密告者

infuriating hidoku haradatashī ひどく腹立たしい

ingenious kōmyō (na) 巧妙(な)

ingredient zairyō 材料

inhabit … ni sumu …に住む

inhabitant jūmin 住民

inhale *v/t & v/i* suikomu 吸い込む

inhaler kyūnyūki 吸入器

inherit sōzoku suru 相続する

inhibition yokusei 抑制

in-house *adv work* shanai de 社内で

inhuman zankoku (na) 残酷(な)

initial 1 *adj* hajime (no) 始め(の) **2** *n* inisharu イニシャル

initiate *v/t* kaishi suru 開始する

initiative shudōken 主導権

inject MED chūsha suru 注射する; *capital* tōnyū suru 投入する

injured 1 *adj* kega o shita 怪我をした; *feelings* kizutsuita 傷ついた **2** *n: the ~* fushōsha 負傷者

injury kega 怪我

ink inku インク; *(Chinese ~)* sumi 墨

in-laws inseki 姻せき

inmate *(prison)* jukeisha 受刑者; *(mental hospital)* nyūin-kanja 入院患者

inn ryokan 旅館

inner *courtyard* uchigawa (no) 内側(の)

inner city toshinbu 都心部

innocence mujaki 無邪気; JUR muzai 無罪

innocent mujaki (na) 無邪気(な); JUR muzai 無罪(の)

innovative kakushinteki (na) 革新的(な)

in-patient nyūin-kanja 入院患者

input *n (to project)* enjo 援助; COMPUT nyūryoku 入力

inquest chōsa 調査

inquire toiawaseru 問い合わせる

inquiry toiawase 問い合わせ

inquisitive shiritagari (no) 知りたがり (の)

insane kyōki (no) 狂気(の)

insanity kyōki 狂気

inscription mei 銘

insect konchū 昆虫

insecticide satchūzai 殺虫剤

insect repellent mushiyoke
虫よけ

insecure *(anxious)* fuan ni
omotte iru 不安に思っている

insensitive donkan (na) 鈍感
(な); *remark* mushinkei (na)
無神経(な)

insert *v/t* sashikomu 差し込む

inside 1 *n* naka 中; **~ out**
uragaeshi ni 裏返しに
2 *prep* ... no naka ni ...の中
に 3 *adv stay* naka ni 中に; *go*
naka e 中へ; *play* naka de 中
で 4 *adj* naka (no) 中(の);
~ information naibu-jōhō 内
部情報

insider shōsokutsū 消息通

insides o-naka おなか

insight dōsatsu 洞察

insist iharu 言い張る

insistent shitsukoi しつこい

insomnia fumin 不眠

inspect *tickets* kensa suru 検
査する; *school* shisatsu suru
視察する

inspiration insupirēshon イン
スピレーション

inspire *respect etc* yobiokosu
呼び起こす

instability fuantei 不安定

installment ichiwa 一話;
(payment) ikkaibun no shiharai
一回分の支払い

instant 1 *adj* sokuji (no) 即時
(の) 2 *n* shunkan 瞬間

instant coffee insutanto-kōhī
インスタントコーヒー

instantly sokuza ni 即座に

instead sono kawari ni その代
わりに; **~ of** ... no kawari ni
...の代わりに

instinct honnō 本能

instinctive honnōteki (na) 本
能的(な)

institute *n* SCHOOL kyōiku-kikan
教育機関; *(research)* kenkyū-
kikan 研究機関

institution POL kikan 機関

instruct *(teach)* oshieru 教える

instruction shiyō-setsumei 使
用説明

instrument MUS gakki 楽器;
(tool) kigu 器具

insulation ELEC zetsuen 絶縁;
(against cold) dannetsu 断熱

insulin inshurin インシュリン

insult 1 *n* bujoku 侮辱 2 *v/t*
bujoku suru 侮辱する

insurance hoken 保険

insurance company hoken-
gaisha 保険会社

insurance policy hoken-
shōsho 保険証書

insure … ni hoken o kakeru
…に保険をかける; **be ~d**
hoken ni haitte iru 保険に入
っている

intact mukizu (no) 無傷(の)

integrity kōketsu 高潔

intellectual **1** adj chiteki (na)
知的(な) **2** n chishikijin
知識人

intelligence chinō 知能; MIL
jōhō 情報

intelligent rikō (na) 利口(な)

intend: ~ **to** … … suru tsumori
de aru …するつもりである

intense mōretsu (na) 猛烈
(な)

intensive shūchūteki (na) 集
中的(な)

intensive care (unit) ai-shī-yū
I C U

intention ito 意図

intentional itoteki (na) 意図
的(な)

interactive taiwashiki (no) 対
話式(の)

intercept *ball* intāseputo suru
インターセプトする;
message bōju suru 傍受する;
missile tochū de geigeki suru
途中で迎撃する

intercom intāhon インタ
ーホン

intercourse seikō 性交

interest **1** n kyōmi 興味;

(*financial*) rishi 利子 **2** v/t
kyōmi o motaseru 興味を持
たせる

interesting omoshiroi おも
しろい

interfere kanshō suru 干渉
する

♦ **interfere with** *plans* jama
suru邪魔する

interference kanshō 干渉;
RADIO jushin-shōgai 受信障害

interior **1** adj naibu (no) 内部
(の) **2** n (*of house*) interia イ
ンテリア

intermediary n chūkaisha
仲介者

intermediate adj chūkyū (no)
中級(の)

internal naibu (no) 内部(の)

international adj kokusaiteki
(na) 国際的(な)

Internet intānetto インター
ネット

interpret v/t & v/i tsūyaku suru
通訳する

interpretation tsūyaku 通訳;
(*of meaning*) kaishaku 解釈

interpreter tsūyaku 通訳

interrogate jinmon suru 尋
問する

interrupt **1** v/t … no hanashi
ni warikomu …の話に割り
込む **2** v/i jama o suru 邪魔
をする

interruption jama 邪魔

intersection AUTO kōsaten 交差点

interval kankaku 間隔; THEAT kyūkei-jikan 休憩時間

intervene kainyū suru 介入する

interview 1 *n* (on TV) intabyū インタビュー; (for job) mensetsu 面接 **2** *v/t* (on TV) … ni intabyū suru …にインタビューする; (for job) mensetsu suru 面接する

intimacy shitashisa 親しさ, (sexual) nikutai-kankei 肉体関係

intimidate odosu 脅す

into … no naka ni …の中に; *translate ~ English* Eigo ni hon'yaku suru 英語に翻訳する; *be ~ infml* (like) … ga suki de aru …が好きである

intolerable taerarenai 耐えられない

intolerant henkyō (na) 偏狭(な)

intricate fukuzatsu (na) 複雑(な)

intriguing omoshiroi おもしろい

introduce shōkai suru 紹介する

introduction (to person) shōkai 紹介; (in book) jobun 序文;

(of new technique) dōnyū 導入

intruder shinnyūsha 侵入者

invade shinryaku suru 侵略する

invalid *n* MED byōnin 病人

invaluable *help* kakegae no nai かけがえのない

invasion shinryaku 侵略

invent hatsumei suru 発明する

inventor hatsumeisha 発明者

invest *v/t & v/i* tōshi suru 投資する

investigate chōsa suru 調査する

investigation chōsa 調査

investment tōshi 投資; (amount) tōshigaku 投資額

invisible me ni mienai 目に見えない

invitation shōtai 招待; (card) shōtaijō 招待状

invite shōtai suru 招待する

invoice *n* seikyūsho 請求書

involve *work* hitsuyō to suru 必要とする; (concern) … ni kankei suru …に関係する

invulnerable fujimi (no) 不死身(の)

inwardly (in one's heart) kokoro no naka de 心の中で

iron 1 *n* tetsu 鉄, (for clothes) airon アイロン **2** *v/t* airon o kakeru アイロンをかける

ironic hiniku (na) 皮肉(な)

irony hiniku 皮肉

irrational fugōri (na) 不合理 (な)

irrelevant mukankei (na) 無関係 (な)

irrigation kangai かんがい

irritable okorippoi 怒りっぽい

irritate *(annoy)* iraira saseru いらいらさせる

irritating iraira suru yō (na) いらいらするよう (な)

irritation iradachi いらだち

Islam Isuramukyō イスラム教

island shima 島

isolate *(cut off)* koritsu saseru 孤立させる

isolated *house* koritsu shita 孤立した; *occurrence* tandoku (no) 単独 (no)

issue 1 *n (matter)* mondai 問題; *March ~* sangatsu-gō 三月号 **2** *v/t visa* hakkō suru 発行する; *supplies* shikyū suru 支給する

it ◇ *(subject)* sore wa / ga それは / が; *(object)* sore o それを ◇ *(not translated)*: *~'s me* watashi desu 私です; *I don't like ~* watashi wa kirai desu 私は嫌いです; *that's ~!* *(right)* sono tōri そのとおり; *(finished)* kore de o-shimai これでおしまい

italics shatai de 斜体で

Italy Itaria イタリア

itch *n* kayumi かゆみ

item shinamono 品物; *(on agenda)* kōmoku 項目

itemize *invoice* kajōgaki ni suru 箇条書にする

its sore (no) それ (の)

itself jishin 自身; *by ~* *(alone)* jishin de 自身で; *(automatically)* sorejishin de それ自身で

J

jacket jaketto ジャケット

jade *n* hisui ひすい

jail keimusho 刑務所

jam *(for bread)* jamu ジャム

January ichigatsu 一月

Japan Nihon 日本

Japanese 1 *adj* Nihon (no) 日本 (の) **2** *n (person)* Nihonjin 日本人; *(language)* Nihongo 日本語

jar *n (container)* bin びん

jasmine tea jasumin-cha ジャスミン茶

jaw *n* ago あご

jazz jazu ジャズ

jealous shittobukai しっと
深い

jeans jīnzu ジーンズ

jellyfish kurage くらげ

jeopardize kiken ni sarasu 危
険にさらす

jerk v/t guitto hiku ぐいっ
と引く

jet 1 n (plane) jettoki ジェット機

jetlag jisaboke 時差ぼけ

Jew Yudayajin ユダヤ人

jeweler hōsekishō 宝石商

jewelry hōsekirui 宝石類

job shoku 職; (task) shigoto
仕事

jog n/i (as exercise) jogingu suru
ジョギングする

join 1 v/i (of roads etc) gōryū
suru 合流する; (as member)
kanyū suru 加入する
2 v/t (connect) tsunagu つな
ぐ; person ... to issho ni naru
…と一緒になる; club ... ni
kanyū suru …に加入する

joint n ANAT kansetsu 関節; (in
wood) tsugime 継ぎ目

joint account kyōdō-yokin-
kōza 共同預金口座

joint venture gōben-jigyō 合
弁事業

joke n jōdan 冗談; (practical ~)
itazura いたずら

jolt 1 n (jerk) yure 揺れ 2 v/t

(push) ... ni butsukaru …に
ぶつかる

jostle v/t osu 押す

journalism jānarizumu ジャー
ナリズム

journalist kisha 記者

journey n ryokō 旅行

joy yorokobi 喜び

judge 1 n JUR saibankan 裁判
官; (in competition) shinpan
審判 2 v/t handan suru 判
断する

judgment JUR hanketsu 判決;
(opinion) iken 意見; (good
sense) handan 判断

judo jūdō 柔道

juice jūsu ジュース

July shichigatsu 七月

jumble n yoseatsume 寄せ
集め

jump 1 n jampu ジャンプ;
(increase) kyūjōshō 急上昇
2 v/i tobu 跳ぶ; (in surprise)
dokitto suru どきっとする

jumpy bikubiku shite iru びく
びくしている

June rokugatsu 六月

junior 1 adj (subordinate) shita
(no) 下(の) 2 n (in rank)
kōhai 後輩

junk (trash) garakuta がら
くた

junk food janku-fūdo ジャン
クフード

junkie mayaku-jōshūsha 麻薬
常習者
junk mail dairekuto-mēru ダイ
レクトメール
juror baishin-in 陪審員
jury baishin 陪審
just adv (exactly) chōdo ちょ
うど; (only) tada ただ; **I've ~
got here** watashi wa koko ni
tsuita bakari desu 私はここに
着いたばかりです; **~ now**
(a few moments ago) tsui sakki
ついさっき; (at the moment)
chōdo ima ちょうど今
justice shihō 司法; (of cause)
seigi 正義
justify seitōka suru 正当化する
juvenile delinquent hikō-
shōnen 非行少年; (female)
hikō-shōjo 非行少女

K

karaoke karaoke カラオケ
karate karate 空手
keep 1 v/t totte oku 取って
おく; (not give back) motte
iru 持っている; (not lose)
tamotsu 保つ; (in specific
place) shimatte oku しまって
おく; **~ a promise** yakusoku
o mamoru 約束を守る; **~
trying** tsuzukete miru 続けて
みる **2** v/i (remain) … no
mama de iru …のままでい
る; (of food) motsu もつ
◆**keep down** v/t costs etc
osaeru 抑える
◆**keep up 1** v/i (running etc)
tsuite kuru ついてくる **2** v/t
pace tsuzukeru 続ける
ketchup kechappu ケチャップ
kettle yakan やかん

key 1 n (to door) kagi 鍵;
COMPUT, MUS kī キー **2** adj
(vital) jūyō (na) 重要(な)
3 v/t COMPUT nyūryoku suru 入
力する
keyboard COMPUT, MUS kī-bōdo
キーボード
keycard kādo-shiki no kagi カ
ード式の鍵
keyring kī-horudā キーホ
ルダー
kick 1 n kikku キック **2** v/t &
v/i keru ける
kid infml **1** n (child) kodomo 子
供 **2** v/t karakau からかう
kidnap yūkai suru 誘拐する
kidney ANAT jinzō じん臓;
(food) kidonī キドニー;
kill v/t korosu 殺す; time
tsubusu つぶす

kilogram kiroguramu キログラム

kilometer kiromētā キロメーター

kimono kimono 着物

kind¹ adj shinsetsu (na) 親切 (な)

kind² n shurui 種類; (brand) kata 型; what ~ of...? donna どんな; ~ of sad infml nandaka sabishī

kindness shinsetsu 親切

king kokuō 国王

kiss 1 n kisu キス 2 v/t ... ni kisu suru …にキスする 3 v/i kisu o suru キスをする

kit dōgubako 道具箱; (to assemble) kumitateyō buhin-setto 組み立て用部品セット

kitchen daidokoro 台所

kitten koneko 子猫

knack kotsu こつ

knee n hiza ひざ

kneel hizamazuku ひざまずく

knife n naifu ナイフ

knock 1 n (at door) nokku ノック; (blow) shōgeki 衝撃 2 v/t (hit) butsukeru ぶつける 3 v/i (on the door) nokku suru ノックする

♦**knock down** (of car) haneru はねる; wall torikowasu 取り壊す

♦**knock out** nokku-auto suru ノックアウトする

knot n musubime 結び目

know 1 v/t shitte iru 知っている; language ... ga dekiru …ができる 2 v/i shitte iru 知っている; I don't ~ shirimasen 知りません

knowhow nōhau ノウハウ

knowledge chishiki 知識

Korea (South) Kankoku 韓国; (North) Kita-chōsen 北朝鮮

L

lab jikkenshitsu 実験室

label n raberu ラベル

labor n rōdō 労働; (in pregnancy) bunben 分べん

lace n rēsu レース; (of shoe) kutsuhimo 靴ひも

lack 1 n ketsubō 欠乏 2 v/t

... ni kakeru …に欠ける 3 v/i: be ~ing kakete iru 欠けている

lacquerware shikki 漆器

ladder hashigo はしご

ladies' room joseiyō toire 女性用トイレ

lady shukujo 淑女

♦**lag behind** okureru 遅れる

lake mizūmi 湖

lamb kohitsuji 子羊; (meat) ramu ラム

lame person bikko (no) びっこ(の)

lamp ranpu ランプ

land 1 n tochi 土地; (shore) riku 陸; (country) kuni 国 **2** v/i (of plane) chakuriku suru 着陸する; (of ball) ochiru 落ちる

landing (top of staircase) ichiban ue no odoriba 一番上の踊り場

landlady (of hostel) onna-shujin 女主人

landlord (of hostel) shujin 主人

landmark mokuhyō 目標

landscape n keshiki 景色

lane (in country) komichi 小道; (alley) roji 路地; AUTO shasen 車線

language kotoba 言葉; foreign ~ gaikokugo 外国語

Laos Raosu ラオス

lap¹ n (of track) isshū 一周; (in athletics) rappu ラップ

lap² n (of person) hiza ひざ

laptop COMPUT rapputoppu ラップトップ

large ōki 大きい

largely shu to shite 主として

laryngitis kōtōen こう頭炎

laser rēzā レーザー

last¹ adj (in series) saigo (no) 最後(の); (preceding) kono mae (no) この前(の); ~ but one saigo kara nibanme 最後から二番目; ~ night sakuban 昨晩; at ~ tsui ni ついに

last² v/i tsuzuku 続く; (of food) nagamochi suru 長持ちする

lastly saigo ni 最後に

late osoi 遅い; (behind time) okureta 遅れた; (for meeting) chikoku shita 遅刻した

lately saikin 最近

later adv ato de あとで

latest news saishin (no) 最新(の)

latter: the ~ kōsha 後者

laugh 1 n warai 笑い **2** v/i warau 笑う

♦**laugh at** (mock) azawarau あざ笑う

laughter waraigoe 笑い声

launch n (boat) ranchi ランチ; (of rocket) hassha 発射; (of ship) shinsui 進水; (of product) hatsubai 発売

launch pad hasshadai 発射台

laundromat koinrandorī コインランドリー

laundry kurīninguten クリーニング店; (clothes) sentakumono 洗濯もの

lavatory toire トイレ

law hōritsu 法律; *(subject)* hōgaku 法学

lawn shibafu 芝生

lawsuit soshō 訴訟

lawyer bengoshi 弁護士

lay *v/t (put)* oku 置く; *eggs* umu 産む

layer *n* sō 層

layout reiauto レイアウト

lazy *person* namakete iru 怠けている; *day* nonbiri shita のんびりした

lead[1] *v/t (conduct)* ... sentō ni tatsu ...の先頭に立つ; *team* hikīru 率いる 2 *v/i (in race)* rīdo suru リードする; *(give leadership)* rīdā ni naru リーダーになる

lead[2] *n (for dog)* kusari 鎖

lead[3] *n (metal)* namari 鉛

leader *n (of group)* rīdā リーダー; *(in race)* sentō 先頭

leadership rīdāshippu リーダーシップ

leading-edge *adj technology* saisentan (no) 最先端(の)

leaf happa 葉っぱ

leaflet chirashi ちらし

leak 1 *n* more 漏れ; *(of information)* rōei 漏えい 2 *v/i* moru 漏る

lean[1] *v/i (at angle)* katamuku 傾く; *~ against* ... ni yorikakaru ...に寄りかかる; *(of object)*

... ni tatekakaru ...に立てかかる

lean[2] *adj meat* akami (no) 赤身(の)

leap 1 *n (jump)* chōyaku 跳躍 2 *v/i* tobu 跳ぶ

learn narau 習う

learning *n (knowledge)* gakushiki 学識

lease *n (to lend)* chintai-keiyaku 賃貸契約; *(document)* chintai-keiyakusho 賃貸契約書

least 1 *adv: the ~ expensive car* ichiban yasui kuruma 一番安い車 2 *n: at ~* sukunaku tomo 少なくとも

leather *n* kawa 皮

leave 1 *n (vacation)* kyūka 休暇; *on ~* kyūka de 休暇で 2 *v/t town* hanareru 離れる; *company* saru 去る; *college* sotsugyō suru 卒業する; *husband, wife* ... to wakareru ...と別れる; *food* nokosu 残す; *(forget)* okiwasureru 置き忘れる; *~ X alone (not interfere with)* X o hotte oku Xをほっておく; *be left* nokoru 残る 3 *v/i (of person)* tachisaru 立ち去る; *(of plane)* shuppatsu suru出発する

lecture *n* kōgi 講義

lecturer kōshi 講師

ledge tana たな

left 1 *adj* hidari (no) 左(の); POL saha (no) 左派(の) **2** *n* hidari 左; POL saha 左派; **on the ~** hidarigawa ni 左側に **3** *adv* turn hidari ni 左に

left-handed hidarikiki (no) 左利きの

left-wing POL sayoku (no) 左翼(の)

leg ashi 足

legacy isan 遺産

legal gōhōteki (na) 合法的(な); *(relating to the law)* hōritsu (no) 法律(の)

legality gōhōsei 合法性

legalize gōhōka suru 合法化する

legend densetsu 伝説

legible yomeru 読める

legislature POL rippōfu 立法府

legitimate gōhōteki (na) 合法的(な)

leisure hima 暇

lemon remon レモン

lemonade remonēdo レモネード

lemon juice remon-jūsu レモンジュース

lend: *~ Y to X* X ni Y o kasu XにYを貸す

length nagasa 長さ; **at ~** *explain* kuwashiku 詳しく; *(eventually)* tsui ni ついに

lengthen nobasu 伸ばす

lenient kandai (na) 寛大(な)

lens renzu レンズ

leopard hyō ひょう

lesson jugyō 授業; *(piano, swimming)* ressun レッスン

let *v/t (allow)*: *~ X do Y* X ni Y saseru XにYさせる; *~ me go!* hanashite 放して; *~'s go* ikō 行こう; *~ go (of rope)* hanasu放す

lethal chishi (no) 致死(の)

letter *(of alphabet)* moji 文字; *(in mail)* tegami 手紙

lettuce retasu レタス

leukemia hakketsubyō 白血病

level 1 *adj field* taira (na) 平ら(な); *(in score)* dōten (no) 同点(の) **2** *n (standard)* suijun 水準; *(in hierarchy)* chi-i 地位; *(amount)* reberu レベル

lever *n* rebā レバー

liability insurance songai-baishō-hoken 損害賠償保険

liable sekinin no aru 責任のある; *be ~ to (likely)* … shigachi de aru …しがちである

♦**liaise with** … to no renrakuyaku o tsutomeru …との連絡役を務める

liar usotsuki うそつき

liberal *adj (broad-minded)* kokoro no hiroi 心の広い; POL jiyū-shugi (no) 自由主義(の)

liberate jiyū ni suru 自由
にする

liberty jiyū 自由

library toshokan 図書館

license 1 n menkyo 免許; (for
car) unten-menkyoshō 運転
免許証 2 v/t: be ~d ninka o
ukeru 認可を受ける

license number AUTO nanbā
ナンバー

license plate nanbāpurēto ナ
ンバープレート

lick v/t nameru なめる

lid futa ふた

lie¹ 1 n (untruth) uso うそ **2** v/i
uso o tsuku うそをつく

lie² n (of person) yoko ni naru
横になる; (of object) aru ある

♦**lie down** yoko ni naru 横
になる

life inochi 命; (way of living)
seikatsu 生活; (lifetime) isshō
一生

life insurance seimei-hoken
生命保険

life jacket kyūmei-dōi 救
命胴衣

life-threatening inochi ni
kakawaru 命にかかわる

lift 1 v/t mochiageru 持ち上
げる **2** v/i (of fog) hareru 晴
れる **3** n: give ... a ~ (in car)
kuruma de okuru 車で送る

light¹ 1 v/t hikari 光; (lamp)
akari 明り **2** v/t cigarette
... ni hi o tsukeru …に火を
つける; (illuminate) raitoappu
suru ライトアップする
3 adj (not dark) akarui 明る
い; color usui 薄い

light² adj (not heavy) karui 軽い

light bulb denkyū 電球

lighter (for cigarette) raitā ラ
イター

lighting shōmei 照明

lightning inabikari 稲光

like¹ prep ... no yō (na) …の
よう(な)

like² v/t ... ga suki da …が好
きだ; I ~ her kanojo ga suki
da 彼女が好きだ; I would
~ ... ... ga hoshī …が欲し
い; I would ~ to ... ... shitai
…したい; would you ~ ...?
... ga hoshī desu ka …が欲し
いですか; would you ~ to
...? ... shitai desu ka …した
いですか; if you ~ yokereba
よければ

likeable sukareru 好かれる

likelihood mikomi 見込み

likely (probable) arisō (na) あ
りそう(な)

lily yuri ゆり

limit 1 n (of speed) seigen 制限
2 v/t seigen suru 制限する

limp adj arm etc darari to shita
だらりとした

line n (on paper) sen 線; (of people) retsu 列; (of text) gyō 行; TEL denwasen 電話線

line v/t clothes … ni ura o tsukeru …に裏をつける

♦ **line up** v/i seiretsu suru 整列する

lining (of clothes) uraji 裏地

link 1 n kanren 関連; (in chain) wa 輪 **2** v/t kanren saseru 関連させる

lion raion ライオン

lip kuchibiru 唇

lipstick kuchibeni 口紅

liqueur rikyūru リキュール

liquid n ekitai 液体

liquor sake 酒

liquor store sakaya 酒屋

list n risuto リスト; (of people) meibo 名簿

listen kiku 聞く

♦ **listen to** kiku 聞く

literature bungaku 文学

litter gomi ごみ

little 1 adj house chīsai 小さい; problem sasai (na) ささい(な); child osanai 幼い **2** n: a ~ sukoshi 少し; a ~ bread sukoshi no pan 少しのパン **3** adv: ~ by ~ sukoshi zutsu 少しずつ; a ~ better sukoshi yoi 少しよい

live v/i sumu 住む; (be alive) ikiru 生きる

live adj broadcast nama (no) 生(の)

livelihood seikei 生計

lively nigiyaka (na) にぎやか(な)

liver MED kanzō 肝臓; (food) rebā レバー

livestock kachikurui 家畜類

living 1 adj ikite iru 生きている **2** n kurashi 暮し

living room ribingu-rūmu リビングルーム

lizard tokage とかげ

load 1 n tsumini 積荷 **2** v/t car … ni noseru …にのせる

loaf: a ~ of bread ikkin no pan 一斤のパン

loan 1 n rōn ローン; on ~ karite iru 借りている **2** v/t kasu 貸す

lobby robī ロビー; POL atsuryoku-dantai 圧力団体

local 1 adj jimoto (no) 地元(の) **2** n (person) tochi no hito 土地の人

local call TEL shinai-tsūwa 市内通話

local time genchi-jikan 現地時間

locate factory etc oku 置く

lock 1 n kagi 鍵 **2** v/t door … ni kagi o kakeru …に鍵をかける

locker rokkā ロッカー

log *(wood)* maruta 丸太;
(record) kiroku 記録

logic ronri 論理

logical ronriteki (na) 論理
的(な)

logo rogo ロゴ

London Rondon ロンドン

lonely kodoku (na) 孤独(な);
place sabishī 寂しい

long¹ 1 *adj* nagai 長い; *it's a
~ way* tōi 遠い **2** *adv* nagaku
長く; *will it take ~?* nagaku
kakarimasu ka 長くかかりま
すか; *~ before then* sore yori
daibu mae ni それよりだい
ぶ前に; *before ~* mamonaku
まもなく; *so ~ as (provided)*
… de aru kagiri …である
限り; *so ~!* sayōnara さよ
うなら

long² *v/i*: *~ for*
machinozomu 待ち望む

long-distance *adj* chōkyori
(no) 長距離(の)

long jump habatobi 幅跳び

long-range *missile* chōkyori
(no) 長距離(の); *forecast*
chōki (no) 長期(の)

long-term *adj* chōki (no) 長
期(の)

look 1 *n (appearance)* mikake
見かけ; *(glance)* ikken 一見;
have a ~ at chotto miru ちょ

っと見る; *can I have a ~?*
chotto mite mo ī desu ka ち
ょっと見てもいいですか
2 *v/i* miru 見る; *(seem)* ni
mieru …に見える

♦**look after** *kids* … no sewa
o suru …の世話をする;
property … no kanri o suru
…の管理をする

♦**look at** miru 見る; *(examine)*
shiraberu調べる

♦**look for** sagasu 探す

♦**look out** *v/i (of window)* soto
o miru 外を見る; *~!* abunai
危ない

♦**look up to** *(respect)* sonkei
suru 尊敬する

loose *connection* yurui ゆる
い; *clothes* yuttari shita ゆっ
たりした; *morals* fushidara
(na) ふしだら(な)

loosen yurumeru ゆるめる

lorry *Br* torakku トラック

lose 1 *v/t object* nakusu なく
す; *game* … ni makeru …に
負ける **2** *v/i* makeru 負け
る; *(of clock)* okureru 遅れ
る; *I'm lost* michi ni mayotta
道に迷った

loser SPORTS haisha 敗者

loss *(of object)* funshitsu
紛失; *(through death)* sōshitsu
喪失; *(in business)* sonshitsu
損失

lost ushinawareta 失われた

lotion rōshon ローション

loud *noise* ōkī 大きい; *music* urusai うるさい

loudspeaker supīkā スピーカー

love 1 *n* ai 愛; *(for child, pet)* aijō 愛情; *(romantic)* ren'ai 恋愛; *(in tennis)* rabu ラブ; **be in ~** ...ni koi shite iru ...に恋している; **fall in ~** horeru ほれる 2 *v/t* aisuru 愛する

love affair ren'ai-kankei 恋愛関係

lovely *face* utsukushī 美しい; *color* kirei (na) きれい(な); *weather* subarashī すばらしい

lover aijin 愛人

low *adj* hikui 低い; *price etc* yasui 安い

loyal chūjitsu (na) 忠実(な)

luck un 運; *good* ~ kōun 幸運; *bad* ~ fu-un 不運; *hard* ~! zannen 残念; *good* ~! ganbatte がんばって

luckily un'yoku 運よく

lucky *person* un no ī 運のいい; *number* kōun (no) 幸運(の)

luggage tenimotsu 手荷物

lukewarm nurui ぬるい

lull *n (in storm)* koyami 小やみ

lullaby komoriuta 子守歌

lump *(of sugar)* kakuzatō ikko 角砂糖一個; *(swelling)* kobu こぶ

lump sum ikkatsubarai 一括払い

lunar tsuki (no) 月(の)

lunatic *n* ōbaka 大ばか

lunch hirugohan 昼ごはん

lunch box *(packed lunch)* o-bentō お弁当; *(at station)* ekiben 駅弁

lung hai 肺

lung cancer haigan 肺がん

lust *n* yokubō 欲望

luxury 1 *n* zeitaku ぜいたく 2 *adj* gōka (na) 豪華(な)

M

machine *n* kikai 機械

macho otokoppoi 男っぽい

mad ki no kurutta 気の狂った

made-to-measure ōdāmeido (no) オーダーメイド(の)

madness kyōki 狂気

magazine zasshi 雑誌

magic 1 *n* mahō 魔法; *(tricks)* tejina 手品 2 *adj* mahō no yō (na) 魔法のよう(な)

magician majishan マジシャン

magnet jishaku 磁石

magnetic jishaku (no) 磁石(の)

magnificent sōdai (na) 壮大(な)

magnify kakudai suru 拡大する

magnifying glass mushimegane 虫眼鏡

mah-jong mājan 麻雀

maid (in hotel) kyakushitsu-gakari 客室係

mail 1 n yūbin 郵便 **2** v/t letter yūsō suru 郵送する

mailbox posuto ポスト; (of house) yūbin'uke 郵便受け; COMPUT mērubokkusu メールボックス

mailman yūbin'yasan 郵便屋さん

main adj omo (na) 主(な)

mainland hondo 本土

mainly omo ni 主に

main street ōdōri 大通り

maintain iji suru 維持する; speed jizoku suru 持続する; innocence shuchō suru 主張する

major 1 adj shuyō (na) 主要(な) **2** n MIL shōsa 少佐

majority daitasū 大多数; POL tokuhyō sa 得票差

make 1 n (brand) shurui 種類 **2** v/t dress, cake tsukuru 作る; tea ireru 入れる; movie seisaku suru 制作する; speech etc suru する; bed totonoeru 整える; hole akeru 開ける; (manufacture) seizō suru 製造する; ~ X do Y X ni Y saseru XにYさせる; ~ X happy X o shiawase ni suru Xを幸せにする; made in Japan Nihonsei 日本製

♦ **make out** v/t list tsukuriageru 作り上げる; (see) miwakeru 見分ける; (imply) ... to honemakasu …とほのめかす

♦ **make up 1** v/i (after quarrel) nakanaori suru 仲直りする **2** v/t story tsukuridasu 作り出す; face ... ni keshō o suru …に化粧をする; (constitute) kōsei suru 構成する; ~ one's mind kesshin suru 決心する

♦ **make up for** ... no umeawase o suru …の埋め合せをする

maker seizō-gaisha 製造会社

make-up (cosmetics) keshōhin 化粧品

Malaysia Marēshia マレーシア

Malaysian Marēshia (no) マレーシア(の)

male 1 *adj* dansei (no) 男性
(の); *animal* osu (no) 雄(の)
2 *n* dansei 男性; *(animal)*
osu 雄

male chauvinist pig danson-
johi no butayarō 男尊女卑の
ブタ野郎

malfunction *n* fuchō 不調

malignant *tumor* akusei (no)
悪性(の)

mall *(shopping)* shoppingu-sentā
ショッピングセンター

malnutrition eiyō-shitchō 栄
養失調

maltreatment gyakutai 虐待

mammal honyū-dōbutsu ほ
乳動物

man *n* otoko 男; *(human)* hito
人; *(humanity)* ningen 人間

manage 1 *v/t business* keiei
suru 経営する; *money* kanri
suru 管理する; ~ **to** nantoka
... suru 何とか…する **2** *v/i*
(cope) dō ni ka kurashite iku
どうにか暮らしていく

manageable *hair* atsukaiyasui
扱いやすい; *work* dō ni ka
shori suru どうにか処理
できる

management 1 *n* keiei 経営;
(managers) keieisha-gawa 経
営者側

manager *(of restaurant, hotel)*
shihainin 支配人; *(of shop)*
tenchō 店長

managing director senmu-
torishimariyaku 専務取締役

mandatory hissu (no) 必
須(の)

maneuver 1 *n* sakusen 作戦
2 *v/t* takumi ni ugokasu 巧み
に動かす

maniac kyōjin 狂人

manipulate *person* ayatsuru
操る

man-made jinkō (no) 人
工(の)

manner *(way)* hōhō 方法;
(attitude) taido 態度

manners: *good / bad* ~
yoi / warui gyōgi よい/悪
い行儀; *have no* ~ gyōgi ga
warui 行儀が悪い

manpower jin'in 人員

mansion daiteitaku 大邸宅

manual 1 *adj* tesagyō (no) 手
作業(の) **2** *n* manyuaru マ
ニュアル

manufacture *v/t* seizō suru 製
造する

manufacturer seizō-gyōsha
製造業者

many 1 *adj* takusan (no) たく
さん(の); ~ *times* nando mo
何度も **2** *pron* tasū 多数; *a
good* ~ kanari takusan no か
なりたくさんの

map *n* chizu 地図

marathon *(race)* marason マ
ラソン

March sangatsu 三月

march 1 *n* kōshin 行進;
(protest) demo-kōshin デモ行
進 **2** *v/i* kōshin suru 行進す
る; *(in protest)* demo-kōshin
suru デモ行進する

margin *(of page)* yohaku 余白;
(profit ~) rizaya 利ざや

marine 1 *adj* umi (no) 海(の)
2 *n* MIL kaihei-tai-in 海兵隊員

maritime umi (no) 海(の)

mark 1 *n (stain)* shimi 染
み; *(sign, token)* shirushi 印;
SCHOOL tensū 点数 **2** *v/t (stain)*
ato o tsukeru 跡をつける;
SCHOOL saiten suru 採点する;
(indicate) shimesu 示す

market 1 *n* ichiba 市場; *on
the ~* shijō de 市場で **2** *v/t*
shijō ni uri ni dasu 市場に売
りに出す

marketing māketingu マーケ
ティング

market research shijō-chōsa
市場調査

mark-up rihaba 利幅

marriage kekkonshiki 結婚
式; *(institution)* kekkon 結
婚; *(being married)* kekkon-
seikatsu 結婚生活

marriage certificate kekkon-
shōmeisho 結婚証明書

married kekkon shita 結婚
した

marry ... *to* kekkon suru
...と結婚する; *get married*
kekkon suru 結婚する

martial arts bujutsu 武術

marvelous subarashī すば
らしい

mascara masukara マスカラ

masculine dansei (no) 男性
(の); *appearance* danseiteki
(na) 男性的(な)

mass *n (amount)* tairyō 大量

massacre *n* daigyakusatsu
大虐殺

massage *n* massāji マッ
サージ

massive taihen (na) 大変(な)

mass media masumedia マス
メディア

master 1 *n (of dog)* shujin 主
人 **2** *v/t skill* shūtoku suru 習
得する

masterpiece kessaku 傑作

mastery jukutatsu 熟達

match[1] *n (for cigarette)* matchi
マッチ

match[2] **1** *n (competition)* shiai
試合 **2** *v/t (be the same as)* ...
to chōwa suru ...と調和する
3 *v/i (of colors etc)* chōwa suru
調和する

matching osoroi (no) おそ
ろい(の)

mate 1 n (of animal) tsugai no aite つがいの相手 **2** v/i tsugai ni naru つがいになる

material n (substance) busshitsu 物質; (fabric) kiji 生地

materials (for specific activity) yōgu 用具

maternal boseiteki (na) 母性的(な)

maternity bosei 母性

math sūgaku 数学

mathematical sūgaku (no) 数学(の)

matter (affair) mondai 問題; (physical) busshitsu 物質; what's the ~ (with you)? dō shita no どうしたの **2** v/i jūyō de aru 重要である; it doesn't ~ taishita koto de wa nai たいしたことではない

mattress mattoresu マットレス

mature adj (grown-up) seijuku shita 成熟した

maturity seijuku-ki 成熟期; (in behavior) seijuku 成熟

maximum 1 adj size saidai (no) 最大(の); speed saikō (no) 最高(の) **2** n saidaigen 最大限

May gogatsu 五月

may ◊ (possibility) ... ka mo shirenai …かもしれない

◊ (permission) ... shite mo ī …してもいい; ~ I? shite mo ī desu ka してもいいですか

maybe tabun たぶん

May Day Mēdē メーデー

mayonnaise mayonēzu マヨネーズ

me watashi 私; with ~ watashi to 私と; he doesn't know ~ kare wa watashi o shiranai 彼は私を知らない; can you mail it to ~? watashi ni okutte moraemasu ka 私に送ってもらえますか

meal shokuji 食事

mean¹ (with money) kechi (na) けち(な); (nasty) iji no warui 意地の悪い

mean² v/t imi suru 意味する; (intend) tsumori de aru つもりである

meaning imi 意味

means (financial) zaisan 財産; (way) hōhō 方法

meanwhile sono aida ni その間に

measure 1 n (step) taisaku 対策 **2** v/t hakaru 測る

measurement sunpō 寸法; (action) sokutei 測定

meat niku 肉

mechanic AUTO jidōsha-shūrikō 自動車修理工

mechanism (device) kikai

機械

medal medaru メダル

media: the ~ masukomi マスコミ

median strip chūō-bunritai 中央分離帯

mediator chōteisha 調停者

medical 1 *adj* college igaku (no) 医学(の); *insurance* iryō (no) 医療(の); **~ treatment** iryō 医療 **2** *n* kenkō-shindan 健康診断

medicine kusuri 薬; *(science)* igaku 医学

mediocre heibon (na) 平凡(な)

medium 1 *adj* chūgurai (no) 中位(の) **2** *n (in size)* emu-saizu エムサイズ

meet 1 *v/t … ni au* …に会う; *(encounter) … ni deau* …に出会う; *(at airport etc)* demukaeru 出迎える; *need* mitasu 満たす; *deadline* mamoru 守る **2** *v/i* au 会う; *(get to know each other)* shiriau 知り合う; *(in competition)* taisen suru 対戦する; *(of committee)* kaigō suru 会合する **3** *n* kyōgikai 競技会

meeting deai 出会い; *(in business)* kaigi 会議; *(of committee)* kaigō 会合

melon meron メロン

melt 1 *v/i* tokeru 溶ける **2** *v/t* tokasu 溶かす

member ichi-in 一員; *(of organization)* menbā メンバー

membership kai-in-shikaku 会員資格; *(of UN etc)* kai-in no chi-i 会員の地位; *(members)* kai-insū 会員数

memo memo メモ

memoirs kaikoroku 回顧録

memorable wasurerarenai 忘れられない

memorial *n* kinenhi 記念碑

memorize anki suru 暗記する

memory kioku 記憶; *(of vacation, childhood)* omoide 思い出; *(power of recollection)* kiokuryoku 記憶力; COMPUT memorī メモリー

memory stick yū-esu-bī memori USBメモリ

mend *v/t* shūri suru 修理する

meningitis nōmakuen 脳膜炎

men's room danseiyō toire 男性用トイレ

mental seishin (no) 精神(の); *ability* chinō (no) 知能(の

mentality *(intellect)* chisei 知性; *(mindset)* kangaekata 考え方

mention *v/t … no koto o hanasu* …のことを話す; **don't ~ it** dō itashimashite どういたしまして

menu *also* COMPUT menyū メニュー

merchandise shōhin 商品

mercy jihi 慈悲

merger gappei 合併

merit *n (worth)* kachi 価値; *(advantage)* chōsho 長所

merry yōki *no* 陽気(な)

merry-go-round merīgōraundo メリーゴーラウンド

mess: *be a ~ (of room, desk)* chirakatte iru 散らかっている

message messēji メッセージ

messy *room* torichirakashita 取り散らかした; *person* darashi no nai だらしのない

metabolism shinchin-taisha 新陳代謝

metal 1 kinzoku 金属 **2** *adj* kinzoku *(no)* 金属(の)

meteor ryūsei 流星

meteorology kishōgaku 気象学

meter[1] *(for measuring)* mētā メーター; *(parking)* pākingu-mētā パーキングメーター

meter[2] *(length)* mētoru メートル

method hōhō 方法

methodical soshikiteki *(na)* 組織的(な); *person* kichōmen *(na)* きちょうめん(な)

meticulous *person* kichōmen *(na)* きちょうめん(な)

metropolitan *adj* daitoshi *(no)* 大都市(の)

microphone maiku マイク

microwave denshi-renji 電子レンジ

midday shōgo 正午

middle 1 *adj* mannaka *(no)* 真ん中(の) **2** *n (of room)* mannaka 真ん中; *(of week etc)* nakaba 半ば

middle-aged chūnen *(no)* 中年(の)

middle-class chūryū-kaikyū *(no)* 中流階級(の)

Middle East Chūtō 中東

midnight mayonaka 真夜中

Midwest Chūseibu 中西部

midwife josanpu 助産婦

might ... ka mo shirenai …かもしれない; *I ~ be late* okureru ka mo shirenai 遅れるかもしれない

migraine henzutsū 偏頭痛

migration idō 移動

mild *weather* odayaka *(na)* 穏やか(な); *voice* otonashī おとなしい

mile mairu マイル

militant *n* tōshi 闘士

military 1 *adj* guntai *(no)* 軍隊(の) **2** *n: the ~* guntai 軍隊

milk *n* gyūnyū 牛乳

millionaire hyakuman-chōja 百万長者

mimic v/t ... no monomane o suru …の物まねをする

mind 1 n chisei 知性; **change one's ~** kangae o kaeru 考えを変える **2** v/t (object to) kamau かまう; (look after) ... no sewa o suru …の世話をする; (heed) ... no iu koto o kiku …の言うことを聞く **3** v/i: **~!** ki o tsukete 気をつけて; **never ~!** ki ni shinai 気にしない; **I don't ~** dotchi demo ī desu どっちでもいいです

mine¹ pron watashi no mono 私のもの

mine² n (coal ~ etc) kōzan 鉱山

mine³ n MIL jirai 地雷

mineral kōbutsu 鉱物

mineral water mineraru-wōtā ミネラルウォーター

miniature adj kogata (no) 小型(の)

minimal saishōgen (no) 最小限(の)

minimum 1 adj saitei (no) 最低(の) **2** n: **a ~ of 10 people** saitei jū nin 最低十人

minister POL daijin 大臣; REL bokushi 牧師

ministry POL shō 省

minor 1 adj chīsa (na) 小さ(な); operation karui 軽い

2 n miseinensha 未成年者

minority shōsū 少数

minute¹ n (of time) fun 分; **in a ~** sugu すぐ

minute² adj (tiny) kiwamete chīsai きわめて小さい; (detailed) shōsai (na) 詳細(な)

minutes (of meeting) gijiroku 議事録

miracle kiseki 奇跡

mirror n kagami 鏡; AUTO bakkumirā バックミラー

miscarriage MED ryūzan 流産

miserable mijime (na) みじめ(な); life aware (na) 哀れ(な); weather iya (na) いや(な)

misfortune fu-un 不運

misjudge ... no handan o ayamaru …の判断を誤る

misleading magirawashī 紛らわしい

mismanagement (of company) ayamatta keiei 誤った経営

misprint n goshoku 誤植

mispronounce hatsuon o machigaeru 発音を間違える

miss¹: *Miss Smith* Sumisusan スミスさん

miss[2] *v/t (not hit)* hazusu はずす; *(not meet)* … to ikichigau …と行き違う; *(emotionally: person)* … ga inaku natte sabishiku omou …がいなくなって寂しく思う; *(emotionally: place)* … ga natsukashī …がなつかしい; *bus, train* … ni norisokonau …に乗りそこなう; *(not notice)* miotosu 見落とす; *(not be present at)* kesseki suru 欠席する **3** *v/i* hazusu はずす

missile misairu ミサイル

missing: be ~ yukue-fumei de aru 行方不明である

mist kiri 霧

misspell … no tsuzuri o machigaeru …のつづりを間違える

mistake *n* machigai 間違い; **make a ~** machigau 間違う

mistress *(lover)* aijin 愛人; *(of dog)* kainushi 飼い主

mistrust 1 *n* fushinkan 不信感 **2** *v/t* shin'yō shinai 信用しない

misty kiri no kakatta 霧のかかった

misunderstand gokai suru 誤解する

misunderstanding gokai 誤解

mitt *(in baseball)* mitto ミット

mix 1 *n* kongō 混合; *(in cooking)* mazeawaseta mono 混ぜ合わせたもの **2** *v/t* mazeru 混ぜる **3** *v/i (socially)* tsukiau 付き合う

mixed *feelings* fukuzatsu (na) 複雑(な)

mixture *(in cooking)* mazeawaseta mono 混ぜ合わせたもの; *(medicine)* kongōyaku 混合薬

moan *v/i (in pain)* umeku うめく

mob *n* gunshū 群衆; *(violent)* bōto 暴徒

mobile *adj* *person* ugoku koto no dekiru 動くことのできる

mobile phone *Br* keitai-denwa 携帯電話

mock *v/t* baka ni suru ばかにする; *(by mimicking)* … no mane o suru …のまねをする

mockery azakeri あざけり

model 1 *adj* *boat etc* mokei (no) 模型(の) **2** *n (miniature)* mokei 模型; *(fashion)* fasshon-moderu ファッションモデル

modem modemu モデム

moderate *adj* *heat* hodoyoi ほどよい; *success, salary* māmā (no) まあまあ(の); POL onken (na) 穏健(な)

modern kindaiteki (na) 近代的(な)

modernize kindaika suru 近代化する

modest *house* sasayaka (na) さ さやか(な); *amount* tekido (na) 適度(な); *(not conceited)* kenkyo (na) 謙虚(な)

modify *machine* kaizō suru 改造する; *system* kaisei suru 改正する

moist shimetta 湿った

moisturizer moisucharaizā モイスチャライザー

mold[1] *n (on food)* kabi かび

mold[2] **1** *n* igata 鋳型 **2** *v/t clay etc* katadoru かたどる

mom *n infml* mama ママ; *(talking to outsiders about one's own ~)* haha 母

moment shunkan 瞬間; *at the ~* ima no tokoro いま のところ; *for the ~* sashiatari 差し当たり

monastery shūdōin 修道院; *(Buddhist)* sōbō 僧坊

Monday getsuyōbi 月曜日

monetary *policy* kin'yū (no) 金融(の)

money o-kane お金

Mongolia Mongoru モンゴル

monitor[1] *n* COMPUT sukurīn スクリーン **2** *v/t* kanshi suru

monk shūdōshi 修道士; *(Buddhist)* sō 僧

monkey saru さる

monolog monorōgu モノローグ

monopolize dokusen suru 独占する

monopoly senbai 専売

monotonous *voice* tanchō (na) 単調(な); *job* taikutsu (na) 退屈(な)

monster *n* kaibutsu 怪物

month tsuki 月

monthly *adj payment* maitsuki (no) 毎月(の); *magazine* gekkan (no) 月刊(の)

monument kinenhi 記念碑

mood *(frame of mind)* kigen 機嫌; *be in a good / bad ~* kigen ga yoi / warui 機嫌がよい/悪い

moon *n* tsuki 月

moral 1 *adj standards* dōtokuteki (na) 道徳的(な); *person* seigikan no tsuyoi 正義感の強い **2** *n (of story)* kyōkun 教訓; **~s** dōtoku 道徳

morale shiki 士気

morality dōtoku 道徳

more 1 *adj* motto ōku (no) もっと多く(の); *some ~ tea?* kōcha no o-kawari wa いかが; 紅茶のおかわりは; *there is*

no ~ money o-kane wa mō
arimasen お金はもうあり
ません 2 *adv* motto もっ
と; *~ important* motto daiji
(na) もっと大事(な); *once
~* mō ichido もう一度; *~
than* 以上; *I don't live there
any ~* mō soko ni wa sunde
imasen もうそこには住ん
でいません 3 *pron: do you
want some ~?* mō sukoshi
ikaga desu ka もう少しいか
がですか

moreover sara ni さらに

morning asa 朝; *this ~* kesa け
さ; *good ~* o-hayō gozaimasu
おはようございます

morphine moruhine モルヒネ

mosquito ka 蚊

most 1 *adj* taitei (no) たいて
い(の) 2 *adv (very)* taihen た
いへん; *the ~ interesting*
mottomo omoshiroi 最もおも
しろい; *~ of all* nani yori mo
何よりも 3 *pron* hotondo ほ
とんど; *at (the) ~* seizei せ
いぜい

mostly omo ni おもに

mother *n* o-kāsan お母さん;
*(talking to outsiders about one's
own)* haha 母

mother-in-law giri no o-kāsan
義理のお母さん; *(talking to
outsiders about one's own)* giri

no haha 義理の母

mother tongue bokokugo
母国語

motivation dōki 動機

motive dōki 動機

motor mōtā モーター

motorbike ōtobai オートバイ

motorcyclist raidā ライダー

mountain yama 山

mountain bike mauntenbaiku
マウンテンバイク

mountaineering tozan 登山

mourn *v/t* nageki-kanashimu
嘆き悲しむ

mouse nezumi ねずみ;
COMPUT mausu マウス

mouth *n* kuchi 口; *(of river)*
kakō 河口

move 1 *n (in chess)* te 手; *(step,
action)* ugoki 動き; *(change
of house)* hikkoshi 引っ越し
2 *v/t object* ugokasu 動かす;
(transfer) idō saseru 移動させ
る; *(emotionally)* kandō saseru
感動させる 3 *v/i* ugoku 動
く; *(of traffic)* nagareru 流
れる; *(transfer)* idō suru 移
動する

movement ugoki 動き;
(organization) undō 運動

movie eiga 映画; *go to the ~s*
eiga ni iku 映画に行く

movie theater eigakan 映画館

moving *(emotionally)* kandōteki

(na) 感動的(な)

mph (= miles per hour) jisoku
… mairu 時速…マイル

Mr … san …さん

Mrs … san …さん

Ms … san …さん

much 1 adj ōku (no) 多く
(の); she doesn't have ~
money kanojo wa amari kane
o motte inai 彼女はあまりお
金を持っていない 2 adv
hijō ni 非常に; better, smaller
haruka ni はるかに; very ~
hontō ni 本当に; as ~ as … to
onaji dake …と同じだけ
3 pron takusan たくさん;
nothing ~ taishita koto ja nai
たいしたことじゃない

mud doro 泥

mug¹ n (for drink) magukappu
マグカップ

mug² v/t (attack) osotte kane o
ubau 襲って金を奪う

multinational n takokuseki-
kigyō 多国籍企業

multiple adj fukusū (no) 複
数(の)

multiply v/t: ~ 3 by 4 san ni
yon o kakeru 3に4を掛ける

murder 1 n satsujin 殺人 2 v/t
satsugai suru 殺害する

murderer satsujin-hannin 殺
人犯人

muscle kinniku 筋肉

museum hakubutsukan 博物館

mushroom n kinoko きのこ;
(small white) masshurūmu マ
ッシュルーム

music ongaku 音楽; (score)
gakufu 楽譜

musician ongakuka 音楽家;
(pop, jazz) myūjishan ミュー
ジシャン

must nakereba naranai なけれ
ばならない; (with negatives)
…te wa naranai … てはなら
ない; I ~ n't be late chikoku
shite wa naranai 遅刻しては
ならない

mustache kuchihige 口ひげ

mustard masutādo マスター
ド; (Japanese) karashi からし

mutter v/t & v/i tsubuyaku つ
ぶやく

mutual sōgo (no) 相互(の);
(shared) kyōtsū (no) 共通(の)

my watashi no 私の

myself jishin 自身; I ~ watashi
jishin 私自身; by ~ jibun de
自分で; (alone) hitori de ひ
とりで

mysterious nazomeita なぞ
めいた

mystery nazo なぞ

myth shinwa 神話; fig henken
偏見

N

nag *v/i (of person)* kogoto o iu 小言を言う

nail *(for wood)* kugi くぎ; *(on finger)* tsume つめ

nail file tsume-yasuri つめやすり

nail polish manikyua マニキュア

nail scissors tsume-kiri-basami つめ切りばさみ

naive sekenshirazu (na) 世間知らず(な)

naked hadaka no 裸(の)

name *n* namae 名前; *(family ~)* myōji 名字; *(of movie)* taitoru タイトル; *what's your ~?* o-namae o o-negai shimasu お名前をお願いします

nametag nafuda 名札

nanny *n* uba 乳母

nap *n* utatane うたた寝

napkin *(table ~)* napukin ナプキン

narrator narētā ナレーター

narrow semai 狭い; *views* kyōryō na 狭量(な)

narrow-minded kokoro no semai 心の狭い

nasty iji no warui 意地の悪い; *smell, weather* iya (na) い

や(な); *cut* hidoi ひどい

nation kokka 国家

national 1 *adj* kokka (no) 国家(の) **2** *n: a Japanese ~* Nihonjin 日本人

national anthem kokka 国歌

nationality kokuseki 国籍

nationalize kokuyūka suru 国有化する

native *adj* umarekokyō (no) 生まれ故郷(の); *~ language* bokokugo 母国語

native speaker neitibu-supīkā ネイティブスピーカー

natural shizen (no) 自然(の); *(obvious)* tōzen (no) 当然(の)

natural gas tennengasu 天然ガス

naturally *(of course)* tōzen 当然; *behave* shizen ni 自然に; *(by nature)* motomoto もともと

nature shizen 自然; *(of person)* seishitsu 性質; *(of problem)* honshitsu 本質

naughty gyōgi no warui 行儀の悪い

nausea hakike 吐き気

nauseous: *feel ~* hakike ga suru 吐き気がする

nautical umi (no) 海(の)

naval kaigun (no) 海軍(の)

navigate v/i (in ship, plane) kōkō suru 航行する

navigator (on ship) kōkaishi 航海士; (in airplane) kōkūshi 航空士

navy kaigun 海軍

navy blue adj kon'iro (no) 紺色(の)

near 1 adv chikaku ni 近くに 2 prep ... no chikaku ni ...の近くに; *the bank* ginkō no chikaku ni 銀行の近くに 3 adj chikai 近い

nearby adv chikaku ni 近くに

nearly hotondo ほとんど

neat room seiton sareta 整とんされた; person kichin to shita きちんとした; whiskey sutorēto (no) ストレート(の); solution tekisetsu (na) 適切(な); infml (terrific) suteki (na) すてき(な)

necessary hitsuyō (na) 必要(な)

necessity hitsuyō 必要; (thing) hitsujuhin 必需品

neck kubi 首

necklace nekkuresu ネックレス

necktie nekutai ネクタイ

need 1 n hitsuyō 必要; in ~ komatte 困って 2 v/t hitsuyō

to suru 必要とする; *you don't ~ to wait* anata wa matanakute mo ī desu あなたは待たなくてもいいです

needle hari 針; MED chūshabari 注射針

negative adj GRAM hitei (no) 否定(の); person shōkyokuteki (na) 消極的(な); ELEC mainasu (no) マイナス(の)

neglect 1 n hōchi 放置 2 v/t garden hottarakashi ni suru ほったらかしにする; health mushi suru 無視する

negligence taiman 怠慢

negotiate v/i kōshō suru 交渉する

neighbor kinjo no hito 近所の人

neighborhood chi-iki 地域

neither 1 adj dochira no ... mo ... de nai どちらの...も...でない 2 pron: *which do you want? - ~, thanks* dochira ga hoshī – warui ga dochira mo hoshiku nai どちらが欲しい – 悪いがどちらも欲しくない 3 conj: *~ my mother nor my father knew* haha mo chichi mo shiranakatta 母も父も知らなかった 4 adv: *~ do I* watashi mo desu 私もです

Nepal Nepāru ネパール

nephew oi 甥

nerve shinkei 神経

nervous *(tense)* shinkeishitsu (na) 神経質（な）; *(timid)* ki no chīsai 気の小さい

net *adj weight* shōmi (no) 正味 (の); **~ price** seika 正価

net profit junrieki 純利益

network nettowāku ネットワーク

neurologist shinkeikai 神経科医

neurotic *adj* shinkei-kabin (no) 神経過敏（の）

neutral 1 *adj country* chūritsu (no) 中立（の）; *color* chūkan (no) 中間（の）**2** *n (gear)* nyūtoraru ニュートラル

neutrality chūritsu 中立

never *(future tense)* kesshite nai 決してない; *(past tense)* … koto ga nai … ことがない

nevertheless sore ni mo kakawarazu それにもかかわらず

new atarashī 新しい

newborn *adj* umaretate (no) 生まれたて（の）

news nyūsu ニュース; *(from friend, family)* tayori 便り

newspaper shinbun 新聞

newsreader kyasutā キャスター

news report hōdō-kiji 報道記事

New Year Shōgatsu 正月; *Happy ~!* Akemashite o-medetō gozaimasu 明けましておめでとうございます

New Year's Day Gantan 元旦

New Year's Eve Ōmisoka 大みそか

New York Nyū-Yōku ニューヨーク

next 1 *adj* tsugi (no) 次（の）; *(in space)* tonari (no) 隣（の）; **~ week** raishū 来週 **2** *adv* tsugi ni 次に; **~ to** *(beside)* … no tonari ni …の隣に; *(in comparison with)* hotondo … to onaji ほとんど…と同じ

next-door 1 *adj* tonari (no) 隣 (の) **2** *adv live* tonari ni 隣に

next of kin mottomo chikai shinzoku もっとも近い親族

nice *person* shinsetsu (na) 親切（な）; *weather, smile* ī いい; *party, trip* tanoshī 楽しい; *hair, color* kirei (na) きれい（な）; *meal, food* oishī おいしい

nickname *n* nikkunēmu ニックネーム

niece mei めい

night yoru 夜; *(in hotel)* ippaku 一泊; **11 o'clock at ~** yoru jūichiji 夜十一時; *good ~* o-yasumi nasai おやすみなさい

normal

nightclub naitokurabu ナイトクラブ

nightdress naitodoresu ナイトドレス

nightmare akumu 悪夢

night school yakan-gakkō 夜間学校

no 1 *adv* īe いいえ ◊ *(using 'yes', i.e. yes, that is right)*: *you don't know the answer, do you? – ~, I don't* kotae ga wakaranai n deshō – hai wakarimasen 答えがわからないんでしょう – はい、わかりません 2 *adj*: *there's ~ coffee left* kōhī wa sukoshi mo nokotte inai コーヒーは少しも残っていない; *I have ~ family* watashi ni wa kazoku ga inai 私には家族がいない; *~ smoking* kin'en 禁煙

nobody dare mo ... (+ *negative verb*) だれも…; *~ knows* dare mo shiranai だれも知らない

nod *n* unazuki うなずき

noise oto 音; *(unpleasant)* zatsuon 雑音

noisy yakamashī やかましい

nominate *(appoint)* ninmei suru 任命する; *~ X for a post* X o shoku ni suisen suru X を職に推薦する

nonalcoholic arukōru o fukumanai アルコールを含まない

noncommittal aimai (na) あいまい(な)

none *(people)* ... no dare mo ...nai …のだれも…ない; *(things)* ... no dore mo ...nai …のどれも…ない; *there are ~ left* hitotsu mo nokotte inai ひとつも残っていない

nonetheless sore demo nao それでもなお

non-iron *shirt* airon no iranai アイロンのいらない

nonpayment fubarai 不払い

nonreturnable kaette konai 返ってこない

nonsense tawagoto たわごと

nonsmoker tabako o suwanai hito たばこを吸わない人

nonstop 1 *adj flight, train* chokkō (no) 直行(の) 2 *adv travel* chokkō de 直行で; *chatter* taema naku 絶え間なく

noodles menrui めん類; *(thick, white)* udon うどん; *(brown)* soba そば; *Chinese ~* rāmen ラーメン

noon shōgo 正午

nor: *~ do I* watashi mo desu 私もです

normal futsū (no) 普通(の)

normally futsū wa 普通は; *(in normal way)* seijō ni 正常に

north 1 *n* kita 北 **2** *adj* kita (no) 北(の) **3** *adv* travel *etc* kita no hō ni 北の方に

North America Kita-Amerika 北アメリカ

North American 1 *adj* Kita-Amerika (no) 北アメリカ (の) **2** *n* Kita-Amerikajin 北アメリカ人

northern kita (no) 北(の)

North Korea Kita-chōsen 北朝鮮

nose hana 鼻

nosebleed hanaji 鼻血

nostalgia kyōshū 郷愁

nosy sensakuzuki (na) せんさく好き(な)

not ◊ *(with verbs)* nai ない; *(past tense)* nakatta なかった; *I am ~ finished* watashi wa owatte inai 私は終わっていない; *he didn't help* kare wa tetsudawanakatta 彼は手伝わなかった ◊ *(when using masu)* masen ません; *I don't know* wakarimasen わかりません; *I am ~ American* watashi wa Amerikajin de wa arimasen 私はアメリカ人ではありません ◊: *~ this one, that one* kore de wa nakute, sore desu これではなくて、

それです; *~ there* soko wa dame desu そこはだめです; *~ like that* sō de wa naku そうではなく; *~ for me, thanks* dōmo, demo watashi wa kekkō desu どうも、でも私は結構です; *a lot (degree)* anmari あんまり; *(quantity)* sukoshi dake 少しだけ

note *n (short letter)* mijikai tegami 短い手紙; MUS onpu 音符; *(memo to self)* memo メモ; *(comment on text)* chū 注; *take ~s* nōto o toru ノートをとる

notebook nōto ノート

notepaper binsen 便せん

nothing nani mo ...; *(+ negative verb)* nani mo ...; *there is ~ left* nani mo nokotte inai 何も残っていない; *~ for me thanks* kekkō desu, dōmo 結構です、どうも

notice 1 *n (on board)* keiji 掲示; *(in street)* harigami はり紙; *(advance warning)* keikoku 警告; *(in newspaper)* kōkoku 公告; *(to leave job / house)* tsūkoku 通告; *at short ~* girigiri no tsūtatsu de ぎりぎりの通達で; *take no ~ of* mushi suru 無視する **2** *v/t* ... ni ki ga tsuku ...に気がつく

notify ... ni tsūchi suru ...に

通知する

notorious akumei no takai 悪名の高い

nourishing eiyō no aru 栄養のある

novel n shōsetsu 小説

novelist shōsetsuka 小説家

November jūichigatsu 十一月

novice shoshinsha 初心者

now ima 今; ~ *and again*, ~ *and then* tokidoki 時々; *by* ~ ima made ni 今までに; *from* ~ *on* ima kara 今から

nowadays konogoro wa このごろは

nowhere doko ni mo ... (+ *negative verb*) どこにも ...

nuclear kaku no 核(の)

nuclear energy genshiryoku 原子力

nuclear power station genshiryoku-hatsudensho 原子力発電所

nuclear waste kaku-haikibutsu 核廃棄物

nuclear weapons kakuheiki 核兵器

nude adj hadaka (no) 裸(の)

nuisance (*person*) meiwaku na hito 迷惑な人; (*having to do something*) mendō 面倒

number n sūji 数字; (*of room, house, phone*) bangō 番号

numerous tasū (no) 多数(の)

nurse kangofu 看護婦; (*male*) kangoshi 看護士

nursery (*for plants*) naedoko 苗床

nursing home (*for old people*) rōjin-hōmu 老人ホーム

nut konomi 木の実; (*for bolt*) natto ナット

nutritious eiyō no aru 栄養のある

O

oak (*wood*) ōku-zai オーク材; (*tree*) kashi かし

oar ōru オール

oath JUR sensei 宣誓

obedience fukujū 服従

obedient iu koto o kiku 言うことを聞く

obey *law* ... ni shitagau ...に従う; *parents* ... no iu koto o kiku ...の言うことを聞く

obituary n shibō-kiji 死亡記事

object[1] n (*thing*) mono 物; (*aim*) mokuteki 目的; GRAM mokutekigo 目的語

object[2] v/i hantai suru 反対する

objection igi 異議

objective 1 *adj* kyakkanteki (na) 客観的(な) 2 *n* mokuteki 目的

obligation gimu 義務

obliterate *city* kanzen ni hakai suru 完全に破壊する

obnoxious ki ni sawaru 気にさわる

obscene waisetsu (na) わいせつ(な)

observant chūibukai 注意深い

observation (*of stars etc*) kansatsu 観察; (*comment*) iken 意見

observe *wildlife* kansatsu suru 観察する; (*notice*) ... ni ki ga tsuku ...に気がつく

obsession (*with idea*) kyōhaku-kannen 強迫観念; (*with thing, person*) shūchaku 執着

obsolete sutareta すたれた

obstacle shōgaibutsu 障害物

obstinate ganko (na) 頑固(な)

obstruct fusagu ふさぐ; *police* samatageru 妨げる

obtain eru 得る

obvious akiraka (na) 明らか(な)

occasion bāi 場合; (*event, ceremony*) gyōji 行事

occasional tama (no) た

ま(の)

occasionally tama ni たまに

occupant (*of vehicle*) jōkyaku 乗客

occupation (*job*) shokugyō 職業; (*of country*) senryō 占領

occupy toru 取る; *country* senryō suru 占領する

occur okoru 起こる

ocean umi 海

o'clock: *at five / six* go- / roku-ji ni 五/六時に

October jūgatsu 十月

odd hen (na) 変(な); (*not even*) kisū (no) 奇数(の)

odor nioi におい

of (*possession*) ... no ...の; *the name ~ the hotel* hoteru no namae ホテルの名前; *five minutes ~ twelve* jūniji gofun mae 十二時五分前; *die ~ cancer* gan de shinu がんで死ぬ

off 1 *adv*: *be ~* (*of light, TV*) keshite aru 消してある; (*of lid*) shimete inai 閉めていない; (*canceled*) chūshi ni naru 中止になる; *walk ~* tachisaru 立ち去る 2 *adj*: *the ~ switch* suitchi スイッチ

offend *v/t* okoraseru 怒らせる

offense JUR hanzai 犯罪

offensive 1 *adj* shitsurei (na) 失礼(な) 2 *n* MIL kōgeki 攻

撃; **go onto the ~** ~ kōgeki shihajimeru 攻撃し始める

offer 1 n teikyō 提供 **2** v/t teikyō suru 提供する

office *(building)* jimusho 事務所; *(room)* ofisu オフィス

office block ofisubiru オフィスビル

office hours kinmu-jikan 勤務時間; *(of doctor)* shinsatsu-jikan 診察時間

officer MIL. shikan 士官; *(in police)* keisatsukan 警察官

official 1 adj statement, visit kōshiki (no) 公式(の) **2** n kōmuin 公務員

off-line adj ofurainshiki (no) オフライン式の

often yoku よく

oil n *(for machine)* sekiyu 石油; *(for food)* oiru オイル

oil company sekiyu-gaisha 石油会社

oil tanker sekiyu-tankā 石油タンカー

oil well yusei 油井

ointment nankō 軟こう

ok adv *(as reply)* ōkē オーケー; **are you ~?** *(well, not hurt)* daijōbu desu ka 大丈夫ですか

old *person* toshi o totta 年をとった; *car, building, joke* furui 古い; *custom* mukashi

kara (no) 昔から(の); *(previous)* mae (no) 前(の); **~ man / woman / people** otoshiyori お年寄り; **how is he?** kare wa ikutsu desu ka 彼はいくつですか

old age rōnen 老年

old-fashioned furui 古い; *pej* furukusai 古くさい

olive oil orību-oiru オリーブオイル

Olympic Games Orinpikku オリンピック

omit shōryaku suru 省略する; *person* jogai suru 除外する

on 1 prep *(with verbs of being)* … ni …に; *(with verbs of activity)* … de …で; **it's ~ the table** tēburu ni aru テーブルにある; **I traveled ~ the bus** watashi wa basu de itta 私はバスで行った; **~ TV** terebi de テレビで; **~ Sunday** nichiyōbi ni 日曜日に **2** adv: **be ~** *(of light, TV, computer)* tsuite iru ついている; *(of lid)* shimatte iru 閉まっている; *(of TV program)* hōei sarete iru 放映されている; *(of meeting etc)* yotei sarete iru 予定されている; **what's ~ tonight?** *(on TV etc)* konban wa nani o yatte imasu ka 今晩は何をやっていますか; *(what's* *planned?)* konban no yotei wa nan desu ka 今晩の予定は何ですか **3** *adj:* the ~ switch suitchi スイッチ

once *adv (one time)* ichido 一度; *(formerly)* katsute かつて; *at* ~ *(suddenly)* sugu ni すぐに; *all at* ~ *(suddenly)* totsuzen 突然; *(together)* mattaku dōji ni まったく同時に

one 1 *n (number)* ichi 一 **2** *adj (with things)* hitotsu (no) 一つ(の); *(with people)* hitori (no) 一人(の) **3** *pron: would you like* ~? anata mo hoshī desu ka あなたも欲しいですか; *which* ~? dotchi どっち; *(person)* dare だれ

one-way street ippō-tsūkō 一方通行

one-way ticket katamichi-kippu 片道切符

onion tamanegi たまねぎ

on-line *adj* onrain (no) オンライン(の)

only 1 *adv* ... dake ...だけ; ~ *once* ikkai dake 一回だけ; *he's* ~ *6* kare wa hon no rokusai desu 彼はほんの六歳です; *it's* ~ *one o'clock* mada ichiji desu まだ一時です; ~ *just manage* karōjite かろうじて **2** *adj* yui-itsu (no) 唯一(の); ~ *son* hitori-

musuko 一人息子

onto: *put X* ~ *Y (on top of)* X o Y no ue ni oku X をY の上におく

open 1 *adj* aita 開いた; *shop* eigyōchū (no) 営業中(の); *(frank)* sotchoku (na) 率直 (な) **2** *v/t* hiraku 開く; *door, shop, window, bottle* akeru 開ける **2** *v/i (of door, shop)* hiraku 開く

opera opera オペラ

operate 1 *v/i* MED shujutsu suru 手術する **2** *v/t machine* sōsa suru 操作する

operation MED shujutsu 手術

opinion iken 意見

opponent aite 相手

opportunity kikai 機会

oppose ... ni hantai suru ...に反対する

opposite *adj side* mukōgawa (no) 向こう側(の); *direction* hantai (no) 反対(の); *views* seihantai (no) 正反対(の); *meaning* gyaku (no) 逆(の)

oppressive *rule* asseiteki (na) 圧制的(な); *day* uttōshī うっとうしい

optical illusion me no sakkaku 目の錯覚

optimist rakkan-ronsha 楽観論者

optimistic rakkanteki (na) 楽

観的(な)

option sentaku 選択

optional *subject* jiyū-sentaku (no) 自由選択(の)

or … ka … ka …か…か *(otherwise)* samonaito さもないと

orange 1 *adj (color)* orenji-iro (no) オレンジ色(の) **2** *n (fruit)* orenji オレンジ

orange juice orenji-jūsu オレンジジュース

orchestra ōkesutora オーケストラ

orchid ran らん

order 1 *n (command)* meirei 命令; *(sequence)* jun 順; *(orderliness)* chitsujo 秩序; *(for goods, in restaurant)* chūmon 注文; **out of ~** *(not functioning)* koshōchū de 故障中で; *(not in sequence)* junjo ga kurutte 順序が狂って **2** *v/t (put in sequence)* seiri suru 整理する; *goods, meal* chūmon suru 注文する; **~ X to do Y** X ni Y suru yō ni meijiru XにYするように命じる **3** *v/i (in restaurant)* chūmon suru 注文する

ordinary futsū (no) 普通(の)

organic *food* munōyaku (no) 無農薬(の)

organization soshikitai 組織

体; *(organizing)* kōsei 構成

organize *people* soshiki suru 組織する; *conference* junbi suru 準備する; *data* keitōdateru 系統立てる

Orient Tōyō 東洋

origin kigen 起源

original *adj (not copied)* dokuji (no) 独自(の); *(first)* moto (no) もと(の)

originally motomoto もともと と; *(at first)* hajime wa 始めは

orphanage yōgo-shisetsu 養護施設

orthopedic seikei-geka (no) 整形外科(の)

other 1 *adj* hoka (no) ほか(の) **2** *n*: **the ~s** *(things)* mō ippō no mono もう一方の物; *(people)* mō ippō no hito もう一方の人

otherwise samonaito さもないと; *(differently)* chigau fū ni 違うふうに

our watashitachi no 私たちの

ours watashitachi no mono 私たちのもの

ourselves jishin 自身; **we ~** watashitachi jishin 私たち自身; **by ~** jibuntachi de 自分たちで; *(alone)* watashitachi dake de 私たちだけで

out: be ~ *(of light)* kirete iru 切れている; *(of fire)* kiete iru

消えている; *(of flower)* saite iru 咲いている; *(of sun)* dete iru 出ている; *(not at home)* rusu de aru 留守である; *(not in office)* gaishutsuchū de aru 外出中である; *(no longer in competition)* haitai suru 敗退する; *(in baseball)* auto de aru アウトである; *(get)* ~! dete ike 出ていけ

outbreak *(of violence, war)* boppatsu ぼっ発

outcome kekka 結果

outdoors *adv* soto ni 外に

outer *wall etc* sotogawa (no) 外側(の)

outgoing *personality* gaikōteki (na) 外向的(な); ~ **flight** shuppatsubin 出発便

outlet *(of pipe)* hakeguchi はけ口; *(for sales)* hanbaiten 販売店; ELEC soketto ソケット

outlook *(prospects)* mitōshi 見通し

outof ◊ *(motion)*: **run ~ the house** ie kara hashiridasu 家から走り出る ◊ *(position)*: **20 miles ~ Detroit** Detoroito kara nijūmairu no tokoro de デトロイトから二十マイルの所で ◊ *(cause)*: ~ **curiosity** kōkishin kara 好奇心から ◊ *(without)*: **we're ~ gas** gasorin ga kireta ガソリ

ンが切れた ◊ *(from a group)*: **5 ~ 10** jūnin chū gonin 十人中五人

out-of-date jidai-okure (no) 時代遅れ(の)

output 1 *n (of factory)* seisandaka 生産高 **2** *v/t (produce)* seisan suru 生産する

outrage *n (feeling)* ikidōri いきどおり; *(act)* bōryoku-kōi 暴力行為

outrageous yurushigatai 許しがたい; *prices* akireta あきれた

outside 1 *adj surface, wall* sotogawa (no) 外側(の) **2** *adv sit* soto ni 外に; *go* soto e 外へ **3** *prep* … no soto de / ni …の外で/に

outsider bugaisha 部外者; *(in race, election)* kachime no nai hito 勝ち目のない人

outskirts kōgai 郊外

outstanding kesshutsu shita 傑出した; FIN miharai (no) 未払い(の)

oval *adj* daenkei (no) だ円形(の)

oven ōbun オーブン

over 1 *prep* … *(above)* … no ue ni …の上に; *(across)* … no mukōgawa ni …の向こう側に; *(more than)* … yori ōku …より多く **2** *adv*: **be ~**

(finished) owari de aru 終わりである; *(left)* amatte iru 余っている; *~ here (with verbs of being)* kochira ni こちらに; *(with verbs of activity)* kochira de こちらで; *do X ~ (again)* X o kurikaesu Xを繰り返す

overcoat n ōbā オーバー

overcome *difficulty* ni uchikatsu に打ち勝つ

overdo yari-suguru やりすぎる; *(in frying, grilling)* yaki-suguru 焼きすぎる

overdone *meat* yakisugita 焼きすぎた

overdose n *(of sleeping pills etc)* chishiryō 致死量

overdraft tōza-karikoshi 当座借越

overestimate kadai ni hyōka suru 過大に評価する

overhead n FIN kansetsu-keihi 間接経費

overhear futo mimi ni suru ふと耳にする

overlook *(of building etc)* miorosu 見下ろす; *(not see)*

miotosu 見落とす; *(deliberately)* minogasu 見逃す

overnight adv ippaku 一泊

overrated kadai-hyōka sareta 過大評価された

overseas adv *live* kaigai ni 海外に; *work* kaigai de 海外で

oversight miotoshi 見落とし

overtake *(in work, development)* shinogu しのぐ; *Br* AUTO ... ni oitsuku …に追いつく

overtime adv *(in the evening)* zangyō de 残業で; *(on Sunday, holiday)* kyūjitsu-shukkin de 休日出勤で

owe v/t ... ni shakkin o shite iru …に借金をしている

owing to ... no tame ni …のために

own[1] v/t shoyū suru 所有する

own[2] **1** adj jibun-jishin (no) 自分自身(の) **2** pron: *on my / his* ~ hitori de ひとりで

owner shoyūsha 所有者

ozone layer ozonsō オゾン層

P

pace n *(step)* ippo 一歩; *(speed)* pēsu ペース

Pacific: *the* ~ *(Ocean)*

Taiheiyō 太平洋

Pacific Rim: *the* ~ kan-Taiheiyō 環太平洋

pack 1 *n (back~)* bakku-pakku バックパック; *(of cereal, cigarettes)* hako 箱 2 *v/t* tsumeru 詰める; *bag ... ni nimotsu o tsumeru* …に荷物を詰める 3 *v/i* nizukuri o suru 荷造りをする

package *n (parcel)* kozutsumi 小包; *(of offers etc)* ikkatsu-keiyaku 一括契約

package deal *(for vacation)* setto-hanbai セット販売

packet pakku パック

page[1] *n* pēji ページ

page[2] *v/t (call)* yobidasu 呼び出す

pagoda tō 塔

pain itami 痛み

painful itai 痛い

painkiller itamidome 痛み止め

paint 1 *n (for wall)* penki ペンキ; *(for artist)* enogu 絵の具 2 *v/t wall etc ... ni penki o nuru* …にペンキを塗る; *picture* kaku 描く

painter *(decorator)* penkiya ペンキ屋; *(artist)* ekaki 絵かき, gaka 画家

painting *(picture)* e 絵; *(decorating)* penkinuri ペンキ塗り

pair *(of objects)* tsui 対; SPORTS pea ペア; *a ~ of shoes* kutsu issoku 靴一足

pajamas pajama パジャマ

pale *person* aojiroi 青白い

palm *(of hand)* tenohira 手のひら

pamphlet panfuretto パンフレット

pan *n* furaipan フライパン

panic 1 *n* panikku パニック 2 *v/i* awateru あわてる

pant *v/i* ikigire suru 息切れする

panties pantī パンティー

pants zubon ズボン

pantyhose pantīsutokkingu パンティーストッキング

paper *n* kami 紙; *(news~)* shinbun 新聞; ~**s** *(identity ~s)* mibun-shōmeisho 身分証明書

paperback pēpābakku ペーパーバック

parade *n (procession)* parēdo パレード

paradise tengoku 天国

paragraph danraku 段落

parallel *n (line)* heikō 平行; *fig* ruijiten 類似点

paralyze mahi saseru 麻ひさせる

paramedic iryō-hojoin 医療補助員

paranoia saigishin さいぎ心

paranoid *adj* kangurisugi (no) かんぐりすぎ(の)

paraplegic n kahanshin-mahi no hito 下半身麻ひの人

parcel kozutsumi 小包

parent oya 親; **~s** ryōshin 両親

parental oya (no) 親 (の)

park[1] (area) kōen 公園

park[2] v/t & v/i AUTO chūsha suru 駐車する

parking AUTO chūsha 駐車

parking garage chūshajō 駐車場

parking lot chūshajō 駐車場

parking meter pākingu-mētā パーキングメーター

parking ticket chūsha-ihan no yobidashijō 駐車違反の呼び出し状

parliament gikai 議会

parrot ōmu おうむ

part n (portion) ichibu 一部; (section) bu 部; (area) bubun 部分; (of machine) buhin 部品; (in play, movie) yaku 役; (in hair) wakeme 分け目; **take ~ in** ... ni sanka suru …に参加する

participate sanka suru 参加する

particular (specific) tokutei (no) 特定 (の); (special) tokubetsu (no) 特別 (の); (fussy) yakamashī やかましい

particularly toku ni 特に

partition n (screen) majikiri 間仕切り

partly bubunteki ni 部分的に

partner COMM kyōdō-keieisha 共同経営者; (husband, wife) haigūsha 配偶者; (in long-term relationship) koibito 恋人; (in particular activity) pātonā パートナー

partnership COMM kyōdō-keiei-jigyō 共同経営事業; (in dance, sport) kyōryoku-kankei 協力関係

part-time adv work pātotaimu de パートタイムで

party n pātī パーティー; POL seitō 政党; (group) ichidan 一団

pass n (permit) tsūkōshō 通行証; SPORTS pasu パス; (in mountains) tōge 峠 2 v/t (hand) watasu 渡す; (go past) tōrisugiru 通り過ぎる; AUTO oikosu 追い越す; (go beyond) koeru 越える; (approve) kaketsu suru 可決する; SPORTS pasu suru パスする; **~ an exam** shiken ni gōkaku suru 試験に合格する 3 v/i (of time) tatsu たつ; SPORTS pasu suru パスする

passage tsūro 通路; (from book) issetsu 一節

passenger jōkyaku 乗客

passer-by tsūkōnin 通行人

passion jōnetsu 情熱; *(sexual)* jōyoku 情欲

passive *adj* ukemi (no) 受身(の)

passport pasupōto パスポート

password pasuwādo パスワード

past 1 *adj (former)* izen (no) 以前(の); *the ~ few days* kono sūjitsu この数日 **2** *n* kako 過去; *in the ~* kako ni 過去に **3** *prep (in time)* sugite 過ぎて; *(in position)* tōrisugite 通り過ぎて; *it's half ~ two* niji han desu 二時半です

pastime shumi 趣味

pastry *(for pie)* pai-kiji パイ生地

paternal *pride, love* chichioya (no) 父親(の)

paternity chichioya de aru koto 父親であること

path komichi 小道

pathetic aware (na) 哀れ(な); *infml (very bad)* nasakenai hodo heta (na) 情けないほど下手(な)

patience nintai 忍耐

patient 1 *n* kanja 患者 **2** *adj* gamanzuyoi 我慢強い

patriotic aikokuteki (na) 愛国的(な)

patrol 1 *n* junkai 巡回 **2** *v/t* junkai suru 巡回する

patrolman junsa 巡査

patronizing meuebutta 目上ぶった

pattern *n (on fabric)* moyō 模様; *(model)* mihon 見本; *(in events)* patān パターン

pause 1 *n* ma 間 **2** *v/i (in speaking)* ma o akeru 間をあける; *(in doing sth)* chūdan suru 中断する

pavement *(roadway)* hosō 舗装

paw *n (of animal)* ashi 足

pay 1 *n* kyūryō 給料 **2** *v/t person ...* ni shiharau ... に支払う; *sum, bill* harau 払う **3** *v/i* shiharai o suru 支払いをする; *(be profitable)* mōkaru もうかる

pay check kyūryō 給料日

payday kyūryōbi 給料日

payment *(of bill)* shiharai 支払い; *(money)* shiharai-kingaku 支払い金額

pay phone kōshū-denwa 公衆電話

PC (= personal computer) pasokon パソコン; *(= politically correct)* shakaiteki ni tadashī 社会的に正しい

peace heiwa 平和; *(quiet)* shizukesa 静けさ

peaceful (quiet) shizuka (na) 静か(な); (not violent) heiwa (na) 平和(な)

peach momo 桃

peak n (of mountain) chōjō 頂上

peak hours pīku-ji ピーク時

peanut butter pīnattsu-batā ピーナッツバター

pear (oriental) nashi なし; (western) seiyōnashi 西洋なし

pearl shinju 真珠

peck v/t (bite) tsutsuku つつく

peculiar (odd) myō (na) 妙(な)

pedal (of bike) pedaru ペダル

pedestrian n hokōsha 歩行者

pediatrician shōnikai 小児科医

peel 1 n kawa 皮 **2** v/t fruit … no kawa o muku …の皮をむく **3** v/t (of nose etc) mukeru むける

peer v/i jitto miru じっと見る; ~ at jitto miru じっと見る

pen n (ballpoint) bōrupen ボールペン

penalize (punish) shobatsu suru 処罰する

penalty (punishment) batsu 罰; (fine) bakkin 罰金; SPORTS penarutī ペナルティー

penalty clause iyaku-jōkō 違約条項

pencil enpitsu 鉛筆

penetrate (of knife) kantsū suru 貫通する; market … ni sannyū suru …に参入する

penicillin penishirin ペニシリン

peninsula hantō 半島

penitentiary keimusho 刑務所

pension nenkin 年金

Pentagon: the ~ Amerika-kokubō-sōshō アメリカ国防総省

penthouse saijōkai no apāto 最上階のアパート

people hitobito 人々; (race, tribe) minzoku 民族; two ~ futari ふたり; ten ~ jūnin 十人

pepper (spice) koshō こしょう; (vegetable) pīman ピーマン

percent pāsento パーセント

perception (with senses) chikaku 知覚; (of situation) ninshiki 認識

perfect 1 adj kanpeki (na) 完ぺき(な) **2** v/t kansei suru 完成する

perfection kanpeki 完ぺき

perfectly kanpeki ni 完ぺきに; (totally) mattaku 全く

perform v/t (carry out) okonau

行う; *play* jōen suru 上演
する

performance *(by actor)* engi
演技; *(by theater company)*
kōen 公演; *(by musician)* ensō
演奏; *(of employee, company
etc)* seiseki 成績; *(by machine)*
seinō 性能

perfume kōsui 香水; *(of
flower)* kaori 香り

perhaps tabun たぶん

peril kiken 危険

perimeter shūi 周囲

period kikan 期間; *(woman's)*
seiri 生理; *(punctuation)*
piriodo ピリオド

perjury gishō 偽証

perm *n* pāma パーマ

permanent *adj* eikyūteki (na)
永久的(な)

permanently eikyū ni 永久に

permission kyoka 許可

permit 1 *n* kyokashō 許可証
2 *v/t* kyoka suru 許可する

perpetual *(continual)* taema nai
絶え間ない

persecute hakugai suru 迫
害する

persecution hakugai 迫害

persist *(last)* tsuzuku 続
く; *(keep on)* koshitsu suru
固執する; *~ in doing X*
X shitsuzukeru X し続ける

persistent nebarizuyoi 粘り強

い; *(negative sense)* shitsukoi
しつこい; *rain* itsu made mo
tsuzuku いつまでも続く

person hito 人; *in ~* jibun de
自分で

personal *opinion, life* kojinteki
(na) 個人的(な); *belongings*
kojin (no) 個人(の); *(private)*
shiteki (na) 私的(な)

personal computer pāsonaru-
konpyūta パーソナルコンピ
ューター

personality jinkaku 人格;
(celeb) yūmeijin 有名人

personally *(for my part)*
watashi to shite wa 私とし
ては; *(in person)* jibun de
自分で

personnel shokuin 職員;
(section) jinjibu 人事部

perspiration hakkan 発汗

persuade settoku suru 説
得する

persuasion settoku 説得

pessimist hikan-ronsha 悲
観論者

pessimistic hikanteki (na) 悲
観的(な)

pest *(insect)* gaichū 害虫; *infml
(person)* yakkaimono やっ
かいもの

pester urusaku itte komaraseru
うるさく言って困らせる

pesticide satchūzai 殺虫剤

pet n *(animal)* petto ペット

petition n seigansho 請願書

petrochemical *adj* sekiyu-kagaku (no) 石油化学(の)

petroleum sekiyu 石油

petty *person* kokoro no semai 心の狭い; *detail* toru ni taranai 取るに足らない

pharmaceuticals kusuri 薬

pharmacist yakuzaishi 薬剤師

pharmacy *(store)* yakkyoku 薬局

phase *(stage)* dankai 段階

phenomenal odoroku hodo (no) 驚くほど(の)

philosopher tetsugakusha 哲学者

philosophical tetsugakuteki (na) 哲学的(な); *fig* reisei (na) 冷静(な)

philosophy tetsugaku 哲学

phobia kyōfushō 恐怖症

phone 1 n denwa 電話 2 v/t ... ni denwa o kakeru …に電話をかける 3 v/i denwa o suru 電話をする

phone book denwachō 電話帳

phone booth kōshū-denwa-bokkusu 公衆電話ボックス

phone call denwa 電話

phone number denwa-bangō 電話番号

phon(e)y *adj* *address* uso (no) うそ(の); *accent* nise (no) 偽(の); *person* shin'yō dekinai 信用できない

photo n shashin 写真

photocopier kopīki コピー機

photocopy 1 n kopī コピー 2 v/t kopī suru コピーする

photographer kameraman カメラマン

photography shashin-satsuei 写真撮影

phrase n GRAM ku 句; *(expression)* īkata 言い方

physical *adj* *(bodily)* shintaiteki (na) 身体的(な); *attraction, labor* nikutaiteki (na) 肉体的(な)

physician naikai 内科医

physicist butsurigakusha 物理学者

physics butsurigaku 物理学

physiotherapy butsuri-ryōhō 物理療法

piano piano ピアノ

pick v/t *(choose)* erabu 選ぶ; *flower* tsumu 摘む; *fruit* mogu もぐ

♦ pick up v/t toriageru 取り上げる; *(from ground)* hiroiageru 拾い上げる; *(collect: person)* mukae ni iku 迎えに行く; *dry cleaning etc* tori ni iku 取りに行く; *information* atsumeru 集める; *(in car)* noseru 乗せる; *(in sexual sense)* hikkakeru ひっかける; *skill* oboeru 覚える

pickpocket suri すり

pick-up (truck) kogata-torakku 小型トラック

picnic *n* pikunikku ピクニック

picture *n* e 絵; *(photo)* shashin 写真

picturesque e no yō ni utsukushī 絵のように美しい

pie pai パイ

piece kakera かけら; *(component)* bubun 部分; *a ~ of pie* hitokire no pai 一切れのパイ

pierce *(penetrate)* tsuranuku 貫く; *ears ...* ni piasu o suru ...にピアスをする

pig buta 豚; *(person)* butayarō 豚野郎

pigeon hato はと

pile yama 山

pilgrimage junrei 巡礼

pill kusuri 薬; *the ~* piru ピル

pillar hashira 柱

pillow *n* makura まくら

pilot *n* pairotto パイロット

pilot plant shiken-kōjō 試験工場

PIN *(= personal identification number)* anshō-bangō 暗証番号

pin *n (also bowling)* pin ピン; *(badge)* burōchi ブローチ

pinch *n: a ~ of salt* shio hitotsumami 塩一つまみ

pine *n (tree)* matsu 松

pineapple painappuru パイナップル

pink *adj* pinku-iro (no) ピンク色(の)

pioneering *adj* senkuteki (na) 先駆的(な)

pipe *n (for smoking, gas etc)* paipu パイプ

pipeline yusōkan 輸送管

pirate *v/t software ... no kaizokuban o tsukuru ...*の海賊版を作る

pistol pisutoru ピストル

pitch 1 *v/i (in baseball)* tōkyū suru 投球する **2** *v/t tent* haru 張る

pitcher[1] *(baseball)* pitchā ピッチャー

pitcher[2] *(container)* mizusashi 水差し

pitiful *sight* aware (na) 哀れ(な)

pity *n* awaremi 哀れみ; *it's a ~ that ...* ... wa zannen desu ...とは残念です

pizza piza ピザ

place 1 *n* basho 場所; *(bar, restaurant)* mise 店; *(house)* uchi うち; *(seat)* seki 席; *at*

my ~ watashi no uchi de 私の
うちで 2 *v/t (put)* oku 置く
plain *adj (clear)* meihaku (na)
明白(な); *(not patterned)*
muji (no) 無地(の)
plan 1 *n* keikaku 計画;
(drawing) zumen 図面
2 *v/t* keikaku suru 計画する;
(design) sekkei suru 設計す
る; ~ *to do* … suru tsumori de
aru …するつもりである
plane *n (air~)* hikōki 飛行機
planet wakusei 惑星
plank ita 板
planning keikaku 計画
plant¹ 1 *n* shokubutsu 植物
2 *v/t* ueru 植える
plant² *n (factory)* kōjō 工場;
(equipment) kikai-setsubi 機
械設備
plaque *(on wall)* meiban 銘板
plaster *n (on wall, ceiling)*
shikkui しっくい
plastic 1 *n* purasuchikku
プラスチック 2 *adj*
purasuchikkusei (no) プラス
チック製(の)
plastic bag binīru-bukuro ビ
ニール袋
plastic surgery keisei-geka
形成外科; *(cosmetic)* seikei-
shujutsu 整形手術
plate *n* sara 皿
platform endan 演壇; RAIL

purattohōmu プラットホ
ーム
platinum *n* purachina プラ
チナ
play 1 *n* THEAT geki 劇; *(on TV)*
dorama ドラマ; *(of children)*
asobi 遊び 2 *v/i (of children)*
asobu 遊ぶ; *(of musician)*
ensō suru 演奏する; *(SPORTS:
perform)* suru する; *(SPORTS:
take part)* shutsujō suru 出場
する 3 *v/t music* hiku 弾く;
wind instrument fuku 吹く;
game suru する; *role* enjiru
演じる
player SPORTS senshu 選手;
(musician) ensōsha 演奏者
playing card toranpu トラ
ンプ
playwright geki-sakka 劇作家
plea *n* tangan 嘆願
plead *v/i:* ~ *for* tangan suru
嘆願する; ~ *guilty* tsumi o
mitomeru 罪を認める; ~ *not
guilty* muzai o shuchō suru 無
罪を主張する
pleasant kaiteki (na) 快適
(な); *person* kanji no ī 感じ
のいい; *meal* tanoshī 楽しい
please 1 *adv* dōzo どう
ぞ; *close the door* ~ doa o
shimete kudasai ドアを閉
めてください; *more tea?*
– *yes,* ~ ocha no o-kawari wa

– hai, arigatō お茶のおかわ
りは、はい、ありがとう; ~
do ē, dōzo ええ、どうぞ
2 *v/t* yorokobasu 喜ばす

pleased yorokonda 喜んだ;
~ *to meet you* hajimemashite
はじめまして

pleasure (*satisfaction*)
yorokobi 喜び; (*enjoyment*)
tanoshimi 楽しみ; (*not
business*) asobi 遊び

plenty: ~ *of* (*a lot of*) takusan
(no) たくさん(の); (*enough*)
jūbun (na) 十分(な)

plot 1 *n* inbō 陰謀; (*of novel*)
suji 筋 2 *v/t* & *v/i* takuramu た
くらむ

plow *n* suki すき

plug *n* (*for bath*) sen 栓;
(*electrical*) puragu プラグ;
(*for new book etc*) senden 宣伝

plum *n* puramu プラム;
(*Japanese*) ume 梅

plumber haikankō 配管工

plumbing (*pipes*) haikan 配管

plump *adj* potchari shita ぽっ
ちゃりした

plunge *v/i* tobikomu 飛び込
む; (*of prices*) kyūraku suru
急落する

plus *prep*: 2 ~ 2 *is* 4 ni tasu ni
wa yon da 2足す2は4だ

pneumonia haien 肺炎

poached egg otoshitamago

落し卵

P.O. Box shishobako 私書箱

pocket *n* poketto ポケット

pocketbook (*purse*)
handobaggu ハンドバッグ;
(*billfold*) saifu 財布; (*book*)
bunkobon 文庫本

pocketknife pokettonaifu ポ
ケットナイフ

poem shi 詩

poet shijin 詩人

poetry shi 詩

point 1 *n* (*of knife*) saki 先;
(*in contest, exam*) tensū 点
数; (*purpose*) imi 意味; (*in
discussion*) yōten 要点; (*in
decimals*) ten 点; (*decimal
~*) shōsūten 小数点 2 *v/i*
sasu 指す

♦ **point at** yubisasu 指さす

♦ **point out** *sights* sashishimesu
指し示す; *advantage* shiteki
suru 指摘する

pointless muimi (na) 無意
味(な)

point of view kanten 観点

poison *n* doku 毒

poke *v/t* (*prod*) tsutsuku つ
つく; (*stick*) tsukkomu 突
っ込む

poker (*cards*) pōkā ポーカー

pole (*of wood, metal*) bō 棒

police *n* keisatsu 警察

policeman keikan 警官

police station keisatsusho
警察署

policy[1] POL seisaku 政策; (of
company) hōshin 方針

policy[2] (insurance) hoken-
shōken 保険証券

polish 1 n tsuyadashi つや出
し 2 v/t migaku 磨く

polite reigi-tadashī 礼儀正しい

politeness reigitadashisa 礼
儀正しさ

political seiji (no) 政治(の)

politician seijika 政治家

politics seiji 政治

poll n (survey) seron-chōsa 世
論調査

pollute osen suru 汚染する

pollution osen 汚染

pond ike 池

ponytail ponītēru ポニー
テール

pool[1] (swimming) pūru プー
ル; (of water, blood) tamari
たまり

pool[2] (game) pūru プール

poor 1 adj mazushī 貧しい;
(not good) heta (na) 下手
(な); (unfortunate) aware (na)
哀れ(な) 2 n: the ~ mazushī
hitobito 貧しい人々

pop[1] v/i (of balloon etc) pon to
iu oto o tateru ぽんという音
を立てる

pop[2] n MUS poppusu ポップス

pop[3] infml (father) tōchan 父
ちゃん

popcorn poppukōn ポップ
コーン

pope Rōma-hōō ローマ法王

poppy popī ポピー

Popsicle® aisukyandī アイス
キャンディー

popular ninki no aru 人気の
ある; belief ippan (no) 一
般(の)

popularity ninki 人気

population jinkō 人口

porcelain n jiki 磁器

pork butaniku 豚肉

pornographic poruno (no) ポ
ルノ(の)

pornography poruno ポルノ

port n (town) minatomachi 港
町; (area) minato 港

portable 1 adj keitaiyō (no) 携
帯用(の) 2 n (TV) keitaiyō
terebi 携帯用テレビ

porthole NAUT genső げん窓

portion n (of food) ichininmae
1人前

portrait n shōzōga 肖像画

pose v/i (for artist) pōzu o toru
ポーズをとる

position n 1 ichi 位置; (stance)
shisei 姿勢; (in race) jun'i 順
位; (point of view) iken 意見;
(situation) tachiba 立場 2 v/t
haichi suru 配置する

positive *attitude* sekkyokuteki (na) 積極的(な); *response* maemuki (na) 前向き(な); *results* yōsei (no) 陽性(の); GRAM genkyū (no) 原級(の); ELEC purasu (no) プラス(の)

possession shoyū 所有; *(thing owned)* shoyūbutsu 所有物; ~**s** shoyūbutsu 所有物

possibility kanōsei 可能性

possible kanō (na) 可能(な); *the best* ~ ... dekiru dake yoi ... できるだけよい...

possibly dekiru dake できるだけ; *(perhaps)* osoraku おそらく

post[1] 1 *n (of wood etc)* hashira 柱 2 *v/t notice* haru はる

post[2] *v/t guards* haichi suru 配置する

postage yūsōryō 郵送料

postcard hagaki はがき

postdate sakihizuke ni suru 先日付にする

poster posutā ポスター

posting *(assignment)* haizoku 配属

postmark keshi-in 消印

post office yūbinkyoku 郵便局

postpone enki suru 延期する

posture shisei 姿勢

pot *(for cooking)* nabe なべ; *(for coffee, tea)* potto ポット;

(for plant) uekibachi 植木鉢

potato jagaimo じゃがいも

potato chips poteto-chippusu ポテトチップス

potential 1 *adj* kanō (na) 可能(な); *customer, problem* senzaiteki (na) 潜在的(な) 2 *n* kanōsei 可能性

pothole *(in road)* ana 穴

poultry *(birds)* kakin 家きん; *(meat)* toriniku 鳥肉

pound[1] *n (weight)* pondo ポンド

pound[2] *v/i (of heart)* dokidoki suru どきどきする

pound sterling Igirisu-pondo イギリスポンド

pour *v/t drink* tsugu つぐ

poverty hinkon 貧困

powder *n* kona 粉; *(for face)* o-shiroi おしろい

powder room keshōshitsu 化粧室

power *n (strength)* chikara 力; *(authority)* kenryoku 権力; *(energy)* dōryoku 動力; *(electricity)* denryoku 電力

power cut teiden 停電

powerful *blow* kyōryoku (na) 強力(な); *engine* bariki no aru 馬力のある; *man* yūryoku (na) 有力(な)

powerless muryoku (na) 無力(な)

power station hatsudensho
発電所

PR (= public relations) pīāru
ピーアール

practical *experience* jissaiteki
(na) 実際的(な); *person*
genjitsuteki (na) 現実的(な)

practice 1 *n* jissen 実践;
(training) renshū 練習;
(rehearsal) keiko けいこ;
(custom) shūkan 習慣 2 *v/t*
renshū suru 練習する; ~ *law*
bengoshi o shite iru 弁護士を
している

praise 1 *n* shōsan 称賛 2 *v/t*
shōsan suru 称賛する

pray inoru 祈る

precaution yōjin 用心

precede *v/t (in time)* ... yori
saki ni kuru ...より先に来る

precious kichō (na) 貴重(な)

precise seikaku (na) 正確(な)

precisely seikaku ni 正確に

predecessor *(in job)*
zenninsha 前任者

predict yogen suru 予言する

predominant attōteki (na) 圧
倒的(な)

predominantly attōteki ni 圧
倒的に

preface *n* jobun 序文

prefer ... no hō o konomu
...のほうを好む; ~ X *to*
Y Y yori X no hō ga suki de

aru Y より X のほうが好き
である

preferable nozomashī 望
ましい

preference konomi 好み

preferential yūsen (no) 優
先(の)

pregnancy ninshin 妊娠

pregnant ninshin shite iru 妊
娠している

prejudice *n* henken 偏見

preliminary *adj* yobiteki (na)
予備的(な)

premature baby mijukuji
未熟児

première *n (of movie)* fūkiri
封切り; *(of play)* shonichi
初日

premises *(of business)* shikichi
敷地; *(of store)* mise 店

premium *n (in insurance)*
hokenryō 保険料

prepare *v/t* ... no junbi o suru
...の準備をする

prescription MED shohōsen 処
方せん

presence iru koto 居ること

present¹ 1 *adj (current)* genzai
(no) 現在(の); *be ~* iru い
る; *(at meeting, in class)*
shusseki shite iru 出席して
いる 2 *n: the ~* genzai 現在;
GRAM genzaikei 現在形; *at ~*
ima no tokoro 今のところ

present² 1 *n (gift)* purezento プレゼント 2 *v/t award* okuru 贈る; *program* teikyō suru 提供する

presentation *(of new product)* purezen プレゼン

presently *(at the moment)* ima no tokoro 今のところ; *(soon)* mamonaku まもなく

presidency *(office)* daitōryō no chi-i 大統領の地位; *(term)* daitōryō no ninki 大統領の任期

president POL daitōryō 大統領; *(of company)* shachō 社長

presidential daitōryō (no) 大統領(の)

press 1 *n: the ~* shinbun-zasshi 新聞雑誌; *(journalists)* hōdōjin 報道陣 2 *v/t button* osu 押す; *clothes ...* ni airon o kakeru …にアイロンをかける

pressure 1 *n* atsuryoku 圧力; *(of work)* jūatsu 重圧; *be under ~* puresshā o kanjiru プレッシャーを感じる 2 *v/t* ... ni atsuryoku o kakeru …に圧力をかける

prestige meisei 名声

presumably tabun 多分

pretense misekake 見せかけ

pretext kōjitsu 口実

pretty 1 *adj* kirei (na) きれい(な) 2 *adv (quite)* kanari かなり

prevent fusegu 防ぐ

preview *n (of movie)* shishakai 試写会

previous mae (no) 前(の)

prey *n* emono 獲物

price *n* nedan 値段

priceless hijō ni kichō (na) 非常に貴重(な)

pride *n* jiman 自慢; *(self-respect)* jisonshin 自尊心

priest *(Christian)* shisai 司祭; *(Buddhist)* sōryo 僧侶; *(Shinto)* kannushi 神主

primary 1 *adj* shuyō (na) 主要(な) 2 *n* POL yobi-senkyo 予備選挙

prime minister sōri-daijin 総理大臣

primitive genshi (no) 原始(の); *conditions* genshiteki (na) 原始的(な)

prince ōji 王子

princess ōjo 王女

principal 1 *adj* shuyō (na) 主要(な) 2 *n (of school)* kōchō 校長

principle *(moral)* shugi 主義; *(rule)* genri 原理

print 1 *n (in book)* insatsu sareta moji 印刷された文字 2 *v/t* insatsu suru 印刷する

printer purintā プリンター;

(person) insatsu-gyōsha 印刷業者

prior *adj* engagement saki (no) 先(の)

prioritize *(order)* ... no yūsen-jun'i o kimeru ···の優先順位を決める; *(put first)* yūsen saseru 優先させる

priority *(sth urgent)* yūsen-jikō 優先事項; *(most important thing)* saijūyō-jikō 最重要事項

prison keimusho 刑務所

prisoner shūjin 囚人

privacy puraibashī プライバシー

private *adj* life shiteki (na) 私的(な); *office* kojin'yō (no) 個人用(の); *school* shiritsu (no) 私立(の)

privately hito no inai tokoro de 人のいないところで; *owned* shiteki ni 私的に

privilege *(special treatment)* tokken 特権; *(honor)* meiyo 名誉

prize *n* shō 賞

prizewinner jushōsha 受賞者

probability mikomi 見込み

probable arisō (na) ありそう(な)

probably tabun たぶん

probation JUR shikkō-yūyo 執行猶予; *on ~ (in job)* shiyō-kikanchū de 試用期間中で

probe *n (investigation)* chōsa 調査

problem mondai 問題

procedure tetsuzuki 手続き

process 1 *n* katei 過程
2 *v/t* kakō suru 加工する; *data* shori suru 処理する

proclaim sengen suru 宣言する

produce 1 *n (agricultural)* seisanbutsu 生産物 **2** *v/t* commodity seisan suru 生産する; *(bring about)* motarasu もたらす; *(bring out)* toridasu 取り出す; *play, movie* seisaku suru 製作する

producer *(of commodity)* seisansha 生産者, seizō-gaisha 製造会社; *(of play, movie)* purodyūsā プロデューサー

product seihin 製品

production seisan 生産; *(of play, movie)* seisaku 制作

productive seisanryoku no takai 生産力の高い; *meeting* seisanteki (na) 生産的(な)

productivity seisansei 生産性

profession shokugyō 職業

professional 1 *adj* puro (no) プロ(の); *advice* senmonka (no) 専門家(の); *work* puro-nami (no) プロ並み(の)

2 *n* puro プロ; *(doctor, lawyer etc)* senmonshoku no hito 専門職の人

professor kyōju 教授

profit rieki 利益

profitable mōke ni naru もうけになる

profit margin rizaya 利ざや

program 1 *n* keikaku 計画; *(on radio, TV)* bangumi 番組; THEAT, COMPUT puroguramu プログラム **2** *v/t* COMPUT ... ni puroguramu o ireru …にプログラムを入れる

programmer COMPUT puroguramā プログラマー

progress 1 *n* shinpo 進歩 **2** *v/i (in time)* shinkō suru 進行する; *(move on)* susumu 進む; *(make~)* jōtatsu suru 上達する

prohibit kinshi suru 禁止する

project[1] *n (plan)* keikaku 計画; SCHOOL kenkyū-kadai 研究課題; *(housing area)* jūtaku-danchi 住宅団地

project[2] **1** *v/t figures* yosō suru 予想する **2** *v/i (stick out)* tsukideru 突き出る

projection *(forecast)* mitsumori 見積もり

projector eishaki 映写機

prolong enchō suru 延長する

prom *(dance)* dansu-pātī ダンスパーティー

promise 1 *n* yakusoku 約束 **2** *v/t person* ... ni yakusoku suru …に約束する

promote *employee* shōshin saseru 昇進させる; COMM senden suru 宣伝する

promotion *(of employee)* shōshin 昇進; COMM hanbai-sokushin 販売促進

prompt *adj person* jikan o mamoru 時間を守る; *(speedy)* jinsoku (na) 迅速(な)

pronounce *word* hatsuon suru 発音する

proof *n* shōko 証拠

propaganda puropaganda プロパガンダ

proper *(real)* chanto shita ちゃんとした; *(correct)* tadashī 正しい; *(fitting)* tekitō (na) 適当(な)

properly chanto ちゃんと

property shoyūbutsu 所有物; *(land)* tochi 土地

proportions tsurai つり合い

propose 1 *v/t (suggest)* teian suru 提案する; *(plan)* keikaku suru 計画する **2** *v/i (to marry)* puropōzu suru プロポーズする

prosecute *v/t* JUR kiso suru 起訴する

prosperous seikō shita 成

功した

prostitute *n* baishunfu 売春婦

protect hogo suru 保護する

protection hogo 保護

protein tanpakushitsu たんぱく質

protest 1 *n* kōgi 抗議; *(demo)* kōgi-shūkai 抗議集会 **2** *v/i* kōgi suru 抗議する

protester kōgisha 抗議者

proud hokorashige (na) 誇らしげ(な); *be ~ of* hokori ni omou 誇りに思う

prove shōmei suru 証明する

provide *(for society, school)* kyōkyū suru 供給する; *(for person)* ataeru 与える; *~d (that)* to iu jōken de という条件で

province shū 州

provisional jōkentsuki (no) 条件つき(の)

provoke *(annoy)* okoraseru 怒らせる

proximity chikasa 近さ

psychiatric seishinka (no) 精神科(の)

psychiatrist seishinkai 精神科医

psychiatry seishin-igaku 精神医学

psychoanalysis seishin-bunseki 精神分析

psychoanalyst seishin-

bunseki-i 精神分析医

psychological shinriteki (na) 心理的(な)

psychologist shinrigakusha 心理学者

psychology shinrigaku 心理学

psychopath seishin-ijōsha 精神異常者

public 1 *adj* ōyake (no) 公(の); *(open to ~)* kōkai (no) 公開(の) **2** *n*: *the ~* ippan no hitobito 一般の人々; *in ~* hitomae de 人前で

publication *(of book)* shuppan 出版; *(by newspaper: of photographs)* kōhyō 公表; *(of story)* hōdō 報道

publicity senden 宣伝; *(media attention)* chūmoku 注目

publicly kōzen to 公然と

public relations kōhō-katsudō 広報活動

publish shuppan suru 出版する

publisher shuppansha 出版社; *(person)* hakkōsha 発行者

pull 1 *v/t* hipparu 引っ張る; *tooth* hikinuku 引き抜く; *muscle* itameru 痛める **2** *v/i* hipparu 引っ張る

♦ **pull out** *v/i* *(of agreement, competition)* te o hiku 手を引く

pulse myakuhaku 脈拍

pump *n* ponpu ポンプ

punch 1 *n* (blow) panchi パンチ **2** *v/t* (with fist) kobushi de naguru こぶしで殴る

punctual jikan ni seikaku (na) 時間に正確(な)

punctuate bassuru 罰する

punishment batsu 罰; JUR keibatsu 刑罰

purchase 1 *n* (action) kōnyū 購入; (object) kōnyūhin 購入品 **2** *v/t* kōnyū suru 購入する

purchaser kaite 買い手

pure silk junsui (na) 純粋(な); air, water sunda 澄んだ; (morally) junketsu (na) 純潔(な)

purely tan ni 単に

purify water jōka suru 浄化する

purple *adj* murasaki (no) 紫(の)

purpose mokuteki 目的; on ~ waza to わざと

purse *n* (pocketbook) handobaggu ハンドバッグ

pursue *v/t* person tsuiseki suru 追跡する

pursuer tsuisekisha 追跡者

push *v/t* & *v/i* osu 押す

put oku 置く

♦ **put down** oku 置く; (deposit) atamakin to shite harau 頭金として払う; rebellion chin'atsu suru 鎮圧する

♦ **put off** light, TV kesu 消す; (deter) omoi-todomaraseru 思いとどまらせる

♦ **put on** light, TV tsukeru つける; music, glasses kakeru かける; jacket, shirt kiru 着る; shoes, pants haku はく; make-up suru する

♦ **put out** hand sashidasu 差し出す; fire, light kesu 消す

♦ **put up** *v/t* hand, price ageru 上げる; person tomeru 泊める; (erect) tateru 建てる; poster kakageru 掲げる

♦ **put up with** gaman suru 我慢する

puzzle *n* (mystery) nazo なぞ; (game) pazuru パズル

Q

qualified doctor etc nintei sareta 認定された

qualify *v/i* (get degree etc) shikaku o toru 資格を取る;

SPORTS ...ni susumu …に進む

quality shitsu 質; (trait) tokuchō 特徴

quantity ryō 量

quarrel 1 n kenka けんか **2** v/i kenka suru けんかする

quart kuwōto クウォート

quarter n yonbun no ichi 四分の一; *a ~ of an hour* jūgofun 十五分; *a ~ of 5* goji jūgofun mae 五時十五分前; *~ after 5* goji jūgofun 五時十五分

quarterfinal junjunkesshō 準々決勝

quarterly 1 adj shihanki (no) 四半期(の) **2** adv publish kikan de 季刊で; *pay* shihanki goto ni 四半期毎に

queen joō 女王

query 1 n shitsumon 質問 **2** v/t *(doubt)* ... ni toitadasu ...に問いただす

question 1 n shitsumon 質問; *(matter)* mondai 問題 **2** v/t person ... ni shitsumon suru ...に質問する; *(doubt)* utagau 疑う

question mark gimonfu 疑問符

questionnaire ankēto アンケート

quick hayai 速い

quickly hayaku 早く

quiet shizuka (na) 静か(な); *life* heion (na) 平穏(な); *town, street* kansan to shita 閑散とした

quit v/t & v/i *(leave job)* yameru 辞める

quite *(fairly)* kanari かなり; *(completely)* mattaku まったく; *not ~ ready* mada junbi ga dekite inai まだ準備ができていない; *~ a lot* kanari かなり

quiz n kuizu クイズ

quota wariate 割り当て

quote 1 n *(from author)* in'yō 引用; *(price)* mitsumori 見積もり; *(~ mark)* in'yōfu 引用符 **2** v/t text inyō 引用する; *price* ... no mitsumori o dasu ...の見積もりを出す

R

rabbit usagi うさぎ

race 1 n SPORTS rēsu レース **2** v/i *(run fast)* isoide iku 急いで行く; SPORTS kyōgi ni deru 競技に出る

racial jinshu (no) 人種(の)

racism jinshu-sabetsu 人種差別

racist n jinshu-sabetsu-shugisha 人種差別主義者

rack n (for bikes) rakku ラック; (for bags on train) tana 棚; (for CDs) tate 立て

racket[1] SPORTS raketto ラケット

racket[2] (noise) sōon 騒音; (criminal) sagi 詐欺

radar rēdā レーダー

radiator rajiētā ラジエーター

radical adj konponteki (na) 根本的(な); POL views kyūshinteki (na) 急進的(な)

radio rajio ラジオ

radioactive hōshasei (no) 放射性(の)

rag (for cleaning etc) zōkin ぞうきん

rage n gekido 激怒

raid n (by troops, police) shūgeki 襲撃; (by robbers) gōtō 強盗

rail (on track) rēru レール; (hand~) tesuri 手すり; (for towel) kake kāke 掛け

railings saku さく

railroad tetsudō 鉄道

railroad station eki 駅

rain 1 n ame 雨 **2** v/i ame ga furu 雨が降る; it's ~ing: ame ga futte iru 雨が降っている

raincoat reinkōto レインコート

rainy amemoyō 雨模様

raise 1 n (in salary) shōkyū

昇給 **2** v/t children sodateru 育てる

rally n (meeting) shūkai 集会

ranch daibokujō 大牧場

rancher bokujō-keieisha 牧場経営者

random 1 adj teatari-shidai (no) 手当たり次第(の) **2** n: at ~ teatari-shidai ni 手当たり次第に

range n (of products) haba 幅; (of airplane) kōzoku-kyori 航続距離; (of mountains) sanmyaku 山脈

rank n MIL kaikyū 階級

ransack kumanaku sagasu くまなく探す

ransom minoshirokin 身の代金

rape 1 n gōkan 強かん **2** v/t gōkan suru 強かんする

rapid hayai 速い

rapids kyūryū 急流

rare mare (na) まれ(な); steak rea レア

rarely mettani...nai めったに...ない

rash[1] MED hasshin 発しん

rash[2] action keisotsu (na) 軽率(な)

raspberry razuberī ラズベリー

rat n nezumi ねずみ

rate n rēto レート; (price)

ryōkin 料金

rather *(fairly)* kanari かなり

rational *person* riseiteki (na) 理性的(な); *method etc* gōriteki (na) 合理的(な)

rationalize *v/t production* gōrika suru 合理化する

rattlesnake garagarahebi がらがらへび

raw *food* nama (no) 生(の); *sugar, iron* kakō shite inai 加工していない

raw materials genryō 原料

ray kōsen 光線

razor kamisori かみそり

razor blade kamisori no ha か みそりの刃

reach *v/t city etc* ... ni tsuku ...に着く; *(go as far as)* ... ni todoku ...に届く; *decision* ... ni tassuru ...に達する

react hannō suru 反応する

reaction hannō 反応

reactionary *adj* POL handōteki (na) 反動的(な)

reactor *(nuclear)* genshiro 原子炉

read *v/t & v/i* yomu 読む

reader *(person)* dokusha 読者

readily *admit* susunde 進んで

reading dokusho 読書; *(from meter)* kiroku 記録

ready *(prepared)* junbi ga dekita 準備ができた;

(willing) susunde... suru 進ん で...する

real hontō (no) 本当(の); *gold* honmono (no) 本物(の)

realistic genjitsuteki (na) 現実的(な)

reality jijitsu 事実

realize *v/t* kizuku 気付く

really hontō ni 本当に; *not ~ (not much)* anmari あんまり

realtor fudōsan'ya 不動産屋

rear *adj legs* ushiro (no) 後ろ (の); *seats, wheels* kōbu (no) 後部の

reason *n (faculty)* risei 理性; *(cause)* riyū 理由

reasonable *person* funbetsu no aru 分別のある; *price* datō (na) 妥当(な)

reassuring anshin saseru 安 心させる

rebel *n* POL hangyakusha 反逆 者; *(against parents)* hankō-bunshi 反抗分子

rebellion POL hanran 反乱; *(against parents)* hankō 反抗

recall *v/t ambassador* yobimodosu 呼び戻す; *(remember)* omoidasu 思 い出す

receipt *(for money)* ryōshūsho 領収書, reshīto レシート; *(for goods)* juryōsho 受領書

receive uketoru 受け取る

recent saikin (no) 最近(の)

recently saikin 最近

reception (in company) uketsuke 受付; (in hotel) furonto フロント; (party) resepushon レセプション; (welcome) kangei 歓迎; (for cell phone) jushin 受信

reception desk (in company) uketsuke 受付; (in hotel) furonto フロント

receptionist (in company) uketsuke-gakari 受付係; (in hotel) furonto-gakari フロント係

recession keiki-kōtai 景気後退

recipe reshipi レシピ

recipient uketorinin 受取人

reciprocal sōgo (no) 相互(の)

recite poem anshō suru 暗唱する

reckless mucha (na) 無茶(な)

reckon (consider) omou 思う

recognition (of state, achievements) shōnin 承認

recognize ni oboe ga aru ...に覚えがある; POL state shōnin suru 承認する

recommend susumeru 勧める

recommendation suisen 推薦

reconciliation (of people) wakai 和解

recondition shūri suru 修理する

reconnaissance MIL teisatsu 偵察

reconsider v/t & v/i kangaenaosu 考え直す

record 1 n MUS rekōdo レコード; SPORTS etc saikō-kiroku 最高記録; **~s** kiroku 記録 2 v/t (tape etc) rokuon suru 録音する

record-breaking kiroku-yaburi (no) 記録破り(の)

record holder kiroku-hojisha 記録保持者

recording rokuon 録音

recover 1 v/t sth lost torimodosu 取り戻す 2 v/i med genki ni naru 元気になる

recovery (of sth lost) kaishū 回収; (from illness) kaifuku 回復

recreation goraku 娯楽

recruit 1 n MIL shinpei 新兵; (to company) shinnyūsha-in 新入社員 2 v/t new staff boshū suru 募集する

recruitment boshū 募集

rectangle chōhōkei 長方形

recurrent tabitabi okoru 度々起こる

recycle sairiyō suru 再利

用する

recycling risaikuru リサイクル

red akai 赤い

Red Cross Sekijūji 赤十字

redevelop *part of town* saikaihatsu suru 再開発する

red-handed: catch X ~ X o genkōhan de tsukamaeru X を現行犯で捕まえる

redhead akage no hito 赤毛の人

red light akashingō 赤信号

red tape kanryō-shugi 官僚主義

reduce herasu 減らす

reduction genshō 減少; *(of price)* nesage 値下げ

reel n *(of film)* rīru リール; *(of thread)* maki 巻

♦ refer to *(allude to)* honomekasu ほのめかす

referee SPORTS shinpan 審判

reference *(allusion)* genkyū 言及; *(for job)* suisenjō 推薦状

reference number shōkai-bangō 照会番号

referendum jūmin-tōhyō 住民投票

refinery seiseijo 精製所

reflect 1 *v/t light* hansha suru 反射する **2** *v/i (think)* yukkuri kangaeru ゆっくり考える

reflection hansha 反射; *(thought)* jukkō 熟考

reflex hansha-nōryoku 反射能力

reform 1 n kaikaku 改革 **2** v/t kaikaku suru 改革する

refreshing *drink* sawayaka (na) さわやか(な); *experience* sugasugashī すがすがしい

refrigerate reizō suru 冷蔵する

refrigerator reizōko 冷蔵庫

refuel v/i *(of airplane)* nenryō no hokyū o ukeru 燃料の補給を受ける

refugee nanmin 難民

refund 1 n haraimodoshi 払い戻し **2** v/t haraimodosu 払い戻す

refusal kyozetsu 拒絶

refuse: ~ to do ... ... suru no o kotowaru ... するのを断る

regard 1 n *(allusion)* keigu 敬具 **2** v/t: **~ X as Y** X o Y to omou X を Y と思う

regardless: ~ of ... ... ni mo kakawarazu ...にもかかわらず

regime POL seiji-taisei 政治体制

regiment n rentai 連隊

region chi-iki 地域

regional chihō (no) 地方(の)

register 1 n tōrokubo 登録簿

2 v/t birth, death todokederu
届け出る; vehicle tōroku suru
登録する; letter kakitome ni
suru 書留めにする 3 v/i (for
course) jukōtetsuzuki o suru
受講手続きをする; (with
police) tōroku suru 登録する

regret 1 v/t kōkai suru 後悔す
る 2 n kōkai 後悔

regular 1 adj teikiteki (na) 定
期的(な); pattern taishōteki
(na) 対称的(な); (normal)
tsūjō (no) 通常(の) 2 n (at
bar etc) jōren 常連

regulate machine chōsetsu suru
調節する

regulation (rule) kisoku 規則

rehearsal rihāsaru リハー
サル

rehearse v/i rihāsaru o suru リ
ハーサルをする

reimburse haraimodosu 払
い戻す

reinforce hokyō suru 補強す
る; belief urazukeru 裏付ける

reject v/t kyozetsu suru 拒絶
する; goods uketsukenai 受け
付けない

relapse MED saihatsu 再発

related ketsuen-kankei (no)
血縁関係(の); event, ideas
kankei ga aru 関係がある

relation (family) shinseki 親せ
き; (link) kankei 関係

relationship kankei 関係

relative 1 n shinseki 親せき 2
adj sōtaiteki (na) 相対的(な)

relatively hikakuteki 比較的

relax v/i kutsurogu くつろぐ

relaxation kibarashi 気晴らし

relay n: (race) rirē リレー

release 1 n (from prison)
shakuhō 釈放; (of CD etc)
hatsubai 発売 2 v/t prisoner
shakuhō suru 釈放する; brake
hanasu 放す

relent taido ga nanka suru 態度
が軟化する

relentless shūnen-bukai 執念
深い; rain etc taema no nai 絶
え間のない

relevant kanren suru 関連
する

reliable shinrai dekiru 信頼
できる; information shin'yō
dekiru 信用できる

relief ando 安ど

relieve pressure, pain
yawarageru 和らげる; be ~d
(at news etc) anshin suru 安
心する

religion shūkyō 宗教

relocate v/i idō suru 移動する

reluctance ki ga susumanai
koto 気が進まないこと

reluctant: be ~ to do X X suru
koto ni ki ga susumanai Xする
ことに気が進まない

♦**rely on** *(count on)* shin'yō suru 信用する

remain *(be left)* nokoru 残る; *(stay)* todomaru とどまる

remark n hatsugen 発言

remarkable subarashī すばらしい

remedy n MED, *fig* chiryōhō 治療法

remember 1 *v/t* omoidasu 思い出す **2** *v/i*: *I don't ~* oboete inai 覚えていない

remind: *~ X to do Y* X ni Y o wasurenai yō ni chūi suru XにYを忘れないように注意する; *Tokyo ~s me of ...* Tōkyō wa watashi ni ... o omoidasaseru 東京は私に...を思い出させる

reminder omoidasaseru mono 思い出させる物; COMM saisokujō 催促状

reminisce omoidebanashi o suru 思い出話をする

remnant nokori 残り

remorse hageshī kōkai 激しい後悔

remote *village* henpi (na) へんぴ(な); *ancestor* tōi 遠い

remote control rimōto-kontorōru リモートコントロール

removal jokyo 除去; MED setsujo 切除

remove torinozoku 取り除く; MED setsujo suru 切除する

renew *contract* kōshin suru 更新する; *talks* saikai suru 再開する

renounce hōki suru 放棄する

renowned yūmei (na) 有名(な)

rent 1 n yachin 家賃; *for ~* kashi-ie ari 貸し家あり **2** *v/t* kariru 借りる; *(~ out)* kasu 貸す

rental *(for apartment)* yachin 家賃; *(for TV etc)* chintairyō 賃貸料

rental car renta-kā レンタカー

reopen *v/t & v/i* saikai suru 再開する

rep COMM sērusuman セールスマン

repair *v/t* shūri suru 修理する

repairman shūriya 修理屋

repay *money* haraimodosu 払い戻す

repeal *v/t* law haishi suru 廃止する

repeat 1 *v/t* kurikaeshite iu 繰り返して言う; *experience* kurikaesu 繰り返す **2** n TV etc saihōsō 再放送

repeated saisan (no) 再三(の)

repel *v/t* attack gekitai suru 撃退する; *insects* oiharau 追い払う

repercussions eikyō 影響

repetitive *style* kudoi くどい; *work* kurikaeshi (no) 繰り返し(の)

replace moto ni modosu 元に戻す; *(take place of)* … ni kawaru …に代わる

replacement *(person: permanent)* kōkeisha 後継者; *(temporary)* kōtai-yōin 交代要員

replica repurika レプリカ

reply 1 *n* henji 返事 **2** *v/i* henji suru 返事する

report 1 *n (account)* hōkokusho 報告書; *(by journalist)* hōdō 報道 **2** *v/t (to authorities)* hōkoku suru 報告する

reporter kisha 記者

represent *(act for)* … no dairi o suru …の代理をする; *(stand for)* … no tenkei de aru …の典型である

representative *n* dairi 代理; COMM sērusuman セールスマン; POL kain-gi-in 下院議員

repress *revolt* yokuatsu suru 抑圧する; *feelings* osaeru 抑える; *laugh* koraeru こらえる

reprieve *(act for)* n JUR shikei-shikkō-yūyo 死刑執行猶予 **2** *v/t prisoner* shikei-shikkō o yūyo suru 死刑執行を猶予する

reprimand *v/t* shisseki suru 叱

責する

reprisal hōfuku 報復

reproach *n* hinan 非難

reproduce 1 *v/t document* fukusei suru 複製する **2** *v/i* BIOL hanshoku suru 繁殖する

republic kyōwakoku 共和国

Republican 1 *n* Kyōwatō-in 共和党員 **2** *adj* Kyōwatō (no) 共和党(の)

repulsive ken'o subeki 嫌悪すべき

reputable hyōban no yoi 評判の良い

reputation hyōban 評判

request 1 *n* yōsei 要請 **2** *v/t* o-negai suru お願いする

require …ga hitsuyō de aru が必要である

requirement *(need)* yōkyū 要求; *(condition)* jōken 条件

rescue 1 *n* kyūjo 救助 **2** *v/t* kyūjo suru 救助する

research *n* kenkyū 研究

research and development kenkyū-kaihatsu 研究開発

resemble … ni nite iru …に似ている

resent … ni hara o tateru …に腹を立てる

reservation *(of room, table)* yoyaku 予約

reserve 1 *n (store)* bichiku 備蓄; *(aloofness)* enryo 遠慮;

sports hoketsu 補欠 2 *v/t*
seat, table yoyaku suru 予
約する

residence *(stay)* zaijū 在住

residence permit zairyū-
kyoka 在留許可

resident *n* kyojūsha 居住者;
(in hotel) shukuhaku-kyaku
宿泊客

resign *v/i* jinin suru 辞任する

resignation *(from job)* jinin
辞任

resist *v/t* teikō suru 抵抗する

resistance teikō 抵抗

resolution *(decision)* ketsugi
決議; *(New Year ~)* kesshin 決
心; *(determination)* kyōko na
ishi 強固な意志

resort *n (place)* rizōto リゾ
ート

resource shigen 資源

resourceful rinki-ōhen (no) 臨
機応変(の)

respect 1 *n* sonkei 尊敬;
(consideration) sonchō 尊重
2 *v/t person* sonkei suru 尊敬
する; *law* mamoru 守る

respectable rippa (na) 立
派(な)

respond kotaeru 答える;
(react) ōjiru 応じる

response kotae 答え;
(reaction) hannō 反応

responsibility sekinin 責任;

(duty) gimu 義務; *(in job)*
shokumu 職務

responsible *(liable)* sekinin ga
aru 責任がある; *(in job)* sekinin
no omoi 責任の重い

rest[1] *n* yasumi 休み 2 *v/i*
yasumu 休む; *(lean etc)*
yorikakeru 寄り掛ける; *job* sekinin

rest[2]: *the ~* nokori 残り

restaurant resutoran レス
トラン

restore *building etc* shūfuku
suru 修復する

restrain seishi suru 制止する;
~ oneself jibun o osaeru 自分
を抑える

restraint *(moderation)* setsudo
節度

restrict seigen suru 制限する

restricted area MIL tachi-iri-
kinshi no basho 立ち入り禁
止の場所

restriction seigen 制限

rest room o-tearai お手洗

result *n* kekka 結果; *(of exam)*
seiseki 成績

resume *v/t* ... ni modoru ...に
戻る

résumé rirekisho 履歴書

retail *adv* kourine de 小売値で

retaliate hōfuku suru 報復する

retire *v/i (from work)* taishoku
suru 退職する

retirement taishoku 退職

retract v/t statement tekkai suru 撤回する

retreat v/i MIL taikyaku suru 退却する

retrieve sth lost torimodosu 取り戻す

retrospective n kaiko 回顧

return 1 n kikan 帰還; (giving back) henkyaku 返却; COMPUT, (in tennis) ritān リターン **2** v/t (give back) henkyaku suru 返却する; (put back) modosu 戻す; favor kaesu 返す **3** v/i kaeru 帰る; (of times, doubt etc) modoru 戻る

return flight kaeri no bin 帰りの便

reunion atsumari 集まり

reunite v/t friends saikai saseru 再会させる; country saitōgō suru 再統合する

reveal (make visible) miseru 見せる; (make known) akiraka ni suru 明らかにする

revealing remark akiraka ni suru 明らかにする

revenge n fukushū 復しゅう

revenue shūnyū 収入; (of government) sainyū 歳入

reverse 1 n (opposite) gyaku 逆; (back) ura 裏; AUTO bakku バック **2** v/i AUTO bakku suru バックする

review 1 n (of book, movie)

hihyō 批評 **2** v/t book, movie hihyō suru 批評する; SCHOOL fukushū suru 復習する

reviewer hyōronka 評論家

revise v/t text, figures shūsei suru 修正する; opinion kaeru 変える

revision shūsei 修正

revive 1 v/t custom fukkatsu saseru 復活させる **2** v/i (of business) kaifuku suru 回復する

revolt 1 n hangyaku 反逆 **2** v/i hangyaku suru 反逆する

revolting (disgusting) mukatsukaseru むかつかせる

revolution POL etc kakumei 革命; (turn) kaiten 回転

revolutionary 1 n POL kakumeika 革命家 **2** adj idea kakumeiteki (na) 革命的(な)

revolutionize kakumei o okosu 革命を起こす

revolver riborubā リボルバー

revulsion ken'o 嫌悪

reward n (benefit derived) hōbi ほうび; (financial) shōkin 賞金

rewarding tame ni naru ためになる

rewrite v/t kakinaosu 書き直す

rheumatism ryūmachi リューマチ

rhyme n in 韻

rhythm rizumu リズム

rib n rokkotsu ろっ骨

ribbon ribon リボン

rice kome 米; *(cooked)* gohan ご飯

rice ball o-nigiri おにぎり

rice bowl gohan-jawan ご飯茶碗

rice cooker suihanki 炊飯器

rice cracker senbei せんべい

ricefield suiden 水田

rice wine sake 酒

rich 1 *adj* kanemochi (no) 金持ち(の); *food* kotteri shita こってりした **2** n: *the ~* kanemochi 金持ち

rid: *get ~ of* torinozoku 取り除く

ride 1 n *(on horse)* jōba 乗馬; *(in vehicle)* doraibu ドライブ; *(journey)* ryokō 旅行 **2** v/t *horse, bike …* ni noru …に乗る

ridicule 1 n azakeri あざけり **2** v/t azakeru あざける

ridiculous bakageta ばかげた

rifle n raifuru ライフル

right 1 *adj (correct)* tadashī 正しい; *(morally)* seitō (na) 正当(な); *(fair)* tekisetsu (na) 適切(な); *(proper)* tekitō (na) 適当(な); *(not left)* migi (no) 右(の); *be ~ (be correct)* tadashī 正しい;

that's ~! sono tōri そのとおり **2** *adv (directly)* sugu すぐに; *(correctly)* tadashiku 正しく; *(not left)* migi ni 右に; *~ now (immediately)* ima sugu ni 今すぐに; *(at the moment)* ima 今 **3** n *(civil, legal etc)* kenri 権利; *(not left)* migi 右; POL uha 右派; *on the ~* migi ni 右に

rightful *owner etc* seitō (na) 正当(な)

right-handed migikiki (no) 右利き(の)

right wing n POL uyoku 右翼; *(within party)* uha 右派; SPORTS raito-uingu ライトウイング

rigid katai 固い; *attitude* yūzū no kikanai 融通の利かない

rigorous *discipline* kibishī 厳しい; *tests* genmitsu (na) 厳密(な)

rim *of wheel* rimu リム

ring[1] *wa* 輪; *(on finger)* yubiwa 指輪; *(boxing)* ringu リング

ring[2] 1 n *(of bell)* naru oto ベルの鳴る音 **2** v/t bell narasu 鳴らす **3** v/i *(of bell)* naru 鳴る

ringleader shubōsha 首謀者

rinse 1 n *(for hair)* hea-dai ヘアダイ **2** v/t susugu すすぐ; *hair* rinsu suru リンスする

riot 1 n bōdō 暴動 **2** v/i bōdō o okosu 暴動を起こす

rip 1 *n sakeme* 裂け目 2 *v/t cloth etc saku* 裂く

ripe *fruit ureta* 熟れた

rip-off *n infml sagi* 詐欺

rise *v/i (of sun) noboru* 昇る; *(of price, level) agaru* 上がる

risk *n kiken* 危険

rival *n raibaru* ライバル

rivalry *kyōsō* 競争

river *kawa* 川

road *dōro* 道路

roadblock *kenmonsho* 検問所

road map *dōro-chizu* 道路地図

roadsign *dōro-hyōshiki* 道路標識

roam *samayou* さまよう

roar *v/i (of lion) hoeru* ほえる; *(of person: in anger) wameku* わめく

roast 1 *v/t yaku* 焼く; *nuts, coffee iru* いる 2 *v/i (of food) yakeru* 焼ける

rob ...*kara ubau* …から奪う

robber *gōtō* 強盗

robbery *gōtō* 強盗

robot *robotto* ロボット

robust *person takumashī* たくましい; *structure ganjō (na)* 頑丈(な)

rock 1 *n ganseki* 岩石; *(small) ishi* 石 2 *v/i (of boat) yureru* 揺れる

rocket *n roketto* ロケット

role *yakuwari* 役割

role model *risō no sugata* 理想の姿

roll 1 *n (bread) rōru-pan* ロールパン; *(of film) maki* 巻き 2 *v/i (of ball etc) korogaru* 転がる

roller blade *n rōrā-burēdo* ローラーブレード

roller skate *n rōrā-sukēto* ローラースケート

romantic *romanchikku (na)* ロマンチック(な)

roof *yane* 屋根

room *n heya* 部屋; *(space) basho* 場所; *Japanese-style ~ washitsu* 和室

roommate *rūmu-mēto* ルームメート

room service *rūmu-sābisu* ルームサービス

root *ne* 根

rope *rōpu* ロープ

rose *bara* ばら

rot 1 *n (in wood) fuhai* 腐敗 2 *v/i kusaru* 腐る

rotate *v/i kaiten suru* 回転する

rotten *food etc kusatta* 腐った

rough *adj surface zarazara shita* ざらざらした; *seas areta* 荒れた; *(violent) ranbō (na)* 乱暴(な); *(approximate) daitai no* だいたいの

roughly *(approximately) daitai*

だいたいの

round 1 *adj* marui 丸い **2** *n* (of competition) kaisen 回戦; (in boxing match) raundo ラウンド

round trip ōfuku 往復

rouse (from sleep) okosu 起こす; interest hikiokosu 引き起こす

route rūto ルート; (walking) tōrimichi 通り道

routine 1 *adj* (customary) nichijō 日常(の) **2** *n* (habitual behavior) shūkan 習慣; (set sequence) itsumo no tejun いつもの手順

row (line) retsu 列

rowboat bōto ボート

rub *v/t* kosuru こする

rubber 1 *n* gomu ゴム **2** *adj* gomu (no) ゴム(の)

rude person burei (na) 無礼 (な); behavior gehin (na) 下品(な)

rudeness burei 無礼

rudimentary skill shohoteki (na) 初歩的(な); knowledge kisoteki (na) 基礎的(な)

rug shikimono 敷き物; (blanket) hizakake ひざ掛け

rugged scenery kewashī 険しい

ruin 1 *n*: ~s iseki 遺跡 **2** *v/t* party, vacation dame ni suru だ

めにする; plans kowasu 壊す; be ~ed (financially) hasan suru 破産する

rule 1 *n* (of club, game) rūru ルール; as a ~ gaishite 概して **2** *v/t* country shihai suru 支配する **3** *v/i* (of monarch) tōchi suru 統治する

ruler (for measuring) monosashi 物差し; (of state) shihaisha 支配者

ruling *adj*: ~ party yotō 与党

rumor *n* uwasa うわさ

run 1 *n* (on foot) kakeashi 駆け足; (in pantyhose) dengen 伝線 **2** *v/i* hashiru 走る; (of river, make-up) nagareru 流れる; (of trains etc) unkō suru 運行する; (of nose) hanamizu ga tareru 鼻水が垂れる; (of faucet) deru 出る; (of play) renzoku-kōen suru 連続公演する; (of engine) sadō suru 作動する; (of software) tsukaeru 使える; ~ for President daitōryō-sen ni shutsuba suru 大統領選に出馬する **3** *v/t* race kyōgikai ni deru 競技会に出る; 3 miles etc hashiru 走る; business etc keiei suru 経営する

run-down person hetoheto (no) へとへと(の); area sabirete iru さびれている

runner sōsha 走者

runner-up nichaku no hito 二着の人

running water suidōsui 水道水

runway kassōro 滑走路

rural inaka (no) 田舎 (の)

rush 1 *n* ōisogi 大急ぎ **2** *v/i* isogu 急ぐ

rush hour rasshu-awā ラッシ ュアワー

Russia Roshia ロシア

rust 1 *n* sabi さび **2** *v/i* sabiru さびる

rusty sabita さびた; *French etc* ...ga dame ni natta …がだめ になった

ruthless reikoku (na) 冷酷 (な)

S

sack *n* ōbukuro 大袋

sad kanashī 悲しい

sadist sadisuto サディスト

sadly kanashi-sō ni 悲しそ うに; *(regrettably)* zannen na koto ni 残念なことに

sadness kanashimi 悲しみ

safe 1 *adj* anzen (na) 安全 (な); *(not in danger)* buji (na) 無事 (な) **2** *n* kinko 金庫

safely *arrive* buji ni 無事に; *drive* anzen ni 安全に

safety anzen 安全

safety pin anzenpin 安全ピン

sail 1 *n* ho 帆; *(trip)* kōkai 航海 **2** *v/i* sēringu suru セーリ ングする; *(depart)* shukkō suru 出港する

sailboat yotto ヨット

sailing SPORTS sēringu セー リング

sailor suihei 水兵; SPORTS yottoman ヨットマン

saint seijin 聖人

sake: *for your ~* anata no tame ni あなたのために

sake sake 酒

sake cup choko ちょこ

salad dressing doresshingu ド レッシング

salary kyūryō 給料

sale hanbai 販売; *(reduced prices)* sēru セール; *for ~* urimono 売り物

sales clerk ten'in 店員

salesman sērusuman セールス マン

salmon sake さけ

salt shio 塩

salty shiokarai 塩辛い

salute 1 *n* MIL keirei 敬礼 **2** *v/i* aisatsu suru あいさつする

same 1 *adj* onaji 同じ **2** *pron*: *the ~ (things)* onaji mono 同じ物; *(abstracts)* onaji koto 同じこと **3** *adv*: *look the ~* onaji ni mieru 同じに見える

sample *n* sanpuru サンプル

sanction *n (penalty)* seisai 制裁

sand *n* suna 砂

sandal sandaru サンダル; *Japanese ~* zōri ぞうり

sandwich *n* sandoitchi サンドイッチ

sane shōki 正気(の)

sanitarium ryōyōsho 療養所

sanitary *conditions* eiseiteki (na) 衛生的(な)

sanitary napkin seiriyō napukin 生理用ナプキン

sanitation *(installations)* eisei-setsubi 衛生設備; *(waste removal)* gesui-setsubi 下水設備

sanity shōki 正気

sarcasm hiniku 皮肉

sarcastic iyami (na) 嫌み(な)

satellite jinkō-eisei 人工衛星

satire fūshi 風刺

satirical fūshiteki (na) 風刺的(な)

satisfaction manzoku 満足

satisfactory manzoku no iku 満足のいく; *(just ok)* nami (no) 並み(の)

satisfy manzoku saseru 満足

させる; *conditions, hunger* mitasu 満たす

Saturday doyōbi 土曜日

sauce sōsu ソース

saucer ukezara 受け皿

sauna sauna サウナ

sausage sōsēji ソーセージ

savage *adj animal* dōmō (na) どう猛(な); *attack* zannin (na) 残忍(な); *criticism* zankoku (na) 残酷(な)

save 1 *v/t (rescue)* sukū 救う; *money* tameru ためる; *time* setsuyaku suru 節約する; COMPUT hozon suru 保存する **2** *v/i (put money aside)* chokin suru 貯金する **3** *n* SPORTS sēbu セーブ

saving *(amount)* setsuyaku 節約; *(act)* chochiku 貯蓄

savings chokin 貯金

savory *adj (salty)* shioaji (no) 塩味(の); *(spicy)* piritto shita ぴりっとした

saw *n (tool)* nokogiri のこぎり

say *v/t* iu 言う

saying kotowaza ことわざ

scaffolding ashiba 足場

scale *n (size)* kibo 規模; *(of map)* shukushaku 縮尺; MUS onkai 音階

scales *(for person)* taijūkei 体重計

scan v/t *page* … ni zatto me o tōsu …にざっと目を通す; COMPUT sukyanā o kakeru スキャンをかける; MED sukyan o kakeru スキャンをかける; COMPUT sukyanā o kakete kopī suru スキャナーをかけてコピーする

scandal sukyandaru スキャンダル

scanner MED sukyan スキャン; COMPUT sukyanā スキャナー

scar 1 n kizuato 傷跡 **2** v/t … ni kizuato o nokosu …に傷跡を残す

scarce fujūbun (na) 不十分(な)

scarcely hotondo…nai ほとんど…ない

scare v/t kowagaraseru 怖がらせる; **be ~d of** kowagaru 怖がる

scarf (around neck) mafurā マフラー; (over head) sukāfu スカーフ

scary kowai 怖い

scatter 1 v/t leaflets baramaku ばらまく **2** v/i (of crowd) chirijiri ni naru ちりぢりになる

scenario sujigaki 筋書き; (of movie) shinario シナリオ

scene THEAT ba 場; (view) jōkyō 情況; (of crime etc) genba 現場; (argument)

ōsawagi 大騒ぎ

scenery keshiki 景色; THEAT butai-sōchi 舞台装置

scent n (smell) kaori 香り

schedule n (of events, work) sukejūru スケジュール; (for trains etc) jikokuhyō 時刻表; **be on ~** (of work) yotei dōri de aru 予定どおりである; **be behind ~** yotei yori okureru 予定より遅れる

scheduled flight teikibin 定期便

scheme n keikaku 計画; (plot) takurami たくらみ

schizophrenia seishin-bunretsushō 精神分裂症

scholarship gakumon 学問; (financial award) shōgakukin 奨学金

schoolboy danshi-seito 男子生徒

schoolchildren seito 生徒

school days gakusei-jidai 学生時代

schoolgirl joshi-seito 女子生徒

schoolteacher sensei 先生

science kagaku 科学

science fiction esu-efu SF

scientific kagakuteki (na) 科学的(な)

scientist kagakusha 科学者

scissors hasami はさみ

♦**scoff at** azawarau あざ笑う

scold v/t shikaru しかる

scooter sukūtā スクーター

scope han'i 範囲;
(opportunity) yochi 余地

scorch v/t kogasu 焦がす

score SPORTS **1** n tokuten 得
点 **2** v/t & v/i tokuten suru 得
点する

scorn n keibetsu 軽べつ

scornful keibetsu shita 軽べ
つした

scowl n shikamettsura しか
めっ面

scrap 1 n *(metal)* kuzu くず;
(little bit) sukoshi 少し **2** v/t
plan etc yameru やめる

scrape v/t *paint, arm* kosuru
こする

scratch 1 n *(mark)* hikkakikizu
引っかき傷 **2** v/t *skin, paint*
hikkaku 引っかく; *(because
of itch)* kaku かく

scream 1 n himei 悲鳴 **2** v/i
himei o ageru 悲鳴をあげる

screen 1 n *(in room)* tsuitate つ
いたて, *(decorative)* byōbu
屏風, *(protective)* maku 幕;
(for movie) sukurīn スクリー
ン; COMPUT gamen 画面 **2** v/t
(protect, hide) ōikakusu 覆い
隠す, *(for security)* shinsa suru
審査する

screw n neji ねじ

screwdriver doraibā ドラ
イバー

scribble n hashirigaki 走り
書き

script *(for play)* kyakuhon 脚
本; *(writing)* moji 文字

scriptwriter kyakuhon-ka
脚本家

scroll n makimono 巻き物

scrub v/t *floor, hands*
goshigoshi arau ごしごし
洗う

scruples ryōshin no togame 良
心のとがめ

scrutinize menmitsu ni
shiraberu 綿密に調べる

scuba diving sukyūba daibingu
スキューバダイビング

sculpture n chōkoku 彫刻

sea umi 海; *by the* ~ kaigan
海岸

seafood gyokairui 魚介類,
shīfūdo シーフード

seafront kaigandōri 海岸通り

seal 1 n *(on document)* inshō 印
章 **2** v/t *container* mippei suru
密閉する

♦**seal off** *area* fūsa suru 封
鎖する

sea level: *above* ~ kaibatsu
海抜; *below* ~ kaimenka
海面下

seam n *(on garment)* nuime
縫い目

search 1 n chōsa 調査 2 v/t sagasu 捜す

♦ **search for** sagasu 捜す

searchlight sāchiraito サーチライト

search party sōsaku-tai 捜索隊

seasick funayoi (no) 船酔い(の)

season n (of year) kisetsu 季節; (for tourism etc) shīzun シーズン

seasoning chōmiryō 調味料

season ticket (for bus etc) teikiken 定期券; (for football etc) shīzun chiketto シーズンチケット

seat n zaseki 座席; (of pants) shiri しり

seat belt shīto-beruto シートベルト

seaweed kaisō 海草, (edible) nori のり

secluded hitozato hanareta 人里離れた

second 1 n (of time) byō 秒 2 adj dai-ni (no) 第二 (の) 3 adv come ni-i de 二位で

secondary education chūtō-kyōiku 中等教育

second best adj nibanme ni yoi 二番目によい

second class adj ticket nitō 二等

secondhand adj chūko (no) 中古(の)

secondly dai-ni ni 第二に

second-rate niryū (no) 二流(の)

secrecy himitsu ni suru koto 秘密にすること

secret n himitsu 秘密

secretary hisho 秘書; POL daijin 大臣

Secretary of State Kokumu-chōkan 国務長官

secretive himitsu-shugi (no) 秘密主義(の)

sect shūha 宗派

section bubun 部分; (of text) shō 章; (of company) ...bu …部

sector (of city) kuiki 区域

secure adj shelf etc kotei sareta 固定された; feeling antei shita 安定した

security (in job) hoshō 保証; (guarantee) tanpo 担保; (at airport etc) keibi 警備

security guard keibi-in 警備員

sedan AUTO sedan セダン

sedative n chinseizai 鎮静剤

seduce yūwaku suru 誘惑する

see miru 見る; (understand) wakaru わかる; can I ~ the manager? manējā ni aemasu ka マネージャーに会えますか; **~ you!** mata ne またね

◆**see off** (at airport etc) okuru 送る

seed tane 種

seeing (that) ... de aru kara ...であるから

seek v/t job sagasu 捜す

seem ... no yō ni mieru ...のように見える

seemingly mita tokoro de wa 見たところでは

segment ichibu 一部

segregate bunri suru 分離する

seize tsukamu つかむ; chance toraeru とらえる; (of customs etc) ōshū suru 押収する

seldom mettani ... nai めったに...ない

select 1 v/t erabidasu 選び出す **2** adj (exclusive) erabareta 選ばれた

selection sentaku 選択; (that chosen) senbatsu 選抜

selective sentaku suru chikara no aru 選択する力のある

self-confidence jishin 自信

self-conscious uchiki (na) 内気(な)

self-defense jiko-bōei 自己防衛

self-employed jieigyō (no) 自営業(の)

selfish wagamama (na) わがまま(な)

self-respect jisonshin 自尊心

self-service adj serufu-sābisu (no) セルフサービス(の)

sell v/t & v/i uru 売る

semester gakki 学期

semi (truck) torērā トレーラー

semicircle han'en 半円

semifinal junkesshō 準決勝

seminar seminā セミナー

senate jōin 上院

senator jōin-gi-in 上院議員

send v/t okuru 送る

senile mōroku shita もうろくした

senior nenchō (no) 年長(の); (in rank) jōi (no) 上位(の)

senior citizen kōreisha 高齢者

sensation (feeling) kankaku 感覚; (surprise event) sensēshon センセーション; (sb/sth very good) daininki 大人気

sensational sensēshonaru (na) センセーショナル(な); (very good) subarashī 素晴らしい

sense n (meaning) imi 意味; (purpose, point) ito 意図; (common ~) jōshiki 常識; (of sight, smell etc) kankaku 感覚; (feeling) kanji 感じ

sensible jōshiki no aru 常識
のある; *advice* kenmei (na)
賢明(な)

sensitive *skin* binkan (na) 敏感
(な); *person* shinkeishitsu (na)
神経質(な)

sensuality kōshoku 好色

sentence *n* GRAM bun 文; JUR
senkoku 宣告

sentimental kanshōteki (na) 感
傷的(な)

separate 1 *adj* wakeru 分け
る **2** *v/t* wakeru 分ける;
people hikihanasu 引き離す
3 *v/i* (*of couple*) bekkyo suru
別居する

separated *couple* bekkyo shita
別居した

separation bunri 分離; (*of
couple*) bekkyo 別居

September kugatsu 九月

sequel tsuzuki 続き

sequence *n* renzoku 連続

sergeant MIL gunsō 軍曹;
(*police*) junsa-buchō 巡査
部長

serial *n* rensai 連載

serial number seizō-bangō 製
造番号

series renzoku 連続

serious *situation, damage* jūdai
(na) 重大(な); *illness* omoi
重い; (*earnest*) majime (na)
まじめ(な)

seriously *injured* hidoku ひ
どく

serve 1 *n* (*in tennis*) sābu サ
ーブ **2** *v/t food* dasu 出す;
customer ... no yō o ukagau
…の用をうかがう **3** *v/i*
(*in job*) tsutomeru 勤める; (*in
tennis*) sābu suru サーブする

service 1 *n* (*to customers*)
sābisu サービス **2** *v/t vehicle,
machine* tenken-shūri suru 点
検修理する

service charge sābisuryō サ
ービス料

service industry sābisu-
sangyō サービス産業

service station gasorin
sutando ガソリンスタンド

session kaigi 会議; (*with
consultant etc*) sōdan 相談

set 1 *n* (*of tools, books etc*)
isshiki 一式; THEAT setto セッ
ト; (*for movie*) satsuei-genba
撮影現場; (*in tennis*) setto セ
ット **2** *v/t* (*place*) oku 置く;
date, time sadameru 定める;
alarm clock awaseru 合わせ
る; ~ **the table** shokutaku no
yōi o suru 食卓の用意をす
る **3** *v/i* (*of sun*) shizumu 沈
む; (*of glue*) katamaru 固まる
4 *adj* kata ni hamatta 型
にはまった; ~ **meal** teishoku
定食

setback kōtai 後退

settle 1 *v/i (of dust)* shizumeru 静める; *(to live)* ochitsuku 落ち着く **2** *v/t dispute* ketchaku o tsukeru 決着をつける; *debts* harau 払う

settlement *(of claim, debt)* kessai 決済; *(of dispute)* ketchaku 決着

sever *arm, cable etc* setsudan suru 切断する

several 1 *adj* ikutsu ka (no) 幾つか(の); *people* ikunin ka (no) 幾人か(の) **2** *pron* ikutsu ka 幾つか

severe *penalty, winter* kibishī 厳しい; *teacher* genkaku (na) 厳格(な)

sew *v/t* nū 縫う

sewer gesuidō 下水道

sewing *(skill)* saihō 裁縫

sex *(act)* sekkusu セックス; *(gender)* seibetsu 性別

sexual seiteki (na) 性的(な)

sexy sekushī (na) セクシー(な)

shabby *coat etc* yoreyore (no) よれよれ(の)

shade *n* hikage 日陰; *(for lamp)* kasa かさ; *(of color)* iroai 色合い; *(on window)* buraindo ブラインド

shadow *n* kage 陰

shady hikage (no) 日陰(の);

dealings ikagawashī いかがわしい

shake 1 *v/t* furu 振る; ~ *hands* akushu suru 握手する **2** *v/i* furueru 震える; *(of building)* yureru 揺れる

shallow asai 浅い; *person* asahaka (na) 浅はか(な)

shame 1 *n* haji 恥; *what a ~!* zannen da 残念だ **2** *v/t* hazukashimeru 辱める

shampoo *n* shanpū シャンプー

shape *n* katachi 形

share 1 *n* wakemae 分け前; FIN kabu 株 **2** *v/t* wakeru 分ける; *opinion* wakachiau 分かち合う

shareholder kabunushi 株主

shark same さめ

sharp *adj knife* surudoi 鋭い; *mind* rikō (na) 利口(な); *pain* hageshī 激しい; *taste* piritto shita ピリッとした

shatter *v/t* konagona ni waru 粉々に割る; *illusion* dainashi ni suru 台無しにする

shattering *news, experience* shokkingu (na) ショッキング(な)

shave *v/t & v/i* soru そる

shaver denki-kamisori 電気かみそり

shawl shōru ショール

she ◊ kanojo 彼女
◊ *(omission)*: *who is ~?* are
wa dare desu ka あれは誰
ですか

shed[1] *v/t blood, tears* nagasu
流す

shed[2] *n* koya 小屋

sheep hitsuji 羊

sheer *adj madness, luxury*
mattaku (no) 全くの; *cliffs*
kiritatta 切り立った

sheet *(for bed)* shītsu シーツ

shelf tana 棚; *shelves* tana 棚

shell *n* kaigara 貝殻; *(of egg)*
kara 殻; MIL bakuhatsubutsu
爆発物

shellfish kōkakurui 甲殻類

shelter 1 *n (refuge)* hinansho
避難所; *(construction)*
amayadori no basho 雨宿りの
場所 **2** *v/i* hinan suru 避難す
る **3** *v/t* mamoru 守る

shift 1 *n (in attitude)* henka 変
化; *(at work)* kōtai 交替
2 *v/t (move)* ugokasu 動かす
3 *v/i (move)* ugoku 動く; *(in
opinion)* kawaru 変わる

shift work kōtaisei no shigoto
交替制の仕事

shine *v/i (of sun etc)*
kagayaku 輝く **2** *v/t light*
terasu 照らす

shingles MED obijō-hōshin 帯
状疱疹

Shinto Shintō 神道

Shinto altar kamidana 神棚

Shinto priest kannushi 神主

ship 1 *n* fune 船 **2** *v/t (send)*
okuru 送る; *(by sea)* funabin
de okuru 船便で送る

shipment kamotsu-yusō 貨
物輸送

shipyard zōsensho 造船所

shirt shatsu シャツ

shiver *v/i* furueru 震える

shock 1 *n* shokku ショッ
ク; ELEC dengeki 電撃 **2** *v/t*
shokku o ataeru ショックを
与える

shocking shōgekiteki (na) 衝
撃的(な); *infml (very bad)*
hidoi ひどい

shoe kutsu 靴

shoot *v/t* utsu 撃つ; *(kill)*
uchikorosu 撃ち殺す; *movie*
satsuei suru 撮影する

shop 1 *n* mise 店 **2** *v/i* kaimono
o suru 買い物をする; *go
~ping* kaimono ni iku 買い
物に行く

shopkeeper tenshu 店主

shopper kaimono-kyaku 買
い物客

shopping kaimono 買い物;
(items) katta shinamono 買っ
た品物

shore kishi 岸

short *adj (in height)* se no hikui

背の低い; *distance, time* mijikai 短い; **be ~ of** ... ga tarinai ⋯が足りない

shortage fusoku 不足

shortcoming ketten 欠点

shortcut chikamichi 近道

shorten *v/t* mijikaku suru 短くする

shortfall fusoku 不足

short-lived tsukanoma (no) つかの間(の)

shortly *(soon)* sugu ni すぐに

shorts hanzubon 半ズボン; *(underwear)* pantsu パンツ

shortsighted kingan (no) 近眼(の)

short story tanpen-shōsetsu 短編小説

short-term tankikan (no) 短期間(の)

shot hassha 発射; *(photo)* shotto ショット

shotgun sandanjū 散弾銃

should ...subeki de aru ⋯すべきである; **what ~ I do?** dō shitara ī desu ka どうしたらいいですか; **you ~n't do that** sore o subeki de nai それをすべきでない

shoulder *n* kata 肩

shout 1 *n* ōgoe 大声 **2** *v/i* donaru 怒鳴る **3** *v/t order* ōgoe de iu 大声で言う

shove 1 *n* hito-oshi ひと押し

2 *v/t & v/i* osu

show 1 *n* THEAT. 一; *(display)* hyō 一; *v/t passport* miseru *interest, emotion* arawⁿ す **3** *v/i (be visible)* mieru 見える; *(of movie)* jōei sareru 上映される

shower 1 *n (rain)* niwaka-ame にわか雨; *(to wash)* shawā シャワー **2** *v/i* shawā o abiru シャワーを浴びる

show-off unuboreya うぬぼれや

shred *v/t paper* shureddā ni kakeru シュレッダーにかける; *food* mijingiri ni suru みじん切りにする

shrewd nukeme no nai 抜け目のない

shrimp ebi えび

shrink *v/i (of material)* chijimu 縮む

shrug: ~ (one's shoulders) kata o sukumeru 肩をすくめる

shudder *v/i (of person)* furueru 震える; *(of building)* yureru 揺れる

shun sakeru さける

shut 1 *v/t* shimeru 閉める **2** *v/i* shimaru 閉まる

♦shut up *v/i (be quiet)* damaru 黙る; **~!** damare 黙れ

ttle service orikaeshi-unten 折返し運転

shy hazukashigari (no) 恥ずかしがり (の)

sick byōki (no) 病気(の); *I'm going to be ~ (vomit)* hakisō desu 吐きそうです; *be ~ of …* ni unzari suru …にうんざりする

sick leave byōketsu 病欠

side *n (of box, house)* sokumen 側面; *(of room, field)* gawa 側; *(of mountain)* sanpuku 山腹; *(of person)* waki わき; SPORTS chīmu チーム; *I'm on your ~* watashi wa anata no mikata desu 私はあなたの味方です; *~ by ~* narande 並んで

sideboard shokkidana 食器棚

sideburns momiage もみあげ

side dish tsukeawase 付け合わせ

side effect fukusayō 副作用

side street wakimichi わき道

sidewalk hodō 歩道

sigh 1 *n* tameiki ため息 2 *v/i* tameiki o tsuku ため息をつく

sight *n* kōkei 光景; *(sense)* shiryoku 視力; *~s (of city)* keshiki 景色

sightseeing kankō 観光

sign 1 *n* chōkō 兆候; *(road ~)* hyōshiki 標識; *(on building)*

hyōji 表示 2 *v/t document …* ni shomei suru …に署名する

signal 1 *n* aizu 合図 2 *v/i* AUTO aizu suru 合図する

signature shomei 署名

signature seal inkan 印鑑

significance igi 意義

significant jūyō (na) 重要 (な); *(large)* kanari (no) かなり (の)

sign language shuwa 手話

silence 1 *n* seijaku 静寂; *(of person)* chinmoku 沈黙 2 *v/t* damaraseru 黙らせる

silent shizuka (na) 静か(な)

silk 1 *n* kinu 絹 2 *adj shirt etc* kinu (no) 絹(の)

silly baka (na) ばか(な)

silver 1 *n* gin 銀 2 *adj ring* gin (no) 銀(の)

similar ruiji shita 類似した

similarity ruiji 類似

simple kantan (na) 簡単(な); *person* tanjun (na) 単純(な)

simplicity kantansa 簡単さ

simplify kantan ni suru 簡単にする

simply tan ni 単に; *(absolutely)* mattaku 全く

simultaneous dōji (no) 同時(の)

sin *n* tsumi 罪

since 1 *prep* irai 以来; *~ last week* senshū irai 先週以来

2 *adv* sore irai それ以来

3 *conj* …shite irai …して以来; *(seeing that)* …dakara …だから

sincere seijitsu (na) 誠実 (な)

sincerity seijitsusa 誠実さ

sing *v/t & v/i* utau 歌う

singer kashu 歌手

single *n (sole)* hitotsu dake (no) 一つだけ(の); *(not double)* hitoe no 一重(の); *(not married)* dokushin (no) 独身(の)

single parent family *(father only)* fushi katei 父子家庭; *(mother only)* boshi katei 母子家庭

single room shinguru シングル

sinister ayashige (na) 怪しげ(な)

sink 1 *n* nagashi 流し **2** *v/i (of ship, sun)* shizumu 沈む

sip *v/t* sukoshi zutsu nomu 少しずつ飲む

sir *(to teacher)* sensei 先生; *(to customer)* o-kyakusan お客さん; *excuse me, ~* chotto sumimasen ちょっとすみません

siren sairen サイレン

sister *(own, elder)* ane 姉; *(sb else's, elder)* o-nēsan お姉さ

ん; *(own, younger)* imōto 妹; *(sb else's, younger)* imōtosan 妹さん

sit *v/i* suwaru 座る

♦**sit down** suwaru 座る

sitcom renzoku hōmu komedī 連続ホームコメディー

site *n* basho 場所

sitting room ribingu-rūmu リビングルーム

situated: *be ~* ichi shite iru 位置している

situation jōsei 情勢

size ōkisa 大きさ; *(of jacket, shoes)* saizu サイズ

skate *n* sukēto スケート

skateboard *n* sukēto-bōdo スケートボード

skeptic utagaibukai hito 疑い深い人

skeptical kaigiteki na 懐疑的(な)

skepticism kaigi 懐疑

sketch 1 *n* suketchi スケッチ; THEAT shōhin 小品 **2** *v/t* shasei suru 写生する

ski 1 *n* sukī スキー **2** *v/i* sukī o suru スキーをする

skid 1 *n* surippu スリップ **2** *v/i* surippu suru スリップする

skiing sukī スキー

ski lift sukī-rifuto スキーリフト

skill gijutsu 技術

skilled jukuren (no) 熟練(の)

skillful jōzu (na) 上手(な)

skin n hifu 皮膚

skinny yaseta やせた

skip 1 n (little jump) sukippu スキップ 2 v/t (omit) tobasu 飛ばす

skirt n sukāto スカート

skull zugaikotsu 頭がい骨

sky sora 空

skyscraper chōkōsō-biru 超高層ビル

slack rope yurui ゆるい; discipline tarunda たるんだ; person ikagen (na) いい加減(な); period kakki no nai 活気のない

slacken v/t rope yurumeru 緩める; pace otosu 落とす

slam v/t door batan ni shimeru バタンと閉める

slander n waruguchi 悪口

slang surangu スラング

slant v/i katamuku 傾く

slap 1 n hirateuchi 平手打ち 2 v/t pishatto utsu ピシャッと打つ

slash 1 n (cut) kirikizu 切り傷; (punctuation) surasshu スラッシュ 2 v/t costs kirisageru 切り下げる

slaughter n tosatsu と殺; (of people) gyakusatsu 虐殺

slave n dorei 奴隷

sleazy misuborashī みすぼらしい

sleep 1 n nemuri 眠る; go to ~ neru 寝る 2 v/i nemuru 眠る

sleeping bag nebukuro 寝袋

sleeping pill suimin'yaku 睡眠薬

sleepless night nemurenai 眠れない

sleepy town kakki no nai 活気のない; I'm ~ watashi wa nemui 私は眠い

sleeve sode そで

slender figure hossori shita ほっそりした; margin wazuka (na) わずか(な)

slice 1 n hitokire ひときれ 2 v/t loaf etc usuku kiru 薄く切る

slide 1 n (for kids) suberidai 滑り台; PHOT suraido スライド 2 v/i suberu 滑る

slight adj wazuka (na) わずか(な); person kyasha (na) きゃしゃ(な)

slightly sukoshi 少し

slim 1 adj hossori shita ほっそりした; chance wazuka (na) わずか(な) 2 v/i daietto suru ダイエットする

slip v/i (on ice etc) suberu 滑る; (of quality) teika suru 低

smuggling

下する

slipper heyabaki 部屋ばき

slippery suberiyasui 滑りやすい

slit 1 *n (tear)* sakeme 裂け目; *(in skirt)* suritto スリット **2** *v/t* kirihiraku 切り開く

slogan surōgan スローガン

slope 1 *n* katamuki 傾き; *(of mountain)* sanpuku 山腹 **2** *v/i* naname ni naru 斜めになる

sloppy *work* zusan (na) ずさん(な)

slot *n* tōnyūguchi 投入口

slouch *v/i* maekagami ni naru 前かがみになる

slow osoi 遅い

slowly osoku 遅く

slum *n* suramugai スラム街

slump *n* COMM fukeiki 不景気

slurred *speech* fumeiryō (na) 不明りょう(な)

sly zurui ずるい

small *adj* chīsai 小さい

small hours yonaka 夜中

small talk sekenbanashi 世間話

smart *adj* iki (na) いき(な); *(intelligent)* atama ga ī 頭がいい

smash 1 *n* AUTO shōtotsu 衝突 **2** *v/t (break)* mechamecha ni kowasu めちゃめちゃに壊す; *(hit)* kyōda suru 強打する

3 *v/i (break)* konagona ni naru 粉々になる

smear *n (of ink)* shimi 染み; *(on character)* chūshō 中傷

smell 1 *n* nioi におい **2** *v/t* nioi ga suru においがする **3** *v/i (bad)* niou におう

smile 1 *n* hohoemi ほほ笑み **2** *v/i* hohoemu ほほ笑む

smirk *n* niyaniya-warai にやにや笑い

smoke 1 *n* kemuri 煙 **2** *v/t cigarettes* sū 吸う **3** *v/i* tabako o sū たばこを吸う

smoker kitsuenka 喫煙家

smoking kitsuen 喫煙; *no ~* kin'en 禁煙

smolder *(also fig)* kusuburu くすぶる

smooth *adj* nameraka (na) なめらか(な); *ride* shizuka (na) 静か(な); *transition* junchō (na) 順調(な)

smother *flames* ... ni ...o kabusete kesu …に…をかぶせて消す; *person* chissoku saseru 窒息させる

smug hitoriyogari (no) 独りよがり(の)

smuggle *v/t* mitsuyu suru 密輸する

smuggler mitsuyu-gyōsha 密輸業者

smuggling mitsuyu 密輸

snack n keishoku 軽食

snake n hebi 蛇

snap v/t (break) pokin to oru ぽきんと折る; (say sharply) kamitsuku かみつく

snarl n (of dog) unari うなり

sneakers sunīkā スニーカー

sneer v/i azawarau あざ笑う

sneeze 1 n kushami くしゃみ **2** v/i kushami o suru くしゃみをする

sniff v/t (smell) nioi o kagu においをかぐ

sniper sogekihei 狙撃兵

snob kidoriya 気取り屋

snooty gōman (na) ごう慢 (な)

snore v/i ibiki o kaku いびきをかく

snow 1 n yuki 雪 **2** v/i yuki ga furu 雪が降る

snowball yukidama 雪玉

snowplow josetsuki 除雪機

snowstorm fubuki 吹雪

snub n bujoku 侮辱

so 1 adv: ~ hot totemo atsui とても暑い; not ~ much amari あまり; ~ much better zutto yoi ずっと良い; ~ many ... takusan ...たくさん; ~ am I do I watashi mo sō desu わたしもそうです; and ~ on ... nado ...など; ~ what? sore de それで **2** pron:

I hope ~ sō kibō shimasu そう希望します **3** conj (for that reason) sono kekka その結果; (in order that) ... node ...ので

soak v/t (steep) tsukeru つける; (of rain) nurasu ぬらす

soaked bishonure ni natta びしょぬれになった

soap n sekken 石けん

soap (opera) renzoku merodorama 連続メロドラマ

soar (of rocket etc) maiagaru 舞い上がる; (of prices) kyūjōshō suru 急上昇する

sob v/i nakijakuru 泣きじゃくる

sober shirafu (no) しらふ (の)

soccer sakkā サッカー

sociable shakōteki (na) 社交的 (な)

social adj shakai (no) 社会 (の)

socialism shakai-shugi 社会主義

socialist 1 adj shakai-shugi (no) 社会主義の **2** n shakai-shugisha 社会主義者

socialize tsukiau 付き合う

social worker sōsharu-wākā ソーシャルワーカー

society shakai 社会; (organization) kyōkai 協会

sock kutsushita 靴下

socket ELEC soketto ソケット; *(of arm)* kataguchi 肩口

soda *(~ water)* sōda ソーダ; *(ice-cream ~)* kurīmu sōda クリームソーダ; *(soft drink)* saidā サイダー

sofa sofa ソファ

soft yawarakai 柔らかい; *(lenient)* yasashii 優しい

soft drink seiryō-inryōsui 清涼飲料水

software sofuto ソフト

soil *n (earth)* tsuchi 土

solar energy taiyō-enerugī 太陽エネルギー

soldier gunjin 軍人

sole *n* ashi no ura 足の裏; *(of shoe)* kutsu no soko 靴の底

solemn *(serious)* genshuku (na) 厳粛(な)

solid *adj* katai 固い; *gold* junsui (no) 純粋(の); *(sturdy)* ganjō (na) 頑丈(な); *support* shikkari shita しっかりした

solidarity kessoku 結束

solitaire *(game)* hitori toranpu 一人トランプ

solitary *life* kodoku (na) 孤独 (な); *(single)* tatta hitori dake (no) たった一人だけ(の)

solitude kodoku 孤独

solo 1 *n* MUS dokusō 独奏 **2** *adj*

tandoku (no) 単独(の)

solution kaitō 解答; *(mixture)* yōeki 溶液

solve toku 解く

somber *dark* kurai 暗い; *(serious)* shinkoku (na) 深刻(な)

some 1 *adj* aru ある; *(a few, little)* sukoshi no 少しの; **~ people** aru hito ある人 **2** *pron (people)* aru hito ある人; *(things)* aru mono あるもの; *(a few, little)* sukoshi 少し

somebody dareka 誰か

someday itsu no hi ka いつの日か

somehow nantoka shite 何とかして; *(for unknown reason)* nazeka なぜか

someone → *somebody*

someplace → *somewhere*

something nanika 何か

sometimes tokidoki 時々

somewhere *adv (with verbs of being)* dokoka ni どこかに; *(with verbs of activity)* dokoka de どこかで

son musuko 息子

song uta 歌

son-in-law giri no musuko 義理の息子

soon mō sugu もうすぐ; *(a short time after)* sugu ni すぐに; **as ~ as possible** dekiru dake hayaku できるだけ早く

soothe *person* nagusameru なぐさめる

sophisticated senren sareta 洗練された; *machine* kōdo (na) 高度(な)

sore *adj (painful)* itai 痛い

sorrow *n* kanashimi 悲しみ

sorry *sight* sabishisō (na) さびしそう(な); *(I'm) ~! (apologizing)* summimasen すみません; *I'm ~ (regretting)* summimasen ga すみませんが; *I feel ~ for her* kanojo ni dōjō suru 彼女に同情する

sort 1 *n* shurui 種類 2 *v/t* bunrui suru 分類する; COMPUT sōto suru ソートする

sound 1 *n* oto 音 2 *v/i: that ~s interesting* sore wa omoshiro-sō da それはおもしろそうだ

soundproof *adj* bō-on (no) 防音(の)

soup sūpu スープ

sour *adj* suppai 酸っぱい; *milk* suppaku natta 酸っぱくなった

source *n* minamoto 源; *(of river)* suigenchi 水源地

south 1 *adj* minami (no) 南 (の) 2 *n* minami 南; *(of country)* nanbu 南部 3 *adv* minami ni 南に; *(travel)*

minami e 南へ

South Africa Minami-Afurika 南アフリカ

South America Nanbei 南米

Southeast Asia Tōnan Ajia 東南アジ

southern nanbu (no) 南部(の)

South Korea Kankoku 韓国

souvenir o-miyage おみやげ

sovereignty *(of state)* shuken 主権

soy sauce shōyu しょうゆ

space *n (outer ~)* uchū-kūkan 宇宙空間; *(area)* yohaku 余白; *(room)* basho 場所

spacecraft uchūsen 宇宙船

space shuttle supēsushatoru スペースシャトル

spacious hirobiro to shita 広々とした

spade sukoppu スコップ

Spain Supein スペイン

spare 1 *adj* yobi (no) 予備 (の) 2 *n (part)* kōkan-buhin 交換部品

spare ribs supearibu スペアリブ

spare room yobi no heya 予備の部屋

spare time yoka 余暇

spare tire, spare wheel supea taiya スペアタイヤ

spark *n* hibana 火花

spark plug tenka-puragu 点

火プラグ

sparse *vegetation* tenzai suru 点在する

speak *v/i* hanasu 話す; *~ing* TEL watashi desu 私です

speaker *(at conference)* enzetsusha 演説者; *(of sound system)* supīkā スピーカー

special tokubetsu (na) 特別(な)

specialist senmonka 専門家; MED senmon-i 専門医

♦ **specialize in** senmon ni suru 専門にする; *subject* senkō suru 専攻する

specially → **especially**

specialty tokushoku 特色; *(food)* jiman-ryōri 自慢料理

species shu 種

specific tokutei (no) 特定(の)

specify shitei suru 指定する

specimen mihon 見本; MED hyōhon 標本

spectacle *(impressive sight)* supekutakuru スペクタクル

spectator kankyaku 観客

speculate *v/i* okusoku suru 憶測する; FIN tōki suru 投機する

speech *(address)* supīchi スピーチ

speed 1 *n* hayasa 速さ; *(of car, plane etc)* supīdo スピード **2** *v/i* isogu 急ぐ; AUTO

ihan-sokudo de hashiru 違反速度で走る

speeding fine supīdo-ihan no bakkin スピード違反の罰金

speed limit seigen-sokudo 制限速度

**spell² ** *v/t & v/i* tsuzuru つづる

**spell² ** *n (period)* sukoshi no aida 少しの間

spelling superingu スペリング

spend *money* tsukau 使う; *time* sugosu 過ごす

spice *n* kōshinryō 香辛料

spider kumo くも

spill 1 *v/t* kobosu こぼす **2** *v/i* koboreru こぼれる

spin 1 *v/t* kaiten saseru 回転させる **2** *v/i (of wheel)* kaiten suru 回転する

spinach hōrensō ほうれん草

spine sebone 背骨; *(of book)* se 背

spin-off fukusanbutsu 副産物

spiral *n* rasenkei ら旋形

spirit *n (not body)* seishin 精神; *(of dead)* rei 霊; *(energy)* katsuryoku 活力; *(courage)* kiryoku 気力

spirits¹ *(alcohol)* jōryūshu 蒸留酒

spirits² *(morale)* shiki 士気

spiritual *adj* reiteki (na) 霊的(な)

spit v/i (of person) tsuba o haku つばを吐く

spite n akui 悪意

spiteful ijiwaru (na) 意地悪(な)

splash v/t person mizu o tobichirasu 水を飛び散らす; water hanekakeru 跳ねかける

splendid gōka (na) 豪華(な)

splendor gōka 豪華さ

splinter n hahen 破片

split 1 n (in wood) wareme 割れ目; (disagreement) bunretsu 分裂; (division, share) bunpai 分配 **2** v/t logs waru 割る; party etc bunretsu saseru 分裂させる; (divide) wakeru 分ける

spoil v/t dame ni suru だめにする; child amayakasu 甘やかす

spoilsport infml za o shirakesaseru hito 座を白けさせる人

spoilt adj child amayaka sareta 甘やかされた

spokesperson supōkusu-pāson スポークスパーソン

sponsor n (for immigration) hoshōnin 保証人; (of program, event) suponsā スポンサー

sponsorship kōen 後援

spontaneous jihatsuteki (na) 自発的(な)

spoon n supūn スプーン

sporadic barabara (no) バラバラ(の)

sport n supōtsu スポーツ

sportscar supōtsu-kā スポーツカー

sportsman supōtsu-man スポーツマン

sportswoman supōtsu-ūman スポーツウーマン

spot[1] (pimple) nikibi にきび; (from measles etc) dekimono できもの; (in pattern) mizutama 水玉

spot[2] (place) basho 場所

spot[3] v/t (notice, identify) mitsukeru 見つける

spot check nukitori-kensa 抜き取り検査

spotlight n supottoraito スポットライト

sprain 1 n nenza ねんざ **2** v/t nenza suru ねんざする

sprawl v/i (of city) zatsuzen to shita basho 雑然とした場所

spray n (water) shibuki しぶき; (paint, for hair) supurē スプレー

spread 1 n (of disease, religion) hirogari 広がり **2** v/t (lay) hirogeru 広げる; butter nuru 塗る; news, disease hiromeru

広める 3 *v/i* hiromaru 広
まる

spring[1] *n (season)* haru 春

spring[2] *n (device)* bane ばね

springboard tobi-ita 飛び板

sprinkle *v/t* furikakeru ふり
かける

sprint 1 *n* SPORTS tankyori-
kyōsō 短距離競走 **2** *v/i*
zensokuryoku de hashiru 全速
力で走る

spurt 1 *n (in race)* supāto スパ
ート **2** *v/i (of liquid)* fukidasu
噴き出す

spy *n* supai スパイ

♦**spy on** saguru さぐる

squalid fuketsu (na) 不潔(な)

squander *money* rōhi suru 浪
費する

square 1 *adj* seihōkei (no)
正方形(の); **~ mile** heihō
mairu 平方マイル **2** *n*
seihōkei 正方形; *(in town)*
hiroba 広場

squash[1] *n (vegetable)* urirui
うり類

squash[2] *n (game)* sukasshu
スカッシュ

squash[3] *v/t (crush)* tsubureru
つぶれる

squat shagamu しゃがむ;
(illegally) fuhō-kyojū suru 不
法居住する

squeak *v/i (of mouse)* chūchū

naku チューチュー鳴く;
(of hinge) kīkī naru キーキー
一鳴る

squeeze *v/t (press)* gyutto
nigirishimeru ぎゅっと握り
締める; *orange* gyutto shiboru
ぎゅっと絞る

squint *n* shashi 斜視

stab *v/t* sasu 刺す

stability antei 安定

stable *adj* antei shita 安定した

stadium kyōgijō 競技場

staff *n (employees)* sha-in 社員;
(teachers, in government office)
shoku-in 職員

stage[1] *(in project)* dankai 段階;
(of journey) kōtei 行程

stage[2] *n* THEAT butai 舞台

stagger *v/i* yoromeku よろ
めく

stain 1 *n (mark)* shimi 染み;
(for wood) chakushokuzai 着
色剤 **2** *v/t (dirty)* yogosu 汚
す; *wood* chakushoku suru 着
色する

stainless steel *n* sutenresu ス
テンレス

stair dan 段; *the ~s* kaidan
階段

stake *n (of wood)* kui くい;
(gambling) kakekin 賭け金;
(investment) tōshi 投資

stale *bread* furuku natta 古く
なった

stall *v/i (of vehicle)* ensuto
suru エンストする; *(for
time)* jikankasegi suru 時間
稼ぎする

stamina sutamina スタミナ

stammer 1 *n* domori どもり
2 *v/i* domoru どもる

stamp 1 *n (for letter)* kitte 切
手 **2** *v/t passport* sutanpu o osu
スタンプを押す

stance *(position)* shisei 姿勢

stand 1 *n (at exhibition)*
sutando スタンド **2** *v/i
(not sit)* tatsu 立つ; *(rise)*
tachiagaru 立ち上がる
3 *v/t (tolerate)* gaman suru 我
慢する

♦ **stand by** *v/i (be ready)* taiki
suru 待機する **2** *v/t person*
shiji suru 支持する; *decision*
koshu suru 固守する

♦ **stand for** *(represent)* ... no
ryaku de aru ...の略である

♦ **stand up** *v/i* tachiagaru 立
ち上がる

standard 1 *adj (usual)* tsūrei no
通例(の) **2** *n (level)* suijun 水
準; *(norm)* kikaku 規格

standardize *v/t* kikakuka suru
規格化する

standard of living seikatsu-
suijun 生活水準

standby: on ~ *(for flight)* キャン
kyanseru machi (no) キャン

seru machi (no)
セル待ち(の)

standpoint kanten 観点

standstill: be at a ~ teishi shite
iru 停止している

staple diet shushoku 主食

stapler hotchikisu ホッチ
キス®

star 1 *n* hoshi 星; *fig* sutā スタ
ー; *four-~ hotel etc* yotsuboshi
(no) 四つ星(の) **2** *v/i (in
movie)* shuen suru 主演する

stare: ~ at niramu にらむ

Stars and Stripes Seijōki
星条旗

start 1 *n* hajimari 始まり
2 *v/i* hajimaru 始まる; *(of
car)* shidō suru 始動する
3 *v/t* hajimeru 始める; *engine*
shidō suru 始動する; *business*
sōritsu suru 創立する

starter *(of meal)* zensai 前菜;
AUTO sutātā スターター

starvation kiga 飢餓

starve *v/i* ueru 飢える

state¹ 1 *n (condition)* jōtai
状態; *(of country)* shū 州;
(country) kokka 国家; *the
States* Beikoku 米国 **2** *adj
capital etc* shū (no) 州(の)

state² *v/t* noberu 述べる

State Department
Kokumushō 国務省

statement *(police)* chinjutsu
陳述; *(announcement)* seimei

声明書; (bank) kōza-shūshi-hōkokusho 口座収支報告書

state-of-the-art *adj* saishin-gijutsu (no) 最新技術(の)

statesman ōmono-seijika 大物政治家

station *n* RAIL eki 駅; RADIO, TV channeru チャンネル

stationary tomatte iru 止まっている

statistics (science) tōkeigaku 統計学; (figures) tōkei 統計

statue zō 像

status chi-i 地位; (class) mibun 身分

status symbol suteitasu-shinboru ステイタスシンボル

stay 1 *n* taizai 滞在 **2** *v/i* taizai suru 滞在する; (in a condition) ... no mama de iru …のままでいる; **~ in a hotel** hoteru ni tomaru ホテルに泊まる; **~ right there!** soko o ugokanaide そこを動かないで

steady *adj* (not shaking) shikkari shita しっかりした; (regular) antei shita 安定した

steak sutēki ステーキ

steal *v/t* nusumu 盗む

steam *n* suijōki 水蒸気

steamer (for cooking) mushiki 蒸し器

steel *n* kōtetsu 鋼鉄

steep *adj* hill etc kewashii 険しい

steer *v/t* unten suru 運転する

steering wheel handoru ハンドル

step *n* (pace) ippo 一歩; (stair) dan 段; (measure) kōdō 行動

♦ **step down** (from post) jinin suru 辞任する

stereo *n* sutereo ステレオ

stereotype *n* sutereotaipu ステレオタイプ

sterilize hinin-shujutsu o suru 避妊手術をする; equipment sakkin suru 殺菌する

stern *adj* kibishī 厳しい

steroids suteroido ステロイド

stew *n* shichū シチュー

steward (on plane, ship) suchuwādo スチュワード

stewardess suchuwādesu スチュワーデス

stick *n* bōkire 棒切れ; (of policeman) konbō こん棒

stick² **1** *v/t* (glue) haritsukeru はり付ける **2** *v/i* hittsuku 引っ付く; (jam) ugokanaku naru 動かなくなる

sticky betobeto shita べとべとした; label nori no tsuita のりの付いた

stiff *adj* leather katai 堅い; muscle kowabatta こわばっ

た; *(in manner)* katakurushī 堅
苦しい; *competition* kibishī
厳しい

stifle v/t *yawn* osaeru 抑え
る; *debate* yokuatsu suru 抑
圧する

stifling ikigurushī 息苦しい

stigma omei 汚名

still¹ 1 *adj* shizuka (na) 静か
(な) 2 *adv* ugokanaide 動か
ないで; *keep ~!* ugokanaide
動かないで

still² *adv (yet)* mada まだ;
(nevertheless) sore demo それ
でも; *~ more* sara ni さらに

stillborn: be ~ shizan shita 死
産した

stimulant kakuseizai 覚せい剤

stimulate *person* kōfun saseru
興奮させる

stimulation shigeki 刺激

stimulus *(incentive)* shigeki
刺激

sting 1 v/t *(of bee, jellyfish)* sasu
刺す 2 v/i *(of eyes)* hirihiri
suru ひりひりする

stipulate jōken to suru 条件
とする

stir v/t kakimazeru かき混
ぜる

stir-fry v/t tsuyobi de itameru
強火でいためる

stitch 1 n *(sewing)* hitohari 一
針; *(knitting)* hitoami 一編

み; *~es* MED hōgō 縫合 2 v/t
(sew) nū 縫う

stock 1 n *(reserves)* shigen 資
源; *(COMM: in store)* shōhin 商
品; FIN kabushiki 株式; *be
in ~* zaiko ga aru 在庫があ
る 2 v/t COMM mise ni oku 店
に置く

stockbroker kabushiki-
nakagainin 株式仲買人

stock exchange shōken-
torihikisho 証券取引所

stockholder kabunushi 株主

stock market kabushiki-shijō
株式市場

stockpile n bichiku 備蓄

stomach n i 胃; *(abdomen)*
o-naka おなか

stomach-ache fukutsū 腹痛

stone n *(material)* ishi 石;
(pebble) koishi 小石

stony *ground* ishi darake (no)
石だらけ(の)

stoop v/i *(bend)* kagamu かが
む; *(have bent back)* koshi ga
magaru 腰が曲がる

stop 1 n *(for train)* eki 駅; *(for
bus)* teiryūjo 停留所 2 v/t *(put
an end to, prevent)* yamesaseru
やめさせる; *(cease)* yameru
やめる; *car* tomeru 止める
3 v/i tomaru 止まる; *(of rain,
snow)* yamu やむ

stopover *(in air travel)* tochūkōki 途中降機

stop sign ichiji-teishi-hyōshiki
一時停止標識

storage hokan 保管

store 1 n mise 店; (stock)
takuwae 蓄え; (storehouse)
sōko 倉庫 **2** v/t shimau しまう

storm n arashi あらし

stormy aremoyō (no) 荒れ模
様(の); relationship hageshī
激しい

story[1] monogatari 物語; (in
newspaper) kiji 記事

story[2] (of building) kai 階

stove (for cooking) renji レン
ジ; (for heating) sutōbu ス
トーブ

straight 1 adj massugu (na) ま
っすぐ(な); (honest) shōjiki
(na) 正直(な); whiskey etc
sutorēto (no) ストレート
(の) **2** adv (in a straight
line) massugu ni まっすぐ
に; (directly) sugu ni すぐに;
carry ~ on (of driver etc) sono-
mama massugu iku そのま
ままっすぐ行く; ~away sugu
ni すぐに

straighten v/t massugu ni suru
まっすぐにする

straightforward shōjiki (na)
正直(な); (simple) tanjun (na)
単純(な)

strand v/t: be ~ed ashidome

sareru 足留めされる

strange (odd) hen (na) 変
(な); (unknown) shiranai 知
らない

stranger mishiranu hito 見知
らぬ人

strap n (of purse, dress)
katahimo 肩ひも; (of watch)
bando バンド

strategy senryaku 戦略

straw mugiwara 麦わら

strawberry ichigo いちご

stream n ogawa 小川

street tōri 通り

streetcar romen-densha 路
面電車

strength tsuyosa 強さ; (of
emotion, currency, physical
~) chikara 力; (strong point)
tsuyomi 強み

strengthen v/t tsuyoku suru
強くする

stress 1 n (emphasis) jūten 重
点; (tension) sutoresu ストレ
ス **2** v/t importance etc kyōchō
suru 強調する

stressful sutoresu no ōi スト
レスの多い

stretch 1 n (of land, water)
hirogari 広がり **2** v/t material
nobasu 伸ばす; income
yarikuri suru やりくりす
る **3** v/i (to relax) nobi o suru
伸びをする; (to reach sth)

karada o nobasu 体を伸ばす;
(extend) hirogaru 広がる
strict kibishī 厳しい; *orders*
genmitsu (na) 厳密(な)
stride n ōmata 大また
strike 1 n *(of workers)* sutoraiki
ストライキ; *(in baseball)*
sutoraiku ストライク; *be
on* ~ sutoraikichū de aru ス
トライキ中である **2** v/i *(of
disaster)* osou 襲う **3** v/t *(hit)*
utsu 打つ; *oil* hakken suru 発
見する
string n himo ひも; *(of violin
etc)* gen 弦; *(of tennis racket)*
gatto ガット
strip 1 v/t *(remove)* hagasu は
がす **2** v/i *(undress)* hadaka ni
naru 裸になる
stripe shima しま
strive: ~ *for* ... no tame ni
doryoku suru …のために
努力する
stroke n MED nōshukketsu 脳
出血; *(in writing)* kaku 画; *(in
Chinese characters)* kakusū 画
数; *(swimming)* eihō 泳法
2 v/t naderu なでる
stroll n sanpo 散歩
stroller *(for baby)* isugata-
bebīka いす型ベビーカー
strong tsuyoi 強い; *structure*
ganjō (na) 頑丈(な); *tea,
coffee, taste* koi 濃い; *views*

kyōko (na) 強固(な)
structural kōzōteki (na) 構造
的(な)
structure n kōsei 構成; *(sth
built)* kōzō 構造
struggle 1 n *(fight)* arasoi 争
い; *(hard time)* kutō 苦闘 **2** v/i
(have a hard time) kurō suru
苦労する
stub n *(of cigarette)* suigara
吸い殻
stubborn ganko (na) 頑固
(な); *defense* kyōko (na) 強
固(な)
stuck-up infml kōmanchiki
(na) 高慢ちき(な)
student *(at high school)* seito
生徒; *(at university)* gakusei
学生
studio *(of artist)* atorie アトリ
エ; *(recording, TV)* sutajio ス
タジオ; *(film)* satsueisho 撮
影所; *(apartment)* wanrūmu-
manshon ワンルームマン
ション
study 1 n *(in room)* shosai 書
斎; *(learning)* benkyō 勉強;
(investigation) kenkyū 研究
2 v/t *(at school)* benkyō
suru 勉強する; *(examine)*
shiraberu 調べる **3** v/i benkyō
suru 勉強する
stuff n mono 物
stuffing tsumemono 詰め物

stuffy *room* mutto shita むっ
とした; *person* furukusai 古
くさい

stumble *vi* tsumazuku つ
まずく

stumbling block shōgai 障害

stun kizetsu saseru 気絶させ
る; *(of news)* shokku o ataeru
ショックを与える

stupid baka (na) ばか(な)

stupidity orokasa 愚かさ

stutter *vi* domoru どもる

style *n* yōshiki 様式; *(fashion)*
ryūkō 流行; *(elegance)* sutairu
スタイル

subconscious: *the ~* senzai-
ishiki 潜在意識

subcontract *v/t* shitauke saseru
下請けさせる

subcontractor shitauke-gaisha
下請け会社

subdued shizuka (na) 静
か(な)

subject *n (topic)* shudai 主題;
(of learning) kamoku 科目;
GRAM shugo 主語

subjective shukanteki (na) 主
観的(な)

submarine sensuikan 潜水艦

submissive jūjun (na) 従
順(な)

submit *v/t plan* teishutsu suru
提出する

subordinate *n* buka 部下

♦**subscribe to** *magazine* teiki-
kōdoku suru 定期購読する

subscription kōbai-keiyaku
購買契約

subside *(of flood)* hiku ひく;
(of wind) yamu やむ; *(of
building)* chinka suru 沈下する

subsidiary *n* kogaisha 子会社

subsidy joseikin 助成金

substance *(matter)* busshitsu
物質

substantial sōtō (na) 相当
(な); *meal* tappuri shita たっ
ぷりした

substitute *n (person)* dairi 代
理; *(commodity)* daiyōhin 代
用品; SPORTS hoketsu 補欠

subtitle *n* jimaku 字幕

subtle bimyō (na) 微妙(な);
person kōmyō (na) 巧妙(な)

subtract *v/t* hiku 引く

suburb kōgai 郊外; *the ~s*
kōgai 郊外

subway chikatetsu 地下鉄

succeed *vi* seikō suru 成
功する

success seikō 成功

successful seikō shita 成
功した

successive renzoku shite 連
続して

successor kōninsha 後任者

such 1 *adj*: *~ a (so much of
a)* sonna そんな; *it was ~*

a surprise! sore wa hontō ni odoroki datta それは本当に驚きだった **2** *adv* totemo とても; *~ a nice day* totemo o-tenki no ī hi とてもお天気のいい日

suck *candy* nameru なめる

sudden totsuzen (no) 突然(の)

suddenly totsuzen 突然

sue *v/t* kiso suru 起訴する

suffer *v/i* kurushimu 苦しむ

sufficient jūbun (na) 十分(な)

suffocate *v/i* chissoku suru 窒息する

sugar *n* satō 砂糖

suggest teian suru 提案する

suggestion teian 提案

suicide jisatsu 自殺; *commit ~* jisatsu suru 自殺する

suit 1 *n* sūtsu スーツ **2** *v/t (of clothes, color)* … ni niau …に似合う

suitable tekitō (na) 適当(な)

suitcase sūtsukēsu スーツケース

suite *(rooms)* suīto-rūmu スイートルーム; *(furniture)* kagu-isshiki 家具一式

sulk *v/i* suneru すねる

sum *(total)* gōkei 合計; *(amount)* kingaku 金額; *(in arithmetic)* keisan-mondai 計算問題

summarize *v/t* yōyaku suru 要

約する

summary *n* yōyaku 要約

summer natsu 夏

summit chōjō 頂上; POL samitto サミット

summon yobu 呼ぶ

sumo wrestler sumōtori 相撲取り

sun taiyō 太陽; *in the ~* hinata de 日なたで

sunbathe nikkōyoku suru 日光浴する

sunblock hiyakedome 日焼け止め

sunburn hiyake 日焼け

Sunday nichiyōbi 日曜日

sunglasses sangurasu サングラス

sunrise hinode 日の出

sunset nichibotsu 日没

suntan hiyake 日焼け

superb subarashī 素晴らしい

superficial hyōmenteki (na) 表面的(な); *person* usupperai 薄っぺらい

superfluous yokei (na) 余計(な)

superintendent *(of apartments)* kanrinin 管理人

superior 1 *adj (better)* yori sugureta よりすぐれた **2** *n (in organization)* jōshi 上司

supermarket sūpāmāketto スーパーマーケット

superpower POL chōtaikoku
超大国

superstitious meishin-bukai
迷信深い

supervise kantoku suru 監
督する

supervisor *(at work)* kantoku
監督

supper yūshoku 夕食

supplier COMM nōnyū-gyōsha
納入業者

supply 1 *n* kyōkyū 供給 **2** *v/t*
kyōkyū suru 供給する

support 1 *n* shichū 支柱;
(backing) shien 支援
2 *v/t structure* sasaeru 支える;
(financially) yashinau 養う;
(back) shiji suru 支持する

supporter shijisha 支持者;
SPORTS fan ファン

supportive kyōryokuteki (na)
協力的(な)

suppose *(imagine)* …da to
omou …だと思う; *be ~d to*
… *(be meant to)* … suru hazu
ni natte iru …するはずに
なっている; *(said to be)* …
to iwarete iru …と言われて
いる; *you are not ~d to* …
(not allowed) …shite wa ikenai
koto ni natte iru …しては
けない事になっている

suppress *feelings* osaeru 抑
える

Supreme Court Saikō-
saibansho 最高裁判所

sure 1 *adj*: *I'm ~* hontō desu
本当です; *I'm not ~* yoku
wakarimasen よくわかりま
せん **2** *adv*: *~!* mochiron も
ちろん

surely *(in negative sentence)*
masaka まさか; *(in affirmative
sentence)* kitto きっと;
(gladly) mochiron もちろん

surf 1 *n (on sea)* uchiyoseru
nami 打ち寄せる波 **2** *v/t*: ~
the Net netto sāfin o suru ネ
ットサーフィンをする

surface *n* hyōmen 表面; *(of
water)* suimen 水面

surfing sāfin サーフィン

surge *n (growth)* kyūzō 急増

surgeon gekai 外科医

surgery geka 外科

surname myōji 名字

surplus *adj* yojō (no) 余剰(の)

surprise 1 *n* odoroki 驚き
2 *v/t* odorokasu 驚かす; *be
~d* odoroita yō da 驚いた
ようだ

surprising odoroku beki 驚
くべき

surrender *v/i* MIL kōfuku suru
降伏する

surround *v/t* kakomu 囲む

surroundings kankyō 環境

survival seizon 生存

survive 1 *v/i (of species)* ikinokoru 生き残る
2 *v/t accident* ikinobiru 生き延びる

survivor seizonsha 生存者

suspect 1 *n* yōgisha 容疑者 **2** *v/t person* utagau 疑う; *(suppose)* ... to omou …と思う

suspend *(from duties)* teishoku-shobun ni suru 停職処分にする

suspense sasupensu サスペンス

suspicion utagai 疑い

suspicious *(causing suspicion)* ayashī 怪しい; *(feeling it)* utagai-bukai 疑い深い

swallow *v/t & v/i* nomikomu 飲み込む

swan hakuchō 白鳥

swear *v/i* akutai o tsuku 悪態をつく; JUR sensei suru 宣誓する

swearword akutai 悪態

sweat 1 *n* ase 汗 **2** *v/i* ase o kaku 汗をかく

sweater sētā セーター

sweatshirt torēnā トレーナー

sweep *v/t floor* haku 掃く

sweet *adj taste* amai 甘い

sweet and sour *adj* amazuppai 甘酸っぱい

sweetcorn tōmorokoshi とうもろこし

sweetener *(for drink)* kanmiryō 甘味料

swell *v/i* hareru 腫れる

swelling *n* MED hare 腫れ

swerve *v/i* soreru それる

swim 1 *v/i* oyogu 泳ぐ **2** *n* suiei 水泳

swimming pool pūru プール

swimsuit mizugi 水着

swindle *n* sagi 詐欺

swing 1 *n (for child)* buranko ブランコ **2** *v/t furu* 振る **3** *v/i* yureru 揺れる; *(turn)* muki ga kawaru 向きが変わる; *(of opinion)* kawaru 変わる

switch 1 *n (for light)* suitchi スイッチ; *(change)* tenkan 転換 **2** *v/t & v/i (change)* kirikaeru 切り替える

♦**switch off** *v/t lights, TV* kesu 消す; *engine, PC* kiru 切る

♦**switch on** *v/t lights, TV, PC* tsukeru つける; *engine* kakeru かける

swollen hareta 腫れた

sword katana 刀

syllabus kōgi-gaiyō 講義概要

symbol *(character)* kigō 記号; *(in poetry etc)* shōchō 象徴

symbolic shōchōteki (na) 象徴的(な)

symmetric(al) taishōteki (na) 対称的(な)

sympathetic *(showing pity)*
dōjōteki (na) 同情的(な);
(understanding) kōiteki (na) 好
意的(な)
sympathizer POL shiensha
支援者
sympathy dōjō 同情;
(understanding) kyōkan 共感

symphony kōkyōkyoku 交
響曲
symptom MED shōjō 症状; *fig*
kizashi 兆し
synthetic gōsei (no) 合成(の)
syringe chūshaki 注射器
system soshiki 組織; *(method)*
hōhō 方法

T

table *n* tēburu テーブル; *(of
figures)* hyō 表
tablespoon tēburu-supūn テー
ブルスプーン
table tennis takkyū 卓球
tablet MED jōzai 錠剤
taboo *adj* tabū (no) タブ
ー(の)
tact kiten 気転
tactful josainai 如才ない
tactics sakusen 作戦
tactless kiten no kikanai 気転
の利かない
tag *(label)* fuda 札
tail *n* shippo 尻尾
tailor yōfukuya 洋服屋
Taiwan Taiwan 台湾
take *(remove)* toru 取る;
(transport, accompany) tsurete
iku 連れて行く; *(accept:
credit cards)* tsukau 使う;
photo toru 撮る; *exam* ukeru

受ける; *(endure)* gaman
suru 我慢する; *(require)*
hitsuyō to suru 必要とする;
(time) kakaru かかる; *how
long does it ~?* dorekurai
kakarimasu ka どれくら
いかかりますか; *I'll ~ it
(shopping)* kaimasu 買います

♦**take out** *(from bag)* toridasu
取り出す; *appendix* toru
取る; *tooth* nuku 抜く; *(to
dinner etc)* shokuji ni tsurete
iku ... 食事に連れて行く;
insurance ... ni kanyū suru
…に加入する

♦**take over** *v/t company*
nottoru 乗っ取る **2** *v/i (of
new management etc)* hikitsugu
引き継ぐ

♦**take up** *carpet* hagasu は
がす; *(carry up)* motte iku
持って行く; *judo etc* narai

hajimeru 習い始める; *space,*
time shimeru 占める

takeoff *(of plane)* ririku 離陸

takeover COMM baishū suru 買
収する

tale monogatari 物語

talented sainō ga aru 才能
がある

talk 1 *v/t & v/i* hanasu 話す
2 *n (conversation)* kaiwa 会話;
(lecture) kōgi 講義

talk show tōkushō トーク
ショー

tall se ga takai 背が高い

tame *animal* kainarasareta
飼い慣らされた; *joke etc*
tsumaranai つまらない

tampon tanpon タンポン

tangerine mikan みかん

tank tanku タンク; AUTO
tankusha タンク車; MIL
sensha 戦車

tanker *(ship)* tankā タンカ
ー; *(truck)* tanku rōrī タンク
ローリー

tanned hi ni yaketa 日に
焼けた

tap 1 *n* jaguchi 蛇口 **2** *v/t*
(knock) karuku utsu 軽く打
つ; *phone* tōchō suru 盗聴
する

tape 1 *n* tēpu テープ **2** *v/t*
(record) rokuon suru 録音す
る; *(stick)* hittsukeru 引っ

つける

tape measure makijaku 巻尺

tape recorder tēpu-rekōdā テ
ープレコーダー

target 1 *n* mato 的; *(for sales)*
mokuhyō 目標 **2** *v/t market*
mato ni suru 的にする

tarmac *(at airport)* kūkō-
epuron 空港エプロン

tart *n* taruto タルト

task shigoto 仕事

taste 1 *n (sense)* mikaku 味覚;
(of food etc) aji 味; *(in clothes*
etc) konomi 好み **2** *v/t* ajimi
suru 味見する

tattoo *n* irezumi いれずみ

taunt *n* azakeri あざけり

taut pin ni hatta ぴんと張った

tax *n* zeikin 税金

tax-free menzei (no) 免税
(の)

taxi takushī タクシー

tax payer nōzeisha 納税者

tax return kakutei-shinkokusho
確定申告書

tea *n* cha 茶; *Japanese* ~ o-cha
お茶; *green* ~ ryokucha 緑茶

teabag tībaggu ティーバッグ

tea ceremony sadō 茶道

teach 1 *v/t* oshieru 教える
2 *v/i* kyōshi o suru 教師を
する

teacher kyōshi 教師, sensei
先生

teacup kōcha-jawan 紅茶茶碗; *(for green tea)* yunomi ゆのみ

team chīmu チーム

teamwork chīmuwāku チームワーク

teapot tīpotto ティーポット

tear¹ 1 *n (in cloth etc)* sakeme 裂け目 **2** *v/t* hikisaku 引き裂く **3** *v/i (run fast)* mōretsu na ikioi de hashiru 猛烈な勢いで走る

tear² *(in eye)* namida 涙

tearful namida de ippai (no) 涙でいっぱい(の)

tear gas sairuigasu 催涙ガス

tease *v/t* ijimeru いじめる

teaspoon tīspūn ティースプーン

technical senmonteki (na) 専門的(な)

technician gishi 技師

technique gijutsu 技術

technological kagaku-gijutsu (no) 科学技術(の)

technology kagaku-gijutsu 科学技術

teenager tīn'eijā ティーンエイジャー

telecommunications denki-tsūshin 電気通信

telephone 1 *n* denwa 電話 **2** *v/t person* … ni denwa o kakeru …に電話をかける

3 *v/i* denwa suru 電話する

telephone call denwa 電話

telephone number denwa-bangō 電話番号

telephoto lens bōen-renzu 望遠レンズ

television terebi-hōsō テレビ放送; *(set)* terebi テレビ

television program terebi-bangumi テレビ番組

tell *v/t story* hanasu 話す; *difference* wakaru わかる; ~ *X Y* X ni Y o iu XにYを言う; ~ *X to do Y* X ni Y suru yō ni iu XにYにするように言う

teller madoguchi 窓口

temp *n (employee)* haken 派遣

temper *(bad)* kigen 機嫌; *keep one's ~* heisei o tamotsu 平静を保つ; *lose one's ~* hara o tateru 腹を立てる

temperamental *(moody)* kimagure (na) 気まぐれ(な)

temperature ondo 温度; *(fever)* netsu 熱

temple REL shinden 神殿; *(Japanese)* tera 寺

temporary ichiji (no) 一時(の)

tempting miwakuteki (na) 魅惑的(な)

tenant shakuchinin 借地人

tendency keikō 傾向

tender¹ *adj (sore)* itai 痛い;

(affectionate) yasashī 優しい;
steak yawarakai 柔らかい

tender² *n* COMM nyūsatsu 入札

tennis tenisu テニス

tennis court tenisu-kōto テニ
スコート

tense *adj muscle* pin to hatta ピ
ンと張った; *person* kinchō
shita 緊張した

tension hariguai 張
りぐあい; *(in atmosphere)*
kinchō 緊張; *(in movie)*
kinpaku 緊迫

tent tento テント

tentative shikenteki (na) 試
験的(な)

tepid *water* namanurui なま
ぬるい

term *(time)* kikan 期間;
(condition) jōken 条件

terminal 1 *n (airport, bus)*
tāminaru ターミナル **2** *adj*
MED makki (no) 末期(の)

terminate *v/t contract*
owaraseru 終わらせる;
pregnancy chūzetsu suru 中
絶する

terminus tāminaru ターミナル

terrain chikei 地形

terrible hidoi ひどい

terrific sugoi すごい

terrify totemo kowagaraseru と
ても怖がらせる

terrifying osoroshī 恐ろしい

territory ryōdo 領土

terrorism tero テロ

terrorist terorisuto テロリスト

terrorize obiesaseru おびえ
させる

test 1 *n* tesuto テスト **2** *v/t*
tamesu 試す

testify *v/i* JUR shōgen suru 証
言する

tetanus hashōfū 破傷風

text 1 *n* honbun 本文; *(~
message)* mēru メール **2** *v/t*
mēru suru メールする

textbook kyōkasho 教科書

textile orimono 織物

texture tezawari 手触り

Thailand Tai タイ

than …yori …より; *bigger
~ me* watashi yori ōkī 私よ
り大きい

thank *v/t* … ni kansha suru
…に感謝する; *~ you* arigatō
gozaimasu ありがとうござ
います; *no ~* kekkō desu
結構です

thankful kansha shite iru 感謝
している

thanks kansha 感謝; *~!* arigatō
ありがとう

Thanksgiving (Day) Kanshasai
感謝祭

that 1 *adj* sono その; *(further
away)* ano あの; *~ one* sore
それ; *are* あれ **2** *pron* ◊ sore

それ; *(further away)* are あれ; *what's ~?* are / sore wa nan desu ka あれ/それは何ですか◇ *who's ~?* ano hito / sono hito wa dare desu ka あの人/その人はだれですか; *(when there's a noise outside)* dochirasama desu ka どちら様ですか◇ *(relative)*: *the person – you saw* anata ga mita hito あなたが見た人

3 *conj*: *I think ~ …* watashi wa … to omou 私は…と思う

thaw *v/i* tokeru 溶ける; *(of frozen food)* kaitō suru 解凍する

the *no equivalent*

theater gekijō 劇場

theft nusumi 盗み

their karera no 彼らの; *(of things)* sorera no それらの

theirs karera no mono 彼らのもの

them ◇ karera 彼ら; *(things)* sorera それら◇ *(direct object)* karera o 彼らを; *(things)* sorera o それらを◇ *(indirect object)* karera ni 彼らに; *(things)* sorera ni 彼らに

theme tēma テーマ

theme park tēma-yūenchi テーマ遊園地

themselves: *they hurt ~* karera wa kega o shita 彼

らはけがをした; *by ~* jibuntachi de 自分達で; *(alone)* jibuntachi dake de 自分達だけで

then sono tōji その当時; *(after)* sorekara それから; *(deducing)* sorenara それなら

theory riron 理論

therapist serapisuto セラピスト

therapy serapī セラピー

there *(with verbs of being)* asoko ni あそこに; *(with verbs of activity)* asoko de あそこで; *over ~* asoko あそこ; *~ is / are* … ga iru …がいる; *(of things)* … ga aru …がある; *is / are ~?* … ga imasu ka …がいますか; *(of things)* … ga arimasu ka …がありますか; *~ is / are not* …ga inai …がいない; *~* *(of things)* … ga nai …がない; *– you are (giving sth)* hai dōzo はいどうぞ; *~ he is!* imashita います

therefore shitagatte 従って

thermometer MED taionkei 体温計

thermos flask mahōbin 魔法瓶

these **1** *adj* kono この **2** *pron* kore これ

they karera 彼ら; *(things)*

sorera それら ◊ *(omission of pronoun)*: **where are ~?** **~ ~ have left** karera wa doko desu ka—mō ikimashita 彼らはどこですかーもう行きました

thick *hair* ōi 多い; *soup, fog* koi 濃い; *wall* atsui 厚い

thief dorobō 泥棒

thigh momo もも

thin *hair, soup* usui 薄い; *person, line* hosoi 細い

thing mono もの; **~s** *(belongings)* mochimono 持ち物

think omou 思う; **I ~ so** sō omoimasu そう思います

thirst nodo no kawaki 喉の渇き

thirsty: **I'm ~** nodo ga kawaite iru 喉が渇いている

this 1 *adj* kono この; **~ one** kore これ **2** *pron* kore これ; **~ is...** *(introducing)* kochira wa ... san desu こちらは...さんです; TEL **... to mōshimasu ga ...to mōshimasu ga** ...と申します

thorough *search* tetteiteki (na) 徹底的(な); *person* tettei shite iru 徹底している

those 1 *adj* sono その; *(further away)* ano あの **2** *pron* sore それ; *(further away)* are あれ

though 1 *conj* (*although*) keredomo けれども; **as ~ ...**

no yō ni ...のように **2** *adv* demo でも

thought kangae 考え; *(collective)* shisō 思想

thoughtful kangaekonda 考え込んだ; *(considerate)* omoiyari no aru 思いやりのある

thoughtless keisotsu (na) 軽率(な)

thousand sen 千; **ten ~** man 万; **~s of** tasū no 多数の

thread *n* ito 糸

threat kyōhaku 脅迫; *(to security, environment)* kyōi 脅威

threaten kyōhaku suru 脅迫する; *security, environment* obiyakasu 脅かす

thrill 1 *n* suriru スリル **2** *v/t*: **be ~ed** wakuwaku suru わくわくする

thriller surirā-mono スリラー物

thrilling wakuwaku saseru わくわくさせる

thrive *(of plant)* sodatsu 育つ; *(of economy)* sakaeru 栄える

throat nodo のど

throb *n* *(of heart)* kodō 鼓動; *(of music)* rizumu リズム

throne ōza 王座

through 1 *prep* ◊ *(across)* yokogitte 横切って ◊ *(with*

time): **~ *the winter*** fuyu jū 冬中; ***Monday ~ Friday*** getsuyōbi kara kin'yōbi made 月曜日から金曜日まで **2** *adv*: **wet ~** bishonure de びしょぬれで **3** *adj*: **be ~ (of couple)** owaru 終わる

throw **1** *v/t* nageru 投げる **2** *n* nage 投げ

♦ **throw out** *all things* suteru 捨てる; *person* oidasu 追い出す

thumb *n* oyayubi 親指

thumbtack gabyō 画びょう

thump *n* (*blow*) naguru koto 殴ること; (*noise*) gotsun to iu oto ゴツンという音

thunder *n* kaminari 雷

thunderstorm raiu 雷雨

Thursday mokuyōbi 木曜日

thwart dame ni suru だめにする

Tibet Chibetto チベット

ticket kippu 切符

ticket machine kippu-hanbaiki 切符販売機

ticket office kippu-uriba 切符売場

tickle *v/t* kusuguru くすぐる

tidy *person* kichin to shita きちんとした; *room* kogirei (na) こぎれい(な)

♦ **tidy up** *v/t* katazukeru 片づける

tie 1 *n* (*necktie*) nekutai ネクタイ; (SPORTS: *even result*) hikiwake 引き分け **2** *v/t knot* musubu 結ぶ; *hands* tsunagu つなぐ

tiger tora トラ

tight *adj clothes* kitsui きつい; *security* kibishī 厳しい; (*hard to move*) katai 堅い; (*not leaving time*) kitsui きつい

tighten *screw* kataku shimeru 堅く絞める; *security* kibishiku suru 厳しくする

time jikan 時間; (*occasion*) kai 回; **have a good ~!** tanoshinde ne 楽しんでね; **what's the ~?** ima nanji desu ka 今何時ですか; **the first ~** hajimete 初めて; **on ~** jikan dōri 時間どおり; **be in ~** ma ni au 間に合う

time limit shimekiri 締め切り

timetable (*at school*) jikanwari 時間割

time zone jikantai 時間帯

timid okubyō (na) 憶病(な)

timing taimingu タイミング; (*of actor, dancer*) ma no torikata 間の取り方

tinted *glasses* iro no tsuita 色のついた

tiny totemo chīsai とても小さい

tip¹ *n* (*of stick*) saki 先; (*of*

cigarette) sentan 先端

tip² _n (advice)_ mimiyori no jōhō 耳寄りの情報; _(money)_ chippu チップ

tippy-toe: _on ~_ tsumasakidachi de つま先立ちで

tire _n_ taiya タイヤ

tired tsukareta 疲れた; _be ~ of ... ni_ unzari shita …にうんざりした

tissue ANAT soshiki 組織; _(paper)_ tisshu-pēpā ティッシュペーパー

title dai 題

to 1 _prep: ~ Japan_ Nihon e 日本へ; _from Monday ~ Wednesday_ getsuyōbi kara suiyōbi made 月曜日から水曜日まで **2** _(with verbs): ~ speak_ hanasu koto 話すこと **3** _adv: ~ and fro_ ittari kitari 行ったり来たり

toast 1 _n_ tōsuto トースト; _(drinking)_ kanpai 乾杯 **2** _v/t (drinking)_ kanpai suru 乾杯する

tobacco tabako タバコ

today kyō 今日

toe _n_ ashi no yubi 足の指

together issho ni 一緒に; _(at same time)_ dōji ni 同時に

toilet toire トイレ

toilet paper toiretto pēpā トイレットペーパー

toiletries senmen yōgu 洗面用具

token _(sign)_ shirushi しるし

Tokyo Tōkyō 東京

tolerant kan'yō (na) 寛容(な)

tolerate kyoyō suru 許容する

toll _(for bridge etc)_ tsūkōryō 通行料; TEL chōkyori-tsūwaryō 長距離通話料

toll-free TEL furī-daiaru フリーダイアル

tomato tomato トマト

tomato ketchup tomato-kechappu トマトケチャップ

tombstone hakaishi 墓石

tomorrow ashita 明日; _the day after ~_ asatte あさって

ton ton トン

tone _(of color)_ nōtan 濃淡; MUS neiro 音色; _~ of voice_ kuchō 口調

tongue _n_ shita 舌

tonic (water) tonikku wōtā トニックウォーター

tonight konban 今晩

tonsillitis hentōsen-en 扁桃腺炎

too _(also)_ ...mo mata …も また; _(excessively)_ ...sugiru …すぎる; _me ~_ watashi mo 私も

tool dōgu 道具

tooth ha 歯

toothache haita 歯痛

toothbrush haburashi 歯ブラシ

toothpaste hamigaki 歯磨き

top 1 *n* (*of mountain, tree*) sentan 先端; (*upper part*) ue 上; (*lid*) futa ふた; (*of class*) ichiban 一番; (*clothing*) uwagi 上着; (AUTO: *gear*) toppu gia トップギア; *on ~ of* … no ue ni …の上に **2** *adj branches* saikō (no) 最高 (の); *floor* saijōkai 最上階; *management* saikō-kanbu 最高 幹部; *speed* saikō 最高

topic wadai 話題

top secret *adj* saikō-kimitsu (no) 最高機密(の)

torment 1 *n* kurushimi 苦し み **2** *v/t* itametsukeru 痛め つける

torrential doshaburi (no) 土砂 降り(の)

torture 1 *n* gōmon 拷問 **2** *v/t* gōmon ni kakeru 拷問 にかける

toss *v/t ball* nageru 投げる; *~ a coin* koin o nagete kimeru コインを投げて決める

total 1 *n* gōkei 合計 **2** *adj amount* gōkei (no) 合計 (の); *disaster* hidoi ひど い; *stranger* mattaku (no) ま ったく(の) **3** *v/t infml car*

mechamecha ni kowasu めち ゃめちゃに壊す

totally mattaku まったく

touch 1 *n* (*of hand*) tezawari 手ざわり; (*sense*) kanshoku 感触; SPORTS tatchi タッチ; *keep in ~ with* … to renraku shite iru …と連 絡している; *we kept in ~* yaritori o tsuzukeru やりとり を続ける **2** *v/t* sawaru 触る; (*emotionally*) kandō saseru 感 動させる **3** *v/t* sawaru 触る

touching *adj* mune o utsu 胸 をうつ

touchy *person* shinkeishitsu (na) 神経質(な)

tough *person* ki no tsuyoi 気 の強い; *meat* katai 固い; *question* muzukashī 難し い; *material* tsuyoi 強い; *punishment* omoi 重い

tour 1 *n* ryokō 旅行 **2** *v/t* ryokō suru 旅行する

tourism kankō-jigyō 観光 事業

tourist kankōkyaku 観光客

tourist (information) office kankō-annaisho 観光案内所

tour operator ryokō-gaisha 旅行会社

tow *v/t* hipparu 引っ張る

toward *prep* … no hō e …の 方へ

towel taoru タオル

tower n tō 塔

town machi 町

town hall shiyakusho 市役所

toxic yūdoku (na) 有毒(な)

toy o-mocha おもちゃ

trace v/t (find) sagashidasu 捜し出す

track n (path) komichi 小道; (racing) kōsu コース; RAIL tetsudō-senro 鉄道線路

tractor torakutā トラクター

trade 1 n bōeki 貿易; (profession) shokugyō 職業 2 v/i (do business) torihiki suru 取り引きする

trade fair mihon'ichi 見本市

trademark tōroku-shōhyō 登録商標

tradition dentō 伝統

traditional dentōteki (na) 伝統的(な)

traffic n kōtsū 交通

traffic circle rōtarī ロータリー

traffic cop infml kōtsū-keisatsukan 交通警察官

traffic jam kōtsū-jūtai 交通渋滞

traffic light shingō 信号

tragedy higeki 悲劇

tragic higeki (no) 悲劇(の)

trail 1 n (path) michi 道 2 v/t (follow) ato o tsukeru 跡をつける; (tow) hipparu 引っぱる

trailer torērā トレーラー;

(mobile home) torērā hausu トレーラーハウス; (of movie) yokokuhen 予告編

train[1] n ressha 列車

train[2] 1 v/t team kitaeru 鍛える; dog chōkyō suru 調教する 2 v/i (of athlete) kitaeru 鍛える; (of teacher etc) kenshū suru 研修する

trainee kenshūsei 研修生

trainer SPORTS torēnā トレーナー

training renshū 練習; (of staff) kenshū 研修

train station eki 駅

traitor hangyakusha 反逆者

tranquilizer seishin-anteizai 精神安定剤

transaction torihiki 取引

transfer 1 v/t idō saseru 移動させる 2 v/i (switch) kirikaeru 切り替える; (in travel) idō suru 移動する 3 n idō 移動; (of money) sōkin 送金

transform v/t henkei saseru 変形させる

transformer ELEC hen'atsuki 変圧器

transfusion yuketsu 輸血

transition utsurikawari 移り変わり

transitional katoki (no) 過渡期(の)

translate hon'yaku suru 翻

訳する

translation hon'yaku 翻訳

translator hon'yakusha 翻訳者

transmission *(of program)* dentatsu 伝達; *(of disease)* densen 伝染; AUTO hensokuki 変速機

transmit *program* okuru 送る; *disease* utsusu うつす

transpacific Taiheiyō-ōdan (no) 太平洋横断(の)

transparent tōmei (no) 透明(の)

transplant *n* MED ishoku 移植

transport 1 *v/t* yusō suru 輸送する **2** *n* yusō 輸送

trap 1 *n (for animal)* wana わな; *(question)* sakuryaku 策略 **2** *v/t*: **be ~ped** hamatta はまった

trash kuzu くず; *(poor product)* garakuta がらくた

trashy kudaranai くだらない

traumatic shōgekiteki (na) 衝撃的(な)

travel 1 *n* ryokō 旅行 **2** *v/i* ryokō suru 旅行する

travel agency ryokōsha 旅行社

traveler ryokōsha 旅行者

traveler's check toraberāzu-chekku トラベラーズチェック

travel expenses shutchō-ryohi 出張旅費

travel insurance ryokō-hoken 旅行保険

tray *(for food etc)* bon 盆

treacherous fuseijitsu (na) 不誠実(な)

tread 1 *n* ashioto 足音; *(of tire)* toreddo トレッド **2** *v/i* aruku 歩く

treason hangyakuzai 反逆罪

treasure *n* takara 宝

Treasury Department Ōkurashō 大蔵省

treat 1 *n* tanoshimi 楽しみ **2** *v/t materials* shori suru 処理する; *illness* chiryō suru 治療する; *(behave toward)* atsukau 扱う

treaty jōyaku 条約

tree ki 木

tremble furueru 震える; *(of building)* yureru 揺れる

tremendously hijō ni 非常に

tremor *(of earth)* shindō 震動

trend keikō 傾向; *(fashion)* ryūkō 流行

trendy hayari (no) はやり(の)

trial JUR saiban 裁判; *(of equipment)* tesuto テスト; **on ~** JUR saiban ni kakerarete 裁判にかけられて

triangle sankakkei 三角形

trick 1 n keiryaku 計略 **2** v/t damasu だます

trigger n hikigane 引き金
♦ **trigger off** ... no hikigane ni naru ...の引き金になる

trip 1 n (journey) ryokō 旅行
2 v/i (stumble) tsumazuku つまずく **3** v/t (make fall) ... no ashi o sukū ...の足をすくう

triumph n shōri 勝利

trivial sasai (na) ささい(な)

troops guntai 軍隊

trophy torofī トロフィー

tropical nettai (no) 熱帯(の)

trouble 1 n (difficulty) kurō 苦労; (inconvenience) mendō 面倒; no ~! daijōbu 大丈夫 **2** v/t (worry) nayamaseru 悩ませる; (disturb) meiwaku o kakeru 迷惑をかける

troublemaker toraburu-mēkā トラブルメーカー

trousers Br zubon ズボン

trout masu ます

truce kyūsen 休戦

truck torakku トラック

truck driver torakku no untenshu トラックの運転手

true hontō (no) 本当(の); come ~ genjitsu ni naru 現実になる

truly hontō ni 本当に; Yours ~ keigu 敬具

trunk (of tree) miki 幹; (of body) dō 胴; (of elephant) hana 鼻; (of car) toranku トランク

trust 1 n shinrai 信用 **2** v/t shin'yō suru 信用する

trustworthy ate ni naru 当てになる

truth shinjitsu 真実

truthful seijitsu (na) 誠実(な)

try 1 v/t tamesu 試す; JUR saiban suru 裁判する **2** v/i tamesu 試す

T-shirt tīshatsu ティーシャツ

tub (bath) furo-oke 風呂おけ; (for yoghurt) iremono 入れ物

tube (pipe) kuda 管; (of toothpaste etc) chūbu チューブ

Tuesday kayōbi 火曜日

tug n NAUT tagubōto タグボート

tuition: private ~ katei-kyōshi 家庭教師

tulip chūrippu チューリップ

tummy o-naka おなか

tumor shuyō しゅよう

tuna maguro まぐろ; (canned) tsuna ツナ

tune n merodī メロディー

tunnel n tonneru トンネル

turbulence (in air travel) rankiryū 乱気流

turkey shichimenchō 七面鳥

turn 1 n (rotation) kaiten 回転; (in road) kābu カーブ; it's

my ~ watashi no junban desu 私の順番です **2** *v/t wheel* kaiten saseru 回転させる; *corner* magaru 曲がる **3** *v/i (of driver)* magaru 曲がる; *(of wheel)* kaiten suru 回転する

♦ **turn down** *v/t offer* kotowaru 断る; *volume, TV* chīsaku suru 小さくする; *heat* yowaku suru 弱くする

♦ **turn off 1** *v/t TV etc* kesu 消す; *faucet, heater, engine* tomeru 止める **2** *v/i (of driver)* waki e hairu わきへ入る

♦ **turn on 1** *v/t TV, engine* tsukeru つける; *faucet, heater* ireru 入れる; *infml (sexually)* kōfun saseru 興奮させる

♦ **turn up 1** *v/t collar* orikaesu 折り返す; *volume* ageru 上げる; *heat* tsuyoku suru 強くする **2** *v/i (arrive)* arawareru 現れる

turnover FIN uriage 売り上げ

turnpike yūryō-kōsoku-dōro 有

料高速道路

turnstile kaitenshiki-kido 回転式木戸

turtle kame かめ

tuxedo takishīdo タキシード

TV terebi テレビ

tweezers pinsetto ピンセット

twice nikai 二回; ~ *as much* nibai 二倍

twin futago 双子

twin beds tsuin-beddo ツインベッド

twinge *(pain)* uzuki うずき

twins futago 双子

twist 1 *v/t* nejiru ねじる; ~ *one's ankle* nenza suru ねんざする **2** *v/i (of road)* magarikuneru 曲がりくねる

two ni 二; futatsu 二つ

tycoon ōmono 大物

type 1 *n (sort)* taipu タイプ **2** *v/i (use keyboard)* taipu o utsu タイプを打つ

typical tenketeki (na) 典型的(な)

tyrant bōkun 暴君

U

ugly minikui 醜い

UK (= United Kingdom) Eikoku 英国

ulcer kaiyō かいよう

ultimate *(best)* kyūkyoku (no)

究極(の)

ultimatum saigo-tsūchō 最後通ちょう

umbrella kasa 傘

umpire *n* shinpan 審判

UN (= *United Nations*)
Kokuren 国連

unanimous *verdict* manjō-itchi (no) 満場一致(の)

unassuming kidoranai 気取らない

unavoidable sakerarenai 避けられない

unaware: *be ~ of* ... ni ki ga tsukanai …に気が付かない

unbalanced PSYCH kurutta 狂った

unbearable taerarenai 耐えられない; *person* gaman dekinai 我慢できない

unbelievable shinjirarenai 信じられない; *infml heat, value* sugoi すごい

uncertain *future* hakkiri shinai はっきりしない

uncle o-ji おじ; *(sb else's)* o-jisan おじさん

uncomfortable *chair* kokochi-warui 心地悪い

unconditional mujōken (no) 無条件(の)

unconscious MED ishiki-fumei (no) 意識不明(の); PSYCH muishiki (no) 無意識(の)

uncontrollable *emotion* osaerarenai 抑えられない

uncover ... no ōi o toru …の覆いを取る; *plot* bakuro suru 暴露する

undamaged higai o ukete inai 被害を受けていない

undeniable hitei dekinai 否定できない

under *prep* ... no shita ni …の下に; *(less than)* ...miman de …未満で

undercarriage chakuriku-sōchi 着陸装置

undercut *v/t* COMM ...yori yasui ne de uru …より安い値で売る

underdog jakusha 弱者

underdone *meat* namayake (no) 生焼け(の)

underestimate *v/t* mikubiru 見くびる

underground *adj* chika (no) 地下(の); POL chika-soshiki (no) 地下組織(の)

undergrowth shitabae 下生え

underline *v/t text* kasen o hiku 下線を引く

underlying *problems* kihonteki (na) 基本的(な)

underneath 1 *prep* ... no shita ni …の下に **2** *adv* shita ni 下に

underpants pantsu パンツ

underskirt pechikōto ペチコート

understaffed hitode-busoku (no) 人手不足(の)

understand 1 *v/t* rikai suru 理解する

解する 2 v/i wakaranai わからない

understanding 1 adj person omoiyari no aru 思いやりのある **2** n (of situation) rikai 理解; (agreement) gōi 合意

understatement hikaeme na hyōgen 控えめな表現

undertaking (enterprise) jigyō 事業; (promise) yakusoku 約束

underwear shitagi 下着

underworld (criminal) ankokugai 暗黒街

undisputed monku nashi (no) 文句無し(の)

undoubtedly utagau yochi naku 疑う余地なく

unearth remains hakkutsu suru 発掘する

unemployed 1 adj shitsugyō shita 失業した **2** n: **the ~** shitsugyōsha 失業者

unemployment shitsugyō 失業

uneven quality fuzoroi (no) 不ぞろい(の); surface dekoboko (no) でこぼこ(の)

unexpected omoigakenai 思いがけない

unfair futō (na) 不当(な)

unfaithful uwaki (na) 浮気(な)

unfavorable report, conditions yoku nai 良くない

unfit undō-busoku (no) 運動

不足(の); (morally) ... ni fumuki (na) …に不向き(な)

unforeseen omoigakenai 思いがけない

unforgettable wasurerarenai 忘れられない

unforgivable yurusenai 許せない

unfortunately zannen nagara 残念ながら

unfriendly fushinsetsu (na) 不親切(な)

ungrateful onshirazu (no) 恩知らず(の)

unhappiness fukō 不幸

unhappy fukō (na) 不幸 (な); customers fuman (na) 不満(な)

unharmed buji (na) 無事(な)

uniform n seifuku 制服

unify tōitsu suru 統一する

uninhabited mujin (no) 無人(の)

unintentional koi de nai 故意でない

union POL rengō 連合; (labor ~) rōdō-kumiai 労働組合

unique dokutoku (no) 独特(の)

unite 1 v/t hitotsu ni suru 一つにする **2** v/i danketsu suru 団結する

United Nations n Kokusai-rengō 国際連合

unity kessoku 結束

universal fuhenteki (na) 普遍的(な)

university daigaku 大学

unkind fushinsetsu (na) 不親切(な)

unleaded *adj* muen (no) 無鉛の

unless: *don't say anything ~ you're sure* moshi tashika de nakereba nanimo iu na もし確かでなければ何も言うな

unlikely arisō mo nai ありそうもない

unload *goods* …kara ni o orosu …から荷を下ろす

unlucky *number* engi no warui 縁起の悪い; *person* fukō (na) 不幸(な)

unmistakable machigaeyō no nai 間違えようのない

unnatural fushizen (na) 不自然(な)

unnecessary fuhitsuyō (na) 不必要(な)

unofficial kōhyō sarete inai 公表されていない

unpack *v/i* nimotsu o dashite katazukeru 荷物を出して片づける

unpaid *work* mukyū (no) 無給(の)

unpleasant fuyukai (na) 不愉快(な)

unpopular *person* ninki no nai 人気のない; *decision* fuhyō (no) 不評(の)

unpredictable yosō dekinai 予想できない

unproductive hiseisanteki (na) 非生産的(な)

unprofessional shokugyō-rinri ni hansuru 職業倫理に反する; *work* shirōto (no) 素人(の)

unprofitable rieki no nai 利益のない

unqualified *doctor etc* shikaku no nai 資格のない

unrealistic higenjitsuteki (na) 非現実的な

unreasonable *person* riseiteki de nai 理性的でない; *demand* futō (na) 不当(な)

unreliable shinrai dekinai 信頼できない; *car* ate ni naranai 当てにならない

unrest fuan 不安

unruly te ni oenai 手に負えない

unsatisfactory fumanzoku (na) 不満足(な)

unscrew … no neji o nuku …のネジを抜く; *top* nejitte akeru ねじって開ける

unsettled *weather, market* kawariyasui 変わりやすい; *lifestyle* ochitsukanai 落ち着

かない

unskilled mijuku (na) 未熟 (な)

unsuitable futekitō (na) 不適当 (な)

untidy chirakatta 散らかった

until *prep* …made …まで;
from Monday ~ Friday
getsuyōbi kara kin'yōbi made
月曜日から金曜日まで

untiring *efforts* tayumanu たゆまぬ

untrue uso (no) うそ (の)

unusual mezurashī 珍しい

unusually mezurashiku 珍しく

unwell kibun ga warui 気分が悪い

unwilling: *be ~ to do X* X suru no o iyagatte iru Xするのを嫌がっている

up *adv* ue e 上へ; *~ on the roof* yane no ue ni 屋根の上に; *be ~ (out of bed)* okite iru;
(of sun) nobotte iru 昇っている; *(of price)* agatte iru; *what's ~?* nani ka atta 何かあった

upbringing shitsuke しつけ

update *v/t file* kōshin suru 更新する

upheaval *(emotional)* dōyō 動揺; *(social)* dōran 動乱

uphold *rights* mamoru 守る

upkeep *n* iji-kanri 維持管理

upper *part* jōbu (no) 上部 (の)

uprising bōdō 暴動

uproar ōsawagi 大騒ぎ; *(protest)* kōgi 抗議

upscale *adj hotel etc* kōshotoku-sō (no) 高所得層 (の)

upset 1 *v/t glass* hikkurikaesu ひっくり返す; *(emotionally)* kanashimaseru 悲しませる **2** *adj (emotionally)* kanashimu 悲しむ

upstairs *adv* ue no kai ni 上の階に

up-to-date saishin (no) 最新 (の)

upturn *(in economy)* kōten 好転

uranium uraniumu ウラニウム

urban toshi (no) 都市 (の)

urge *n* shōdō 衝動

urgency kinkyūsei 緊急性

urgent kinkyū (na) 緊急 (な)

USA (= *United States of America*) Amerika-gasshūkoku アメリカ合衆国

use 1 *v/t tool, word* tsukau 使う; *skills* katsuyō suru 活用する; *sb's car* kariru 借りる **2** *n* shiyō 使用; *be of no ~* zenzen yaku ni tatanai 全然役に立たない

used[1] *car etc* chūko (no) 中古 (の)

used[2]: *be ~ to* … ni narete iru …に慣れている; *get ~ to*

useful

... ni narete kuru …に慣れ
てくる
useful yaku ni tatsu 役に立つ
useless *information* yaku ni
tatanai 役に立たない; *infml*
person yakutatazu (no) 役立
たず (の)
user shiyōsha 使用者
user-friendly tsukaiyasui 使
いやすい

usual itsumo (no) いつも
(の); *(customary)* futsū (no)
普通 (の); **as ~** itsumo no yō
ni いつもの様に
usually futsū wa 普通は
utterly mattaku 全く
U-turn yū-tān Uターン; *fig*
hyakuhachijūdo no hōkō-
tenkan 百八十度の方向
転換

V

vacant aite iru 空いている;
look utsuro (na) うつろ (な)
vacate akeru 空ける
vacation *n* kyūka 休暇; **be
on ~** kyūkachū de aru 休暇
中である
vacationer kōrakukyaku 行
楽客
vaccinate ... ni yobō-sesshu o
suru …に予防接種をする
vaccine wakuchin ワクチン
vacuum *n* shinkū 真空
vacuum cleaner denki-sōjiki
電気掃除機
vague *answer* aimai (na) あい
まい (な)
vain 1 *adj person* unuborete iru
うぬぼれている **2** *n*: **in ~**
munashiku むなしく
valid *visa* yūkō (na) 有効 (な);

reason datō (na) 妥当 (な)
valley tani 谷
valuable 1 *adj help* kichō (na)
貴重 (な); *jewel* kōka (na)
高価 (な) **2** *n*: **~s** kichōhin
貴重品
value *n* kachi 価値; *(financial)*
kakaku 価格
van ban バン
vanilla *n* banira バニラ
vanish kieru 消える
vapor jōki 蒸気
variable *adj* sadamaranai 定ま
らない; *moods* kawariyasui
変わりやすい
variation henka 変化
variety henka 変化; *(type)*
shurui 種類
various *(several)* samazama
(na) 様々 (な); *(different)*

iroiro (na) 色々 (な)

varnish *n* nisu ニス;; *(for nails)* manikyua マニキュア

vary *v/i* henka suru 変化する; *it varies* sono toki ni yotte chigau その時によって違う

vase kabin 花瓶

vast kōdai (na) 広大 (な); *knowledge, sum* bakudai (na) ばく大 (な)

VCR (= **video cassette recorder**) bideo ビデオ

veal koushiniku 子牛肉

vegetable yasai 野菜

vegetarian *n* saishoku-shugisha 菜食主義者

vehicle kuruma 車

velvet *n* berubetto ベルベット

vending machine jidō-hanbaiki 自動販売機

venereal disease seibyō 性病

ventilation kanki 換気

venture *n* benchā-jigyō ベンチャー事業; COMM tōki tōki 投機

venue kaisaichi 開催地

verb dōshi 動詞

verdict JUR hyōketsu 評決; *fig* iken 意見

♦verge on ...dōzen de aru ...同然である

verify *(check)* shōmei suru 証明する; *(confirm)* kakunin suru 確認する

vermin gaijū 害獣; *(fleas, lice)* gaichū 害虫

versatile tasai (no) 多才(の); *gadget* tsukaimichi no ōi 使い道の多い

verse setsu 節; *(poetry)* shi 詩

very *adv* totemo とても; *was it cold? – not – samukatta? – anmari* 寒かった? – あんまり

vessel NAUT fune 船

veteran *n* beteran ベテラン; *(war)* taieki-gunjin 退役軍人

veterinarian jūi 獣医

via keiyu de 経由で

viable *plan* jikkō-kanō (na) 実行可能(な)

vibrate *v/i* shindō suru 振動する

vice akutoku 悪徳

vice president COMM fukushachō 副社長; POL fuku-daitōryō 副大統領

vice versa gyaku no bāi mo onaji 逆の場合も同じ

vicinity kinjo 近所

vicious *dog* dōmō (na) どう猛 (な); *attack, temper* zankoku (na) 残酷(な)

victim giseisha 犠牲者

victory shōri 勝利

video 1 *n* bideo ビデオ 2 *v/t* bideo ni rokuga suru ビデオに録画 する

video camera bideo-kamera ビデオカメラ

video cassette bideo-tēpu ビデオテープ

video recorder bideo-tēpu-rekōda ビデオテープレコーダー

Vietnam Betonamu ベトナム

view n keshiki 景色; (of situation) iken 意見; **in ~ of ...** ... kangaeru と ... 考えると

viewer TV shichōsha 視聴者

viewpoint mikata 見方

vigor genki 元気

village mura 村

villager murabito 村人

vindictive fukushūshin ni moeta 復しゅう心に燃えた

vine budō no ki ぶどうの木

vinegar su 酢

vintage n (of wine) budō-shūkakunen ぶどう収穫年

violate rules ihan suru 違反する

violence bōryoku 暴力

violent bōryokuteki (na) 暴力的(な); storm hageshī 激しい

violin baiorin バイオリン

VIP (= very important person) VIP ブイアイピー

virtual jijitsujō (no) 事実上(の)

virtually jisshitsuteki ni wa 実

質的には

virus MED, COMPUT uirusu ウイルス

visa biza ビザ

visibility shikai 視界

visible me ni mieru 目に見える

vision shiryoku 視力; REL maboroshi 幻

visit 1 n hōmon 訪問; (to place) kenbutsu 見物 2 v/t person hōmon suru 訪問する; place tazuneru 訪ねる

visitor kyaku 客; (to museum etc) nyūkansha 入館者; (tourist) kankōkyaku 観光客

visual shikakuteki (na) 視覚的(な)

visualize sōzō suru 想像する

vital jūyō (na) 重要(な)

vitamin bitamin ビタミン

vitamin pill bitamin-zai ビタミン剤

vivid color azayaka (na) 鮮やか(な); imagination kappatsu (na) 活発(な)

vocabulary goi 語い; (list) yōgoshū 用語集

voice n koe 声

voicemail rusuban-denwa sābisu 留守番電話サービス

volcano kazan 火山

voltage den'atsu 電圧

volume (of container) yōseki 容積; (of work) ryō 量; (of

book) satsu 冊; *(of radio etc)* boryūmu ボリューム

voluntary *adj* jihatsuteki (na) 自発的 (な); *work* borantia (no) ボランティア (の)

volunteer *n* borantia ボランティア

vomit *v/i* haku 吐く

voracious *appetite* ōsei (no) 旺盛 (の)

vote 1 *n* tōhyō 投票 **2** *v/i* POL tōhyō suru 投票する; *~ for / against …* … ni sansei / hantai no tōhyō o suru …に賛成/反対の投票をする

voyage funatabi 船旅

vulgar gehin (na) 下品 (な)

vulnerable kōgeki sareyasui 攻撃されやすい

W

wad *n (of paper)* taba 束; *(of cotton)* katamari 固まり

♦ **wade across** mizu no naka o aruite wataru 水の中を歩いて渡る

wag *v/t* furu 振る

wage *n* kyūryō 給料

wagon: *be on the ~ infml* sake o tatte iru 酒を断っている

waist koshi 腰

wait *v/i* matsu 待つ

waiter ueitā ウエイター; *~!* sumimasen すみません

waiting list junban-machi no meibo 順番待ちの名簿

waiting room machiaishitsu 待合室

waitress ueitoresu ウエイトレス

♦ **wake up** *v/i* me ga sameru

目が覚める **2** *v/t* okosu 起こす

wake-up call mōningu-kōru モーニングコール

walk 1 *n* toho 徒歩; *go for a ~* sanpo ni iku 散歩に行く **2** *v/i* aruku 歩く; *(not take car etc)* aruite iku 歩いていく; *(hike)* haikingu suru ハイキングする

wall kabe 壁

wallet satsuire 札入れ

wallpaper *n* kabegami 壁紙

Wall Street Wōru-gai ウォール街

walnut kurumi クルミ

wander *v/i* buratsuku ぶらつく; *(of attention)* yokomichi ni soreru 横道にそれる

want *v/t* …ga hoshī …が欲し

い; *(need)* …ga hitsuyō de aru …が必要である; *~ to do X* X ga shitai Xがしたい
want ad kyūjin-kōkoku 求人広告
wanted *(by police)* shimei-tehaichū (no) 指名手配中(の)
war *n* sensō 戦争
warden *(of prison)* shochō 所長
warehouse sōko 倉庫
warfare sensō 戦争
warhead dantō 弾頭
warm *adj* atatakai 暖かい; *welcome* kokoro kara (no) 心から(の)
warmhearted kokoro no atatakai 心の温かい
warmth atatakasa 暖かさ; *(of welcome)* atatakami 温かみ
warn keikoku suru 警告する
warning *n* keikoku 警告
warped *fig* hinekureta ひねくれた
warrant *n* reijō 令状
warranty hoshō 保証
warship gunkan 軍艦
wartime senji 戦時
wash 1 *v/t* arau 洗う; *clothes* sentaku suru 洗濯する **2** *v/i* senmen suru 洗面する
♦ **wash up** *v/i (hands and face)* senmen suru 洗面する
washbasin senmenki 洗面器
washer *(for faucet etc)* zagane 座金
washing machine sentakuki 洗濯機
washroom o-tearai お手洗い
waste 1 *n* rōhi 浪費; *(industrial)* haikibutsu 廃棄物 **2** *v/t* mudazukai suru 無駄使いする
waste basket kuzukago くずかご
watch 1 *n (timepiece)* udedokei 腕時計 **2** *v/t movie, TV* miru 見る; *(look after)* … ni ki o tsukeru …に気をつける **3** *v/i* miru 見る
water 1 *n* mizu 水 **2** *v/t plant* mizu o yaru 水をやる
waterfall taki 滝
watermelon suika スイカ
waterproof *adj* bōsui (no) 防水(の)
wave[1] *n (in sea)* nami 波
wave[2] **1** *v/i (with hand)* te o furu 手を振る **2** *v/t flag* furu 振る
way 1 *n (method, manner)* hōhō 方法; *(route)* iku michi 行く道; *this ~ (like this)* kono yarikata このやり方; *(in this direction)* kono hōkō この方向; *by the ~ (incidentally)* tokoro de ところで; *be in*

the ~ jama ni naru 邪魔になる; *no* ~! jōdan ja nai 冗談じゃない **2** *adv infml (much)* suggoku すっごく

way in iriguchi 入り口

way of life seikatsu-yōshiki 生活様式

way out deguchi 出口; *fig* kaiketsuhō 解決法

we watashitachi 私達
◊ *(omission of pronoun):* ~ *don't know* shirimasen 知りません

weak yowai 弱い; *coffee* usui 薄い

weaken *v/t* yowaku suru 弱くする

wealth zaisan 財産

wealthy yūfuku (na) 裕福(な)

weapon buki 武器

wear *v/t (have on)* kiru 着る; *hat* kaburu かぶる; *shoes, skirt, pants, pantyhose* haku はく; *necktie* shimeru 締める; *gloves, ring* hameru はめる; *make-up* suru する; *glasses* kakeru かける

◆ **wear out** *v/t (tire)* tsukaresaseru 疲れさせる; *shoes* suriherasu 擦り減らす

weary tsukarehateta 疲れ果てた

weather *n* tenki 天気

weather forecast tenki-yohō 天気予報

Web: *the* ~ webu ウェブ

web *(of spider)* kumo no su くもの巣

web page webu-pēji ウェブページ

website webusaito ウェブサイト

wedding kekkonshiki 結婚式

wedding ring kekkon-yubiwa 結婚指輪

Wednesday suiyōbi 水曜日

weed *n* zassō 雑草

week shū 週; *(duration)* shūkan 週間; *a* ~ *tomorrow* raishū no ashita 来週の明日

weekday heijitsu 平日、uīkudē ウイークデー

weekend shūmatsu 週末; *on the* ~ shūmatsu ni 週末に

weekly *adj* maishū (no) 毎週(の)

weep shikushiku naku しくしく泣く

weigh 1 *v/t* omosa o hakaru 重さを量る **2** *v/i* omosa ga … de aru 重さが…である

weight *(of person)* taijū 体重; *(of object)* omosa 重さ

weird hen (na) 変(な)

welcome 1 *adj* kangei subeki 歓迎すべき; *you're* ~! dō itashimashite どういたしまして **2** *n also fig* kangei 歓

迎 3 *v/t* guests kangei suru 歓
迎する; decision etc ureshiku
omou うれしく思う

welfare *(assistance)* fukushi
福祉

well¹ *n* (for water) ido 井戸

well² 1 *adv* yoku よく; *as ~
(too)* ... mo ...も; *as ~ as
(in addition to)* ... no hoka ni
...のほかに; *~, ~!* (surprise)
ē'エーッ; ... ētto ... えー
っと 2 *adj*: *be ~* genki de
aru 元気である

well-behaved gyōgi no ī 行
儀のいい

well-dressed minari no yoi 身
なりの良い

well-known yūmei (na) 有
名 (な)

well-off yūfuku (na) 裕福 (な)

west 1 *n* nishi 西; *the West*
Nishigawa-shokoku 西側諸
国 2 *adj* nishi (no) 西 (の)
3 *adv* nishi ni 西に; *(travel)*
nishi e 西へ

West Coast (of USA)
Nishikaigan 西海岸

western 1 *adj* nishi (no) 西
(の); *Western* Nishigawa
(no) 西側 (の) 2 *n* (movie)
seibugeki 西部劇

Westerner Seiyōjin 西洋人

wet *adj* nureta ぬれた; *(rainy)*
ame no ōi 雨の多い

whale kujira 鯨

what 1 *pron* ◊ *(interrogative)*
nani 何; *~ is it?* (~ do you
want?) nannano 何なの; *~
about some dinner?* yūshoku
ni shimasu ka 夕食にしま
せんか; *so ~?* sore de それ
で 2 *adj* dono どの

whatever 1 *pron* nan demo 何
でも; *(regardless of what)* ...
ni kakawarazu ...にかかわら
ず 2 *adj* donna... demo どん
な...でも

wheat komugi 小麦

wheel *n* sharin 車輪

wheelchair kurumaisu 車いす

when 1 *adv* itsu いつ 2 *conj*
toki 時; *~ I was a child*
watashi ga kodomo datta toki
私が子供だった時

whenever (any time) ... suru
toki wa itsu demo ...する時
はいつでも

where 1 *adv* doko ni どこに
2 *conj*: *this is ~ I used to live*
koko wa watashi ga izen sunde
ita tokoro desu ここは私が以
前住んでいた所です

wherever 1 *conj* doko ni
...shite mo どこに...して
も 2 *adv* ittai doko ni 一体
どこに

whether ...ka dō ka ...か
どうか

which 1 *adj* dono どの **2** *pron* ◊ *(interrogative)* dore どれ; *(referring to people)* dono hito どの人 ◊ *(relative)*: **the house, ~ was designed by ...** ... no dezain shita ie ...のデザインした家

whichever 1 *adj*: **~ style you choose** anata ga dono sutairu o erabu ni shite mo あなたがどのスタイルを選ぶにしても **2** *pron* dore demo どれでも

whip 1 *n* muchi むち **2** *v/t (beat)* muchiutsu むち打つ

whirlpool *(for relaxation)* jakūji ジャクージ

whiskey uisukī ウイスキー

whisper 1 *n* sasayaki ささやき **2** *v/t & v/i* sasayaku ささやく

whistle 1 *n (sound)* kuchibue 口笛; *(device)* fue 笛 **2** *v/i* kuchibue o fuku 口笛をふく

white 1 *n* shiro 白; *(person)* hakujin 白人 **2** *adj* shiroi 白い; *person* hakujin (no) 白人(の)

white-collar worker howaito-karā no sararīman ホワイトカラーのサラリーマン

White House Howaito-hausu ホワイトハウス

white wine shiro wain 白ワイン

who ◊ *(interrogative)* dare 誰 ◊ *(relative)*: **the woman ~ saved the boy** otoko no ko o tasuketa fujin 男の子を助けた婦人

whoever dare demo 誰でも

whole *adj* zentai (no) 全体(の)

wholesale *adv* oroshi de 卸で

wholesome kenkō ni yoi 健康に良い

whose 1 *pron* ◊ *(interrogative)* dare no mono 誰の物 ◊ *(relative)*: **a man ~ wife has left him** tsuma o suterareta otoko 妻に捨てられた男 **2** *adj* dare (no) 誰(の)

why dōshite どうして, naze なぜ

wicked *(evil)* ja-aku (na) 邪悪(な)

wicket *(in station, bank etc)* madoguchi 窓口

wide *adj* hiroi 広い

widely *known* hiroku 広く

wide-open hiroku hiraita 広く開いた

widespread hirogatta 広がった

widow mibōjin 未亡人

widower otokoyamome 男やもめ

width hirosa 広さ

wife tsuma 妻; *(sb else's)* okusan 奥さん

wild *adj animal, flower* yasei (no) 野生(の); *applause* kōfun shita 興奮した

wildlife yasei-dōbutsu 野生動物

will¹ *n* JUR yuigon 遺言

will² *n (~power)* ishi 意志

will³: *I ~ let you know tomorrow* ashita shirasemasu 明日知らせます; *~ you be there too?* anata mo iku no あなたも行くの; *~ you have some more tea?* mō sukoshi o-cha wa ikaga desu ka もう少しお茶はいかがですか

willing: *be ~ to do X* kokoroyoku X suru 快くXする

willingly *(with pleasure)* yorokonde 喜んで

willpower ishi no chikara 意志の力

win 1 *n* shōri 勝利 **2** *v/t ... ni katsu* …に勝つ; *prize* ateru 当てる **3** *v/i katsu* 勝つ

wind¹ *n* kaze 風

wind² *v/i (of path etc)* magaru 曲がる

wind instrument kangakki 管楽器

window mado 窓

windowsill mado no shitawaku

窓の下枠

windshield furontogarasu フロントガラス

wine wain ワイン

wing *n* hane 羽; *(of plane)* tsubasa 翼; SPORTS uingu ウイング

wink *n* uinku ウインク

winner *(of race)* shōsha 勝者; *(of prize)* jushōsha 受賞者

winnings shōkin 賞金

winter *n* fuyu 冬

winter sports uintā-supōtsu ウインタースポーツ

wipe *v/t* fuku ふく; *tape* kesu 消す

wire harigane 針金; ELEC densen 電線

wiring ELEC denki-haisen 電気配線

wisdom chie 知恵

wise kashikoi 賢い

wish 1 *n* nozomi 望み; *best ~es* o-medetō おめでとう **2** *v/t: I ~ that ....* sureba ī no ni to omou …すればいいのにと思う

wit *(humor)* yūmoa ユーモア

witch majo 魔女

with *(accompanied by)* ... to …と ◊ *(proximity)* ... to issho ni …と一緒に; *I live ~ my aunt* watashi wa o-ba to issho ni sunde iru 私はおばと一緒

に住んでいる ◊ *(agency)* … de …で; *stabbed ~ a knife* naifu de sasareta ナイフで刺された ◊ *(cause): shivering ~ fear* kyōfu de furueta 恐怖で震えた ◊ *(possession)* … no …の; *the house ~ the red door* akai doa no uchi 赤いドアの家

withdraw *v/t* torikesu 取り消す; *money* hikidasu 引き出す; *troops* tettai saseru 撤退させる

withdrawn *adj person* hikkomigachi (na) 引っ込みがち(な)

wither kar 枯れる

withhold *consent, pay* horyū suru 保留する; *data* kakusu 隠す

within *prep (inside)* … no naka de …の中で; *(time)* … inai de …以内で; *(distance)* … no han'inai de …の範囲内で

without …nashi de …なしで; *~ looking* nani mo minaide 何も見ないで

withstand … ni taeru …に耐える

witness JUR shōnin 証人; *(of accident)* mokugekisha 目撃者

witty yūmoa no aru ユーモアのある

wolf *n* ōkami おおかみ

woman josei 女性

women's lib ūman ribu ウーマンリブ

wonder 1 *n (amazement)* odoroki 驚き **2** *v/t: I ~ why she said that* naze kanojo ga sō itta no ka na to omou なぜ彼女がそういったのかなと思う

wonderful subarashī 素晴らしい

wood mokuzai 木材; *(forest)* hayashi 林

wooden mokusei (no) 木製(の)

wool keito 毛糸

woolen *adj* ūru (no) ウール(の)

word *n* ◊ *(unit of language)* tango 単語; *a new ~* atarashī tango 新しい単語 ◊ *(with number)* go 語; *500 ~s* gohyaku-go 500語 ◊ *(way of expressing)* kotoba 言葉; *there is no ~ for it in …* … go niwa sono kotoba wa nai …語にはその言葉はない

word processing wāpuro de no bunsho-sakusei ワープロでの文書作成

work 1 *n* shigoto 仕事 **2** *v/i (of person)* hataraku 働く; *(of machine)* ugoku 動く

◆ **work out 1** *v/t solution* mitsukeru 見つける **2** *v/i (at* *gym)* torēningu suru トレーニングする; *(of relationship etc)* umaku iku うまく行く

workaholic *n* shigoto-chūdoku 仕事中毒

workday shūgyō-jikan 就業時間; *(not holiday)* kinmubi 勤務日

worker rōdōsha 労働者

workmanship dekibae 出来栄え

work of art geijutsu-sakuhin 芸術作品

work permit rōdō-biza 労働ビザ

workshop sagyōba 作業場; *(seminar)* wāku-shoppu ワークショップ

world sekai 世界

world war sekaitaisen 世界大戦

worldwide *adj* sekaiteki (na) 世界的(な)

worn-out tsukaifurushita 使い古した; *(of person* hetoheto ni naru へとへとになる

worried shinpaisō (na) 心配そう(な)

worry 1 *n* shinpai 心配 **2** *v/t* shinpai saseru 心配させる; *(upset)* … ga ki ni naru …が気になる **3** *v/i* shinpai suru 心配する

worse 1 *adj* sara ni warui 更に悪い **2** *adv* sara ni waruku 更に悪く

worsen *v/i* akka suru 悪化する

worst 1 *adj* saiaku (no) 最悪(の) **2** *adv* mottomo hidoku 最もひどく

worth *adj*: *be ~* FIN … no kachi ga aru …の価値がある; *be ~ seeing* miru kachi ga aru 見る価値がある

worthless *object* kachi ga nai 価値がない

worthwhile *cause* tame ni naru ためになる

would: *~ you like to go to the movies?* eiga ni ikimasen ka 映画に行きませんか; *~ you tell her that …?* … to kanojo ni tsutaete moraemasu ka …と彼女に伝えてもらえますか

wound *n* kizu 傷

wrap *v/t gift* tsutsumu 包む

wrapping paper hōsōshi 包装紙

wreck 1 *n* zangai 残がい; *(of ship)* nanpasen 難破船 **2** *v/t plans, career, marriage* dainashi ni suru 台無しにする

wreckage *(of car, plane)* zangai 残がい

wrecker rekkāsha レッカー車

wrench *n (tool)* supana スパナ

wriggle *v/i (squirm)* kunekune suru くねくねする

wrinkle *n* shiwa しわ

wrist tekubi 手首

wristwatch udedokei 腕時計

write *v/t* kaku 書く

writer sakka 作家; *(of document etc)* kakite 書き手

writing *(as career)* chojutsugyō 著述業; *(hand~)* hisseki 筆跡; *(words)* bunshō 文章; *(script)* moji 文字

writing paper binsen 便せん

wrong 1 *adj* machigatta 間違った; *(morally)* yokunai 良く

ない; **be ~** *(of person, answer, clock)* machigatte iru 間違っている; *there is something ~ with the car* kono kuruma wa dokoka okashii この車はどこかおかしい **2** *adv* machigatte 間違って; **go ~** *(of person)* machigau 間違う; *(of marriage, plan)* umaku ikanai うまくいかない

wrong number bangōmachigai 番号間違い

X

X-ray *n (picture)* rentogen-shashin レントゲン写真

Y

yacht yotto ヨット

yard¹ *(of prison etc)* kōnai 構内; *(behind house)* uraniwa 裏庭

yard² *(measure)* yādo ヤード

yawn 1 *n* akubi あくび **2** *v/i* akubi suru あくびする

year toshi 年; *(with count word)* nen 年; *this ~* kotoshi 今年; *next ~* rainen 来年; *last ~* kyonen 去年

yell *v/i* sakebu 叫ぶ

yellow *adj* ki-iro (no) 黄色(の)

yen FIN en 円

yes hai はい ◊ *(using 'no' i.e. no, that is not right)*: *you don't know the answer, do you? – oh ~, I do* kotae ga wakaranain deshō – ie wakarimasu 答えがわからないんでしょう – いいえ、わかります

yesterday kinō 昨日; *the day before* ~ ototoi おととい

yet *adv* kore made de これまでで; *as* ~ mada まだ; *is he here* ~? – *not* ~ mō kare wa kimashita ka – mada desu ka もう彼は来ましたか – まだです

yield 1 *n* FIN rieki 利益 **2** *v/i* (give way) yuzuru 譲る

yoghurt yōguruto ヨーグルト

you ◊ (singular: polite) anata あなた; (familiar) kimi きみ; (plural: polite) anatatachi あなたたち; (familiar) kimitachi きみたち; *he knows* ~ kare wa anata o shitte imasu 彼はあなたを知っています; *I told* ~ *before* anata ni mae ni hanashimashita あなたに前に話しました ◊ (omission of pronoun): *are* ~ *sure?* honto? ほんと?

young wakai 若い

your ◊ anata no あなたの; (plural) anatatachi no あなたたちの ◊ (omission of possessive): *did you bring* ~ *passport?* pasupōto motte kimashita ka パスポート持ってききましたか

yours anata no mono あなたのもの; (plural) anatatachi no mono あなたたちのもの; *Yours* (in letter) keigu 敬具

yourself jishin 自身; *you* ~ anata jishin あなた自身; *by* ~ jibun de 自分で; (alone) hitori de ひとりで

yourselves jishin 自身; *you* ~ anatatachi jishin あなたたち自身; *by* ~ jibuntachi de 自分達で; (alone) anatatachi dake de あなた達だけで

youth (young man) seinen 青年; (young people) seishōnen 青少年

youth hostel yūsu-hosuteru ユースホステル

Z

zap *v/t* COMPUT (delete) sakujo suru 削除する

zebra shimauma しまうま

Zen Buddhism Zenshū 禅宗

zero zero ゼロ

zip code yūbin-bangō 郵便番号

zipper fasunā ファスナー

zone chitai 地帯

zoo dōbutsuen 動物園

Numbers

0	zero, rei	ゼロ，零
1	ichi	一
2	ni	二
3	san	三
4	yon, shi	四
5	go	五
6	roku	六
7	nana, shichi	七
8	hachi	八
9	kyū	九
10	jū	十
11	jū-ichi	十一
12	jū-ni	十二
13	jū-san	十三
20	ni-jū	二十
21	ni-jū-ichi	二十一
30	san-jū	三十
35	san-jū-go	三十五
40	yon-jū	四十
50	go-jū	五十
60	roku-jū	六十
70	nana-jū	七十
80	hachi-jū	八十
90	kyū-jū	九十
100	hyaku	百
101	hyaku-ichi	百一

200	ni-hyaku	二百
300	san-byaku	三百
400	yon-hyaku	四百
500	go-hyaku	五百
600	rop-pyaku	六百
700	nana-hyaku	七百
800	hap-pyaku	八百
900	kyū-hyaku	九百
1,000	sen	千
2,000	ni-sen	二千
3,000	san-zen	三千
4,000	yon-sen	四千
5,000	go-sen	五千
6,000	roku-sen	六千
7,000	nana-sen	七千
8,000	hass-sen	八千
9,000	kyū-sen	九千
10,000	ichi-man	一万
20,000	ni-man	二万
100,000	jū-man	十万
1,000,000	hyaku-man	百万
2,000,000	ni-hyaku-man	二百万
10,000,000	sen-man	千万
100,000,000	ichi-oku	一億

yourself slim

The most enjoyable way to lose weight

by
Imah Goer

3 Edgar Buildings,
George Street,
Bath,
BA1 2FJ

www.crombiejardine.com

First published by Crombie Jardine Publishing Limited in 2004
20th reprint 2014

ISBN 10: 1-905102-03-8
ISBN 13: 978-1-905102-03-7

Concept and design by Alastair Williams
Written by Stewart Ferris
Printed and bound by CPI Group (UK) Ltd, Croydon, CR0 4YY

Contents

Introduction

Losing weight isn't rocket science. Eat less and move more and it will happen. So why are so many rocket scientists obese? Simple. It's because rocket scientists are geeks and geeks don't get any sex.

The only well-shafted rocket scientists were the Nazi war criminals who built the moon rockets, but they're all long since buried with a smile on their National Socialist faces.

The link between sex and slimming is simple: a good hard rogering burns calories. If you roger hard enough then that's enough exercise to lose weight.

But do you know how much weight you'll burn up? Which positions offer the greatest slimming opportunities? Where to find a fellow slimmer willing to work with you?

No, nor did I. But that's why I researched this book. Well, that and the offer of fifty quid and a dozen free copies. Now, after literally minutes of in-depth study, you too can lose weight with a smile, just like the dead Nazis.

Self-shagging with a porn mag

Walking to the newsagent
for a porn mag
40 calories

Carrying home lots of computer
mags to hide the porn mag
50 calories

The actual hand shandy
35 calories

☆ **TOTAL: 125 calories** ☆

Self-shagging with a washing machine

Loading the washing machine
and switching it on
10 calories

Sitting on it during the
fastest spin cycle
30 calories

Ironing the clothes afterwards
30 calories

☆ **TOTAL: 70 calories** ☆

Self-shagging with the Internet

Clicking the mouse to find a
suitable porn site
3 calories

The actual hand shandy
35 calories

Wiping clean the
computer screen
10 calories

☆ **TOTAL: 48 calories** ☆

Self-shagging with a vibrator

Replacing the batteries that
short-circuited last time due to
damp conditions
10 calories

Letting the machine do the work
2 calories

A far bigger orgasm than your
boyfriend ever gives you
100 calories

☆ **TOTAL: 112 calories** ☆

Self-shagging with an inflatable doll

Blowing up the doll by mouth
35 calories

Repairing leaks with sticky tape
5 calories

Doing it doggy style because
the doll's face stinks from
a previous encounter
40 calories

☆ **TOTAL: 80 calories** ☆

Self-shagging with a banana

Walking to the supermarket
45 calories

Peeling, inserting and
shagging the banana
5 calories

Spending ages trying get
bits of semi-dissolved
banana out of your twat
10 calories

☆ **TOTAL: 60 calories** ☆

Self-shagging with a steak & kidney pie

Buying the ingredients with a
dirty grin on your face
25 calories

Making a pie with a hole in the
crust for 'ventilation'
10 calories

Giving the pie a good seeing-to
40 calories

☆ **TOTAL: 75 calories** ☆

Finding a shag partner in a club

Pretending to be able to
dance in a nightclub
70 calories

Plucking up the courage
to use a chat-up line
15 calories

Running away from
her boyfriend
85 calories

☆ **TOTAL: 170 calories** ☆

Finding a shag partner on holiday

Holding your stomach in whilst
walking along the beach
looking for a suitable partner
40 calories

Buying an ice-cream and
sharing it with a stranger
minus 200 calories

Holding your stomach in even more
50 calories

☆ **TOTAL: minus 110 calories** ☆

Finding a shag partner in the gym

Twenty minutes on the treadmill
getting ignored by everyone
300 calories

10 minutes on the bike
getting ignored by everyone
150 calories

Giving up and staggering home
50 calories

☆ **TOTAL: 500 calories** ☆

Preparing for a shag

Taking a shower or bath
even though you weren't due
to have one for another week
10 calories

Brushing your teeth *and* flossing
and using mouthwash
5 calories

Trying on kinky underwear
10 calories

☆ **TOTAL: 25 calories** ☆

Preparing for a shag

Trying on 15 different outfits,
none of which disguise
your extra pounds
20 calories

Squeezing your arse into tiny
trousers meant for a 10 year old
5 calories

Taking it all off again now that
you've seduced him
10 calories

☆ **TOTAL: 35 calories** ☆

Preparing for a shag

Undoing her bra with one hand
5 calories

Removing her arse from
too-tight jeans with the help
of some margarine and a
team of firemen
20 calories

Shaking hands with the
firemen as they leave
5 calories

☆ **TOTAL: 30 calories** ☆

Preparing for a shag

Starting to undo his jeans
before he's turned on
5 calories

Removing his jeans
once he gets excited
10 calories

Undressing the rest of
him with your teeth
10 calories

☆ **TOTAL: 25 calories** ☆

Safe shagging - security

Locking the bedroom door
5 calories

Constructing an alibi so
your wife doesn't find out
5 calories

Giving your shag partner a false
telephone number so she can't
track you down if you give her
anything besides pleasure
5 calories

☆ **TOTAL: 15 calories** ☆

Safe shagging - tight condoms

Unwrapping the condom
10 calories

Struggling to put on the condom
when it's an impressively tight fit
15 calories

Hiding the used condom behind the
radiator so scientists in the future
can clone you from your spunk
5 calories

☆ **TOTAL: 30 calories** ☆

Safe shagging
- loose condoms

Unwrapping the condom
10 calories

Slipping on a condom that's
embarrassingly loose and
blaming the room temperature
5 calories

Groping yourself repeatedly
during the performance to try to
hold the condom in place
20 calories

☆ **TOTAL: 35 calories** ☆

Foreplay - dancing

Dancing a strip-tease
around the room while singing
'You can leave your hat on'
60 calories

Throwing your clothes
across the bedroom floor
15 calories

Putting everything back on again
because this was just a rehearsal
and your partner hasn't arrived yet
5 calories

☆ **TOTAL: 80 calories** ☆

Foreplay - oiling

Covering your body
with lavender oil
10 calories

Covering your woman's
body with lavender oil
20 calories

Putting a towel on the bed
so your sheets don't get
covered in lavender oil
5 calories

☆ **TOTAL: 35 calories** ☆

Foreplay - massage

Giving your man a full length
massage on his back
60 calories

Waking your man up
after the massage
sends him to sleep
5 calories

Rolling your sleepy man
over for the good bits
10 calories

☆ **TOTAL: 75 calories** ☆

Foreplay - groping

Groping one erogenous zone
(fully clothed)
10 calories

Groping two erogenous zones
at the same time (fully clothed)
20 calories

Groping three erogenous zones
at the same time (fully clothed)
30 calories

☆ **TOTAL: 60 calories** ☆

Foreplay - kissing

Kissing your partner's neck
5 calories

Kissing your partner's lips
5 calories

Kissing with tongues
10 calories

Wiping the saliva off your lips
using your partner's hair
5 calories

☆ **TOTAL: 25 calories** ☆

Foreplay - nibbling

Nibbling your partner's ears
5 calories

Nibbling your partner's fingers
5 calories

Nibbling your partner's nipples
5 calories

Nibbling your partner's
cream cakes
minus 300 calories

☆ **TOTAL: minus 285 calories** ☆

Foreplay - stimulating

Countering the effects of
brewer's droop in your drunk
partner by using your hand
5 calories

Countering the effects of
brewer's droop in your drunk
partner by using your mouth
5 calories

Jumping on top of him quickly
before he passes out
10 calories

☆ **TOTAL: 20 calories** ☆

Foreplay
- golden shower

Persuading your partner
to let you piss on her
2 calories

Pissing on your partner
5 calories

Running after your angry
partner who thought you
were only kidding
100 calories

☆ **TOTAL: 107 calories** ☆

Foreplay - bondage

Putting on various items
of leather clothing
5 calories

Locking your partner to the bed
with a pair of furry handcuffs
5 calories

Cutting off the handcuffs with
a hacksaw after you realise
you've lost the keys
100 calories

☆ **TOTAL: 110 calories** ☆

Foreplay - S&M

Making your man lick
your shoes while you
spank his bare bottom
5 calories

Making your man sit in a dog
kennel while you watch telly
2 calories

Opening a tin of dog food
and making him eat out of the
dog's bowl with his face
5 calories

☆ **TOTAL: 12 calories** ☆

FOR HIM

Foreplay - M&S

Choosing new M&S underwear
5 calories

Winking at your woman to join
you in the changing rooms
2 calories

Realising this store doesn't
have changing rooms and
being forced to have sex at
home like everyone else
5 calories

☆ **TOTAL: 12 calories** ☆

Foreplay
- whilst driving

Getting her tits out with
one hand on the wheel
10 calories

Having a fish and finger pie whilst
keeping an eye on the road
20 calories

Thinking of an excuse for
the accident to write on
the insurance form
5 calories

☆ **TOTAL: 35 calories** ☆

Foreplay
- whilst driving

Undoing his trousers with
one hand on the wheel
5 calories

When faced with two
sticks remembering which
one to use to change gear
2 calories

Realising windscreen wipers
won't clean on the inside
2 calories

☆ **TOTAL: 9 calories** ☆

Foreplay - oral

Chucking your woman
in the shower,
especially if she's French
5 calories

Giving her a good seeing-to
with your tongue
50 calories

Rinsing the pubes out
of your mouth
5 calories

☆ **TOTAL: 60 calories** ☆

Foreplay - oral

Chucking your man
in the shower,
whether or not he's French
5 calories

Licking his lollipop
until it explodes
50 calories

Bravely deciding to swallow
instead of spitting
minus 200 calories

☆ **TOTAL: minus 145 calories** ☆

Foreplay - 69

Getting into position
5 calories

Stopping to explain that
she's meant to being gobbling
you while you gobble her
5 calories

Enjoying a hairy pie while
your lollipop is licked
40 calories

☆ TOTAL: 50 calories ☆

Foreplay - 69

Getting into position
5 calories

Enjoying yourself even
though his nob keeps
bashing you in the face
20 calories

Sucking his snake while
your bean enjoys a good
tongue flicking
40 calories

☆ **TOTAL: 65 calories** ☆

Shagging
- doggy style

Taking her from behind
20 calories

Moving her around a bit so
you can still see the telly
10 calories

Giving her the best session
she's had since she once got
too friendly with an Alsation
75 calories

☆ **TOTAL: 105 calories** ☆

Shagging
- doggy style

Letting him take you
from behind
10 calories

Straining your neck up so
you can see the telly too
10 calories

Wishing you still lived
next door to that Alsation
5 calories

☆ **TOTAL: 25 calories** ☆

Shagging
- missionary

Spreading her legs
5 calories

Enjoying yourself while
she pretends to
75 calories

Rolling over, farting,
and falling asleep
5 calories

☆ **TOTAL: 85 calories** ☆

Shagging
- missionary

Spreading your legs
5 calories

Faking pleasure and an
orgasm whilst thinking about
what to wear tomorrow
50 calories

Getting up and going out to have
some fun once he's passed out
200 calories

☆ **TOTAL: 255 calories** ☆

Shagging
- in the car

Climbing into the back seat
5 calories

Contorting yourself into an
uncomfortable position
ready to attempt entry
10 calories

Pulling your clothes back on quickly
when a friendly neighbour taps on
the window to see if you're OK
20 calories

☆ **TOTAL: 35 calories** ☆

Shagging
- in the car

Lying awkwardly on the back seat
5 calories

Trying to stop him squashing you
while he gets into position
20 calories

Hiding your face when the
neighbour opens the door and sees
your knickers round your ankles
5 calories

☆ **TOTAL: 30 calories** ☆

Shagging
- on the car bonnet

Helping her onto the bonnet
5 calories

Doing it to her gently in
case the bonnet gets dented
55 calories

Panicking when you see the
shape of her bum cheeks
embedded into the metal
25 calories

☆ **TOTAL: 85 calories** ☆

Shagging
- on the car bonnet

Enjoying the feeling of the warm
engine under your arse
5 calories

Enjoying the feeling of the fresh
night air on your twat
5 calories

Helping him to straighten out
the dent in the bonnet
100 calories

☆ **TOTAL: 110 calories** ☆

Shagging
- at the movies

Walking to a subtle back
row seat in the corner
5 calories

Eating a gallon of popcorn
minus 300 calories

Timing your shag noises to
the sounds in the film
30 calories

☆ **TOTAL: minus 265 calories** ☆

Shagging
- at the movies

Lifting up your skirt
and sitting on him
5 calories

Waiting for him to finish his
popcorn
2 calories

Trying to show no expression
when people turn round to see
what the noise is all about
40 calories

☆ **TOTAL: 47 calories** ☆

Shagging
- her on top

Lying on your back groping her
tits while she sits on you
10 calories

Letting her do all the work
0 calories

Making a few token thrusts so
she doesn't get bored and stop
25 calories

☆ **TOTAL: 35 calories** ☆

Shagging
- her on top

Climbing onto him while
he gropes your tits
15 calories

Doing all the work
150 calories

Getting bored and stopping
because he's making no effort
0 calories

☆ **TOTAL: 165 calories** ☆

Shagging
- in a porn film

Having to 'keep wood' for hours
at a time during multiple takes
300 calories

Having to shag dozens
of birds in a day's work
500 calories

Feeling guilty that you have
such a great job while your
mates work in a pie factory
10 calories

☆ **TOTAL: 810 calories** ☆

Shagging
- in a porn film

Allowing access to parts of you
that are normally exits only
20 calories

Trying to keep moist under
the hot studio lights
100 calories

Faking orgasm twenty
times in a day
300 calories

☆ **TOTAL: 420 calories** ☆

Shagging - silently

Trying to find a sexual position
that won't make the bed creak
and wake up your housemates
40 calories

Forcing yourself to pump slowly
so that you don't grunt too much
40 calories

Muffling the sound of your
orgasm by burying your
face into her tits
20 calories

☆ **TOTAL: 100 calories** ☆

Shagging - silently

Lying still, not needing
to fake enjoyment
5 calories

Bracing your arms against
the wall to muffle
the bed's vibrations
60 calories

Worrying that your friends will
think you're having an epileptic
fit and storm in to save you
10 calories

☆ **TOTAL: 75 calories** ☆

Shagging
- noisily

Thrusting as hard as possible
with the aim of breaking the bed
200 calories

Howling with delight at
the top of your voice
10 calories

Repairing the wooden
slats under the bed
70 calories

☆ **TOTAL: 280 calories** ☆

Shagging
- noisily

Rolling over every couple of
minutes to change positions
in a fervour of passion
200 calories

Thumping the mattress
in orgasmic ecstasy
30 calories

Phoning your boyfriend to tell
him you're ready to see him now
5 calories

☆ **TOTAL: 235 calories** ☆

Shagging
- a prostitute

Asking various women how
much they charge before
finding an actual prozzie
20 calories

Explaining to her that your wife
doesn't understand you
10 calories

Stopping half way through to
see if you have enough cash
to touch both nipples
20 calories

☆ **TOTAL: 50 calories** ☆

Shagging
- a client

Explaining the tariff
5 calories

Listening to his bullshit about his
wife not understanding him
5 calories

Removing his hands from
your breasts and explaining
they're optional extras
20 calories

☆ **TOTAL: 30 calories** ☆

Shagging
- up the arse

Persuading her you got the
wrong hole by accident
but now you're there...
10 calories

Giving her one right up there
70 calories

Washing your nob, your
duvet, your pillowcases
and sheets...twice.
20 calories

☆ **TOTAL: 100 calories** ☆

Shagging
- up the arse

Recoiling in horror when you
realise what he's doing
10 calories

Letting him give you one right up
there whilst wondering whether to
mention your diarrhoea problem
40 calories

Apologising to him while he washes
everything in the room twice.
5 calories

☆ **TOTAL: 55 calories** ☆

Shagging
- your teacher

Reading her your crappy
poems to seduce her
10 calories

Indulging in sexual techniques
you never dreamed
were possible
250 calories

Trying to chat up your
replacement teacher after the first
one gets fired for shagging you
10 calories

☆ **TOTAL: 270 calories** ☆

Shagging
- your teacher

Flirting in class by pointing your
breasts provocatively at him
10 calories

Getting disillusioned by his lack
of sexual imagination in bed
50 calories

Blackmailing him to give
you good grades in return
for keeping his job
10 calories

☆ **TOTAL: 70 calories** ☆

Shagging
- a sheep

Seducing it by wearing your
favourite woolly jumper and talking
knowledgeably about grass
20 calories

Mounting it from behind while
it's still thinking about your
comments on lawn upkeep
50 calories

Running away from
the jealous farmer
300 calories

☆ **TOTAL: 370 calories** ☆

Shagging
- a sheep

Putting on several sets
of false breasts to attract
a male sheep
20 calories

Letting your chosen ruminant
mammal take you from behind
30 calories

Running away from
the excited farmer
300 calories

☆ **TOTAL: 350 calories** ☆

Shagging
- a nervous virgin

Spending three days giving her
foreplay and still she won't relax
500 calories

Trying to persuade her
that you're the best person
to lose her cherry to
20 calories

Giving up and heading into
the loo for a wank instead
50 calories

☆ **TOTAL: 570 calories** ☆

Shagging
- a nervous virgin

Wondering why you're
bothering to go to bed with
such a nerd in the first place
10 calories

Intimidating him with your sexual
confidence and experience
20 calories

Telling him it's quite normal
to ejaculate before he's
even got his pants off
10 calories

☆ **TOTAL: 40 calories** ☆

Shagging
- a desperate virgin

Trying to restrain her enthusiasm
before she wears out your nob
50 calories

Persuading her that all men
are as bad as you in bed
10 calories

Carving a notch in your
bedpost to record the event
30 calories

☆ **TOTAL: 90 calories** ☆

Shagging
- a desperate virgin

Explaining what foreplay is for
whilst holding him away from you
5 calories

Enjoying a full 30 seconds
of foreplay from him before
he gets down to it
20 calories

Enjoying a further 30 seconds
of full-blown bonking
before he explodes
40 calories

☆ **TOTAL: 65 calories** ☆

Shagging
- two birds

Almost creaming your pants
when you realise two birds are
prepared to go to bed with you
20 calories

Worrying they won't be satisfied
with you and might demand a
second bloke to help
10 calories

Working twice as hard as normal
to keep them both satisfied
330 calories

☆ **TOTAL: 360 calories** ☆

Shagging
- two blokes

Offering up both ends of
yourself at the same time
200 calories

Offering two modes of access to
your lower end at the same time
200 calories

Not being able to sit
down for a week
400 calories

☆ **TOTAL: 800 calories** ☆

Shagging
- with another couple

Introducing 'er indoors
to his missus
5 calories

Making polite conversation
about house prices in your area
5 calories

Giving his missus a full
10,000 mile service while he
takes a ride in the loan car
150 calories

☆ **TOTAL: 160 calories** ☆

Shagging
- with another couple

Worrying whether the men
prefer her boobs to yours
5 calories

Worrying whether your man will
feel inadequate when he sees
you enjoying a bigger cock
5 calories

Worrying whether the
other woman might really
be a tuppence licker
5 calories

☆ **TOTAL: 15 calories** ☆

Shagging
- orgies

Awkwardly removing your
suit, wondering if you've
turned up at the right house
10 calories

Groping more people at
once than you can count
100 calories

Realising this isn't the
wake you were invited to and
putting your clothes back on
30 calories

☆ **TOTAL: 140 calories** ☆

Shagging
- orgies

Living out your every fantasy
in the anonymity of a mass
of heaving bodies
250 calories

Realising with horror that
you forgot to take your pill today
10 calories

Narrowing the father of the baby
down to just 15 possible men
40 calories

☆ **TOTAL: 300 calories** ☆

Shagging
- with a celebrity

Working out in the gym for
three months to get fit
enough to attract a celebrity
50,000 calories

Showing your six-pack to a famous
bird at a glamorous London party
5 calories

Giving her the night of her
life by taking her back to your
bedsit for a shag and a pizza
300 calories

☆ **TOTAL: 50,305 calories** ☆

Shagging
- with a celebrity

Putting on a transparent top that reveals your invisible bra and your pneumatic knockers
5 calories

Rubbing your jugs up against an unsuspecting TV presenter while asking him the way to the bogs
20 calories

Selling your story to the *The Sun* the next day
10 calories

☆ **TOTAL: 35 calories** ☆

Shagging
- like a celebrity

Building a swimming pool
in your back garden
25,000 calories

Inviting loads of birds to come
and party with you in the pool
50 calories

Giving up waiting for them to
arrive and paying for prostitutes to
provide your glamour instead
30 calories

☆ **TOTAL: 25,080 calories** ☆

Shagging
- like a celebrity

Finding a man so much
younger than you that you'd
be too embarrassed to
introduce him to your friends
70 calories

Doing it in the garden so that the
paparazzi can photograph you
100 calories

Enrolling at a clinic to
treat your sex addiction
40 calories

☆ **TOTAL: 210 calories** ☆

Shagging
- on Big Brother

Practising by choking
your chicken under the
duvet without making any
noise or visible movement
100 calories

Carrying out foreplay with her in
the hot tub under the bubbles
60 calories

Giving up hiding and shagging
live in front of millions of students
300 calories

☆ **TOTAL: 460 calories** ☆

Shagging
- on Big Brother

Talking endlessly about your boyfriend
back home whilst massaging a naked
fellow contestant
100 calories

Denying to the other housemates
that you two are an item
20 calories

Giving him one secretly under
the duvet while the whole world
thinks he's just having a wank
200 calories

☆ **TOTAL: 320 calories** ☆

Shagging
- swingers

Realising you're lower middle
class, middle aged and slightly ugly
10 calories

Realising your equally ugly
wife no longer turns you on
10 calories

Coupling with swingers
because it's the only way
you can get it up at your age
300 calories

☆ **TOTAL: 320 calories** ☆

Shagging
- swingers

Making much more effort to
clean and polish yourself than
you ever did for your husband
100 calories

Making sure your husband
washes his balls
20 calories

Doing it with other couples
because you still have needs but
don't fancy the hassle of divorce
300 calories

☆ **TOTAL: 420 calories** ☆

Shagging - in front of a romantic fire

Chopping the romantic wood
200 calories

Lighting the romantic firelighters
10 calories

Shagging her on a nice
rug whilst keeping an eye
on the romantic flames in
case they die down
200 calories

☆ **TOTAL: 410 calories** ☆

Shagging
- in front of a
romantic fire

Watching telly while he's
outside chopping the firewood-
0 calories

Drinking a glass of plonk while he
struggles to get the damn thing lit
minus 80 calories

Being rogered on the floor whilst
worrying if the rug will catch fire
200 calories

☆ **TOTAL: 120 calories** ☆

Shagging
- a really fat bird

Helping her up the stairs
into your bedroom and
administering oxygen
100 calories

Heaving her up onto the
bed and hoping the
floorboards hold
100 calories

Humping her as if
you're on a bouncy castle
100 calories

☆ **TOTAL: 300 calories** ☆

Shagging
- a really fat bloke

Undoing the long rope that's
holding up his trousers
5 calories

Helping him locate his
nob somewhere under
his sagging stomach
20 calories

Insisting that it's probably
better if *you* go on top
10 calories

☆ **TOTAL: 35 calories** ☆

Shagging
- up against a wall

Building a wall
(best to use bricks and mortar -
it's stronger than plasterboard)
500 calories

Leaning your lady up
against it and lifting her skirt
10 calories

Entering her gently in case
the wall gives way
60 calories

☆ **TOTAL: 570 calories** ☆

Shagging
- up against a wall

Bracing yourself against a wall
with your knickers round one
ankle and your skirt lifted high
20 calories

Hoping someone will come
along soon to give you a good
shagging before you catch a chill
10 calories

Realising you can't put much into
the shag from that position
10 calories

☆ **TOTAL: 40 calories** ☆

Shagging
- the wheelbarrow
position

Locating your
nearest garden centre
50 calories

Putting your naked woman
into a wheelbarrow
30 calories

Admitting to the security guard
that you didn't really understand
what this sex position involves
30 calories

☆ **TOTAL: 110 calories** ☆

Shagging
- the wheelbarrow
position

Getting down on all fours and
pointing your arse up at him
10 calories

Letting him lift your legs so your
weight is all on your hands
30 calories

Collapsing forwards onto
your arms as he tries to
roger you from behind
10 calories

☆ **TOTAL: 50 calories** ☆

Shagging
- cyber sex

Positioning your webcam so that
your irresistible body can be seen
by all those men pretending to be
girls on the Internet
5 calories

Spending many hours
online trying to find a
genuine bird to cyber-shag
10 calories

Making do with a Thai ladyboy
30 calories

☆ **TOTAL: 45 calories** ☆

Shagging
- cyber sex:

Setting up your webcam
in front of your bed
5 calories

Re-setting your computer when
it turns out your naked presence
has overloaded the servers with
too many masturbating males
5 calories

Touching yourself watched by a
million lonely men with their dicks out
100 calories

☆ **TOTAL: 110 calories** ☆

Shagging
- side by side

Deciding you can't be bothered to
go on top and wondering whether
you can enter her from the side
5 calories

Trying to lift her chubby
thighs out of the way
20 calories

Wiggling your backside a bit
while you try to enter before giving
up and going down the pub
30 calories

☆ **TOTAL: 55 calories** ☆

Shagging
- side by side

Persuading him not to
go to the pub just yet
5 calories

Sliding close to him and
wrapping your legs around him
10 calories

Deciding it would have been
better to make the effort to
go on top in the first place
5 calories

☆ **TOTAL: 20 calories** ☆

Shagging
- spoons position

Cuddling up behind your
partner while she's asleep
5 calories

Trying to take her gently from
behind in rhythm to her snores
20 calories

Feeling insulted that
your erection wasn't enough
to disturb her sleep
5 calories

☆ **TOTAL: 30 calories** ☆

Shagging
- spoons position

Lying in bed quietly minding
your own business,
pretending to be asleep
5 calories

Trying not to react to feeling a
small prick between your legs
5 calories

Lying in bed gloating that
he thinks his nob is too
small to wake you up
5 calories

☆ **TOTAL: 15 calories** ☆

Shagging
- in the shower

Getting the water
temperature right
10 calories

Soaping her up
10 calories

Trying not to slip over while
you're slipping her one
80 calories

☆ **TOTAL: 100 calories** ☆

Shagging
- in the shower

Standing on a chair so he can
enter you without slipping a disc
10 calories

Soaping him up
10 calories

Enjoying five minutes of
precarious passion
80 calories

☆ **TOTAL: 100 calories** ☆

Shagging
- mile high club

Queuing up for the bogs
at the back of the plane
10 calories

Squeezing into the tiny cubicle
with your woman while other
passengers stare suspiciously
10 calories

Shagging her on the sink so
vigorously that the pilot illuminates
the 'fasten seat belts' sign
150 calories

☆ **TOTAL: 170 calories** ☆

Shagging
- mile high club

Having a quick piss
before inviting your man into
the cubicle to join you
10 calories

Sitting on the sink with the tap poking
into your arse while he porks you
120 calories

Sheepishly walking back past
the queue of angry passengers
about to wet themselves
10 calories

☆ **TOTAL: 140 calories** ☆

Shagging
- faking orgasm

Hiding a small sachet of salad
cream in your underpants
5 calories

Screaming loudly while bursting
the salad cream packet over her
20 calories

Wishing you hadn't just spanked
your monkey before meeting her
5 calories

☆ **TOTAL: 30 calories** ☆

Shagging
- faking orgasm

Howling like a dog (whose tail
has just been trodden on)
10 calories

Thumping the bed
with your arms
10 calories

Forcing a contented grin
on your unsatisfied face
10 calories

☆ **TOTAL: 30 calories** ☆

Shagging
- real orgasm

Grunting like a pig
20 calories

Shafting her like a
steam piston engine
until the boiler blows up
200 calories

Falling asleep and snoring
5 calories

☆ **TOTAL: 225 calories** ☆

Shagging
- real orgasm

Getting a warm feeling
around your backside
10 calories

Feeling electricity running
through every nerve in your body
40 calories

Realising you've ripped
open the old electric blanket
10 calories

☆ **TOTAL: 60 calories** ☆

Shagging
- telephone sex

Dialling a pervy line from the
back of the *Sunday Sport*
5 calories

Tapping your foot impatiently
while a recorded voice
reminds you that the cost of
this call will bankrupt you
5 calories

Jerking off to the voice of a
rancid warty former whore
50 calories

☆ **TOTAL: 60 calories** ☆

Shagging
- telephone sex

Dialling a dodgy sex line
number because your
girlfriends dared you to
5 calories

Finding the voice on the other
end surprisingly dishy and
wishing you could flick your bean
10 calories

Flicking your bean anyway and
hoping they won't notice
40 calories

☆ **TOTAL: 55 calories** ☆

Extra calorific benefits of shagging

Looking for the condom
afterwards
20 calories

Being forced to change
the bedsheets before your
wife comes home
50 calories

Walking to the clap clinic
40 calories

☆ **TOTAL: 110 calories** ☆

Extra calorific benefits of shagging

Losing your appetite at
the mere thought of him
seeing your love handles
200 calories

Being shagged so hard it
takes an extra effort just to
walk for the next two days
100 calories

Walking to your friend's house to
tell her about your sordid night
40 calories

☆ **TOTAL: 340 calories** ☆

Negative calorific aspects of shagging

Drinking 5 pints of lager to
pluck up the courage to
ask her out in the first place
minus 300 calories

Licking chocolate and
cream off her boobs
minus 400 calories

Having a big fry-up the next
morning when you sober up
minus 500 calories

☆ **TOTAL: minus 1200 calories** ☆

Negative calorific aspects of shagging

Being seduced with rich food
and lots of alcohol
minus 600 calories

Swallowing instead of spitting
minus 150 calories

Getting the munchies after
a good hard rogering
minus 300 calories

☆ **TOTAL: minus 1050 calories** ☆

Shagging diary
day 1

Sex positions attempted	Calories burned

TOTAL CALORIES:

Shagging diary
day 2

Sex positions attempted	Calories burned

TOTAL CALORIES:

Shagging diary
day 3

Sex positions attempted	**Calories burned**

TOTAL CALORIES:

Shagging diary
day 4

Sex positions attempted

Calories burned

TOTAL CALORIES:

Shagging diary
day 5

Sex positions attempted	**Calories burned**

TOTAL CALORIES:

Shagging diary
day 6

Sex positions attempted	Calories burned

TOTAL CALORIES:

Shagging diary
day 7

Sex positions attempted | **Calories burned**

TOTAL CALORIES:

Shagging diary
day 8

Sex positions attempted	Calories burned

TOTAL CALORIES:

Shagging diary
day 9

Sex positions attempted	Calories burned

TOTAL CALORIES:

Shagging diary
day 10

Sex positions attempted	Calories burned
TOTAL CALORIES:	

125

The Little Book of

Chavs

The Branded Guide to Britain's New Elite

LEE BOK

ISBN 1-905102-01-1, £2.99

The Little Book of ...

Wanking

The definitive guide to man's ultimate relief

DICK PALMER

ISBN 1-905102-00-3, £2.99

www.crombiejardine.com